WAR FOR AMERICA

THE FIGHT FOR INDEPENDENCE 1775–1783

For Peter and Peter
friends with an interest in the past

By the Same Author
British Foreign Policy in the Age of Walpole
The British and the Grand Tour
Natural and Necessary Enemies: Anglo-French Relations in the Eighteenth Century
The English Press in the Eighteenth Century
The Collapse of the Anglo-French Alliance, 1727–31
Eighteenth-Century Europe, 1700–89
Robert Walpole and the Nature of Politics in Early Eighteenth-Century Britain
The Rise of the European Powers, 1679–1793
A System of Ambition? British Foreign Policy 1660–1800
A Military Revolution? Military Change and European Society 1550–1800
Culloden and the '45

Edited
Britain in the Age of Walpole
The Origins of War in Early-Modern Europe
Knights Errant and True Englishmen. British Foreign Policy 1660–1800
British Politics and Society from Walpole to Pitt, 1742–89

Co-edited
Essays in European History in Honour of Ragnhild Hatton
The Jacobite Challenge
The Royal Navy and the Use of Naval Power in the Eighteenth Century
Press and Politics in Hanoverian Britain
Culture, Politics and Society in Britain, 1660–1800

WAR FOR AMERICA

THE FIGHT FOR INDEPENDENCE 1775–1783

Jeremy Black

ST. MARTIN'S PRESS · New York

All rights reserved. For information, write:
Scholarly and Reference Division,
St. Martin's Press Inc., 175 Fifth Avenue, New York, NY 10010

First published in the United States of America in 1991
Paperback edition first published 1994

ISBN 0-312-06713-5 (cloth)
ISBN 0-312-12346-9 (paper)

Library of Congress Cataloging-in-Publication Data

Black, Jeremy.
    War for America: the fight for independence, 1775–1783 /
Jeremy Black
        p. cm.
    Includes bibliographical references and index.
    ISBN 0-312-06713-5 (cloth) 0-312-12346-9 (paper)
    1. United States – History – Revolution, 1775–1783. I. Title.
    E208.B6 1991
    973.3 – dc20

Cover illustration : detail from the Death of General Warren *by John Trumbull.*
(photograph courtesy of Peter Newark's Military Pictures)

Typeset in Ehrhardt 11/12.
Typesetting and origination by
Alan Sutton Publishing Limited
Printed in Great Britain by
The Bath Press, Avon.

CONTENTS

LIST OF ILLUSTRATIONS   vii

PREFACE   xi

ABBREVIATIONS   xii

  1 Prologue   1

  2 The Problems of Suppressing Rebellion   13

  3 The Revolutionary War Effort   41

  4 Conflict   58

  5 1775: The First Year of the War   71

  6 1776: The British Attack   93

  7 1777: Philadelphia and Saratoga   114

  8 1778: France Enters the War   146

  9 1779: Georgia and the Highlands   170

10 1780: The Siege of Charleston; Impasse in the North   183

11 1781: Yorktown   203

12 Epilogue   234

SELECT BIBLIOGRAPHY   250

NOTES   254

INDEX   263

LIST OF ILLUSTRATIONS

Endpapers:
  Front: The battle of Lexington
  Back: The surrender of Lord Cornwallis

1 Accounts listing sums spent on the upkeep of the Thirteen   4
   Colonies and the cost of maintaining an army there, 1776
2 A line-cut depicting America spewing tea back into George III's   5
   face, 1775
3 Woodcut of the 'wicked statesman', 1774   6
4 A cartoon lampooning the repeal of the Stamp Act, 1766   7
5 Charles Townshend, Chancellor of the Exchequer   8
6 A line-cut of 'A Prospective View of the Town of Boston', showing   9
   the landing of British troops in 1768
7 *Journal of the Proceedings of Congress* held in Philadelphia,   10
   5 September 1774
8 Frederick, Lord North, First Lord of the Treasury   11
9 A copy of a petition brought before George III by the General   12
   Congress listing their grievances against the Crown
10 Charles, 1st Marquis Cornwallis, 1783   14
11 Sir Henry Clinton   16
12 A comparison of British and Loyalist strength with that of the   30
   French and Americans, 1783
13 Contemporary American cartoon depicting British bounty   35
   payments to the Indians for taking American scalps
14 Medal given to Indian chiefs by the British in recognition of their   36
   aid during the War of Independence
15 The Declaration of Independence   43
16 Patrick Henry   45
17 A Delaware State one shilling note, printed 1777   46
18 A page from the North Carolina Revolutionary army accounts   51
19 An address by Nathanael Greene to the people of Salisbury   52
   District, North Carolina, 1781
20 An American rifleman and general   54
21 Wooden canteens used by the Continental army during the   57
   Revolution
22 'Kentucky' or 'Pennsylvania' long rifle *c.* 1760   60
23 British Marine rifle with bayonet, dated 1762   63
24 Silver-gilt sword of the type used by many British officers   65

25	General Anthony Wayne	68
26	Battle at Lexington, 19 April 1775	72
27	Plan showing Boston and Bunker Hill, 1781	73
28	'A Correct View of the Late Battle at Charlestown', 17 June 1775, engraved *c.* 1780	74
29	Pages from 'An Impartial and Authentic Narrative' of the battle of Bunker Hill, 17 June 1775	76
30	A cartoon entitled 'Bunkers Hill or America's Head Dress', 1 March 1776	77
31	Early engraving of George Washington	81
32	Proclamation, 'for suppressing Rebellion and Sedition', 1775	84
33	A reply to an address 'A Candid Examination of the Mutual Claims of Great Britain and her Colonies'	85
34	Benedict Arnold, March 1776	89
35	'Old View of Quebec', 1730	91
36	Plan of the attack on Quebec, 1775	91
37	Richard, Viscount Howe, 1799	102
38	'The entry of royal troops into New York', 1776	106
39	Battle of Harlem Heights, 16 September 1776	107
40	The battle of Princeton	112
41	General Sir William Howe	118
42	General 'Gentleman Johnny' John Burgoyne	121
43	A chart of the Delaware Bay and River, 1776	124
44	'Provincial General Buttons marching to Saratoga with plunder'	127
45	The surrender of General Burgoyne to Horatio Gates at Saratoga, 17 November 1777	133
46	The battle of Brandywine	137
47	'An East Perspective View of the City of Philadelphia', 1778	138
48	Plan of Philadelphia, 1777	139
49	The Delaware River, with inset of the attack on Fort Mifflin, 1778	141
50	A caricature entitled 'A view in America in 1778'	143
51	Lord George Germain, 1760	149
52	A cartoon entitled 'The Commissioners', 1778	152
53	4th Earl of Sandwich, *c.* 1763	153
54	The capture of General Charles Lee	158
55	Battle of Monmouth Court House	159
56	A summary of the main events of the War of Independence	161
57	A line-cut of a 'Prospect of the City of New-York', 1771	163
58	General John Sullivan	164
59	Rt. Hon William Eden, 1786	171
60	General Benjamin Lincoln	185
61	Colonel Banastre Tarleton	186
62	General Horatio Gates	191
63	Plan of the battle of Camden, 16 August 1780	193
64	West Point, *c.* 1786	198
65	Facsimile of a miniature of Major André, drawn by himself on 1 October 1780	200

66 The taking of Pensacola, Florida, 9 May 1781   205
67 Thomas Jefferson *c.* 1800   207
68 General Daniel Morgan   209
69 Sketch map of the vicinity of Cowan's ford, 1 February 1781   211
70 Battle of Eutaw Springs, North Carolina, 8 September 1781   218
71 Marie Joseph Paul Yves Roch Gilbert du Motier, Marquis de   220
    Lafayette
72 Plan of the siege of Yorktown   229
73 Letter from Cornwallis to Washington concerning the surrender of   231
    Yorktown and the Treaty of Capitulation, 18 October 1781
74 The surrender of Lord Cornwallis' army at Yorktown, 19 October   232
    1781
75 Revolutionary correspondance concerning a British landing at   237
    Beaufort, South Carolina, 5 April 1782
76 George III *c.* 1767   239
77 A French engraving produced to commemorate the peace treaty,   241
    signed at Versailles, 3 September 1783
78 A French map of the Thirteen Colonies, 1783   242
79 A perspective of the reign of George III   244

Maps:

 1 The American Revolution   21
 2 Bunker Hill   75
 3 Siege of Boston   80
 4 Invasion of Canada   90
 5 New York operations   103
 6 New Jersey and Pennsylvania   109
 7 The war in 1777   116
 8 Burgoyne's advance to the Hudson   126
 9 The Highlands forts   130
10 Brandywine   136
11 The South   184
12 Charleston   186
13 Camden   192
14 Guilford Court House   213
15 Yorktown   223

Photographs and illustrations were supplied by, or are reproduced by kind permission of the following: American Antiquarian Society (2, 3, 6, 58); Board of Trustees of the Royal Armouries (23, 24, 25); Bodleian Library, Oxford (Endpapers, 1, 8, 9, 13, 27, 30, 31, 32, 34, 46, 51, 53, 57, 67, 74, 75, 78, 79, 80); Delaware State Archives (18, 44); Historical Society of Pennsylvania (29, 35, 41,

47, 48, 49, 50, 60, 65, 66); Mansell Collection (4, 12, 16, 45, 73); National Army Museum, London (39, 42, 55); National Portrait Gallery, London (5, 10, 11, 38, 52, 54, 62, 77); North Carolina Division of Archives and History (17, 19, 20, 22, 33, 64, 68, 70, 76); Peter Newark's Historical Pictures (14, 15, 21, 26, 28, 36, 37, 40, 43, 56, 59, 61, 63, 69, 71, 72).

PREFACE

It has been instructive to turn from the Jacobite cause discussed in my *Culloden and the '45* to resume an old interest in the American War of Independence. Both were struggles that have been contrasted with the bulk of pre-Revolutionary eighteenth-century European warfare, being more 'political', bitter and decisive. In each it is necessary to consider the question of inevitability: victory for the British regulars against the Jacobites, defeat for their successors, and in some cases the same men, against the American Revolutionaries. The fate of the '45 confirmed the Anglo-centric nature of Britain and the solidity of the British empire in its native archipelago; that of 'the glorious cause' the rending asunder of the English speaking world. It is understandable that American scholars have devoted so much attention to this war and it is appropriate at the outset to pay tribute to their scholarly insights and industry which have ensured that the conflict is the most thoroughly studied of all eighteenth-century wars.

On a personal note I would like to thank numerous Americans for their many kindnesses on my recent visits to their invigorating country and to express the wish that British libraries would emulate their opening hours, without which this study could not have been possible. I owe a great debt to those who have commented on earlier drafts: Ian Christie, Harry Coles, Bill Deary, John Morgan Dederer, John Derry, Ira Gruber, Tony Hayter, Don Higginbotham, J. Michael Hill, Piers Mackesy and John Plowright. I would like to thank Alan Sutton for asking me to write the book and Olive, Countess Fitzwilliam's Wentworth Settlement Trustees and the Director of Libraries Sheffield for permission to quote from the Wentworth Woodhouse Muniments. I am very grateful for assistance from the British Academy, the American Embassy, London and the University of Durham. This book is about brave men in unpredictable circumstances faced with difficult tasks without the resources they required: troops for the generals, food, shelter, clothes and footwear for so many of the soldiers. These men were Americans, both Revolutionaries and Loyalists, British and French. For each the war was different and far from predictable, and in offering an overall account it is necessary not to lose sight of this.

ABBREVIATIONS

Adams Family Corresp.	L.H. Butterfield (ed.), *Adams Family Correspondence* (Cambridge, Mass., 1961).
BL. Add.	London, British Library, Department of Manuscripts, Additional Manuscripts.
Cobbett	W. Cobbett (ed.), *Parliamentary History of England from . . . 1066 to . . . 1803* (36 vols., London, 1806–20).
Cornwallis	C. Ross (ed.), *Correspondence of Charles 1st Marquess Cornwallis* (London, 1859).
Diplomatic Correspondence	F. Wharton (ed.), *The Revolutionary Diplomatic Correspondence of the United States* (Washington, 1889).
Durham, Grey	Durham, England, University Department of Paleography, papers of 1st Earl Grey.
Fortescue	J.W. Fortescue (ed.), *Correspondence of King George the Third 1760–83* (London, 1927–8).
Franklin	L.W. Labaree et al. (eds.), *The Papers of Benjamin Franklin* (New Haven, 1959–).
HMC	Historical Manuscripts Commission.
Halifax	Halifax, Calderdale District Archives.
Hamilton	H.C. Syrett and J.E. Cooke (eds.), *The Papers of Alexander Hamilton* (New York, 1961–79).
Jefferson	J.P. Boyd et al. (eds.), *The Papers of Thomas Jefferson* (Princeton, 1950–).
LC	Washington, Library of Congress.
Madison	W.T. Hutchinson et al. (eds.), *The Papers of James Madison* (Chicago, 1962–).
Me	Nottingham, University Library, Mellish papers.
NeC	Nottingham, University Library, Newcastle, Clumber papers.
NRO	Northumberland Record Office.
PCC	Washington, Papers of the Continental Congress.
PRO	London, Public Record Office.
SRO	Edinburgh, Scottish Record Office.
WMQ	*William and Mary Quarterly*.
WO	Public Record Office, War Office.
WW	Sheffield City Libraries, Wentworth Woodhouse Muniments.

1 Prologue

*. . . a state of anarchy and the dominion of a mob, who not only terrify the
magistracy, but may put the match to the powder of discontent, that threatens to
blow up all the provinces . . . they will suffer no man to execute any law to raise
internal taxes unimposed by their own Assemblies . . . the newspapers . . . thunder
out their weekly execrations against all the authors of the real or supposed grievances
of the country, and the printers . . . inflame the whole continent.*

Governor Thomas Boone, New York, 8 November 1765

*I am more and more grieved at the accounts from America where this spirit will end
is not to be said; it is undoubtedly the most serious matter that ever came before
Parliament it requires more deliberation, candour and temper than I fear it will
meet with.*

George III, 6 December 1765

*. . . although the violent effusions are and will be suppressed by the navy and army
– yet I verily think a far more dangerous spirit is thereby rooting in the minds of the
people – who begin to think Great Britain intends to enslave and destroy them, by
mere force whence it is easy to see a settled gloom and inquietude take place
everywhere; which will shortly alienate all the affection by which this country might
for ever be rendered anything that Great Britain can wish them to be. I confess the
present temper and increasing prejudices in America, appear much more important,
than all the noise and reprehensible violences that have proceeded this time.*

Sir John Wentworth, Governor of New Hampshire, 2 November 1770[1]

In the half century that started with the clashes at Concord and Lexington in
1775, Europe's empires in the New World collapsed. The vast colonial
territories which had been claimed and fought over since Columbus set foot in
the Bahamas in 1492, that had helped fuel European political and economic
activity for over three centuries, were no more. What had taken more than three
hundred years to create, took less than fifty to dismantle. By 1825 Guiana,
divided among the British, Dutch and French, was the only part of South
America still ruled by a European power. In Central America, only British
Honduras (modern Belize) was under European control, although the British

still claimed suzerainty over the Mosquito Coast of Nicaragua. Far to the north, Britain still held Canada, and the Russians controlled Alaska until 1867. Only in the Caribbean had little changed; save for Haiti, all of the islands remained European possessions.

The swift collapse of the European empires does not look exceptional by the standards of post-1945 decolonization, but it was unprecedented in the late eighteenth century. In South America, most of the revolts were a consequence of the French Revolution and the Napoleonic Wars, although Simon Bolivar and other leaders looked north to George Washington as a role model. After abortive republican risings in 1789, 1798 and 1817 the Portuguese colony of Brazil became an independent empire in 1822. This came about largely because of the willingness of the regent, the eldest son of the King of Portugal, to place himself at the head of the separatist movement. In the British and Spanish empires, movements for independence ran more violent courses. Argentina declared independence in 1810. A revolt against Spanish colonial rule was staged in Venezuela in 1811, but the Spaniards were not finally defeated until 1821 at Carabobo. The Peruvian war of independence did not begin until 1821, the Spaniards being defeated at Ayacucho in 1824.

Compared to the conflict in Spanish America, the American War of Independence was shorter, less diffuse and more affected by external intervention. However, once France entered the American war it became part of a global struggle between Britain and France, while the movements for independence in Spanish America benefited from official and unofficial British support, including the despatch as 'volunteers' of veterans from Wellington's army in the Peninsular War. The value of comparing the two wars is naturally limited by their different contexts. The exercise can, however, be a useful reminder of the need not to treat the American war as unique, a need that is underlined by the notion of the American struggle as one of a number of revolutions in an age of revolution.[2] This idea has been criticized, yet it serves as a reminder of the tensions within the Euro-centric world and suggests that the individual steps by which Anglo-American tension increased, though very important, should not be exaggerated.

The American Revolution may also be seen in more familiar terms as a struggle within the British Empire in which the clash of different ideological traditions played a major role. One of the most famous episodes in the pre-history of the Revolution, the Boston Tea Party of 16 December 1773, was properly symbolic in its setting, Boston harbour; and focus, customs duties and imperial finance; in its opposition of local sentiment to imperial interests; illegal, but limited, mass action to outnumbered authority; land power to maritime links. Tea was actually dumped in several ports, but events in Boston received the most attention. The British political establishment, faced by heavy government indebtedness after mid-century conflicts with the Bourbons in 1739–48 and 1756–63 (the latter, the Seven Years War, is usually dated in North America from the outbreak of hostilities in 1754 and called the French and Indian War) sought a contribution towards the burden of defence in future. This led to the highlighting of differences over colonial government and imperial links.

In the American colonies of the European powers many problems stemmed from the fact that the powerful section of the population and the internal colonial power structure were primarily European in origin, parts of a political community that was united as well as divided by the Atlantic, rather than from the original indigenous population. If American interests could lead colonists to clash with their home governments over the division of the profits and responsibilities of the Atlantic trading systems, European ideas could provide them with justification for resistance. The abortive plot of 1787 to expel the Portuguese and declare their Indian colony of Goa a republic was inspired by those Goan clergy who had returned from France with radical ideas. The republican conspiracy in Minas Gerias in Brazil in 1789 similarly failed. In Spanish America the clash between *peninsulares* (natives of Spain) and *creoles* (Spaniards born in America) was exacerbated by the Bourbon reforms of the eighteenth century, pragmatic devices by officials concerned to maximize governmental revenues rather than the expression of a new enlightened ideology on the part of government. Spanish reforms generally ignored *creole* aspirations and senior officials were mostly *peninsulares*. Though the Latin American wars of liberation were not to begin until the following century and owed much to the Napoleonic subjugation of Spain, nationalist feeling was already developing in eighteenth-century South America.[3]

The revolt of the thirteen British colonies owed as much to disagreements over the nature of the colonial bond as to specific colonial grievances. Disagreement revealed uncertainty as to the meaning of key terms, a crucial problem in an age when constitutional and legal issues played a major role in the definition of political identity and interest. In addition, the British and the colonists had grown apart. By 1775 the colonists were increasingly a new colonial hybrid, Americans. Furthermore, the Americans remained wedded to ideological traditions that were increasingly out of fashion in Britain. The role of imperial issues in the cause and conduct of the Seven Years War and its fiscal consequences helped to make America an important topic of British governmental concern, and thus of political debate thereafter. After a long period of benign neglect of their colonies, the British were increasingly coming to think in imperial terms. The observations made in 1755 by Lord Cathcart, a colonel and a confidant of George II's son, the influential Duke of Cumberland, were symptomatic of new attitudes towards America.

I should imagine that the resources in that country have been hitherto so little examined, and turned so little to advantage that with proper powers, which the present emergency will enforce, a great deal might be done that has never been thought of . . . If we do make peace and are no longer afraid of our colonies falling into the enemy's hands, I am persuaded our next care will be to rescue them from themselves at least it ought to be so: that will never be done by a set of governor merchants who give up the nation on many occasions in complaisance to the colony that pays them . . . the very great importance of our colonies in America, which appears stronger now than it ever did, [and] the difficulties which they have made on some late critical occasions will certainly make it necessary either to ascertain their privileges and subordination by an act of Parliament or to leave them independant.

Between 1763 and 1775 nearly 4 per cent of the entire British national budget was spent on maintaining the army in North America. Keen to make the

A P P E N D I X.

An ACCOUNT of what SUMS have been GRANTED to the different PROVINCES in NORTH-AMERICA, as far as appears from the ESTIMATES for the SUPPORT of the CIVIL GOVERNMENT of each PROVINCE, diſtinguiſhing each Year. And alſo of what SUMS have been GRANTED for the SUPPORT of the PROVINCIAL FORCES in NORTH-AMERICA.

Years	NEW-YORK Forces.	CAROLINA. Not diſtinguiſhed whether North or South.	GEORGIA. Settling and Securing.	GEORGIA Military.	SOUTH CAROLINA	NOVA-SCOTIA Civil Government.	EAST-FLORIDA Civil Government.	WEST-FLORIDA Civil Government.	AMERICA Forces.	AMERICA Rewards and Compenſations.

Accounts listing sums spent on the upkeep of the Thirteen Colonies and the cost of maintaining an army there. These costs were used as justification by the British government for the imposition of extra duties and taxes. Printed in 1776

colonists contribute more to the cost of their defence, the government sought both to increase taxation by the Stamp Act of 1765, and to improve the effectiveness of commercial regulations. These attempts clashed with a traditionally lax enforcement, associated smuggling to non-British territories and the sense that the levying of taxation for revenue purposes by a parliament that included no colonial representatives was a dangerous innovation. A feeling of shared community with Britain had for long been matched by one of particular interests shown, for example, by Maryland and Virginia which tried to encourage local shippers by giving them preferential treatment over the British. In December 1774 Viscount Stormont, the British envoy in Paris, reported the widely-held view there that:

> ... from the prodigious increase of the population, trade, and strength of North America, there must come a period when the spirit of independency will be generated throughout our colonies, and when actuated by that spirit, and conscious of their own superior strength, they

will shake off all dependency on their Mother-Country, and form an immense Empire of their own. These men pretend that no human policy can prevent this, that all the greatest wisdom could do would be to palliate, what cannot be cured, and keep off, for a time, what must inevitably come at last, and whenever it does come must give Great Britain a fatal blow. They add that our conduct is directly opposite to what it should be, that by bringing on these discussions, we have raised in our colonies a spirit of opposition, and now by vainly attempting to subdue that unconquerable spirit, we shall of course increase it, make the flame general, and by our own fault accelerate that fatal period, which upon every principle of political wisdom, it should be our utmost endeavour to retard.[4]

American opposition to the new fiscal policy led to mob violence, which the colonial authorities failed to control, despite the deployment of naval and military forces. Force, however, was inappropriate. There was no equivalent of the regular regiments supported by substantial forces of militia that could be found in the Spanish empire after 1763, valuable supports when the colonial authorities wished to raise taxation and introduce administrative reforms. In America British troops were used for tasks for which they had no particular training and the navy was unable to police the entire coastline, lacked sufficient small vessels and was able to concentrate ships in Boston harbour and along the New England coast in 1774–5 only by abandoning the rest of the coast to virtually unregulated trade, although this was not surprising, as their purpose was to 'overawe', rather than defeat, their opponents.[5]

As the Emperor Joseph II, ruler of the Habsburg territories, was to discover in the late 1780s, when faced by rebellion in the Austrian Netherlands (Belgium) and Hungary, force was no substitute for consensus, and the military effort

A line-cut by Nathan Daboll for Freebetter's New England Almanack. It depicts America spewing back into George III's face the tea he is pouring down her throat while she is held down. The British fleet cannonading Boston can be seen in the background. Printed and sold by T. Green, 1775

Woodcut of the 'wicked statesman', by Paul Revere in The Massachusetts Calendar, *1774*

required to suppress disaffection posed serious political, military and financial problems. Though only a minority of the colonists wished for independence when real hostilities began in 1775, the strength of separatist feeling within this minority was such that compromise on terms acceptable to the British government and British political opinion appeared increasingly unlikely. When, for example, Americans subscribed to resolutions rejecting tea drinking, in response to the Tea Act of 1773, designed to facilitate sales of East India Company tea, and enforced these resolutions by terror, tarring and feathering taxmen, they were publicly rejecting in a highly charged atmosphere the structure and rationale of empire. The issue could no longer be discussed in purely British mercantilist terms. The emptiness of the imperial ethos for many was revealed in the paranoia and symbolic and practical acts of defiance that led to a spiral of violence. In 1776 a congress of colonial representatives at Philadelphia declared the colonies independent. British action had led the colonists into doing something that had been hitherto very uncommon: co-operating and compromising. The European origin of the rebels aided them in obtaining support from other European powers, and indeed from British opposition circles, to an extent that non-whites would not have received. Their search for foreign, particularly French, support, typical of the European rebellious movements of the century, helped to internationalize the struggle, and to make compromise more difficult.

While stressing factors that led to rebellion it is also important to point out that numerous Americans did not rebel and many fought the rebels. About a fifth of the politically active section of the population has been described as Loyalist, but Loyalist sentiment and activity, like its Revolutionary counterpart, is difficult to assess and varied greatly, as local studies demonstrate.[6] This is generally the case with civil wars, and helps to ensure that there are essentially two problems to explain, first why so many became critical of governmental measures and alleged intentions, as was the case in England by 1640 and America by 1774, and secondly why people took different sides. A number of issues can be probed, including increasing democratization in American society,[7] which was related to the emergence of new political groups in the 1770s;[8] a millenarian rejection of British authority;[9] concern about British policy in Canada; the borrowing of British conspiracy theories about the supposed autocratic tendencies and intentions of Court Whiggery and George III; specific constitutional, ideological[10] and commercial[11] concerns about relations with Britain that arose from the disputes and economic difficulties of the 1760s and 1770s; and British policies whose firmness could be interpreted as tyranny and changes as sinister inconsistencies. The fact that Britain's most important colonies in the western hemisphere, those in the West Indies, did not rebel, despite the sensitivity of their élites on questions of constitutional principle, suggests that it was the increasingly serious social, economic and political crises in the continental colonies that were crucial, rather than primarily their ideological and political traditions.[12]

As fighting resulted from the determination of the British government to employ force, and the refusal of sufficient Americans to be intimidated and their willingness to organize to use force themselves, then it is clear that both aspects

A contemporary British cartoon by Benjamin Wilson lampooning the repeal of the Stamp Act, 1766. The coffin is carried by George Grenville, who is followed by Bute, the Duke of Bedford, Temple, Halifax, Sandwich and two bishops

Charles Townshend, Chancellor of the Exchequer 1766–7, attributed to Isaac Gosset

have to be considered. Large numbers of Americans had become familiar between 1754 and 1763 with organized warfare involving European-style armies,[13] as opposed to conflict with Indians and between colonists, both of which were also important. American society was also wealthy,[14] sufficiently so to sustain and endure several years of expensive and destructive war. Institutions, habits and ideas of self-government provided a basis for organizing such activity. The potential for an organized armed struggle was present, although that, of course, did not make its outbreak inevitable. It was the anxieties engendered by the British attempt to strengthen imperial bonds when the common cement of fear of France was lacking that made the situation volatile. The authority of the Crown became increasingly involved in the internal political struggles within individual colonies. These struggles helped to determine not only the pace of events, but also the different responses within and between colonies.[15] The unwillingness of British politicians to compromise parliamentary sovereignty, their refusal to make concessions on questions of principle, was demonstrated by the Stamp Act crisis of 1765–6; thereafter, this refusal helped to make a genuine reconciliation impossible. In the mid-1760s many American critics of the British government accepted the distinction between parliamentary taxation for the purposes of controlling trade, which they were prepared to accept, and parliamentary taxation for the raising of revenue, which they were not. Parliamentary sovereignty was fundamental to the British point of view,

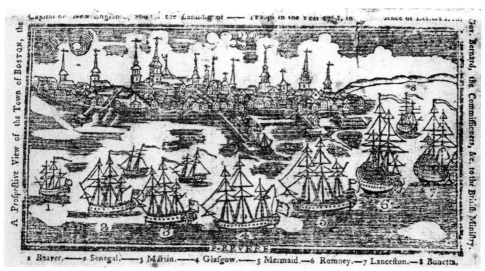

A line-cut of 'A Prospective View of the Town of Boston', showing the landing of British troops there in 1768. Cut by Paul Revere, it was published in Edes & Gill Almanac, *1770*

however, so when the Stamp Act was repealed in 1766 a Declaratory Act was passed stating parliament's authority to legislate for the colonies in all matters.

The British were fortunate that, because Spain's French ally did not support her, the Falkland Islands confrontation with Spain of 1770 did not lead to war with the Bourbons, as that would have raised the issue of colonial military and financial contributions to the imperial war effort anew; but it was to be the problems of another part of the empire, those of the British East India Company, that led to trouble in America. The Revenue Act of 1767, drawn up by Charles Townshend, the Chancellor of the Exchequer, had imposed American customs duties on a variety of goods including tea, which was brought from India by the East Indian Company, a monopolistic trading concern whose financial viability was seen as crucial to British government finances and the reduction of the national debt. This had led to a serious deterioration in relations between the British government and its American critics. The Americans responded with a trade boycott and action against customs officials, leading the British ministry to send troops to Boston. This was followed by the 'Boston Massacre' of 5 March 1770, a bloody incident that caused the death of five Bostonians and widespread hostility towards governmental methods. In some respects it was an overblown event, the consequence of drunken soldier-baiting that got out of hand and was exploited for propaganda purposes by Samuel Adams, but to many Americans it demonstrated the militarization of British authority and proved the harmful consequences of a standing army.

The British ministry had decided in 1769 to abandon all the duties save that on tea, whose retention was seen as a necessary demonstration that they would not yield to colonial views. Tension, however, remained high with serious constitutional disputes of varied cause in a number of colonies, particularly in

JOURNAL

OF THE

PROCEEDINGS

OF THE

CONGRESS,

Held at PHILADELPHIA, September 5th, 1774.

CONTAINING,

The Bill of Rights; A List of Grievances;
Occasional Resolves; The Association; An
Address to the People of Great Britain; A
Memorial to the Inhabitants of the British
American Colonies; and, An Address to
the Inhabitants of the Province of Quebec.

Published by ORDER of the CONGRESS.

TO WHICH IS ADDED,

(Being now first printed by Authority)

AN AUTHENTIC COPY

OF THE

PETITION TO THE KING.

LONDON:

Printed for J. ALMON, opposite Burlington-House, in
Piccadilly.

M.DCC.LXXV.

*Journal of the Proceedings of Congress held in
Philadelphia, 5 September 1774. Printed in London
in 1775*

A LIST *of the* DEPUTIES *or* DELEGATES
who attended the CONGRESS *held at* Philadelphia,
September 5th, 1774.

From NEW HAMPSHIRE.
Major *John Sullivan*, Col. *Nathaniel Folsom*, Esqrs.

From MASSACHUSETTS-BAY.
Hon. *Tho. Cushing*, Esq; Mr. *Samuel Adams*,
John Adams, *Robert Treat Paine*, Esqrs.

From RHODE-ISLAND.
Hon. *Stephen Hopkins*, Hon. *Samuel Ward*, Esqrs.

From CONNECTICUT.
Hon. *Eliphalet Dyer*, *Silas Deane*,
Hon. *Roger Sherman*, Esqrs.

From NEW-YORK.
James Duane, *John Jay*,
Philip Livingston, *Isaac Low*,
John Alsop, Col. *William Floyd*,
Henry Wisner, *John Herring*,
S. Boerum, Esqrs.

From NEW-JERSEY.
James Kinsey, *William Livingston*,
John De Hart, *Stephen Crane*,
Richard Smith, Esqrs.

From PENNSYLVANIA.
Hon. *Joseph Galloway*, *Samuel Rhoads*,
Thomas Mifflin, *Charles Humphreys*,
John Morton, *George Ross*,
Edward Biddle, *John Dickinson*, Esqrs.

From the Government of the Counties of NEW-
CASTLE, KENT, and SUSSEX on DELAWARE.
Hon. *Cæsar Rodney*, *Thomas M'Kean*,
George Read, Esqrs.

From MARYLAND.
Hon. *Matthew Tilghman*, *Thomas Johnson*,
Robert Goldsborough, *William Paca*,
Samuel Chase, Esqrs.

From VIRGINIA.
Hon. *Peyton Randolph*, *Richard Henry Lee*,
George Washington, *Patrick Henry*, jun.
Richard Bland, *Benjamin Harrison*,
Edmund Pendleton, Esqrs.

From NORTH-CAROLINA.
William Hooper, *Joseph Hewes*,
Richard Caswell, Esqrs.

From SOUTH-CAROLINA.
Hon. *Henry Middleton*, *John Rutledge*,
Thomas Lynch, *Christopher Gadsden*,
Edward Rutledge, Esqrs.

JOURNAL

Frederick, Lord North, First Lord of the Treasury 1770–82, by Nathaniel Dance, 1775

Massachusetts, and a growing hostility towards parliamentary claims of authority over American affairs. The Boston Tea Party of December 1773 forced the British government to confront the growing problems of law and order and the maintenance of authority. They believed these arose from the actions of a small coterie of radicals, rather than from widespread disaffection in America. Thus, the ministry mistakenly hoped that tough action against Massachusetts, the so-called 'Coercive' or 'Intolerable' Acts of early 1774, would lead to the restoration of order. The Boston Port Act was designed to protect trade and customs officials from harassment, the Massachusetts Charter Act to strengthen the executive, the Administration of Justice and Quartering Acts to make it easier to enforce order. These measures were criticized by the parliamentary opposition in Britain as oppressive, but passed by overwhelming majorities. More troops were sent to Massachusetts and General Thomas Gage, the Commander-in-Chief in America, was appointed its Governor.

Far from leading to submission, these measures provoked outrage both in Massachusetts and, crucially, in the other colonies as well. A Continental Congress to organize opposition was established and met in Philadelphia in September 1774. Although British politicians feared the contrary, the delegates at that stage were interested not in independence, an idea which threatened the fragile unity of the colonies, but in the traditional constitutional process of redress of grievances, a process no longer adequately provided for by the imperial governmental system.[16] By British standards, their view of the world was arcane, but prohibitions on trade with Britain and the creation of an

Philadelphia, October 26th, 1774.

TO THE

KING'S

MOST EXCELLENT MAJESTY.

Moft Gracious Sovereign,

WE Your Majefty's faithful fubjeas of the Colonies of New-Hampfhire, Maffachu-fetts-Bay, Rhode-Ifland and Providence Planta-tions, Connecticut, New-York, New-Jerfey, Pen-fylvania, the Counties of New-Caftle Kent and Suffex on Delaware, Maryland, Virginia, North-Carolina, and South-Carolina, in behalf of our-felves, and the inhabitants of thofe Colonies, who have deputed us to reprefent them in General Congrefs, by this our humble Petition, beg leave to lay our grievances before the throne.

A ftanding army has been kept in thefe Colonies, ever fince the conclufion of the late war, without the confent of our Affemblies ; and this army, with a confiderable naval armament, has been employed to enforce the collection of taxes.

The first pages of a petition brought before George III by the General Congress listing their grievances against the Crown, 1774

institutionalized union of opposition to Britain were clearly both threats and challenges to imperial interests and pretensions. The Intolerable Acts were defied in Massachusetts and politicians and officials regarded as sympathetic to the royal administration were harried and forced to resign. The British government, led by Lord North, the First Lord of the Treasury, viewed the claims of Congress as an unacceptable challenge to parliamentary authority. Well supported in parliament, but keenly aware that a show of weakness towards the colonies might well alienate decisive elements of that support, they decided to use force, although at the same time they hoped to assuage grievances, as indicated by the conciliatory propositions North put before parliament in February 1775. However, the government was determined to retain control of the constitutional position and reimpose order in America. While there are hints that some compromise over the imposition of taxation might have been possible, there was little ministerial interest in negotiating over constitutional and political arrangements. The outbreak of fighting should have come as no surprise, though the ministry was to be startled by the scale and extent of resistance they encountered.

2 The Problems of Suppressing Rebellion

Suppressing a rebellion within the dominions of the British Crown was not a novel problem for the British armed forces in the eighteenth century. Major risings on behalf of the Jacobite claimant to the throne had occurred in 1715 and 1745. Prior to that the succession crisis of 1685–91 had involved warfare in England, Ireland and Scotland. In 1798 there would be a major rising in Ireland, which was encouraged by the revolutionary government of France. A French invasion force landed to assist the rebels, but it quickly surrendered that September at Ballinamuck to the British Viceroy and Commander-in-Chief, Charles, 1st Marquis Cornwallis. He had himself commanded the British army whose surrender to the Americans and French at Yorktown in 1781 marked the effective end of British hopes of defeating the American Revolutionaries. Unlike Yorktown, however, French intervention in Ireland went for naught.

Nevertheless, the presence or likelihood of foreign intervention played a major role in rebellions within the British dominions. None received the sustained assistance provided by the French to the American Revolutionaries. They hoped to profit from Britain's problems in order to reverse the Peace of Paris of 1763, the territorial settlement that had followed the overwhelming British victories in the Seven Years War (1756–63). If this factor is seen as crucial then the central military problem for the British can be presented as that of countering the fact of French intervention. There is no doubt that that intervention was of great consequence. It denied the British the clear naval superiority that had enabled them in the first years of the conflict to concentrate their military resources in North America, neglecting the defence of the West Indies, let alone Britain, in order to centre their efforts on the Thirteen Colonies and the defence of contiguous possessions: Canada and West and East Florida. Naval superiority enabled Britain to reinforce and supply her forces in North America untroubled save for a few American privateers, to move units along the American seaboard and to seek to blockade the Revolutionaries, although it was very difficult to sustain a blockade in eighteenth-century conditions.

French naval power obviously played a central role in the Yorktown campaign, and it is easy therefore to see it as decisive in the defeat of British plans in

Charles, 1st Marquis Cornwallis, by Thomas Gainsborough, 1783

America. A British officer wrote from New York in July 1781, that 'this city and district are seriously menaced with a general attack, whenever a French fleet shall arrive on the coast, superior to ours, without which we have little to fear, notwithstanding the French and rebels are gathering round us'. Victory for the Americans, in the sense of a decisive defeat of the main British army in the field, can be presented as having been impossible without French intervention. It can, and has, been argued, however, that the British had failed well before Yorktown and that by then they were fighting on for no clear purpose.

This raises the question of British objectives in the conflict, their practicality and the consequent judgment of British military planning and operations. A confusion of purpose (or a strategy bereft of any solid attainable goals) in British intentions has been discerned, between the desire to end the revolution by conciliation, through negotiations in which they would yield many of the pretensions and prerogatives of royal government while denying independence, and the wish to achieve a military solution. It has been argued that this confusion, and especially the wish to negotiate while fighting, inhibited British operations, in particular by lessening the desire for a striking military victory. Attention has been directed to the ambiguous position of the Howe brothers, given military command of the navy and army in America in 1776 and at the same time entrusted with powers to negotiate a reconciliation. It has been suggested that this lessened their determination to crush the Americans. On the other hand, the clear purpose was to bring the war to an acceptable conclusion as rapidly as possible. As the scene of action was 3,000 miles from London it made sense to combine war-making and peace-making powers.

The alleged confusion over objectives has been linked to another over means: specifically the British attitude towards the Loyalists. A large number of Americans did not support the cause of independence, generally due to local considerations, such as opposition to regional élites and leaders. The attitude that the British should take towards them was controversial. The extent to which military use could be made of these loyal Americans, the best means to obtain it and the relationship that this should have with British strategy, were unclear. In general, British hopes of Loyalist assistance increased during the war, especially after France's entry in 1778, and this was linked to the growing concentration of British hopes and efforts on the southern colonies, Georgia and the Carolinas. The British hoped to use regulars to drive the Revolutionaries out of the south, leaving mopping up and the re-establishment of the civil government to Loyalists. As regulars were sent to the Caribbean, while few reinforcements arrived from Britain, British commanders became dependent on Loyalist units to make up their combat forces. The men left for mopping up were more marginal soldiers, men who were more interested, and justifiably considering the harsh way they had been treated in their country, in revenge, than pacification. Reliance on Loyalists posed a major problem, however, for the Loyalists were in turn greatly dependent on military help. In this there was a clear parallel with the '45. Loyal forces in Scotland had played a considerable role, but they were most successful when the major Jacobite force under Charles Edward Stuart (Bonnie Prince Charlie) was in England engaged in operations against the royal army. In addition, loyal irregular units in England had little impact. Although the Jacobite retreat through Cumbria was harassed, their advance had encountered no resistance once the garrison at Carlisle had surrendered. Possibly the major role of the loyal units was in discouraging Jacobite sympathizers from acting, a role that was to prefigure that of the militia in limiting Loyalist action during the American War of Independence.[1]

In the American war it was clear to both loyal generals and Revolutionaries that organized and significant Loyalist activity would require the presence of British forces. The British advance into New Jersey in late 1776 was followed by an upsurge of Loyalist activity, with nearly 2,500 Loyalists volunteering for action. In January 1777 John Adams, a member of Congress, wrote of Sussex County in New Jersey, 'If the British army should get into that county in sufficient numbers to protect the Tories, there is no doubt to be made they would be insolent enough and malicious and revengeful. But there is no danger at present and will be none until that event takes place'. He had described what was to happen in Georgia and South Carolina in 1779 and 1780. In June 1777 another prominent revolutionary, Robert Livingston, a landowner in New York State, wrote of:

. . . the spirit of disaffection being lower now than it has been in this state since the beginning of the controversy owing to the vigilance of the government, the punishment of some capital offenders, and above all to the weakness and languor of the enemies' measures. Some very conscientious persons have declared [when they took the oath to the state] that they held themselves absolved from all allegiance to a power that was no longer able to protect them. Though I do not think such conversions greatly to be relied on, yet they are of use in stopping the progress of disaffection and giving an appearance of strength and unanimity to our government on which more depends than is generally imagined.

Tenants of the Livingstons in the Hudson valley had been dissatisfied with their landlords for a decade and, when the family supported the revolution, they took up arms for George III, rising in 1776 and 1777. Throughout the colonies local Revolutionary committees, supported by the militia, drove many Loyalists from their homes, confiscating property and making life hard for them. These committees and such action were the revolution across much of America.

In May 1776 Henry Clinton, then commander of a British expedition on its way to Charleston, suggested 'we may possibly conquer by the assistance of our friends. Those friends will maintain afterwards with little support from the King's troops'. The defeat of the North Carolina Loyalists at Moore's Creek Bridge that February did not appear to invalidate this claim, as they had not received any support from British troops. In October 1778 Clinton, by now commander-in-chief, wrote, 'We wished to have it clearly understood that military force is not to be employed in this country, but with an ultimate purpose of enabling His Majesty's faithful subjects to resume their civil government'. This was a clearly stated objective, but it was unclear how best to gain and maintain Loyalist support. Lieutenant-Colonel Archibald Campbell, who was sent in late 1778 at the head of nearly 3,000 troops to attack Savannah, was given such authority for Georgia and South Carolina with the hope that 'the re-establishment of Georgia may if well supplied by the loyal inhabitants in the back settlements of South Carolina lead to the possession of this province likewise'.[2]

Yet the Loyalist option posed major problems of strategic choice. The dispersal of troops to protect Loyalist areas would make operations difficult, for

Sir Henry Clinton

it was only through the maintenance of large concentrated forces able to manoeuvre that major attacks could be countered. Loyalist units could help in this, although they were likely to have only a secondary military role, as with the loyal Highlanders at the Jacobite defeat at Culloden in 1746. Alexander Innes, the Inspector General of Provincial Forces, reported from New York on two of the leading units in September 1779, 'Both the Queen's Rangers and New York Volunteers want a good many men to be complete but the nature of the constant service they have been on . . . renders it almost impossible their losses have been so great and are so frequent'. Both were tough units fighting bravely for what they saw as their country. The Caledonian Volunteers, composed of Loyalist Scottish settlers, was another such unit. Furthermore, the Loyalist option offered little assistance if the war was to be taken into areas where there were relatively few Loyalists, especially New England and Virginia. Aside from the problem of protecting Loyalist areas, there was also the question of how far the war should be conducted in a manner calculated neither to offend Loyalist opinion nor to make the task of conciliation more difficult. This would entail the abandonment, not merely of any attempt to live off the country, but, more seriously, of ideas of terrorizing the Americans into submission by savage measures, such as devastating their property or laying them under contribution. When his generalship in America in 1776–8 was investigated in parliament in 1779, Sir William Howe asked a sympathetic witness, Lieutenant-General Charles, Earl Cornwallis, a series of leading questions:

> If I had laid waste the country would not every degree of inconvenience have arisen from it to the King's army, had it been necessary to return with the army into the same country, from the want of refreshments of all kinds, carriages and horses?
>
> Would it not have had the effect of alienating the minds of the Americans from his Majesty's government, rather than terrifying them into obedience?
>
> Would not such a measure have distressed the inhabitants under the protection of the army, and the troops in winter quarters, by reducing the supply of provisions?

Such policies were suggested by some British officers and commentators. When, in September 1775, he realized that the Americans sought independence, Major Francis Sill of the 63rd Foot, hungry and exhausted in Boston, abandoned his earlier sympathy for his opponents and expressed his support for 'harsh, absolute and severe methods'. Four months earlier it had been reported from Boston that 'the whole army are dissatisfied with the conduct of the commander-in-chief [Gage] who all along has treated the seditious Bostonians with unequalled lenity and indulgence . . . The officers think with reason that he is too much of an American . . . Two months past had he only secured six of the most violent of the demagogues, this rebellion would have been crushed in the bud', a familiar illusion. Major Robert Donkin wanted to shoot smallpox-tipped arrows at the Americans. John Hayes, the army physician in charge of medical services at Charleston, wrote in April 1781 to Charles Mellish, an MP who supported the ministry of Lord North until the end:

> . . . this country is in a state of rebellion and destruction. Nine-tenths of the people who had taken protection and those paroled, have joined the enemy and in small bands, infest the

province with a degree of rigour. Murders in cold blood are hourly committed; and they are become so numerous, that it is not safe to travel ten miles . . . they are nineteen out of twenty disaffected; and no ties except extreme rigour can influence them . . . where they used to live they are apt to resort, the more to see their wives and children, who they leave behind. If something of the same nature, as that exercised by Lord Chatham [Pitt the Elder], when he removed the Acadians from Nova Scotia is not adopted, this country will remain in enmity against us – It would be a wise and politic measure to remove the family of every absent, and the men most disaffected to you. New York can furnish refugees sufficient to people the province, and whose loyalty have been proved.[3]

Such tactics were not to be attempted, but they indicate a willingness to consider radical solutions. In part such suggestions can be seen as a bitter response to failure and to the apparently intractable nature of the revolution, but the willingness of European armies to resort to such tactics against recalcitrant populations should not be overlooked. It was certainly shared by the British army. Devastation was employed on a systematic basis in the Highlands of Scotland during and after the '45. Lord George Germain, who was, as Secretary of State for the American colonies from November 1775 until February 1782, to direct British operations, played an active role as an army officer in the '45; and later Irish prisoners were slaughtered in 1798, as they had been on earlier occasions. In this, however, the British army was following the traditional means of dealing with rebels. Parliamentary scrutiny and a generalized sense of the rule of law probably ensured that, on the whole, the British army behaved better than their continental counterparts. There was certainly no comparison between their conduct and that of the Russians, either during the Russo-Turkish War of 1768–74, or in Poland, where, for example, over 10,000 Poles died on one day when the Warsaw suburb of Praga was stormed in 1794. Nevertheless, rebellion altered both the legal and the psychological context and, although Americans were not presented as contemptible aliens, in the fashion of the barbarian Scottish Highlanders or the 'wild' Catholic Irish, a strong antipathy was aroused by their being rebels. Since all Americans looked alike to British and German troops, many Loyalists were driven to the Revolutionary side by depredations. Major Carl Leopold Baurmeister, a Hessian, claimed that such actions by British troops exacerbated popular hostility. The attitude of many of the British troops counteracted attempts at conciliation and ensured that British administration of occupied areas was not such that it would inspire loyalty or retain the support of Loyalists. However, though Britain might have lost the battle for the hearts and minds in, for example, Queen's County, New York, through the army's abuse of private property and its demands on residents for supplies, and the arbitrary and abusive conduct of British officers, enthusiasm for the cause of independence proved difficult to sustain and opposition to the demands of the new government increased.

However different the cases might be, contrasting British conduct towards the Jacobites with that towards the American Revolutionaries highlights another aspect of an important element in the American war; the range of options facing the British. These were not only strategic, but also related to the means by which the conflict could be conducted. Given that much of the stress in accounts of the war has been on how Britain lost it, on mismanaged campaigns, poor generalship and strategic direction and missed oportunities, it is worth considering the question of the options facing the British and placing it in the contexts of the nature of eighteenth-century warfare and of the military problems the British faced.

Eighteenth-century European warfare has traditionally been described (and generally dismissed) as limited and inconsequential, a war of manoeuvre that lacked a determination to destroy the enemy. It is held to have emphasized manoeuvre over battle, a wish to preserve armies rather than a willingness to suffer substantial casualties in achieving objectives, in short an avoidance of risk. This caricature has been contrasted with the more dynamic, determined, vigorous and violent tactics, strategy, methods and objectives of the warfare of revolutionary France and, as in so much else, the American revolution is held to have anticipated that of France.

The novelty of the military methods of the American Revolutionaries is questionable. George Washington sought to create an *ancien régime* army. Given the constraints created by the nature of American society and the federal and anti-militarist political culture of a revolutionary new state, Washington, by necessity, created an American army suited for war in America. It has been argued that Washington was eminently successfully, especially due to the social, political and cultural restraints imposed by American society. The nature of the American achievement, as of the range of options available to the British, can be better appreciated if the over-simplified view of European warfare in the period is dismissed. War could be far from limited, campaigns could be decisive, casualties high, sometimes extraordinarily high. There was no common experience, no uniform model of operations.[4] Generals were affected by a number of factors, among which those summarized by the term logistics (or lack thereof) were paramount, but they had a variety of tactical and strategic options to choose from. The British army had not campaigned since 1762, but the operations of that year indicated that they could look back on a wealth of varied experience. In 1762 British forces campaigned around the globe. They helped the Portuguese resist a Bourbon invasion – a campaign in which Burgoyne distinguished himself by bold action and Grey served – fought the French in Westphalia (part of Germany) and captured Martinique from the French and Havana and Manila from the Spaniards. 1762 was the last campaigning year in the Seven Years War (1756–63), a conflict that had also seen the British defeat French forces in India, crush the French navy in European waters, capture the French bases of Goree (West Africa) and Guadeloupe, and drive the French from Canada.

However, a major part of the problem facing the British is suggested by contrasting their conquests during the Seven Years War and the task facing them in the War of American Independence. During the Seven Years War they were essentially obliged in their colonial warfare to defeat small armies composed of regular European units supported by native irregulars. Campaigns centred on the capture of major fortresses and centres of government, such as Louisbourg and Quebec, all of which could be reached by water. Experience with sieges was obviously important. Operations in the hinterlands around fortresses were limited. The British captured Manila and Havana, not the Philippines or Cuba, but they gave effective political and military control of what

Britain sought, bargaining counters for the inevitable peace treaty. The same was even more true of those French bases that lacked any real hinterland: Goree, Pondicherry, Louisbourg and the principal fortresses in the West Indies. The whole of French Canada fell into British hands with the surrender of Montreal in 1760. The military objective necessary to secure victory in colonial campaigns was therefore clear: assured naval superiority sufficient to permit the landing and supply of an amphibious force that would successfully besiege the major fortress whose capture would lead to the effective end of Bourbon strength.

Such a strategy was one option in dealing with the American Revolution, complementing the naval blockade of the American coast by seizing the major cities. Without occupying coastal bases no magazines (supply dumps) could be developed for operations in the interior. Capturing the leading ports was possible as British successes at New York (1776), Savannah (1779) and Charleston (1780) demonstrated, although the value of this strategy was only assured if the American forces in the region sought to defend the city and could be decisively defeated, as was the case at Charleston and, although not to a decisive extent, New York. Unless such a decisive defeat, accompanied by the surrender of the defeated unit, occurred, the principal effect of gaining a base was to oblige the army to devote much of its resources to defending a fixed target.

This was true of Boston in 1775, Newport in 1776–9 and Philadelphia in the winter of 1777–8. After the French entry into the war in 1778 this was especially dangerous, as the possibility of concerted operations by a French fleet and an American army made British bases vulnerable, as British fears on behalf of their principal base, New York, demonstrated. A British memorandum of March 1779 claimed that the major British posts were poorly fortified and that therefore they:

> . . . would be in a critical situation, if four or five ships of force were to arrive, when we were without men of war, as at present, as such a naval force might cover a numerous descent of the New England and Continental troops . . . in one week might prove fatal to our detached cantonments and decide the war.

In November 1779 Sir George Yonge, a prominent opponent of the war, told the House of Commons that 'the last campaign in America [the 1779 campaign] was not only a defensive, but a disgraceful campaign. Instead of gaining a single foot of ground, we had lost what we possessed in the beginning of it . . . Sir Henry Clinton, with the grand army, had called in all his distant posts, and was in a great measure besieged in New York, or so straitened in his quarters, as to be pretty much in a similar situation'. The American, James Duane, coming to the same conclusion, referred to the British in New York that September as a 'grand army cooped up in a garrison'. In December Sir Charles Bunbury urged the cost and intractability of the American conflict as a reason for abandoning war. He told the Commons that Britain had no hope of conquering America, that she might as well seek to conquer Turkey, a clearly impossible goal, and that in the last campaign the army had 'showed itself incapable of any one offensive

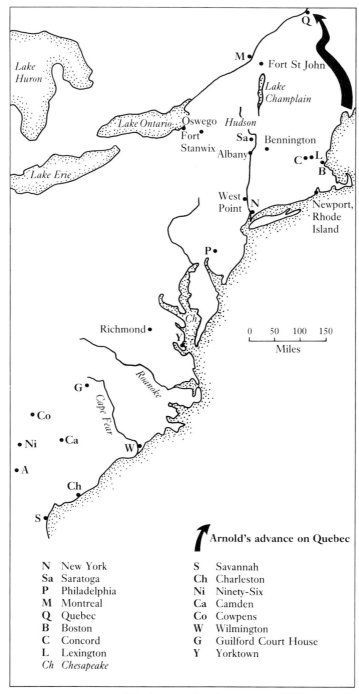

N   New York
Sa Saratoga
P   Philadelphia
M   Montreal
Q   Quebec
B   Boston
C   Concord
L   Lexington
Ch *Chesapeake*

S   Savannah
Ch Charleston
Ni Ninety-Six
Ca Camden
Co Cowpens
W   Wilmington
G   Guilford Court House
Y   Yorktown

The American Revolution

operation, and even of maintaining and defending the small part of America which we had for some late years held, for the army had evacuated Rhode Island, on the news of d'Estaing's approach'. Admiral Viscount Howe had already in April 1779 highlighted the vulnerability of the British defensive position in the face of French naval power when he told the Commons that the previous year:

> ... the army could never have made their retreat good from Philadelphia, if d'Estaing had arrived a few days earlier; that the Delaware would have been blocked up; and that the supply of provisions being cut off, the army under Sir Henry Clinton must either have been starved or be compelled to force their way to New York under every possible disadvantage: or supposing that the army might have gained New York without any considerable loss, the force under his command in the Delaware, deprived of their co-operation must have fallen into the enemy's hands.

Even without considering the impact of French naval power, however, the need to defend these ports was an obvious strategic encumbrance. To a certain extent it encapsulated the problems presented by the defence of Loyalist areas, although the task of defending ports allowed a more concentrated use of British forces. Charles, 1st Earl Grey, who served in America as a major general from 1776 to 1782, calculated that 14,700 men were required for the defence of New York and 6,000 or at least 4,000 for that of Rhode Island.

Capturing ports without destroying American forces might have its drawbacks, but it was nevertheless not without value. The centres of American life were on or close to the Atlantic seaboard. Some 75 per cent of the American population lived within 75 miles of the sea. The economy depended on maritime communications, not only for exports to and imports from foreign markets, principally Europe and the West Indies, but also for inter-colonial trade. A British pamphlet of 1756 had dismissed the possibility that American economic growth might lead to independence by arguing that 'it will be always in our power to subject them by our fleets, and still more by refusing them supplies of many of the necessaries of life'. It might be true that the British conquest of the centres of maritime American life did not give them victory, but it is important not to discount its impact. Although Boston, where the British army was hemmed in, was evacuated in 1776, Philadelphia in 1778 and Newport in 1779, the British were always, with a brief exception in the summer of 1776, in control of at least one major port: 1775: Boston; 1776: Boston and later New York and Newport; 1777: New York, Newport, and later Philadelphia; 1778: New York, Newport, and for a while Philadelphia; 1779: New York, Newport for most of the year, and Savannah; 1780: New York, Savannah and later Charleston; 1781 until the end of the war: New York, Savannah and Charleston. Bourbon naval intervention made the British position vulnerable, but as these major bases were held it is difficult to see how the Americans can be seen as having won the war other than in the very important negative sense of denying victory to the British.

It is arguable that a 'seaboard strategy', a concentration of effort on gaining control of ports and blockading the rest of the coast, was the most sensible one for the British, as it took advantage of their major strength, naval power, and minimized two of their principal difficulties: logistics and the problems of operating and fighting inland, where the terrain was often unfavourable for conflict and transportation. By sticking to the seaboard British forces could lessen the need to move supplies overland and to protect them when thus being moved. Attacking the American coastline would make it harder for the Americans to mount amphibious operations of their own. In January 1779 the movement of some of the garrison of Halifax, Nova Scotia to join the army around New York was approved in part because 'the sea coasts of the New England provinces' were to be attacked and therefore the Americans would be in a poor position for mounting any attack on Halifax.[5] It is unclear what such a 'seaboard strategy' would have led to had it been followed, although speculation is not idle as such a course was urged by some commentators, while critics of the North ministry, after the Bourbons entered the war, suggested that the government retain its coastal possessions in America and concentrate offensive operations against Spanish America. The British navy could land the army where it chose and there was little that the Americans could do about it. Once inland, and forced to rely on either a waggon-drawn or foraged logistical network, the army, however, was in a different position. The British pummelled the Americans in both the middle colonies and the south, but the Americans, became increasingly adept at trading space for time.

A fully-developed 'seaboard strategy' was, however, never followed for a number of reasons the importance of which varied. There were several goals for which significant inland operations appeared to be necessary. These included the need to defend the ports from American forces, and that of protecting Canada, a need that led to the stationing of forces whose use in offensive operations from Canada appeared logical; a sense of obligation towards the Loyalists that was matched by a belief that they could become a militarily valuable force; domestic pressures for victory; the wish to defeat the Americans decisively and speedily in a setpiece battle in order to inhibit foreign support for them; and the fact that the 'seaboard strategy' had already failed in New England in 1775. After the French entry into the war Britain could no longer plan on assured naval superiority in American waters and it was largely the French refusal and inability to fulfil American hopes that they would concentrate their naval forces there that provided the British with a precarious superiority for most of the following two years. Grey argued that 'it must ever be understood that Rhode Island can only belong to that power who rules the ocean', as a garrison there would be dependent on sea-borne supplies. The dangers posed by French naval forces were suggested by the panic over a possible attack on New York in 1778 and by the French role in the unsuccessful siege of Savannah the following year. France, however, devoted more effort to the unsuccessful invasion of England in 1779 and to operations in the West Indies, where d'Estaing took Grenada in 1779. These represented a more obvious, successful and profitable revenge for French losses in the Seven Years War than intervention in the American conflict. To a certain extent the British acted in America after 1778 as if the French had not intervened, although they were very conscious of this intervention. Operations in the south were dependent, at least initially, on naval support, as well as on sea-borne supplies, while the increasing British presence in Virginia was reliant on the backing of the Royal Navy. On the other hand,

Clinton's generally cautious use of his substantial forces based in New York was a consequence not only of personal temperament, but also of a sense of the vulnerability of his base.

America could not have been conquered by a 'seaboard strategy', although the Revolutionary government could have been overturned. At any one time, however, the British were never in control of more than a part of the Thirteen Colonies and, as the war in the north increasingly stabilized after 1777 and that in the centre after the retreat from Philadelphia in 1778, it became more likely that she would never conquer many of the areas in rebellion. Nevertheless, that did not make failure inevitable, nor should the numerous problems that can be enumerated, ranging from logistics and terrain to the sheer scale of America, be used to arrive at the same conclusion. Instead it is necessary to consider the possibility that the American conflict would have ended, as the wars of the period commonly did, with a compromise peace.

The eventual settlement was in part such a peace, less obviously in the case of the new American republic, which gained recognition and extensive territories, but had to accept the failure to gain Canada, than in that between Britain and her European rivals. It is worth considering, however, the possibility that a settlement might have been negotiated that would have left a constitutional relationship between America and the British Crown and even, in the case of a preferential system of foreign trade, with the British parliament. During the war a new relationship was defined between Britain and Ireland, one in which the Westminster parliament and the government in London surrendered most of their prerogatives. It is not impossible that British victory over the American Revolutionaries would have created the basis for a new political settlement, either as a result of negotiation or as a consequence of an upsurge of Loyalism and a falling away of revolutionary spirit under the strain of defeat. In December 1774 Ensign Jeremy Lister offered one alternative. He wrote from Boston, 'I hope next summer, we shall humble them in such a manner, as they will be glad, to accept of such terms, as government will think proper to grant them'. He was, however, to be wounded on the retreat from Concord. In July 1776 the Marquis of Rockingham suggested another, 'if this campaign ends without complete victory on either side, there may be some chance of more temper prevailing', while British victories later in the year led not only ministerial supporters but also their opponents, such as Charles James Fox and the Duke of Richmond, to speculate on the chance of negotiations.

It is easy to dismiss such a suggestion. There is little doubt of the determination of many of the Revolutionaries and although the Howes were appointed peace commissioners, as well as commanders-in-chief in 1776, they were expected to crush the revolution, to force the colonists to accept that they were subjects and to lay down their arms, before they negotiated such an accord. The British offer of pardon upon submission, however, was rejected. Benjamin Franklin wrote to Viscount Howe in July 1776:

> It is impossible we should think of submission to a government, that has with the most wanton barbarity and cruelty, burnt our defenceless towns in the midst of winter, excited the savages to massacre our farmers, and our slaves to murder their masters, and is even now bringing foreign mercenaries to deluge our settlements with blood.[6]

Five months later, with Congress having fled from Philadelphia to Baltimore, many individual rebels wavering or making terms with the British and Loyalism ascendant, the situation looked different. The British military effort still faced formidable problems but that had not prevented victory in battle. Aside from the political reverberations within America, the strategy of cutting America in twain that was to be advanced in 1777 was already a prospect. The Americans had been thrown out of Canada and defeated at the naval engagement off Valcour Island on Lake Champlain in October 1776. The possibility of a British advance via Ticonderoga to the Hudson valley was made more attractive by the establishment of Howe's army at New York. His defeat of Washington and pursuit of him across New Jersey ensured that New York would serve as a base for offensive operations, rather than being a target. In such a context it was not implausible to hope that Congress or individual states would negotiate. European independence wars had been ended by peace settlements, as in Hungary in 1711, and indeed a feature of early-modern European political violence involving members of the social élite had been conciliation rather than brutal suppression.

If such conciliation is treated as impossible in the American case, the military task facing the British was indeed formidable, especially once the opportunities created in the 1776 campaign had been lost. However, that does not imply that the British position was hopeless, militarily or politically. Militarily, it was still possible to hold and gain coastal enclaves, to retain Canada and Florida, to launch offensives into the interior and to hope to defeat the main American army, although these objectives were complicated by the French intervention. Politically, it could be hoped that the continued British presence and war-weariness on the part of the Revolutionaries would lead to an attrition of will, to an upsurge of Loyalist sentiment and activity, to conciliation by degrees of a substantial part of America. The eventual consequences of such military and political activity were unclear to contemporaries. They were worth pursuing, however, in the hope that they would bring victory or provide Britain with bargaining counters in any eventual negotiations. In addition, it was feared that abandoning America would allow the Revolutionaries to attack nearby British possessions: Canada, Nova Scotia, Newfoundland and Florida, and would permit the Bourbons to concentrate their efforts elsewhere.

Thus the war was not lost because of Bunker Hill, Washington's dramatic counter-attack in the last days of 1776, or Burgoyne's surrender at Saratoga in 1777. Each made it very much less likely that the conflict could be brought to a close by the conquest of most of America, but none of these defeats left Britain without objectives, options and possessions in America. The question of what policy to follow, given the possibility of achieving goals short of widespread conquest, was a difficult one and it was confused by the continued lure of such conquest. This tension can be seen in the growing interest in the south from late 1778.

The south offered not one strategic option but a number, including most obviously, the contrasting objectives of gaining Savannah and Charleston and of seeking to control a large portion of the interior. If the latter was intended it was unclear which areas should be sought, whether simply Georgia, the state in which it was easiest to operate, not least because of the British position in neighbouring Florida, or more territory: all or part of the Carolinas and Virginia. Linked to the temperamental clashes between Clinton and Cornwallis was an important difference over the extent to which British successes in the south should be followed up and operations extended. Cornwallis pressed in April 1781 for a war of conquest, an offensive war centring on the over-running of Virginia, and made it clear that he had little time for a defensive plan centred on raiding expeditions despatched from a heavily defended New York. As a result of the winter campaign of January–March 1781, Cornwallis was physically and emotionally spent and, arguably, somewhat confused about the wider strategic situation. Clinton was more cautious, writing to Cornwallis the same month:

> I shall be sorry to find your Lordship continue in the opinion that our hold of the Carolinas must be difficult, if not precarious until Virginia is in a manner subdued, as that is an event which I fear would require a considerable space of time to accomplish, and . . . it might be not quite so expedient at this advanced season of the year to enter into a long operation in that climate.[7]

The tension between Clinton and Cornwallis seriously hindered coordination of the British war-effort in 1781. Clinton never understood Cornwallis' state of mind. This tension was related to markedly different strategic conceptions. Clinton was more cautious, stressing the significance of naval power and troop numbers, and was convinced of the importance of the New York region. He had written in January 1781, 'My situation is critical, Washington's not less so. I have, however, all to hope. He all to fear . . . if we are properly reinforced, if we remain superior at sea, and have an active co-operating naval commander, I think rebellion will be staggered the course of next campaign, without the French should be reinforced also, or these people subsidized with money, but if we are starved, all our golden dreams will vanish'. Two months later Clinton again stressed the need for reinforcements and naval control when he wrote to Cornwallis, 'there seems little wanting to give a mortal stab to rebellion, but a proper reinforcement, and a permanent superiority at sea for the next campaign, without which any enterprise depending on water movements must certainly run great risk', while in May 1781 he emphasized the difference between his problem in defending New York and Cornwallis' situation by directing attention to the position on land, 'Lord Cornwallis has not, nor ever had 1,500 Continentals opposed to him', whereas Clinton felt himself threatened by Washington 'and five inveterate war-like provinces at his call – very different, in their appearance and conduct in war, from the poor heartless militia of the Southern provinces'.[8]

The clash between Clinton and Cornwallis both raises the question of what would have happened had Clinton really controlled the British campaign in 1781 and highlights the range of options confronting British commanders and the fact that they could choose. Their choices have been scrutinized by historians with great attention, as indeed they were examined by contemporaries, and much criticism has been directed both at individual commanders and at the general calibre of British generalship. Blame has been widely distributed: Gage for failing to adopt an adequate defensive posture around Boston and for his tactics at Bunker Hill; Howe for his failure to destroy Washington's army and capture Philadelphia in late 1776, and for over-extending his forces in New Jersey then, and in 1777 for failing to coordinate operations with Burgoyne and taking so long to capture Philadelphia; Burgoyne for plunging ahead towards Albany in 1777 despite being outnumbered and unsupported; Clinton for his caution as commander-in-chief and Cornwallis for his invasion of Virginia in 1781. These are only the most conspicuous instances of a list that could be easily lengthened to take account of the numerous strategic and tactical mistakes and faults that have been ascribed to individual commanders. In addition, British generals as a group have been criticized for unimaginative leadership and poor and confused strategic planning, an analysis that has been extended to much of the naval command, particularly the First Lord of the Admiralty, the Earl of Sandwich, and to Germain, the minister who was principally responsible for the conduct of operations.

It would be idle to dismiss these charges. Specific failures can be ascribed in large part to poor generalship and the individual and cumulative effects of these disappointments and defeats was to deny Britain victory. However, before it is concluded that poor leadership lost Britain the war, it is important to note first that this was not restricted to the British forces; secondly, that the British did enjoy a number of important successes which helped to keep them in the war, thus ensuring that victory was a possibility and a compromise peace likely; thirdly, that British operations in earlier conflicts, as against the French in Canada in 1755–9, had not always been conducted brilliantly and yet victory had been achieved eventually, and fourthly, that the task facing the British leaders was formidable. It is easy to contrast them unfavourably with such eighteenth-century generals as Frederick the Great of Prussia or the French Marshal Saxe, but these continental counterparts neither had to coordinate land and sea operations nor to operate at such a distance from their home bases. It is also worth noting that they made mistakes and even Frederick was defeated. His conduct of Prussian operations in the War of the Bavarian Succession (1778–9) was less than brilliant and, as in America, logistical problems played a major role. Aggressive plans of campaign were not realized by an unresponsive army and the Austrians achieved a defensive victory in the field,[9] indicating the importance of avoiding manoeuvres or battles that might lead to defeat, a lesson that Cornwallis could have profited from two years later.

One obvious problem with contrasting European and American operations to the detriment of the British generals was the different size of their armies. In 1778 Frederick fielded about 202,000 men. His rival the Austrian Field-Marshal Lacy kept most of his 100,000 strong *Elbe Armée* in a single mass. The peacetime Austrian establishment in 1775 was 175,000 men, but by 1779 297,000 were ready to take the field and by 1783 the establishment was 307,000 strong. Furthermore, the Austro-Prussian theatre of war in 1778–9 was not extensive and neither side had to divert resources to naval conflict.

In contrast British forces in America were relatively small and very spread out. Lieutenant-General Edward Harvey pointed out in November 1776 that troops should not be wasted as it was 'difficult to replace them'. The British and Irish army establishment at the beginning of 1775 was about 36,000 strong. The envisaged strength of British land forces for 1776 was 96,314, comprising 24,811 in Britain, 8,003 in Ireland, 5,635 in Gibraltar and Minorca, including 2,373 Hanoverians, 3,501 in Africa and the West Indies, 40,522 men with Howe, including 2,000 marines, 1,038 Loyalists and 12,982 Hessians, and 13,842 in Canada, including 615 Loyalists and 5,780 Germans. The Army Estimates provided to the Commons in December 1779 noted a rise to 179,500 troops, but of these 42,000 men were in the militia, while of the 90,000 deployed abroad, 15,000 were in the West Indies and Africa and 12,000 in Gibraltar and Minorca.

A force of over 60,000 in North America might sound substantial, but they were spread out from Canada to Florida, many units were committed to garrison duties, and others were operating in hostile terrain. Due to American attacks, each foraging unit had to be accompanied by strong detachments. Individual British armies were far smaller than 60,000 strong. Howe sailed with 9,000 men from Halifax to New York in June 1776. By the end of 1776 he had 27,000 effectives and was calling for 15,000 reinforcements. A 'State and Distribution of the Troops under the Command of Sir H. Clinton' on 21 November 1778 recorded:

Posts	Rank & File fit for duty	Effectives
New York	13,800	16,943
Rhode Island	4,627	5,740
Nova Scotia	2,396	3,073
Floridas	1,062	1,679
Sailed under General Campbell [for Pensacola]	941	1,102
Sailed under Colonel Campbell [for Georgia]	2,290	3,303
Bermuda	211	
Providence	179	
	25,506	31,840
Sailed under Grant [for West Indies]	4,369	5,262

On 1 September 1779 the rank and file present and fit for duty in New York and its 'depending posts' were 16,184, in Rhode Island 3,781, in the south 3,587, in West Florida 1,241 and in Halifax 1,750. In October 1780 the comparable figures were: 15,739 under Clinton and 3,838 under Haldimand in Canada, but 34,977 in Britain. Clinton's units were 4,986 under-strength. The British were dependant on being able to hire German soldiers, among whom troops from Hesse-Cassel were most important. German auxiliaries provided 33 per cent of the British strength in America in 1778–9 , a percentage that rose

to 37 in 1781. The British spent substantially more on hiring Germans than the French provided to the Americans

The British forces operating in the field were often quite small, and therefore especially vulnerable to casualties. There were only 3,252 British and 3,007 German rank and file fit for duty, alongside 500 Indians and 145 Canadians, when Burgoyne's army reached Ticonderoga in 1777. Clinton sailed to the relief of Newport in 1778 with 3,000 men, Cornwallis had only 2,043 men, of whom 817 were British regulars, at the battle of Camden in August 1780. He had just over 6,000 rank and file at Yorktown, of whom only 3,273 remained fit for duty when he decided to surrender. These were small forces, a consequence of the need to retain so many men for the defence of bases, an obligation that the French expeditionary force did not share.[10] Given the small size of these armies it is not surprising that British officers sought to conserve their units. Their tactics were certainly different from those of the Russians operating far from their bases against the Turks in 1768–74 and 1787–92. Golitsyn advanced with 80,000 against Khotin in 1769, Rumyantsev and over 35,000 men defeated the Turks at Kagul in 1770, and he crossed the Danube with 55,000 men in 1774. In 1788 the Russians attacked with 130,000 men; in 1790 Suvorov stormed Izmail with 31,000 men, losing 4,260 dead and wounded. British commanders could not afford such losses, and therefore tended to avoid the option of storming, whether Washington's lines outside Boston in 1775–6 or his lines at Brooklyn in 1776. The 1,000 men lost in the frontal assault on Breed's Hill in the battle of Bunker Hill in June 1775 had much to do with these attitudes.

British generals were well aware of the importance of army size. They continually stressed their need for reinforcements and in outlining plans to Germain linked their execution to specific army sizes and to the arrival of fresh units by certain dates. Generals commonly feel they have insufficient resources, but, by contemporary standards, they had a good case. This may well be seen as a crucial constraint on British policy. It was certainly seen as such by the Americans. Replying to a complaint from Brigadier-General Alexander McDougall about a shortage of troops and the inadequacy of the garrisons in the Highlands north of New York, Alexander Hamilton, one of Washington's aide de camps who later became his Secretary of the Treasury and most trusted cabinet member, reassured McDougall in March 1777 that Howe would attack Philadelphia instead, 'not being very numerous it is unlikely they should attempt such an object, without collecting their whole force; and for that reason it is not much to be apprehended they should make any stroke of the kind you mention, which would require a number of men they could not spare, and would probably delay the execution of what clearly appears to be their principal intention'. The following month he wrote to the New York Committee of Correspondence, doubting that Britain could yet attack Philadelphia because of, 'the extreme difficulties they must labour under for want of forage, and the infinite hazard they must run by moving with a small body of about 5,000 men, with an enemy in the rear, incapable of sparing any considerable body of troops to form a post behind, and be an asylum to them in case of accident'. Hamilton returned to the theme of the problems Howe faced as a consequence of the small size of his army. The American use of militia ensured that although Washington was

A VIEW of the STRENGTH of t[he TW]O ARMIES, (Regular and Provincial) acting under the COMMANDER IN CHIEF and Lieutenant-General EARL CORNWALLIS, at different Periods of the Years 1780 a[nd 178]1; and of the REGULAR FORCE of the ENEMY, French and AMERICANS, opposed to each in their respective Districts, according to Calculations drawn from the [best in]formation that could be procured.

Under the immediate Command of Sir Henry Clinton

Under the immediate Command of Sir Henry Clinton at different Periods.	Rank and File for Duty	Average Strength of the Enemy (including French and exclusive of Militia) opposed to Sir Henry Clinton at different Periods.	Rank and File according to the best intelligence received.
In South Carolina, Georgia, and East Florida in the Month of May, 1780	1113	Charles-town, when besieged, were the Virginia, Maryland, and Delaware Brigades	3000
Embarked with Sir Henry Clinton for New-York on the 1st of June, 1780, after the Reduction of Charles-town, and the Submission of the greatest Part of South Carolina	411	Continentals under General Washington in the Vicinage of New-York and in the Forts	14000
At New-York and its Dependencies on the 1st of July, 1780, including the Corps which accompanied Sir Henry Clinton from Charles-town	1430	French Army at Rhode Island under Count Rochambeau arrived July 11, 1780	5800
N. B. Their Recruits very sickly, and spread Contagion through the Army.		Total	19800
At Do. on the 1st of November, 1780, after General Leslie's Expedition had failed, and including 1371 foreign and British Recruits arrived from Europe October 30th, 1780	1286		
At Do. on the 1st of January, 1781, after the Detachment sent to South Carolina under General Leslie, and that to Chesapeak under Brigadier-general Arnold	1151	Continentals under General Washington in the Forts and their Vicinage, after the Revolt of the Pensilvania and Jersey Lines, and the Detachments sent to the Southward under Generals Greene, La Fayette, and Wayne	6000
At Do. on the 1st of June, 1781, after the Detachment sent to the Chesapeak under General Phillips	118[ ]	French Troops who joined him from Rhode Island in July, after which he took the Field	5000
At Do. on the 1st of August, 1781, including 312 British Recruits joined June 27th	1003		
At Do. on the 1st of September, 1781, including 2408 German Recruits joined the 14th of August, and the Foreign Regiment from the West Indies joined the 28th of August	1189	Total	11000

Under the Command of Earl Cornwallis in the whole Southern District

Under the Command of Earl Cornwallis in the whole Southern District at different Periods.	Rank and File for Duty	Average Strength of the Enemy (including French and exclusive of Militia) opposed to Earl Cornwallis at different Periods.	* Rank and File according to the best intelligence received.
Left by Sir Henry Clinton with Earl Cornwallis in the Southern District, after the Embarkation for New-York on the 1st of June, 1780	7215	Regular Continental Troops under General Gates, taken at the highest Calculation before the first Battle of Camden, 16th of August, 1780	2000
Sent to the Chesapeak under General Leslie the 6th of October, 1780, and joined the Army in South Carolina in December, 1780	1206	Regular Troops under General Greene before the Battle of Guildford on the 15th of March, 1781	2000
Recruits sent to Charles-town under General Rose the 4th of November, 1780	571		
Total in South Carolina, Georgia, and East Florida to the Close of the Year 1780	9594	Regular Troops under General Greene before the second Battle of Camden, April 25th, 1781	1500
Marched with Earl Cornwallis into Virginia the 25th of April, 1781	1435		
Third, Nineteenth, and Thirtieth Regiments, and British Recruits arrived at Charles-town the latter End of May, 1781	8459	Regular Troops of the Enemy under General Greene in South Carolina	2000
	2314		
	10791		
Sent to the Chesapeak under Brigadier-general Arnold the 11th of December, 1780	1608	Regular Troops under the Marquis La Fayette in Virginia and Maryland	900
Ditto to ditto under General Phillips, March, 1781	2049		
Ditto to ditto under Colonel De Voit, April 29, 1781	1610	Regular Troops under the Marquis De la Fayette in Virginia	1000
Arrived with Earl Cornwallis from Carolina the 20th of May, 1781	1439		
Guards from their Guards arrived from England and Charles-town in June	130	Joined by a Body of Eighteen-months Men	1000
Convalescents sent to Portsmouth under Lieutenant-colonel Macpherson	500		
In Virginia	7243	Joined by the French Troops under Monsieur St. Simon in the Beginning of September, 1781	3800
In the Carolinas, Georgia, and East Florida	10793		
Total Rank and File for Duty left with Earl Cornwallis, and sent to the Southward between June 1780 and May 1781	18135	Total regular French and American Troops opposed to Lord Cornwallis in Virginia, before the Junction of General Washington	5800

N. B. As Sir Henry Clinton did not receive [Regular] Returns of the Troops in the Southern District, he cannot positively say that their fit for Duty at different Periods exactly corresponded with the above State of them; but he has endeavoured to be as exact as his information would admit. The Militia of the Enemy, (which were a very fluctuating Body) opposed to either Army on particular Occasions, are not noticed in the above View; because, though there can be no Doubt but [that Lo]rd Cornwallis had at Times very considerable Numbers of them acting against him, it is equally notorious that the Militia of the Northern Provinces, who were even more numerous [to]ward, could be collected on Occasion with still greater Facility, and were constantly ready to oppose any Move of the Division of the Army under Sir Henry Clinton's immediate Command.

A comparison of the British and Loyalist strength with that of the French and Americans, printed in 1783 obliged to be reliant on poorly-trained men in order to field a sizeable army, British generals were never sure of the strength of their opponents. Thanks to the militia, American armies seemed to appear out of thin air.

British commentators emphasized the need for substantial forces. It was argued in May 1775 that 'General Gage will not be able to maintain his ground without a reinforcement of double the numbers he has at present: then at least five thousand men must be sent to New York to cut off the communication between the southern and the northern provinces, and as many more will be necessary for the preservation of Canada . . . unless such forces are dispatched speedily, rebellion will gain too great a head'. The following month Rockingham was certain that the army in Boston was 'much too small . . . to subdue and vanquish, the prodigious strength and numbers of all America', however many 'individuals' might be slaughtered. On 4 December 1775 Sir John Wentworth, who had taken refuge in Boston from his governorship of New Hampshire, wrote to Rockingham, 'In or about last spring I wrote your Lordship, that not less than 25,000 men would be requisite to subdue this continent. That number might and probably would have been effective before 1st October last. It now demands at least 40,000', he argued, because of the increase in the strength of the Revolutionaries. Grey wanted about 40,000 men, while one of Howe's leading questions for Cornwallis was, 'did you ever conceive that with the number of troops under my command any other plan than that which was adopted for the campaign of 1777 would have given us a fairer prospect of terminating the war favourably to Great Britain'. In 1778 Clinton complained, 'All the world are witness how mortifying this command has been to me. I was promised an army complete, and a reinforcement of 12,000 British and 2,000 Germans; instead of which 9,000 are taken from me'. The following February he commented on the possibility that the fall of Georgia might affect South Carolina, 'there was a time when this operation must have been attended with every success, but that time is no more. Instead of near 36,000 men [including Burgoyne's army] by detachments etc. I am reduced to little more than 18,000 men of those a great proportion foreigners and provincials'.[11]

Clearly the limited forces at their disposal affected the strategic plans and tactical moves of British generals. In 1777 it was impossible to send a substantial force to the Highlands at the same time as Howe advanced on Philadelphia, a move that might have helped Burgoyne; or to attack New England the same year, a move the Americans feared, and one that might have prevented the militia concentration at Bennington, which had such fatal consequences for Burgoyne's advance. Had the British had more troops they might have been able to operate earlier in the south, frustrating the consolidation of rebel authority, and in 1781 to advance from their base in New York preventing Washington from marching to Yorktown. However, the point should not be pushed too far. Aside from the serious problems of supplying larger forces, bold moves were made, as by Burgoyne or in the south. Indeed, alongside criticisms of timid generalship, indecisive campaigns and cautious conduct on the battlefield, have come charges of over-confidence and insufficient caution. There was certainly no relationship between size of force and boldness of generalship. The British were encouraged by the problems facing their opponents and, although to a varying extent, by the prospect of Loyalist support. Germain wrote to Howe in May 1777 expressing the hope that that year's campaign would end the war:

> I am extremely concerned to find that you do not imagine your force to be as suitable to the operations of the ensuing campaign as you confess it was to those of the last: My concern is however in a great degree diminished by the intelligence which we daily receive of the rebels finding the utmost difficulty in raising an army to face His Majesty's troops . . . there is every reason to expect that your success in Pennsylvania will enable you to raise from among them such a force as may be sufficient for the interior defence of the province, and leave the army at liberty to proceed to offensive operation.

Two years later Major Robert Rogers wrote from New York to Lord Amherst, who was in practice Commander-in-Chief of the British army (although the title was withheld from him to avoid offending the Duke of Gloucester, George III's brother, who had sought the post), 'The face of affairs becomes every day more agreeable to our wishes. The dissensions among the rebels and the great depreciation of their paper, promises the happiest effects. If Great Britain will persevere America must soon be conquered.'[12] The idea that the Revolution was the work of a few miscreants, who had managed to arm some rabble, and that the preponderance of colonials remained loyal subjects of the Crown was the centrepiece of British strategy. It was unclear what the British were fighting for, if not to restore legitimate government, and for what they perceived were the vast majority of still loyal citizens.

Germain's point about difficulties in the American army was a crucial one. It was and is easy to stress problems facing the British, but many of these were shared by their opponents, who also faced serious difficulties of their own. As with other conflicts of the century, it was in part a matter of who succumbed first to their weaknesses and the degree to which they could be coped with. These problems ensured that considerable stress was placed on the attitude of the local population.

This was far from consistent, and British generals were disenchanted with the degree of support they received from the Loyalists, Burgoyne being disappointed in his advance in 1777, as Howe was in Pennsylvania and Cornwallis was to be in North Carolina. Burgoyne subsequently asked why the Loyalists did not rise near Albany or help St Leger's supporting expedition, writing 'A critical insurrection from any one point of the compass within distance to create diversion, would probably have secured the success of the campaign'. In large part the British suffered from their fatal delay in extending the war to Pennsylvania and the south, for in the meantime Loyalists had been isolated by the local militia and cowed into inactivity or submission. On the eastern shore in Maryland, for example, where large numbers of the poor had flouted revolutionary authority, a lack of sustained British support and the activity of revolutionary institutions brought a measure of order. Although defence against Indians had depended on both regulars and militia, the policy after the Seven Years War of entrusting the defence of the colonies to British regulars rather than locally raised units was possibly partly responsible for the weakness of the Loyalists. The fact that Loyalists tended to want peace and quiet affected their willingness to take up arms for the king. On the other hand, there were a number of Loyalist units and in 1780–1 they composed a large portion of the British forces in the south. Ferguson's force, which was destroyed at King's Mountain, were all Loyalists, as, for the most part, were Tarleton's Legion.

Aside from failing to recruit sufficient Loyalists, the British made little attempt to obtain Negro support, although they did use Indians extensively. In November 1774 James Madison, a Virginian, had warned:

> If America and Britain should come to an hostile rupture I am afraid an insurrection among the slaves may and will be promoted. In one of our counties lately a few of those unhappy wretches met together and chose a leader who was to conduct them when the English troops should arrive – which they foolishly thought would be very soon and that by revolting to them they should be rewarded with their freedom. Their intentions were soon discovered and proper precautions taken to prevent the infection. It is prudent such attempts should be concealed as well as suppressed.

He returned to the theme the following June:

> It is imagined our Governor [Lord Dunmore] has been tampering with the slaves and that he has it in contemplation to make great use of them in case of a civil war in this province. To say the truth, that is the only part in which this colony is vulnerable; and if we should be subdued, we shall fall like Achilles by the hand of one that knows that secret.

That summer Jeremiah Thomas, a Negro pilot who himself owned slaves, was sentenced to death in South Carolina for supplying arms to the slaves and encouraging them to flee to the British.[13] In practice the British made relatively little use of Negroes, although slaves made up about a sixth of the colonial population. Lord Dunmore, the Governor of Virginia, had promised freedom to slaves who took up arms against the Revolutionaries, a move that led many undecided whites to join the Revolutionaries, and he created an 'Ethiopian Regiment' of several hundred escaped slaves. The use of Negroes was an important issue only in the south; in contrast they, like the Loyalists, played a relatively minor role in the fighting in New England. General Prevost armed two hundred Negroes at the time of the American–French siege of Savannah in 1779, a step that was criticized by the Americans.[14] When the British threatened Charleston in May 1779 a large number of Negro slaves fled to their camp in search of promised freedom. During the siege of Charleston in 1780 the British encouraged slaves belonging to Revolutionaries to run away, although those of Loyalists were returned to their masters on condition they were not penalized. Slaves of Revolutionaries were to work on sequestered estates or perform other designated tasks in return for which they would receive their freedom at the end of the war. Fleeing slaves were punished by the Revolutionaries. The first three captured attempting to flee to Dunmore in 1776 were publicly hanged, decapitated and quartered. Towards the end of the war there was increased interest in the idea of Negro troops. In January 1782 Dunmore backed John Cruden's proposal for arming 10,000 Negroes, who would receive their freedom under white officers. Two months later James Moncrief, the chief engineer in Charleston, and Lieutenant-General Leslie, the commander there, proposed the raising of a Negro regiment.

Nothing came of these proposals, an obvious contrast to the British use of natives in India, and in the West Indies during the Napoleonic War. Robert Clive's victorious army at Plassey in 1757 consisted of 2,000 sepoys (native troops) and 900 British. By 1765 there were 9,000 Indian troops in the army of the East India Company, and in 1782 the British army in India was 115,000 strong, ninety per cent of it Indian. Negro regiments were raised in the West Indies by the British during the war with revolutionary France. This contrast owed something to the different military environment. Although the West Indian planters, like the American Loyalists, were generally unhappy about the arming of the Negroes and promises of their future freedom in the West Indies, it was an obvious response to the arming of Negroes by the French, while in India the French had pioneered the training and arming of native units. In America, in contrast, Britain's opponent was hesitant about such a course, while the nature of the struggle as in part a civil war ensured that the British were sensitive to Loyalist susceptibilities. Possibly this should be seen as an unimaginative response. Although inexperienced in the use of firearms, Negroes could be trained, and some acted with success as irregulars, fighting on the eastern shore of the Chesapeake alongside Loyalist partisans and, calling themselves 'the King of England's soldiers', fighting on from the Savannah river swamps after the British had evacuated Charleston and Savannah. In May 1786 a combined force of militia and Catawba Indians defeated them, but a year later a governor's message mentioned serious depredations of armed Negroes 'too numerous to be quelled by patrols' in southern South Carolina.[15]

Although the failure to use Negroes on a major scale can be criticized as foolish, it would certainly have complicated the British position in the south and would not necessarily have helped them in New England and the middle colonies. As the British position in the south depended crucially on the winning of Loyalist support, it would have been dangerous to jeopardize this. In November 1779 the Earl of Shelburne warned the House of Lords about the danger of arming Jamaican Negroes.[16] On the other hand, the British were willing to use Indian assistance, despite the outrage that their fighting methods aroused. They were well suited to fighting in the backcountry, an area in which the British military presence was sparse, and, unlike Negroes, were trained in the use of arms and in operating in units. The Indian military potential was considerable given their hunter–warrior training and their not inconsiderable numbers, especially in comparison to the backcountry whites. The independence that made them the great warriors they were, however, also made them uncontrollable in conjunction with regular forces. In addition, the Indians were divided and their politics often factionalized. They were also vulnerable to smallpox, which affected the Creeks in Georgia in 1779, uninterested in a defensive strategy involving garrison duty, and disinclined to abandon the winter hunt for campaigning. The British were unsure about how best to use the Indians. In 1775 Gage ordered Guy Johnson and John Stuart, the Superintendents of the Northern and Southern Indian Departments, to obtain Indian help against the Revolutionaries, but Stuart saw the Indians as auxiliaries who should fight in conjunction with regular or Loyalist forces. He wished to avoid a savage frontier war including attacks on women and children that might antagonize Loyalists. The propaganda use the Americans made of the scalping of Jane McCrea by one of Burgoyne's Indian scouts in 1777 suggests that this was wise. The use of Indians was also criticized in parliament, and British soldiers could think them cruel. The Cherokees, however, were under pressure from illegal settlements, and in 1776, rejecting Stuart's request to await the arrival of British troops, they attacked the Virginia and Carolina frontier. However, the isolated Cherokees were badly defeated by large militia forces and forced to cede much of their territory. Inexperienced Americans were given a blooding which would later prove to be beneficial.[17] The following year the British forces invading from Canada under Burgoyne and St Leger were assisted by Indians. They were seen as important in controlling the backcountry. John Hayes wrote of the American garrison at Ticonderoga, 'our savages will hem them in, in such a manner that they all must be taken'. They were, however, to prove a disappointment, although that owed much to their being poorly supplied and supervised. An Indian force of Seneca and Mohawk warriors played the major role in ambushing American militia under General Herkimer sent to relieve Fort Stanwix, but their subsequent decision to decamp obliged St Leger to abandon the siege and they plundered and attacked Loyalist and British soldiers. The Indians at Bennington scattered when attacked by New England militia.

Contemporary American cartoon depicting British bounty payments to the Indians for taking American scalps

Most of the Indians fought on the British side and their attacks put a lot of pressure on the American frontiers, on for example the Pennsylvania–New York frontier in 1778. There the defeat of the militia by an Iroquois–Loyalist force under John Butler in the 'Wyoming Massacre' was followed by the devastation of the Wyoming valley in July, much of the population being scalped. That December Hayes claimed that 'Butler and Brant at the head of Indians and Loyalists have done more to put an end to this rebellion this summer, than all our armies during the war – Desolation must be adopted'.[18] American counter-attacks by George Rogers Clark into the Illinois country in 1778 and 1779 and by John Sullivan into western New York in 1779 brought successes, such as Clark's capture of Vincennes in February 1779 and Sullivan's victory at Newtown in August 1779, but they were indecisive and the Indians maintained the pressure in New York, on the upper Ohio and in Kentucky until the end of the war. In December 1780 John Rutledge, the refugee Governor of South Carolina, wrote, 'I am afraid the mischief lately committed by the Cherokees, in Rutherford County, will prevent our receiving aid from the backcountry, and lessen what we should have from the neighbouring [counties]'. The same month Cornwallis noted that such Indian action was being actively encouraged in order to prevent the frontiersmen from attacking the British.

It is not clear whether Britain could have made more of her Indian allies. They were better at ambushes than at attacking fortified posts, and were vulnerable to attacks on their settlements. Frontier warfare posed particular logistical problems for both sides, as it was difficult to transport supplies and to obtain sufficient food locally. A projected expedition to take the British base at Detroit, in order to blunt the Indian threat, was agreed to in June 1778 but abandoned the following month as impracticable, Patrick Henry, Governor of Virginia, explaining that 'from a scarcity of workmen and materials, from the want of waggons, from the exhausted state of this country, as to several articles called for, and the distressed situation of our people, resources and supplies, I

Medal given to Indian chiefs by the British in recognition of their aid during the War of Independence, from Tancred's Record of Medals

think the next spring is as soon as the march proposed can be thought of '. He also suggested that whereas an attack on the hostile tribes near the frontiers would be useful, Detroit was too far, 'a post will be difficult to maintain while the great intermediate country is occupied by hostile Indians, and from which it seems easy for the enemy to retreat with all their stores while they are superior upon the adjacent waters', a reminder that British naval power was important to their position on the Great Lakes. Conversely the British army in Canada was affected badly by supply failures in 1778–9, which handicapped their ability to mount operations.[19]

Had the British been more successful in uniting and supporting the Indians they could probably have put more pressure on the American frontiers and this might well have affected the operations of Washington's army. As it was, Indian advances to German Flats and Cherry Valley in New York and Forty Fort in Pennsylvania, all in 1778, took them within striking distance of centres of American power and that year two Continental regiments were sent to join the Western Department, which had been created in 1777. In 1779 Sullivan's army included three brigades of regulars. Had Indian pressure been greater it is probable that even more units would have been diverted or, conversely, if Clinton had been more active it would have been harder to spare the men to fend off Indian attacks. State governments kept up a continual pressure for assistance against Indian attacks and this acted as a counterweight to requests for help to the Continental army. The Indians would have been harder to organize and lead than slave units and most of them were further from the principal theatres of operations. Neither group possessed the potential of the Loyalists. Had the British raised the Negroes or placed greater emphasis on the Indians, a course urged by Dunmore, the task of reconciliation would have been far harder. This was important as the government needed to retain the final objective of the war in mind. The restoration of the colonies to royal government would be pointless if they required a substantial garrison and if the embers of rebellion remained among a discontented population. This would have led to a substantial tax burden that would have had to be borne by the Americans or the British, both options that would have been politically hazardous.

Some British commentators were more inclined to favour proposals that might accentuate the bitterness of the conflict. A stress on the need to consider American opinion in the shape of the Loyalists could lead to the same consequence, as support for active Loyalists could entail, as in the south, taking sides in bitter local disputes; a different course from the idea of encouraging people to be Loyalists by following a policy of conciliation. However, just as the American leadership was hesitant about the radical proposals of Charles Lee, so the British did not pursue some of the possibilities open to them. To have done so would have been risky politically, of unknown value militarily, and at variance with the ethos of a military system whose acceptance of new developments was not limitless. If the dramatic expansion in the use of sepoys in India suggests that major changes were possible, this took place outside the structure of the regular army, while the political context in America was very different, as greater sensitivity had to be shown towards local opinion.

British forces operating in America encountered similar problems to those faced by their opponents, such as supply difficulties and a frequently unfavourable terrain and climate. If Burgoyne had to hack a path through a wilderness and cope with waterways with serious natural obstacles on his advance in 1777, Benedict Arnold had faced worse problems when crossing Maine on the way to invade Canada in late 1775. Most Americans were also unused to the backcountry. There were few frontiersmen in the American army. Most of the troops were farmers or townsmen. Nevertheless, the impact of such problems varied. Most of the British forces, both officers and men, were unused to American conditions, while transportation and supply problems were naturally greater for an army dependent in large part on a trans-oceanic base and with only limited local sources of supply. Howe asked Cornwallis during the parliamentary enquiry:

> Is not the country in general so covered with wood, and so fitting for ambuscades, that little knowledge can be had of it by reconnoitring?

> Is any country, considering the circumstances of the American war, so well calculated for the defensive, as the country of America?

> Were not the movements of the King's army much embarrassed, and retarded, by the difficulties of getting provision and from the closeness of the country, which, in general, would not admit of the army marching, but in one column with the baggage?

James Murray reported from America that British troops did not know the country, were oppressed by having to carry a heavy load and were 'living on salt provisions, under a burning sun, to which they are not accustomed'. The troops who attacked Breed's Hill in 1775 carried 70-lb packs in a scorching 90°F Boston heat. The reliance on salt rations that an absence of fresh meat produced could lead to resentment and plundering, as in Westchester County, New York, in the autumn of 1776. Even when British forces were within easy reach of maritime communications, supplies could be a considerable problem. Major Sill was very unimpressed by conditions at Boston in 1775, 'monstrous distress for want of provisions . . . no fresh provisions . . . our army in a most melancholy situation, so much so that I believe half of them would desert if they could get off, the greatest part of us are encamped and the rest in cold bad churches without bedding, fuel or any fresh provisions'. And yet soldiers coped. Lieutenant Ashton Shuttleworth, who was with the artillery at Bunker Hill, recorded, 'the two howitzers . . . had shells plenty, but no cartridges . . . but luckily for us there was a barrel of powder, and some cartridge bags, though of another sort, which our people were dextrous enough to make up'.[20]

The British had, of course, operated extensively in North America during the Seven Years War, and had freed themselves from a total operational dependence on maritime and riverine communications. The logistical problems of acting in the interior had been largely surmounted, although only after much hard work and several major failures. However, the American war posed greater problems. Whereas in the earlier conflict the British had been able to draw on substantial supplies from the American colonies and their forces had operated with the benefit of a secure hinterland, this was not the case in the American war. Secondly, their adversaries enjoyed local sources of supply and manpower.

Thirdly, as operations were increasingly conducted in the south, so British troops found themselves in more difficult circumstances. Humidity and malaria were problems in the coastal lowlands, summer heat throughout the south and the less populous nature of much of the region made supply more difficult. The British had no time to become acclimatized. The heat and the greater distances made their heavy loads and uniforms a greater burden. In addition, there were numerous rivers, the bridges over, and ferries across which could be destroyed. In the middle colonies British forces tended to operate close to major bases and to the sea, but in the south they moved further afield, with detrimental consequences to their effectiveness.

When in August 1777 Howe's force was seen off the Virginia Capes and its destination assumed to be Williamsburg, York or Portsmouth, Thomas Jefferson claimed, 'Here he may destroy the little hamlet of Williamsburg, steal a few slaves and lose half his army among the fens and marshes of our lower country, or by the heats of our climate'. The British force that invaded South Carolina in 1780 was badly affected by illness, Hayes writing, 'A country full of marshes and small rivers, woods and insects, and a sun so powerful in heat, with dews at night most astonishing and to which the soldier must be always exposed, are causes not to be combatted with . . . sickness therefore was general and of the bilious kind mostly tending to a putrescency . . . This sickness has been the reason why we were not in possession of North Carolina'. Clinton noted the results in terms of the dramatic fall in the number of Cornwallis' effectives. In May 1781 Clinton wrote, 'General A. [sic] is arrived, he says that one of the reasons of the reduced numbers before Guildford was the great numbers of soldiers worn down with fatigue. He hints at desertion, which such a march must of course have occasioned. I have been comparing the returns fit for duty of those I last year left with his Lordship, the reinforcements I have since sent him and his last returns, and I find the deficiency nearly 2,445 men at a much healthier season than when I left him'.[21]

Despite these difficulties, the British were able to act effectively, the siege of Charleston in 1780 proving to be one of their most successful operations of the war. The Carolina interior posed a number of problems, although the British grasped the value of cavalry in the Southern Piedmont, an area that was mostly tree-covered but without obstructive undergrowth. The climate in the south led to a reverse of the seasonal preference for major operations further north. Instead of an emphasis on summer and autumn, there was a stress on autumn and spring and an avoidance of summer, whether the enervating heat of the Piedmont or the heat and humidity of the often swampy lowlands. Heat was not only a problem in the south. Hugh Percy, Lord Warkworth, wrote from Boston in 1774, 'We have days here full as hot as Spain, I am at this instant writing to you sweating without clothes. But our climate is horridly inconstant, for we have it sometimes very cold. But I think ever since we landed it has in general been full as hot as the south of France'. Temperatures of 90–100°F during the day, with sudden drops to around 60°F, are not unusual in a New England summer. Advancing from the St Lawrence towards Lake Champlain in June 1776 Lieutenant William Digby complained of 'the great heat', adding in July:

The weather was intensely hot, scarce bearable in a camp, where the tents rather increased, than diminished it, and the great number of men in so small a space, made it very disagreeable, though we all went as thinly cloathed as possible, wearing large loose trousers, to prevent the bite of the mosquito, a small fly which was then very troublesome. Our men in general were healthy and not much troubled with fevers and fluxes so common when encamped in a warm climate, and lying nights on the ground under heavy dews. The tree spruce, which grows there in great plenty, as indeed in most parts of America, is an excellent anti-scorbutic and when made into beer, is far from a disagreeable flavour.

In July 1777 General Leslie wrote to his brother from Staten Island after his return from, 'our marching and counter-marching in the Jerseys . . . the weather was much against us, for we had it very hot and a good deal of rain, and no tents . . . We embark tomorrow . . . I hope it is north, for the climate will be our enemy if we go southward'.[22]

Despite the similarities of the problems posed by terrain and climate, there were marked differences between the situation of the two combatants. Lieutenant James Hadden of the Royal Artillery, campaigning in Virginia in early May 1781, explained the failure to engage the Americans under their French general the Marquis de Lafayette:

> . . . our force is near two thousand, a number fully sufficient to thrash the Marquis, but as the situation of the Southern Army after all their victories has shown that it is not by fighting we must conquer a people who get recruits within ten miles, while ours come three thousand, the general contented himself with effecting the object of his expedition and destroying a quantity of public stores, particularly twelve hundred hog's heads of tobacco immediately in front of the royal army, which the gallant Marquis suffered to be completed without making any opposition.[23]

Manpower was a crucial problem, felt most acutely by Clinton.[24] In May 1779 he contrasted 'a time when the war was young, when the enemy was little accustomed to service, when no decided public assistance to the rebels was apprehended from any foreign power' to his current wretched situation:

> I with an army reduced in numbers exposed in the very point in which we depend for assistance to the assaults of a French perhaps I might add a Spanish fleet . . . The Admiral tells me that the number of ships which he is to have on this coast will not be above a peace establishment and one half of those are detained in the West Indies . . . the divisions at Philadelphia are great and their distresses are so everywhere; let them not flatter themselves however that Washington cannot bring forth an army. He has already a much greater than he had when Sir William Howe marched against him in 1777.[25]

British forces were large enough to confront and defeat American armies, but the need to defend ports and major settlements once seized was both a drain on manpower and a significant limitation of strategic options. The ability of the militia to control most of the country not actually occupied by the British gave the Americans a tremendous advantage. They were also more numerous in most engagements, a factor that was commonly important in deciding which army would win in battles fought in seventeenth and eighteenth-century Europe and was also very significant in those won in the 1790s by the armies of revolutionary France.[26] To concentrate on manpower would, however, be to suggest that British defeat was inevitable. Such a conclusion appears less obvious if the difficulties facing the Americans are considered.

3 The Revolutionary War Effort

Could we but get a good regular army we should soon clear the continent of these damned invaders.

Thomas Nelson, 2 January 1777[1]

It had been determined by a council of war before my arrival to take post at this place. The strength and condition of the army not admitting of further operations. It is fed by daily collections, and has been subsisted with the utmost difficulty the short time it has been here . . . the whole state has been so ravaged by the numerous militia that have been kept on foot accompanied with such a scene of plunder and waste that I am apprehensive it will be next to impossible to form magazines sufficient for the support of the few regular troops we have . . . The regular force that is here is so naked and destitute of everything, that but little more than half of them are fit for any kind of duty.

Major-General Nathanael Greene (Charlotte), 7 December 1780[2]

Any stress on the difficulties confronting the British cannot detract from the immensity of the problems facing the revolutionaries. They were seeking to defeat a highly trained army backed up by both the largest navy in the world and the strongest system of public finance in Europe and supported by about one-fifth of the population of the Thirteen Colonies, as well as by much of the population in nearby colonies, all of which provided the British with bases: Canada, Nova Scotia, Newfoundland, Florida and the British possessions in the West Indies. The Americans were not without a considerable military tradition, borne out of fighting both Indians and the Bourbons, and their success in both spheres had been considerable. Troops from New England had been responsible for the capture of Louisbourg in 1745. American troops had also played a prominent, although less happy, part in operations against Florida and other Spanish possessions in and around the Caribbean.[3] Indeed, given the military aptitude of so many Americans, it could be argued that the British government was foolish not to entrust the bulk of the defence of North America to the colonists. This would not have been a practical option in Canada, where much of the population was Catholic and of French origin, but elsewhere there appeared to be no great need for British troops. However, most British officers loathed the American troops and thought them generally incompetent and awful. Had such a course been followed then it is possible that there would have been no war or, if a conflict had broken out, that it would have ended rapidly with British forces defeated by well-trained and well-armed American units, although much would have depended on the strength of Loyalist sentiment. Instead, the British government had preferred to rely on British regulars, although some American militia units had had a recent role against the Indians. Before, although not after the Seven Years War, the British underestimated the American willingness to serve in regular military units.

Nevertheless, opposition to a standing army, British or their own, was part of the American ethos. The Americans were wedded to the seventeenth-century English polemic against standing armies, a polemic long out of fashion or ignored in imperial Britain. Washington observed in 1777 that he understood how Americans could be against a standing army in times of peace, but not how this could extend to wartime. One of the foremost problems the revolutionaries faced was political. There were three essential ways in which the principles expounded in the Declaration of Independence hindered American unity from the outset: first, the Americans' acceptance of the theory of 'natural rights' or 'natural law', which questioned the legitimacy of all central authority, be it British or American; secondly, the discrediting of executive power; and, thirdly, the decision to choose a plural rather than a single-nation interpretation of independence. The last was reflected in the use of 'they' rather than 'it', when referring to the United Colonies or, later, the United States, at least until after 1865.

The militia were to play a major role in the War of Independence, a subject that has been highlighted in important work over the last three decades.[4] Its role has to be seen alongside the serious difficulties that were encountered in creating, and still more sustaining, a Continental army, a force that would be under the control of the new government of the Thirteen Colonies, the Continental Congress, and that would face the British army in the field. This was a task for which the militia were poorly suited. State militias were ill-equipped, untrained and disorganized. The decision to emphasize the importance of a Continental army represented the rejection of an alternative path of military development advocated by Major-General Charles Lee, but totally disregarded by conservative Americans, one that would have centred on irregular warfare. The respective merits of the militia and the Continental army can be debated at length, and were indeed raised during the period, although the value of each clearly depended on capability, opposing strength and circumstances, matters which varied greatly; but the decision for a Continental army had an important political background. It symbolized the united nature of the struggle by the Thirteen Colonies and was a vital move in the effort to win foreign recognition and support. It was not necessary to have a Continental army, a force that would not dissolve at the end of the year, even if individual terms of service came to an end, in order for states to assist each other militarily. Prior to the Revolution military units had been deployed outside state bound-

The Declaration of Independence, signed at the Congress of 4 July 1776

aries, against both Indian attacks and the Bourbons, in Canada and the Caribbean. During the Revolution militia units under the control of state governments were sent to assist other states, as indeed they were sent to the Continental army. However, by having such an army, military decisions were in large part taken out of the ambit of state government. In theory this made the planning of strategy easier, freeing generals in some measure from the direction of state governments and allowing them to consider clashing demands for action and assistance.

Nevertheless, the creation of a national army, although essential to the dissemination of a new notion of nationhood, did not free military operations from the views of state and national governments, as the Schuyler–Gates controversy in 1777 over the command of the army designed to prevent an invasion from Canada indicates. In addition, the new national army did not enjoy the support of a developed system for providing reinforcements and supplies, let alone the relatively sophisticated one that enabled the British armed forces to operate so far from their bases. The provision of manpower and supplies for the Continental army created major problems, preventing or hindering American operations and producing serious strains in the relationship between the new national government and those of the states. The Continental army had to turn repeatedly to the states for their assistance. Washington had to beg men and supplies from the states. The response varied considerably. Virginia was a state that provided much support for the revolution but when, in April 1777, Congress recommended drafts from the militia to fill the Continental Army, Jefferson opposed it, arguing that it would be a very unpopular move. There were riots against the draft in Virginia in 1780. In 1779 when a boat with 5,000 stand-of-arms imported for use by the Continental Congress arrived in Virginia, the arms were seized by the government of Virginia on the grounds that the state was very short of arms; down to only 3,000 stand in all magazines. There was a serious dispute as a consequence.[5] On the other hand in November 1777 the General Assembly of Virginia resolved that the county lieutenant of each county should collect clothing for the Continental troops raised in the county, such supplies to be sent via the Deputy Quartermaster-General to Washington as soon as possible. Little was. Washington was forced to deal with states reluctant to replace normal camp wastage; a form of government in which Congress could do little more than request men, funds and supplies from the states; and troops who drifted off. Desertion implies furtively sneaking away, but Americans for the most part just walked out of camp.

Had Washington only to complain about the interference of Congress, the obduracy of state governments and continual problems with manpower and supplies, the situation would have been bleak enough, but, in addition, the revolutionaries faced the problem of war-weariness and a measure of declining enthusiasm for the cause of independence. There is a curious parallel between the derogatory remarks of many British officers and those of some of the American leaders. Hugh Percy could write from Boston, 'The people here are a set of sly, artful, hypocritical rascals cruel and cowards. I must own I cannot but despise them completely', but at the very end of 1777, John Harvie complained to Jefferson that the avarice of individuals was more threatening than the enemy, that it was impossible to purchase provisions for the army, that local government provided no assistance, that 'two-thirds of the state of Delaware are notoriously known in their heart to be with our enemies' and that the army bore the consequences, 'thousands are now in the hospitals for the want of even rags to keep them from the cold'.[6] Accounts of how the militia served to suppress or inhibit loyalist activity need to be complemented by an awareness of the extent to which local communities were not therefore disciplined to provide what was deemed to be necessary by Congress, an extra-legal body prior to 1781, and the army.

Patrick Henry, from Art in the United
States Capitol

On the other hand, these demands were considerable and the picture of a
people increasingly unwilling to serve, and dismayed by the demands of the
cause, glorious or otherwise, has to be matched by a realization of the problems
created by supporting the war-effort. From the perspective of Congress and the
army, local communities were obstinate and individuals selfish, and the
collective cause was thus undermined, with serious consequences for the
war-effort. The Continental army was seen to miss opportunities because it
lacked sufficient men and supplies or only received them too late. Richard
Henry Lee complained in April 1777, 'the slow assembling of an army prevents
any attempt from us upon the enemy, and will furnish them with an opportunity
of collecting reinforcements'. In the winter of 1777–8 General Anthony Wayne
blamed what he saw as a lack of support from Pennsylvania on anti-military
feeling in its government. In November 1778 Patrick Henry, then Governor of
Virginia, wrote to the President of Congress, Henry Laurens, concerning:

> ... the marching of the militia from this state to Charleston, which was requested by
> Congress. When the requisition arrived here the Assembly was sitting. It became necessary to
> lay the matter before them as the law gave the power of marching the militia to a sister state
> only in cases of actual invasion. An act was thereupon passed to enable the executive to send
> out the militia when *certain intelligence* of an *intended* invasion should be received. Just in the
> instant when orders were going to be sent to put the men in motion for Charleston, a letter
> from Governor Johnson [Maryland] arrived, by which it was apparent the enemy had no
> designs on that place. Upon this the Council thought with me it was proper to suspend the
> matter.

Congress was thus informed, not consulted. In June 1780 Washington complained about the plan of the New Jersey government for 'a draft from the militia to serve for the campaign, instead of being incorporated with their Continental battalions', while that October Horatio Gates, commanding the army in the south, found his orders to the North Carolina militia countermanded by the state's Board of War. Gates had to threaten officers who obeyed the Board with dismissal, but pressure from the North Carolina legislature played a role in his removal from command.[7]

Critical views are widely accessible because it is the papers of generals in the Continental army and politicians eager for the cause of independence that have been most extensively studied and published and because the general perspective is that of the independence struggle and the war against the British, which leads those who did not lend sufficient support to be presented as selfish hinderers. However, the colonial ethos has to be considered. Lack of intercolonial cooperation was deeply engrained, as can be seen from the failures of coordinated efforts between 1689 and 1760. Furthermore, the American economy had been gravely disrupted by the war. Commercial relations with the British colonies in the West Indies had been close,[8] America serving as their principal foreign source of much needed food supplies and horses, while other American exports flowed to continental Europe and the British Isles, from which in turn much needed imports were received. This economic system was essential to American prosperity, but it was interrupted by the war, because links were cut by edict, the disruption of financial relationships that war brought and the crucial loss of confidence, and because military action, the blockade enforced by the British navy and the depredations of Loyalist and Revolutionary privateers, helped to make commerce dangerous

A Delaware State one shilling note, printed 1777

and thus, in large part, uneconomic. Destroying stores of tobacco in the Chesapeake in May 1781, Lieutenant James Hadden claimed, 'tobacco alone has gained the rebels allies, and I hope the destruction of it will give the rebellion a severe check'.[9]

The war not only interrupted foreign trade; it also severely disrupted commerce within the Thirteen Colonies. Furthermore, the specific demands of supporting the revolutionary war effort placed a severe strain on economic activity. The financing of the war by the over-issue of paper currency, whose value deteriorated rapidly, posed many problems for those who sought to trade products or services and helped to sap economic confidence. The paper value of all certificates issued by the Quartermastership and Commissary departments was over $100 million. Over-issue led to a reluctance to accept American currency or bills which affected both the economy and military activity. Some Revolutionary firebrands, such as Richard Henry Lee, refused to accept Continental money from their own dependants. In July 1780 Gates complained that his troops were having to steal food in North Carolina, because the people refused to accept Revolutionary money or credits. Destruction to transport infrastructure, the breaking up of roads and bridges and the interruption of ferry services, created serious difficulties, although these were arguably less significant than the disruption created by the demands on transport services posed by the need to move military supplies. In July 1780 Washington empowered Greene to impress in New Jersey and Pennsylvania as many waggon teams as he thought necessary. The following April Greene complained 'our operations are very much retarded by a deficiency of teams'. Because Congress set meagre rates of hire, impressment was necessary, which led to the hiding of horses and waggons and to desertion.[10]

Possibly most critical was the demand for manpower which pressed hard on a society which benefitted from few labour-saving devices; and those were largely provided by animals which were also needed for the war effort. Family and communal economies, and thus the war effort as a whole, depended on the time-consuming and arduous tasks of breaking the soil, sowing, hoeing and harvesting, and the absence of men in the army threatened the ever-precarious balance of household economies. It was scarcely surprising that desertion was a serious problem, far more for the Americans than for the British forces, composed as they were of regulars, who were also far from home. American attempts to cause Hessian desertion had an impact, but were less effective than is generally believed. Nearly 3,000 Hessians deserted, but most towards the end of the war when it was clear that the British had lost; and the Hessian desertion rate was higher in 1762 during the Seven Years War, as was that of the Prussian army in 1778 during the War of the Bavarian Succession.

The extent to which the situation in America was misunderstood by British commentators was demonstrated in an anonymous pamphlet of 1776, which argued that:

> The resources of the Americans . . . lie all within their own reach; and the stores, which their country can furnish, may be brought together, as occasion requires, without any very extraordinary cost. When the public contributions shall cease, their armies, not fearing the

control of any civil authority, will provide for themselves the means of subsistence, as long as a single dollar is left in the pockets, or a single measure of corn in the granaries of the people.[11]

Washington was well aware of the strain created by the war. In September 1775 he wrote, 'the state of inactivity, in which this army has lain for some time, by no means corresponds with my wishes, by some decisive stroke to relieve my country from the heavy expence, its subsistence must create'. Certainly the demands of the new armies were substantial. Envisioning an army of 4,000 in order to implement the recent instructions from the Continental Congress that he invade Canada, General Philip Schuyler, the Commander of the Northern Department, urged the New York Congress in July 1775 to provide about six hundred tents, three months' provisions, tools, thirty barrels of pitch and a ton of oakum for boat-building, arms and powder, two tons of musket balls or lead, two tons of bar iron, thirty-five millsaws, hospital supplies, fifty swivel guns, fifty truck carriages and one hundred and twenty artillery carriages.[12]

The principal supply problems facing the Revolutionaries related to man-power, provisions and weapons. The last might seem surprising as several British politicians critical of the war, such as Chatham, asserted that America could not be conquered on the grounds that all Americans possessed guns, and indeed the image of an armed citizenry resisting the redcoats is well established. Charles Mellish MP argued in 1778 that the 'Americans had one advantage as a militia over most nations, the constant use of the firelock from children'. Jefferson asserted in June 1778 that hitherto the losses of the Revolutionaries had been about half only of those of the British, adding 'This difference is ascribed to our superiority in taking aim when we fire; every soldier in our army having been intimate with his gun from his infancy'.[13] Many Americans possessed firearms and were able to use them, in marked contrast to the population of much of Europe who both could not afford firearms and were denied them anyway in order to secure the hunting rights of their social superiors. In Normandy, for example, under an edict of 1766 a simple denunciation by a noble could lead to a peasant's house being searched and the culprit jailed for three months without recourse to the ordinary courts. No such social regime prevailed in America. Firearms were not available to all, and their general lack of familiarity with them was an obvious disadvantage to any plan for arming slaves, but they were more widely owned than in Europe, and most Americans still shot for the table. Yet some individuals did not possess them and the Revolutionaries were faced with severe shortages, especially in the first year of the revolution. Knowing how to load and fire a weapon no more made a man a soldier than giving him a uniform. Also, many militiamen left the family musket or shotgun at home for defence and hunting game, hoping to receive a weapon in camp. In addition, many militiamen were issued weapons which they took home with them.[14] The Loyalists were also very short of arms and ammunition. Governor Martin of North Carolina, who hoped to restore the south to George III through Loyalist action, asked for 10,000 stand-of-arms in September 1775. His hopes of local support proved to be wildly exaggerated, but of the about 1,400 Loyalist Scottish settlers who gathered at Cross Creek on 15 February

1776 only about 520 had firearms and the Loyalist Highlanders were obliged to rely on their broadswords.[15]

The shortage of firearms on the part of the Revolutionaries led both to frenetic attempts to obtain arms from Europe and to experimentation with other weapons. Pikes as weapons first appeared in the general orders for Washington's army in July 1775 and were last mentioned in August 1776, and they were used by Pennsylvania Associators from August 1775. That month Franklin drew up a memorandum for the Pennsylvania Committee of Safety supporting the use of pikes in the rear one or two ranks of units, 'the spirit of our people supplies more men than we can furnish with firearms ... a charge made with [pikes] insupportable by any battalion armed only in the common manner ... each pikeman to have a cutting sword, and where it can be procured, a pistol'. Virginian riflemen sent to help North Carolina in the spring of 1776 were also armed with pikes.[16] Fortunately for the Revolutionaries, this attempt to compensate for the absence of sufficient firearms was not tested in battle. There can be little doubt that the pikemen would have presented unwieldy targets for British musketeers. The poor state of the Revolutionaries' munitions in 1775 suggests that had the British army been able to act more vigorously in the early stages of the war, instead of being substantially confined to Boston, then they might have seriously checked their opponents. On the other hand, Boston appeared initially to be the source and centre of rebellion, while the march on Concord in 1775 hardly encouraged operations in rural areas where the British lacked an assured superiority of force. The abortive expedition to the Carolinas the following year also indicated the difficulty of both combined operations with Loyalists and amphibious attacks on Revolutionary strongholds.

The shortage of firearms, and military supplies, helps to explain why so much importance was attached to supplies from Europe and therefore to the retention of ports and to the capture of British munitions and ordnance ships.[17] The situation gradually improved thanks to foreign support, American ingenuity and the strength of their economy. Foreign arms were obtained, 23,000 French muskets in 1777, thanks to French governmental support for the pro-American initiatives of the playwright Beaumarchais and the fictitious company he created, Roderique Hortalez and Company. Seven of the eight ships he sent to America with munitions in 1777 arrived safely. The French contribution was crucial, but, in addition, armament plants were established, as at Fredericksburg in Virginia and Providence. Foundries were constructed at Easton, East Bridgewater, Lancaster, Principio, Springfield and Trenton, and craftsmen shifted production. In late 1775 all gunsmiths and blacksmiths in North Carolina were ordered to make muskets and bayonets, while in New England makers of muskets sprang 'out of pail makers, boatmen and farmers'. Soon after Nathanael Greene's appointment to command in the South in October 1780, he decided to begin production of musket cartridges at Salisbury. In July 1775 Madison expressed a common complaint when he wrote, 'the scarcity of ammunition is truly alarming', but by December Franklin was able to offer a more balanced account, 'We are using the utmost industry in endeavouring to make saltpetre, and with daily increasing success. Our artificers are also everywhere busy in fabricating small arms, casting cannon etc. Yet both arms and ammunition are much wanted'.[18]

The military situation was found far more serious if specific positions were considered. Fort Constitution was in April 1776 the only fortress in the Highlands, the uplands about forty miles north of New York, that obstructed any advance along the Hudson. It then had a garrison of 124 but only 'about one half of the privates are armed and about 60 bayonets among them . . . The fort on the land-side is entirely open. There is not one gunner or artillery man in the fort . . . The minute men work about 6 hours in the day and that with great reluctance'.[19] Such conditions prevailed elsewhere and explain the importance of determined leadership in retaining and attacking fortresses, for the undoubted advantage that fortified positions provided could often be overcome. European engineers were extremely helpful in the fortification of Revolutionary positions. With time many individual positions were better fortified and manned and, more significantly, the Revolutionary forces were better supplied with firearms, a process aided by the extent to which New England rapidly ceased to be a conflict zone. Nevertheless, in June 1777 Washington refused to provide arms for the militia on the grounds that 'this article is too much wanted for the Continental army to be spared to the militia'.

Although serious problems were still encountered with firearms they were far less severe than those faced in the supply of provisions, clothing and footwear. An army of 20,000 men consumed about 33 tons of food daily,[20] and, despite the vitality of the American agrarian economy, the demands of the war proved difficult to meet, while problems with credit and transportation further exacerbated the situation. The rations established by Congress in 1775 for the rank and file were generous: one pound of beef, three quarters of a pound of pork or one pound of salt fish daily; one pound of bread or flour daily; one pint of milk daily; three pints of peas or beans weekly; one-half pint of rice or one pint of Indian meal weekly; and one quart of spruce beer per man or nine gallons of molasses for one hundred men weekly. However, the gap between aspiration and reality that was such a characteristic feature of eighteenth-century government was rarely wider than in the case of the condition of troops on active service. At Valley Forge the soldiers dined on 'fire cakes', a baked flour-and-water paste. In the south rations were often rice or 'johnny-cake', or hoe cake, mixed quickly from flour and water and baked over a fire on a hoe.

In America the situation was exacerbated by the difficulty in establishing a well-regulated and credit-worthy government. The war was fought largely through credit, not taxation, although the unreliable nature of the credit itself constituted a form of taxation, while commandeering was a very direct form. In Maryland, for example, the local authorities sought to requisition half of every household's extra blankets during the first winter of the war, paying for them in paper currency, and later sought similarly a pair of shoes from every housekeeper. The service departments established to support the Continental army faced difficulties from the outset from reluctance to accept paper currency and from the competing demands of state agencies. In 1779 a massive over-issue of currency produced depreciation and, in reaction, Congress halted the issue of paper money bills, helping to undermine totally the work of the service departments. In the bitter winters of 1779–80 and, even worse, 1780–1, the army had to live from hand to mouth. In early 1780 Congress devised a new

A page from the North Carolina Revolutionary army accounts, vol. 6, p. 11

system under which individual states were to be asked to provide specific supplies which would be credited towards their portion of Congress' debt. This did not work well, because of the growing exhaustion of the population, the reluctance of the states to subordinate their priorities to those of Congress, and their own problems with credit-worthiness. In consequence the army under Washington was in a very poor state during 1780, and Greene realized that he would have to rely on negotiating his own supplies from the states in the south, rather than on any help from the service departments. Greene feared the operational consequences of insufficient supplies, writing to the North Carolina Board of War on 14 December 1780, 'to detach one half of the army for subsistence will leave the other at prey to the enemy and this must be the case if the army is left to subsist itself'. Supply problems played a role in Greene's decision to send half of his army, under Daniel Morgan, into the South Carolina backcountry. As it was Greene's army was small, less than 2,000 strong, mostly militia, poorly equipped and clothed. Greene returned to the theme on 7 January 1781, writing to Governor Nash:

> It is impossible for an army in a country like this to subsist itself any length of time . . . the men may be dispersed about the country . . . but in such a situation they must soon fall a prey

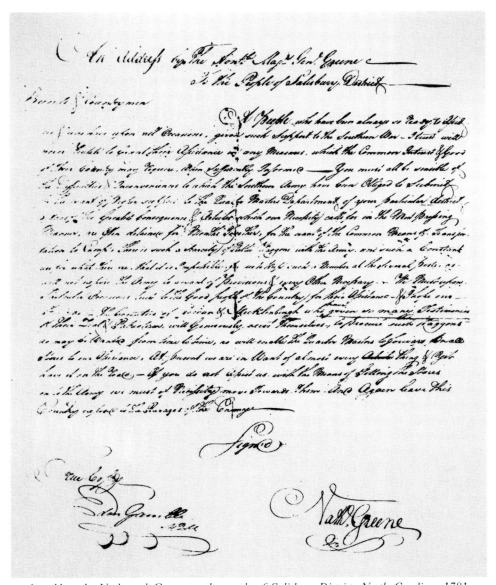

An address by Nathanael Greene to the people of Salisbury District, North Carolina, 1781, appealing for supplies for the Continental army

to their enemies, nor can they give any protection to the inhabitants. Besides which an army, in such a situation, must soon lose its discipline and become not less oppressive to the inhabitants than ungovernable by its officers.

Greene complained that there was no one to superintend the collection and distribution of provisions and forage. The situation led Greene to criticize the relationship between the army and the population, an extension of his concern about the militia. On 7 December 1780 he wrote to a friend, General Henry Knox, who was responsible for the American artillery:

> With the militia every body is a general and the powers of government are so feeble that it is with the utmost difficulty you can restrain them from plundering one another. The people don't want spirit and enterprise but they must go to war in their own way or not at all. Nothing can save this country but a good permanent army conducted with great prudence and caution; for the impatience of the people to drive off the enemy would precipitate an officer into a thousand misfortunes, and the mode of conducting the war which is most to the liking of the inhabitants is the least likely to effect their salvation.

On the last day of 1780 Greene made clear to Governor Lee of Maryland his view that civilian control was unsuited to war:

> It is unfortunate for the public that the business of the two great departments in which they are so deeply interested, Legislation and the Army, cannot be made to coincide better, but the pressing wants of the Army cannot admit of the slow deliberation of Legislation, without being subject to many inconveniences nor can a Legislature with the best intentions always keep pace with the emergencies of war: and thus the common interest suffers from the different principles which influence and govern the two great national concerns.

The following June Greene urged Lafayette not to 'pay any regard to the murmurings of the people'.[21]

Given such concern, diplomatically expressed, at the highest level of command, it is not surprising that the frustration felt by many soldiers led to more direct action. Indeed, it is possibly more remarkable that there had not been widespread mutinies earlier. This could be attributed to the troops' certainty of the justice and necessity of their cause, but it may also have owed much to the relative ease of taking leave without permission, a very frequent occurrence, as well as to a high rate of desertion. There had been disturbances in 1777, when an unpaid New England brigade had refused to join the main army in Pennsylvania, and in 1780, when two hungry Connecticut regiments had to be prevented from ravaging New Jersey, but in January 1781 both the Pennsylvania line and three New Jersey regiments mutinied. Short of pay, food and clothes and seeking discharge, they rejected British approaches, but the Pennsylvania mutiny was ended only by concessions, including the discharge of five-sixths of the men. The New Jersey mutiny, later in the month, was suppressed by firm action, but the entire episode was a salutary warning to the Revolutionary cause and cannot but give rise to speculation as to what would have happened had the army been obliged to endure another harsh winter without the prospect of a victorious close to the conflict that the triumph at Yorktown had brought by the following winter. Hamilton responded to the mutinies by writing to the Secretary of the French legation at Philadelphia, 'the republic is sick and wants powerful remedies. God send that the negotiation abroad for money may succeed; for it is only this that can give success to our interior efforts'. Germain was confident that American weakness would allow Britain to take the strategic initiative, that Cornwallis and Arnold would conquer Virginia without endangering British-held Charleston and New York, because, he argued, Washington's army was weak and Congress lacked authority and money.[22]

It is easy to understand why among the Revolutionaries there was both pressure to do something, to create a stronger government, and a desperate hope that in 1781 the French alliance would finally succeed militarily. However, neither option was free from serious problems. It was difficult to influence French policy, not least because action in the West Indies had already provided better results for the French and appeared likely to offer more. The strong sense of state identity and interests restricted any attempt to lessen state power in favour of Congress, while hostility to uncontrolled army activities was well developed. In New York State in early 1781 several local committees were stirring up opposition to the impressment of supplies by the army. Past experience with the service departments suggested that central control would not necessarily be a panacea.

If the supply of provisions and clothes continued to pose major difficulties and to be a matter of expedients until the end of the conflict, there were also significant difficulties in the manning of the Revolutionary army. The initial force that had blockaded Boston had been essentially a New England army, which dissolved that autumn only to have to be built up again in the face of the

American rifleman (left) and an American general from E. Barnard's History of England, *1790*

British that winter. Congress sought to create a broader-based army, based at first on a one-year term of service. The British decision to send substantial reinforcements, the basis of Howe's army which seized New York in 1776, led Congress to vote to raise eighty-eight battalions, with an intended strength for 1777 of about 75,000 soldiers. Men were offered enlistments for the war, with the eventual reward of 100 acres and 20 dollars, or service for three years. At first voluntary enlistment sufficed, but eventually conscription had to be resorted to, drafts from the militia for a year's service. Thus the states played a major role in raising troops, while, as men could avoid service by paying a fine or providing a substitute, the rank and file were largely drawn from the poorer sections of the community. They sought material benefits, bounties and wages rather than glory.

There were never enough troops in the Continental army. Outside Boston Washington had enjoyed numerical superiority, but next year the situation deteriorated. Washington was outnumbered by Howe in 1776 and, given the respective size and quality of the armies, Howe's decision to delay his invasion of Pennsylvania was crucial to the result of the 1777 campaign. Thereafter Washington, although sorely tempted by the idea of attacking New York, had insufficient men to do so. French troops, as well as sea-power, were crucial in the 1781 campaign. Generals in the Revolutionary army responded with frustration. Angered by the small size of their inadequately-supplied units, they were sceptical about the notion that militia support could compensate. Given the justified scepticism about Cornwallis' strategy of pressing north from South Carolina that has been expressed, it is worth noting Greene's complaint of 31 January 1781 to the President of Congress:

> Twenty thousand men might be in motion in the manner the militia come and go and we not have an operating force in the field of five hundred men . . . The enemy are in force and appear determined to penetrate the country, nor can I see the least prospect of opposing them with the little force we have, naked and distressed as we are for want of provision and forage. Our numbers are greatly inferior to the enemy's when collected and joined by all the militia in the field or that we have even a prospect of getting. The difference in the equipment and discipline of the troops give the enemy such a decided superiority that we can not hope for anything but a defeat. And the enemy being without baggage we cannot avoid an action if we would, especially as we have no place where we can take post for want of provision and forage . . . Nothing can save this country but a well appointed army and I wish conviction may not come too late.[23]

Greene failed to place sufficient weight on Cornwallis' difficulties, but his correspondence offers a salutary qualification to any notion of the British southern strategy as doomed to failure. Looking at the problems facing both sides is always crucial in military history, and in eighteenth-century European conflict it is often the case that the side with the most weaknesses lost, as a consequence of these difficulties, rather than of any strengths on the part of their opponents. Greene's letter highlights two particular problems of the Revolutionaries, which were relatively uncommon in European warfare. Poor logistical support hindered, especially in the south, the adoption of the blocking defensive positions that were so common in Europe, while Greene felt that deficiencies in his army gave the British 'a decided superiority' in the field. One might conclude that, given this army, it was just as well that the Revolutionaries could seek the help of 'a well appointed' fleet, albeit one under French colours, and then suggest that the fate of the war rested ultimately on the arithmetic of naval superiority, the competing appeal of naval operations and commitments in the West Indies and the quality of naval leadership.

There is a measure of truth in this, especially in explaining the fate of the 1781 campaign, but the argument underrates the contribution of Revolutionary forces. There is little doubt that the militia could be unreliable on campaign, keen to return home and not only when their term of service was complete. In the winter of 1778–9 General Lincoln encountered militia desertion and ill-discipline in the south. In 1779 several of the militia commanders refused to obey the order of the South Carolina Assembly to cooperate with Lincoln and at the battle of Stono Ferry in June he was let down by the retreat of the North and South Carolina militia. The following year the South Carolina militia disobeyed orders during the siege of Charleston, while more than 400 of the Virginia militia went home during Gates' advance on Camden. The North Carolina militia has been seen as poorly equipped and lacking in discipline. Greene complained from South Carolina in June 1781, 'the militia of this country will fight only in their own counties and districts, and it is with great difficulty they can be got out of them'.[24] However, not only could the militia defeat regulars under the right circumstances, the South Carolina militia under William Moultrie winning a minor victory at Beaufort on 3 February 1779, but their role in irregular warfare and political surveillance, intimidation and control, became more significant as the war in the south became more important. Pressed for manpower as a consequence of the broadening of the conflict to include the Bourbons, the British placed a greater stress on Loyalist support and it was this that the militia was best suited to counteract. Furthermore, the militia was well placed to seize what Greene called 'all their little outposts', the British positions that offered an appearance of control in the hinterlands of the well-fortified posts. Cornwallis wrote in May 1781 of, 'the clouds of militia which sometimes pour down upon us'.[25] The militia was far more effective operating as a home guard that could turn to guerilla action, than marching with the Continental army for three to six months.

If the militia restricted British control in the south, counteracting the consequences of their success in field operations at Charleston and Camden, the Continental army, poorly-paid, clothed and fed, and demoralized, had by its very presence confined the scope of the British military presence and operations in the middle colonies. Clinton was to be proved correct about the folly of Cornwallis' advance in 1781, but he was himself contributing little to any British chance of victory. Although the immobility and defensive posture of the bulk of the British forces in 1778–81 owed much to the French naval threat and to Clinton's caution, it was also a consequence of Washington's crucial ability to keep the Continental army in the field and undefeated. This was a considerable military and political achievement, one that was of international consequence given the importance of impressing foreign opinion, and one which would not have been obtained by irregular operations, however successful.

Hamilton claimed in April 1781 that by maintaining the Continental army, the British could be obliged to abandon offensive plans and that 'by stopping the progress of their conquests and reducing them to an unmeaning and disgraceful defensive, we destroy the national expectation of success, from which the ministry draws their resources'.[26] This revealed a realistic grasp of the political context of military operations, but that context was not uniformly bleak for Lord North. The general election of 1780 had gone well and in June 1781 Lord Mountstuart, a British diplomat, claimed '. . . the new Parliament has given a decided majority to the minister and the nation seems to have that kind of confidence in him as to assist him with their purses to the utmost extent, indeed as long as our credit can maintain itself we need not fear an enemy'.[27]

Hamilton and Mountstuart were both correct. Britain was willing and able to fight on, but had no real prospect of success. Hamilton thought this would lead to a negotiated peace and it was largely the French role that ensured that, instead, a large British army was defeated decisively for only the second time in the war. In part this defeat was a consequence of a recklessness borne of frustration with the progress of the war that Cornwallis was not alone in revealing. However, that very frustration was a product of American success, though triumph for the Revolutionaries seemed distant in the summer of 1781. As Washington's aide-de-camp Alexander Scammell wrote from Peekskill on 9 June:

> I shudder at the prospect of the ensuing campaign, not from any fear of the enemy, but from apprehensions of starvation. The supplies are so very precarious that the commander-in-chief I believe cannot lay a single plan or commence a single operation for want of the necessary supplies. We have no teams, but very few tents, and I fear by the time that the army ought to take the field that we shall have no provisions unless the states supply us very speedily.[28]

Bleak tidings, but Washington's achievement was to soldier on, to chart a path through his myriad problems, a path constructed of expedients and at times evasions of what might in other circumstances have been opportunities for success in battle, but one that eventually led to the consummation of independence in victory.

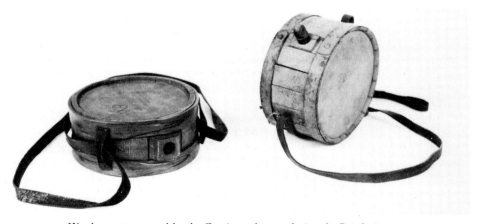

Wooden canteens used by the Continental army during the Revolution

4 Conflict

The War in this country is only fit for savages and robbers, it must be carried on in woods. It is a Petite Guerre, *proper to make good partisans, and the best qualification for a general is to be a good commissary to supply the army with provisions or a good mechanic to build batteries etc.*

Robert Knox, Montreal, 8 July 1776[1]

The War of American Independence can be seen as both revolutionary and traditional: revolutionary in that it was one of the first important instances of the 'nation-in-arms', and traditional in that it was essentially fought on terms that would have been familiar to those who had been engaged in recent wars in Europe and North America. There were significant differences, not least in terms of the role of cavalry and in infantry tactics, but it is important not to exaggerate the extent of novelty. There was little innovation in the technology of war, although there were experiments with new weapons, including the first working submarine, and the hope that new scientific knowledge could be applied to warfare was expressed. In February 1776 William Gosforth, a New York artisan who had become a radical politician, a captain, and the commander of the garrison at Three Rivers, wrote to Franklin:

> I understood you are a great man that you can turn the common course of nature that you have power with the Gods and can rob the clouds of their tremendous thunder. Rouse once more my old Trojan collect the heavy thunders of the united colonies and convey them to the regions of the north and enable us to shake the Quebec walls or on the other hand inform us how to extract the electric fire from the center. Then perhaps we may be able to draw a vein athwart their magazine and send them upwards cloathed as Elijah was with a suit of fire. One or the other of these must be done or we shall be drove to the necessity of another frolic of boarding the town.[2]

Other ideas were scarcely less adventurous. In 1777 Tom Paine worked on a crossbow which would throw an iron arrow across the Delaware, 'enclosing fire in a bulb near the top'. The following year John Stevens attempted to build 'a machine in the river, at West Point, for the purpose of setting fire to any of the enemy's shipping that might attempt a passage up it'. The great chain that was stretched across the Hudson there, one of the longest and largest iron chains ever forged, was a considerable technological triumph. More mundane efforts were made to improve the artillery. In March 1777 a 3-lb field piece made out of wrought iron was manufactured, while that summer Captain Louis O'Hickey d'Arundel, a Frenchman who was the commander of the Virginian artillery, was killed when a wooden mortar he had invented exploded.³ Such developments were but part of the long standing attempt to improve artillery, one that was especially urgent in America because of the need to establish new manufacturies and produce a large number of pieces rapidly using local talent and resources. This was a major problem, Franklin observing in January 1777, 'cannon of iron are casting in different places, as large as 18 pounders; but the workmen not being yet perfect in the business, many of the pieces fail in the proof, which occasions a want of cannon from Europe'.⁴

Experiments with submarine warfare were far more revolutionary. They were a response to the strength and importance of British naval power, but very much the product of the ingenuity of a couple of men. The first known description of a viable submarine was published by the English mathematician William Bourne in 1578, but a Yale graduate, David Bushnell (1740–1824), constructed the first operational machine. In 1774 he began to experiment with a submersible that would plant gunpowder beneath a ship and the following year a prototype was ready for testing and a way had been found to detonate a charge underwater. The wooden submarine contained a tractor screw operated by hand and pedals, a surfacing screw, a drill for securing the explosive charge, fitted with a time fuse, to the hull of the target, a depth pressure gauge, a rudder with a control bar, bellows with tubes for providing ventilation, ballast water tanks with arrangements for flooding and draining, fixed lead ballast, detachable ballast for rapid surfacing and a sounding line. Though Bushnell described the armament as 'a torpedo', after the stinging crampfish of the genus *Torpedinidae*, it was, in fact, a mine. Benjamin Gale described the submarine in August 1775 as:

> . . . a new machine for the destruction of ships . . . it doth not exceed 7 feet in length, and the depth not more than 5½ feet . . . plan is to place the cask containing the powder on the outside of the machine, and it is so contrived, as when it strikes the ship which he proposes shall be at the keel it grapples fast to the keel and is wholly disengaged from the machine. He then rows off. The powder is to be fired by a gun lock fixed within the cask which is sprung by watch work, which he can so order as to have that take place at any distance of time he pleases. He can row it either backward or forward under water about 3 miles an hour, and can steer to what point of compass he pleases . . . At the top he has a pair of glass eyes by which he sees objects under water . . . he has an anchor by which he can remain in place to wait for tide, opportunity etc . . . the whole machine may be transported in a cart.

The same year Joseph Belton of Groton presented to the Pennsylvania Committee of Safety his plan for a submersible, designed, unlike Bushnell's, to carry one or more cannon, which were expected to hole warships below their water-line. These ideas were genuinely revolutionary, offering a mode of warfare against which the British had no defence. Bushnell's *Turtle* could only attack ships at anchor, but, even so, the anchorages of the British fleet at Boston, New York and Newport provided obvious targets. The *Turtle* was not used in Boston harbour in 1775 as originally intended, and was first employed, against HMS *Eagle* in New York harbour, on 6 September 1776. Bushnell, however, encountered serious problems with navigating in the face of the currents and could not attach the charge, which went off harmlessly in the water. The second attempt, against HMS *Phoenix* on 5 October 1776, also failed. The *Turtle* was spotted, Bushnell's depth measurer failed and he lost his target. It is likely that the submarine was destroyed by British warships, when she ran the guns and penetrated the *chevaux de frise* (obstacles) in the Hudson between Mount Washington and Fort Lee on 9 October.

Bushnell had received little financial support from a hard-pressed government and Belton had no luck, finding that Congress 'had no great opinion of such proposals'.[5] This could be seen as a serious failure on the part of the Revolutionary government, although the results of the *Turtle*'s operations were not encouraging and Washington pointed out the difficulty of operating the machine satisfactorily. Alongside the fascination with the novel that helped to explain great public interest in experiments with electricity, there was a great reluctance to adopt new inventions. This was certainly the case with the submarine. Robert Fulton, another American, produced one in 1797 but found neither the French nor the British, then at war with each other, interested in its acquisition.

Belton had more luck in April 1777, seeking congressional support for a musket allegedly able to fire eight rounds with one loading, although there is no sign he ever fulfilled the order. Arms for the battlefield were a more urgent priority, and attempts were made to improve those that were available, David Rittenhouse studying methods of grooving cannon, using telescopic sights and incorporating ammunition compartments in rifles. As far as the British were concerned, the Kentucky or Pennsylvania rifle was itself a formidable weapon, at long range. Employed as a frontier gun, for hunting and Indian fighting, it was used only by frontiersmen. In 1775 ten companies of riflemen from the Maryland, Pennsylvania and Virginia frontier were raised by order of Congress, to help the New England force outside Boston. John Adams described them as 'an excellent species of light infantry. They use . . . a rifle – it has circular . . . grooves within the barrel and carries a ball with great exactness to great distances. They are the most accurate marksmen in the world'. The riflemen from western Maryland under Michael Cresap were armed also with tomahawks and dressed in hunting shirts and moccasins. Fast-moving, the Marylanders marched 550 miles to Boston in three weeks, then started to thin the British sentries, exacerbating the hemmed in and depressed atmosphere in Gage's army. James Murray reported:

> . . . the reason why so many officers fell is that there are amongst the provincial troops a number of enterprising marksmen, who shoot with rifle guns, and I have been assured many of them at 150 yards, will hit a card nine times out of ten . . . though those people in fair action in open field would signify nothing, yet over breast works, or where they can have the advantage of a tree (or a rock) and that may have every 20 yards in this country, the destruction they make of officers is dreadful.

They could actually hit targets at up to 200 yards under optimum conditions. In an echo of fighting against the Jacobites, the *Leeds Mercury* reported on 5 September 1775, 'A correspondent observes that the rifle-men amongst the

'Kentucky' or 'Pennsylvania' long rifle c. *1760*

Americans are held in the same degree of terror, as the broadswords were in the year 1745'. At Bemis Heights in September 1777 the riflemen under Daniel Morgan concentrated on picking off British officers. Burgoyne wrote subsequently:

> The enemy had with their army great numbers of marksmen, armed with rifle-barrel pieces: these, during an engagement, hovered upon the flanks in small detachments, and were very expert in securing themselves, and in shifting their ground. In this action, many placed themselves in high trees in the rear of their own line, and there was seldom a minute's interval of smoke in any part of our line without officers being taken off by single shot.

He found his Indian allies unwilling to help:

> ... not a man of them was to be brought within the sound of a rifle shot ... the best men I had to oppose as marksmen, were the German chasseurs, though their number was so small, as not to be one to twenty of the enemy.

One of the Loyalists in Patrick Ferguson's Loyalist force defeated at King's Mountain in South Carolina in October 1780 recorded that the Revolutionaries:

> ... were armed with rifles, well mounted and of course could move with the utmost celerity: so rapid was their attack ... King's Mountain from its height would have enabled us to oppose a superior force with advantage, had it not been covered with wood which sheltered the Americans and enabled them to fight in their favourite manner in fact after driving in our piquets they were able to advance in three divisions under separate leaders to the crest of the hill in perfect safety until they took post and opened an irregular but destructive fire from behind trees and other cover: Colonel Cleveland's was first perceived and repulsed by a charge made by Colonel Ferguson; Colonel Shelby's next and met a similar fate being driven down the hill; last the detachment under Colonel Campbell and by desire of Colonel Ferguson I presented a new front which opposed it with success: by this time the Americans who had been repulsed had regained their former stations and sheltered behind trees poured in an irregular destructive fire: in this manner the engagement was maintained near an hour, the mountaineers flying whenever there was danger of being charged by the bayonet, and returning again so soon as the British detachment had faced about to repel another of their parties.

After Ferguson was killed, morale broke and the Loyalists surrendered.[6]

It would, however, be mistaken to exaggerate the success of the rifle, or its novelty as far as the British were concerned. A rifle could carry no bayonet, took one minute to load and needed an expert to fire it, of which there were few. When the Duke of Richmond, a lieutenant-general who had served in Germany during the Seven Years War and who by 1779 was an opposition politician supporting the withdrawal of British troops from America, criticized the serious lack of riflemen in the British army, he was able to cite an example from his German days relating to Brunswick troops that would not have been out of place in North American conflict. This underlines the degree of similarity that could exist and the danger of contrasting European and North American warfare too starkly:

> ... his grace mentioned an instance of 800 of this sort of force, being posted by general Imhoff, last war, in a thick wood, near Cassel, directly in the front of the French army. It was astonishing the execution they did, and the difficulty with which they were dislodged was inconceivable. They placed themselves two and two behind the trees, and were such admirable marksmen, that as soon as any of the enemy ventured forward, they dropped them. After trying for a considerable time to dislodge these riflemen, the French general was obliged to march up a large body of his infantry with the utmost rapidity, and by that means, with very great loss on his side, at length dispossessed them of the wood.

Such German riflemen served with the British in North America, the *Jäger* of Hessen-Kassel well experienced in operating in wooded and hilly terrain, although there were only two companies in Howe's army. They had similar weapons to the American riflemen, although they were shorter in length. The *Jägers* wore green uniforms to blend into the woods, unlike the dark blue uniforms of the other Hessian troops. In 1779 more *Jäger* units arrived, bringing their total strength to over 1,000. The Hessian riflemen were reported 'as much superior to those of the rebels as it is possible to imagine', after the battle of Long Island in 1776. *Jägers* were at the front of Cornwallis' column at Brandywine and their sniping harmed the defenders of Charlestown in 1780. In 1779 James Pattison wrote from newly-seized Stony Point, 'The two first days the militia were importunately troublesome by coming down in small bodies, and firing upon our *Jäger* post, but five or six of them having dropped by our rifle shot, they thought fit to disappear, and have given us no further disturbance'.[7] The New York militia were unaccustomed to the range of rifles.

Nevertheless, it was not the fact that British generals could call on German riflemen that lessened the appeal of rifles to their American opponents. Instead, riflemen were seen as vulnerable to musketeers because their guns were not fitted with bayonets. They were also quick to desert, especially early in the war. In June 1776 Major-General Charles Lee, Commander of the Southern District, criticized long-distance firing by riflemen on the grounds that it added 'to the pernicious persuasion of the American soldiers-vizt *that they are no match for their antagonists at close fighting*'. In February 1778 General Wayne of the Pennsylvania Line asked the State Board of War to exchange all the rifles in his division for muskets, 'I don't like rifles. I would almost as soon face an enemy with a good musket and bayonet without ammunition – as with ammunition without a bayonet'. Wayne claimed that riflemen often fled in panic when attacked by soldiers armed with bayonets. The Board of War did not disagree but did not have sufficient muskets, so that Wayne was still trying to replace the rifles three months later. The British fear of American marksmen was therefore matched by American concern about British bayonet charges. As a consequence

British Marine rifle with bayonet, dated 1762. The British troops made effective use of bayonet charges against the American Revolutionary forces

the Inspector General, Baron von Steuben, introduced bayonet practice into the drill of the Continental Army at Valley Forge in early 1778 and at the battle of Monmouth that year the army made its own bayonet attack.[8] The bayonet was also used by the Americans when storming Stony Point, Paulus Hook and the Redoubt at Yorktown. Washington employed riflemen as skirmishers and snipers, not as regular soldiers.

Rifles had other problems. They could be fouled by repeated firing, as at Fort Washington in 1776, and they had a slow rate of fire, one round per minute, not much of a problem if sniping, but a serious problem in close order fighting. Thus, as in other respects, the early impression of a superior American method of warfare that had been engendered by the New England campaign of 1775 was replaced the following year by a sharper realization of weaknesses. This was linked to a major change in the war. For most of 1775 the British had been hemmed in at Boston and had not taken the initiative, but in 1776 they both did so and forced the Revolutionary forces to engage in battle. A Revolutionary song of late 1775, 'The King's Own Regulars', had mocked the British:

It was not fair to shoot at us from behind trees:
If they had stood open as they ought before our great guns we should have beat them with ease.
They may fight with one another that way if they please;
But it is not regular to stand and fight with such rascals as these.

The song had satirized the alleged attitude of the British commander concerning the retreat from Concord:

Of their firing from behind fences, he makes a great pother,
Ev'ry fence has two sides; they [the Americans] made use of one, and we only forgot to use the other.

American sniping was regarded as abhorrent by the British, Jeremy Lister writing after the retreat about 'their skulking way behind hedges and walls' and Digby recording in July 1776:

As brigadier General Gordon . . . was riding . . . he was shot by a scouting party of the enemy from the wood . . . of which he died . . . and in a general order to the army from his excellency

General Carleton after having expatiated on such a cowardly and cruel manner of carrying on the war, he describes the dress, person, etc. of the scout, their captain called Whitcomb a famous ranger from Connecticut, wishing should he be taken, he might be spared for the hands of the hangman, a soldiers death being too honourable for such a wretch.

Alexander Campbell, a Scot who served as a volunteer in the British army at Bunker Hill, wrote to his father, 'the native of this New England was always reckoned a barbarous cruel set and they absolutely prove to be so, they even poison their balls with arsenic and they are a cowardly set that will not fight, but when fenced by trees, houses or trenches'.[9]

However, sniping could not determine campaigns. Riflemen could make an important contribution when they had good cover, either natural, for example north of Fort Washington in 1776 or at Bemis Heights in 1777, or artificial, but these situations arose less frequently than is commonly supposed in American folklore with its romantic notions about frontier riflemen and their rifles. The situation of the outnumbered Revolutionary army in 1776, driven back from New York by Howe, was far from easy and the Americans were obliged to consider both how best to face the British in battle and how to balance regular and irregular warfare. Their response to battle was to adopt the lines of musketeers of European warfare. This was scarcely surprising as numerous Americans had served in the mid-century wars against the Bourbons, over 10,000 as regulars. Three veterans of the British army, Charles Lee, Horatio Gates and Richard Montgomery, were appointed as Revolutionary generals in 1775. Many others were familiar with the methods of European armies, especially the British, through reading, observation or discussion. Linear formations maximized the fire-power of musketeers and could be very flexible on the battlefield, as Frederick the Great had demonstrated in the Seven Years War. In America a more open, less packed, two-deep line was adopted because of the relative unimportance of cavalry. The transportation of horses posed major problems for the British, acquiring sufficient suitable mounts in America was not easy, and the Revolutionaries found cavalry units very expensive. As a result Congress refused to take the three light-horse companies raised by North Carolina into the Continental service, while similar units in South Carolina were converted into infantry regiments.[10]

The infantry therefore dominated the battlefield in the middle colonies, although the potential impact of the trained British musketeers with their bayonets was lessened by the ability of the Revolutionaries to entrench themselves in strong positions. Percy referred to them near New York in November 1776 as 'entrenched up to the eyes in three rows of lines'. In June 1779 Richmond urged the House of Lords to 'learn from America' in considering how to defend Britain from a possible Bourbon invasion:

. . . let the ministers consider to what it was that the long continuance of the war across the Atlantic was ascribable – to their entrenchments. Every Gazette account, from the affair at Bunker Hill to the very last action, told us that the Americans had been uncommonly active in their works of this kind; that they were entrenched up to their teeth; that as soon as one work was demolished, another at a little distance presented itself, and another after that; in short, that the industry displayed in this kind of defensive operation was astonishing.

The value of such positions had been amply demonstrated at Bunker Hill, and British casualties in that battle helped to account for Gage's subsequent caution in the face of steadily more extensive American entrenchments. They were also responsible for Howe's caution, for Howe had commanded the actual assaults on Breed's Hill. The terrain of much of America was appropriate for such defences. Narrow valley routes were flanked by dense woodland, deep rivers often had few crossing points, and in the north the omnipresent stone walls created ready-made defences. British generals were obliged to respond. Howe and Clinton favoured flanking manoeuvres, while Burgoyne, who was very impressed by American entrenchments, argued that they should be bombarded by heavy cannon and howitzers or outflanked by fast-moving light infantry units. He told the House of Commons in May 1779 that:

> ... artillery was extremely formidable to raw troops; that in a country of posts, it was essentially necessary against the best troops; that it was yet more applicable to the enemy we were to combat; because the mode of defence they invariably adopted, and at which they were beyond all other nations expert, was that of entrenchment covered with strong abattis [felled trees with boughs pointing out] when to dislodge them by any other means, might be attended with continued and important losses ... block-houses, a species of fortification unique to America.[11]

Heavily-encumbered regular units manoeuvring and fighting in their accustomed formations were not only vulnerable in the face of entrenched positions and unsuited to the heavily wooded and hilly terrain of the Canadian frontier; they were also not ideal for the vast expanses of the south. In that relatively sparsely-populated region supplies were harder to obtain and, aside from the ports, there were fewer places that it was crucial to hold and therefore less opportunity for positional warfare.

Mounted troops, able to act as both infantry and cavalry, were an obvious response. Lee argued that 'it is a species of troops without which an army is a defective and lame machine' and claimed that each dragoon could also carry an infantryman on his horse. In late 1777 and 1778 Daniel Morgan stressed the desirability of cavalry cooperation with his riflemen. Such troops came into their own as the war increasingly took a southern orientation. The southern states were larger than those of the north, more sparsely populated and had fewer roads. The southern pine, straight and thin with no branches and growth till the top, allowed for easy manoeuvring on horseback, and there were no fences. In October 1780 Lord Rawdon observed that the 'mostly mounted militia' of the

Silver-gilt sword of the type used by many British officers. Made by John Clare II, London

Revolutionaries was 'not to be overtaken by our infantry nor . . . safely pursued in this strong country by our cavalry'. The following month Greene wrote that 'cavalry must be our greatest security till we can form a more respectable body of infantry'. Even in the south, horses were generally a means of transportation and not used in combat. Every militiaman had a horse, but there were few examples of the battlefield use of cavalry, though they did play an important role under Tarleton at the Waxhaws and at Cowpens, while Casimir Pulaski, the commander of a small force of American lancers, was killed at the siege of Savannah in 1779. In the north, however, the more-densely wooded country, with its many stone walls, was not suited to cavalry. In addition, unlikely relatively densely populated western Europe, America had few roads, and rivers, the optimum way of transporting large amounts of forage, ran inland from the sea. Waggon transportation was too valuable to waste on forage when there was barely enough to carry badly needed human sustenance and munitions. Thus, whatever forage could be gleaned locally went for artillery horses and officers' horses. New Jersey saw a lot of raiding, but, generally speaking, the war in the north was primarily an infantry and artillery war.

It might be suggested that the British response was too slow. In January 1776 Burgoyne had argued that the number of dragoons should be increased, while during the next three years Lieutenant-Colonel Thomas Brown, the commander of the East Florida Rangers, a Loyalist provincial corps, had been very successful in his mounted raids on Georgia. The ability of this Loyalist unit to wage irregular warfare successfully suggests that the use of so many Loyalist troops for garrison duty in and around New York might have been a missed opportunity. Despite the potential value of cavalry the proposed disposition of British forces for 1776 included no cavalry in Carleton's army based in Canada, and only two regiments of light dragoons, totalling 982 men, in Howe's force, compared to 4,010 cavalry in Britain. The importance of mobile troops in the south helps to account for the need to win active cooperation from the Loyalists, because the British could not transport or obtain sufficient horses themselves. The movement of horses by sea generally resulted in heavy losses in the eighteenth century. When, in the spring of 1776, Clinton landed in North Carolina, on his way to Charleston, he found no opportunity to secure sufficient horses to draw his artillery. In the positional warfare around New York that Clinton later became involved in horses were of less importance than sea power, and, indeed, the need to transport units sent to Rhode Island or Virginia by sea lessened the appeal of cavalry, which required an enormous quantity of shipping.[12] Had the British armies based in New York contained an appreciable number of cavalry they might have been able to operate more successfully: pursuing the retreating Americans more effectively in 1776, possibly reaching Philadelphia overland in 1777 far earlier than Howe's amphibious force, and giving Clinton's command a greater offensive capability. Flanking manoeuvres would have been more successful had large cavalry forces been able to exploit them, and cavalry attacks might have been more effective than bayonet charges. 'The great want' of cavalry in America was brought home to Germain in October 1780 and as a result he expressed support for the Earl of Lincoln's plan to raise a regiment of cavalry for service there.[13]

British generals usually had, however, to manage without such assistance. Without a considerable depth of country for foraging (and the British bridgeheads were mostly shallow) all the bulky forage had to be imported and remounts could not be obtained locally. Forage was a key problem in both north and south. It was bulky, difficult to transport (the teams ate much of their haul) and precious. The American general Greene complained frequently about militia who rode into camp, ate his dearly-foraged hay and then left.

The British generals devoted their attention to making their infantry more manoeuvrable. They were well aware of the advantages of light infantry and more open formations. In January 1756 Gage, who had commanded the advance column of Braddock's force defeated the previous July by French and Indians taking good advantage of the wooded terrain near Fort Duquesne, criticized the idea that regular troops were useless in America and called for the use of light infantry, rather than the militia:

> I hear no talk of raising irregulars, which, as we have so little interest with the Indians, are very much wanted. Provincials may in some measure answer the end, but a body of light troops, headed by proper officers, and put under subordination and discipline, would be of more service than double the number of the best militia on the Continent. General Braddock's defeat may, in a great measure, be attributed to the want of irregulars; his provincials were armed, clothed, and disciplined, and put on the same footing in every shape with the two [regular] regiments.[14]

The light units Gage called for, echoing the Swiss-born Henry Bouquet, who served under General Forbes, were more along the lines of Rogers' Rangers, disciplined, but flexible.

The Revolutionaries established specifically light units during the war, Morgan being given command of such a unit in 1777, and Wayne of another, which captured Stony Point, in 1779, although Wayne's was essentially a composite unit specific to the task. Greene formed a light infantry detachment under Otho Williams. The first truly innovative unit was Henry 'Light-Horse Harry' Lee's Legion – 300 men, half of whom were cavalry who could also fight as infantry, and half infantry who could ride. American generals frequently used thin skirmish lines, night marches and hit-and-run attacks, and their deployment of troops on the battlefield could be both imaginative and flexible. Charles Lee argued that the Revolutionaries should concentrate on irregular soldiers and increasingly on guerrilla warfare. However, this course was rejected, and light units were not always viewed with favour. Morgan's force only 500 strong, was disbanded in 1778, Wayne's, only 2,000 strong, the following year. If the Revolutionaries subsequently came to rely on such troops and warfare in the south, this was a consequence of the defeat of their regular forces.

In part the rejection of the guerrilla course in favour of the conventional warfare conducted by regular forces advocated by Washington was a consequence of the growing success of Revolutionary forces. In June 1779, after the battle of Stono Ferry, which had become a hand to hand engagement, General Lincoln wrote, 'our men now see that little is to be feared either from musquetry or field pieces; they are full of spirits, and are sure they can beat the enemy on equal grounds at any time'.[15] More important was the fact that guerrilla warfare

General Anthony Wayne

could neither defeat the British nor protect the major centres of American population and the ports that were crucial to the obtaining of funds and supplies through foreign trade. The British had been hemmed in at Boston as a result of their heavy losses at Bunker Hill and the subsequent extensive fortification of the American position. Although guerrilla action had played a role in Burgoyne's defeat, he had in the end been obliged to surrender to a larger regular force. Guerrilla activities could not have preserved New York or Philadelphia, Charleston or Savannah. The Continental Army likewise failed, but the British were obliged to commit considerable forces in order to achieve these objectives.

As the Continental army chose to fight essentially in a manner to which the British were accustomed, they were not obliged to rethink totally their way of fighting on the battlefield, a marked contrast to the unfamiliar logistical and political problems that were faced. The British tended to deploy in two, rather than three, lines and in more open order than in European battles. The Hessian troops hired by the British were also flexible in their tactics, as on Long Island where they advanced first in skirmishing order, while units moved through the woods in open order. This flexibility is not surprising. European manoeuvres were far less inflexible than the idealized pictures of rigid lines would suggest. Translated to America they brought success, strikingly so in 1776, and at Camden where the British soldiers fired accurately as they advanced. Cornwallis wrote then of 'a very heavy and well supported fire on both sides: our line continued to advance in good order, and with the cool intrepidity of experienced British soldiers keeping up a constant fire or making use of bayonets as opportunities offered'. And yet these successes were not always followed up, while Gage, Howe in 1776 and Clinton from 1778 can be criticized for a reluctance to manoeuvre boldly.

Such criticisms have to be advanced with care. Boldly-conceived plans could go wrong, as the Americans discovered at Germantown. Accurate intelligence was not easy to acquire, while coordinating operations, either on land, or, more especially, involving naval transportation or fire-power support, was very difficult. During the parliamentary inquiry in 1779 Howe addressed the question of whether he should have attacked the American lines on Long Island on 27 August 1776. He asked Cornwallis:

> Was it not my duty as far as circumstances would admit, to attend particularly to the preservation of the King's troops during my command? Were there not infinite difficulties attending the recruiting of that army? . . . Was not the knowledge of the country, in a military light extremely difficult to be obtained from the inhabitants?

Again, with reference to the advance on Philadelphia in 1777, 'Should I have been justified in attempting the passage of the Delaware through Jersey with the many difficulties attending that operation and the impracticability of supplying the army with provisions?'[16]

Washington would have understood these arguments, including the problem of gaining accurate intelligence. He blamed being outmanoeuvred after Brandywine on Howe advancing 'through a country from which I could not derive the least intelligence being to a man disaffected'.[17] Possibly Howe was able in 1779 to excuse his generalship excessively on these grounds because of the disastrous loss of an army at Saratoga. The British fought to win, but cautious generalship and the absence of cavalry made it difficult to translate success in the field into overwhelming American losses, and these only occurred when the Revolutionaries held a position whence there was no route for retreat, as at Fort Washington in 1776 and Charleston at 1780. In seeking to exploit success, 'the fatigue of the troops', to which Cornwallis ascribed the limited pursuit after Camden, was a major problem. The effects of minor topographical features were often crucial on the battlefield, as was the tactical flexibility required to take advantage of unexpected developments. These are readily apparent in accounts of battles. At Germantown in October 1777 the 'fog of war' was really pervasive. Washington reported:

> The morning was extremely foggy, which prevented our improving the advantages we gained so well, as we should otherwise have done. The circumstance, by concealing from us the true situation of the enemy, obliged us to act with more caution and less expedition than we could have wished, and gave the enemy time to recover from the effects of our first impression, and what was still more unfortunate, it served to keep our different parties in ignorance of each others movements, and hindered their acting in concert. It also occasioned them to mistake one another for the enemy, which, I believe, more than anything else contributed to the misfortune which ensued. In the midst of the most promising appearances when everything gave the most flattering hopes of victory, the troops began suddenly to retreat; and entirely left the field in spite of every effort that could be made to rally them.

General Mordecai Gist's account stressed the intangible effect of morale:

General Smallwood fell in with their right flank and drove them from several redoubts but the same spirit neglecting to inspire and animate us, the weakness of the human heart prevailed. I suppose the officer commanding against us was acquainted by experience with this defect in nature, who immediately took advantage of our feelings and drove us from the ground. A thick foggy air prevailed throughout the whole of this action as if designed by providence to favour the British arms, which with the smoke of gunpowder prevented our discovering the situation of their line.[18]

As the Revolutionaries became more accustomed to battlefield conditions their ability to repel British attacks or to inflict serious casualties increased. They fought well at Germantown, after which Washington wrote 'our troops . . . have gained what all young troops gain by being in actions', while at Guilford in 1781 Cornwallis' casualties were far greater than his opponent's. In September 1777 John Adams had criticized Washington as too cautious, adding 'I am sick of Fabian systems in all quarters . . . My toast is a short and violent war.'[19] By that stage it was possible to contemplate attacking the major British force, but it is as easy to appreciate Washington's tactical caution as that of Howe and Clinton. All wished to fight if they were likely to win, and the absence of major engagements in the middle colonies in 1779 and 1780 should not be taken to indicate a disinclination to fight. However, the manpower situation in both armies was a testimony to the strains they were suffering from. The British had other pressing commitments and had lost one army at Saratoga; their opponents were finding it increasingly difficult to sustain a major army. As a result both sought new support: the British looking to the Loyalists; their opponents to French intervention in America, rather than the West Indies. The war therefore became a curious interplay of cautious moves and bold aspirations, as increasingly exhausted particpants played for stakes that had been made higher as a consequence of the new factor of French naval power and in an atmosphere that the changing arithmetic of naval strength helped to make volatile for both sides.

5 1775: The First Year of the War

I have always thought and do think our navy sufficient for every purpose in America. Starve their trade and they are all effectually starved. However the friends of government cry out for troops and support; and it is thought reasonable to grant them. Fewer might do.

Sir James Porter, retired diplomat, 14 March 1775[1]

The British were to find that 1775 was to be a disastrous year. They did not appreciate the scale and difficulty of the military task facing them in America until too late, and they allowed the bulk of their forces to become bogged down in an exposed base while the British position collapsed throughout much of North America. By the end of the year the British government faced the possibility that it would lose Canada as well as the Thirteen Colonies. For the Revolutionaries the year was marked by the successful hemming in of the British at Boston, a very creditable performance at the battle of nearby Bunker Hill, the creation of a national army, and the invasion of Canada. At the same time major difficulties had been revealed in the new military force, while the invasion of Canada was not to be a triumph.

The British government had decided the previous November to take a tougher line towards America, George III informing his first minister, Lord North, that: '. . . blows must decide whether they are to be subject to this country or independent.'[2] General Thomas Gage, who was both Governor of Massachusetts, the most rebellious of the colonies, and commander-in-chief of the troops in North America, was ordered to use force to restore royal authority in the colony. He was instructed to arrest the leaders of the provincial Congress. In February North asked the House of Commons to declare Massachusetts in rebellion and to approve the use of troops. The ministry was confident that if there was any popular response it could not be 'very formidable', a view Gage did not share. This attitude in London not only ensured that the news of Concord and Lexington was received with great surprise, but also meant that Gage had not received the major reinforcements he had called for. Furthermore, because the government did not appreciate that the revolution would spread throughout the Thirteen Colonies, they failed to provide the assistance that royal governors elsewhere required. The British war effort in 1775 was therefore too little, too late and too narrowly focussed, though had Gage been successful in his operations near Boston the consequences of this would have been less serious.

CONCORD AND LEXINGTON

Operations began with an attempt to seize a cache of arms reported to be at Concord, a town 16 miles from Boston, past the village of Lexington. Secrecy was lost and when the British reached Lexington at first light on 19 April they found about seventy militia drawn up in two lines. Heavily outnumbered, the militia began to disperse, although not to lay down their arms, when someone, it is not clear who, fired. The shot was followed by two British volleys and the militia scattered. Concord was not such an easy proposition. The British were able to occupy the undefended town but then withdrew in the face of militia pressure. On their route back to Lexington they suffered grievously from sniping, their flanking manoeuvres being insufficient to prevent ambushes. At Lexington a relief column under Brigadier-General Hugh Percy lessened the pressure, although there were renewed attacks on the route back to Boston. Percy reported to Gage the following day:

Battle at Lexington, 19 April 1775, engraved by F. Godefroy for l'Academie Imperiale et Royale de Vienne, 1783

BOSTON AND BUNKER HILL.
(Impartial History, etc., 1781.)

Plan showing Boston and Bunker Hill,
1781

In obedience to your Excellency's orders I marched yesterday morning at 9 o'clock with the 1st brigade and 2 field pieces, in order to cover the retreat of the grenadiers and light infantry in their return from their expedition to Concord. As all the houses were shut up, and there was not the appearance of a single inhabitant, I could get no intelligence concerning them till I had passed Menotomy, when I was informed that the rebels had attacked his Majesty's troops who were retiring, overpowered by numbers, greatly exhausted and fatigued, and having expended almost all their ammunition – and at about 2 o'clock I met them retiring through the town of Lexington – I immediately ordered the 2 field pieces to fire at the rebels, and drew up the brigade on a height.

The shot from the cannon had the desired effect, and stopped the rebels for a little time, who immediately dispersed, and endeavoured to surround us being very numerous. As it began now to grow pretty late and we had 15 miles to retire, and only 36 rounds, I ordered the grenadiers and light infantry to move off first; and covered them with my brigade sending out very strong flanking parties which were absolutely necessary, as there was not a stone wall, or house, though before in appearance evacuated, from whence the rebels did not fire upon us.

'A Correct View of the Late Battle at Charlestown', 17 June 1775. Engraved by Robert Aitken for the Pennsylvania Magazine *c. 1780*

As soon as they saw us begin to retire, they pressed very much upon our rear guard, which for that reason, I relieved every now and then.

In this manner we retired for 15 miles under an incessant fire all round us, till we arrived at Charlestown, between 7 and 8 in the evening and having expended almost all our ammunition.

We had the misfortune of losing a good many men in the retreat, though nothing like the number which from many circumstances I have reason to believe were killed of the rebels.

His Majesty's troops during the whole of the affair behaved with their usual intrepidity and spirit nor were they a little exasperated at the cruelty and barbarity of the rebels, who scalped and cut off the ears of some of the wounded men who fell into their hands.

In fact, no one was scalped and no ears were cropped. Jeremy Lister, who was wounded on the retreat, wrote of 'a general firing upon us from all quarters, from behind hedges and walls'.[3] The news of the shedding of blood produced an outraged response throughout New England and a substantial force soon encircled the British in Boston. Poorly organized and supplied, largely dependent on their personal arms, and short of powder and ball, the Revolutionaries nevertheless benefited from the heavy British losses on 19 April, which discouraged Gage from acting until he received reinforcements and ensured that when he did act it would be in order to improve his defensive position, not to end the encirclement or to attack further afield. Meanwhile the Revolutionaries were entrenching their positions, one British observer, writing on 31 May, that they had strongly fortified 'every road, every pass and every hill within ten miles of Boston' so that even if the British attacked successfully their army would be decimated.[4]

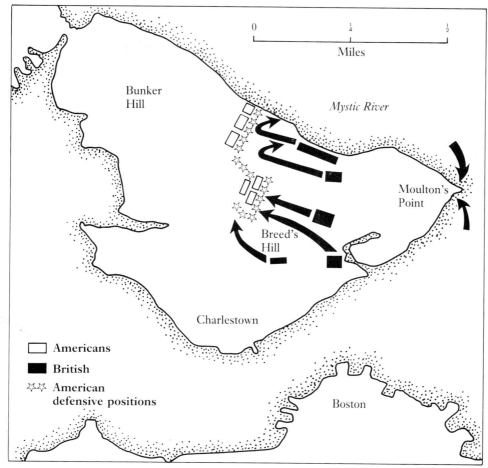

Bunker Hill

BUNKER HILL

This was, in fact, to happen. On 26 May William Howe, Henry Clinton and
John Burgoyne, three major-generals sent from London to lend new energy to
Gage's actions, reached Boston. Reinforced also by several regiments, Gage was
persuaded to address himself to an offensive in order to occupy the heights of
Dorchester and Charlestown from which Boston could be bombarded. The
Revolutionaries discovered the plans and decided to pre-empt them by fortifying
the positions themselves. On the night of 16–17 June they marched to Breed's
Hill on the Charlestown peninsula and began to fortify the position. Clinton,
who made a reconnaissance that night, pressed Gage to attack the new position
at day-break, an idea rejected on the inaccurate grounds that the American

An AUTHENTIC and IMPARTIAL

NARRATIVE

OF THE

BATTLE

Fought on the 17th of June, 1775, &c.

ON Friday the Sixteenth of June, 1775, Lieutenant General Gage, Commander in chief of all his Majesty's Troops in America, and Governor of Boston, received information that the Provincial American Army were erecting a Battery on Bunker's hill contiguous to Charles-Town, with an intent to besiege and annoy the Town of Boston. This information was soon confirmed by their firing several cannon-balls into the town, to the infinite terror and danger of the inhabitants, most of whom then within the town were in general deemed and

(2)

and esteemed the steady Friends of Government.

In consequence of this insult to his Majesty's Troops and Government, Lieutenant-General Gage thought it expedient to give orders for the Men of War, Transports, &c. and the Military, to make every preparation for an action.

On the subsequent day, Saturday the Seventeenth of June, in compliance with these orders, every necessary disposal, from the Fleet and Army, was made by ten in the morning, and such Troops as were ordered upon the expedition were embarked at Hancock's wharf, and effected their landing under the cover of the shipping by one.

Two Transports also with Troops, arrived from England the night before, were ordered to land in the morning on Charles-Town side, to proceed to the engagement.

Immediately

Pages from 'An Authentic and Impartial Narrative' of the battle of Bunker Hill, 17 June 1775, by Lieutenant John Clarke, printed in London in 1775

move was probably only a foray. When, on the contrary, it became clear that Breed's Hill was being fortified, Clinton suggested a bold plan that would take advantage of British maritime strength: the simultaneous landing of a large force on the southern shore of the peninsula, while a separate unit under Clinton landed on the western shore and closed the line of retreat. This was also rejected, possibly because Gage felt such an operation to be risky, and instead Gage decided on a landing at high tide that afternoon followed by an attack on the American entrenchments. The Americans took advantage of the delay to strengthen their position further. The subsequent battle of Bunker Hill, named after the more prominent hill behind Breed's Hill, was described misleadingly in a letter allegedly by a British brigadier-general published in the *Leeds Mercury* on 1 August:

To dislodge them the grenadiers and light-infantry companies, supported by six regiments, attacked them, entrenched to their chins, and flanked by strong redoubts, which they carried,

'*Bunkers Hill or America's Head Dress*',
by Darly, 1 March 1776. This represen-
tation bore no relation to the events of the
battle

putting the rebels to flight, with great slaughter and consternation . . . the rebels forced from their cover, run in a most cowardly manner, not daring to look behind . . . I have seen many actions, but the solemn procession preparative to the last, in embarking the troops into the boats, the order in which they rowed across the harbour, their alertness in making good their landing, their instantly forming in the front of the enemy, and marching on to action, was a grand and interesting sight to all concerned.

Burgoyne was also much struck by the spectacle, writing of Howe's attack:

As his first arm was advancing up the Hill, they met with a thousand impediments from strong fences and were much exposed. They were also extremely hurt by Musketry from *the Town*, of Charles Town, though Clinton and I did not perceive it, till Howe sent us word by a boat and desired us to set fire to Charles Town. No sooner said than done. We threw a parcel of shells and the whole was instantly in flames. Our Battery afterwards kept up an incessant fire on the Heights. It was seconded by a number of frigates, floating batteries, and one ship of the line. And now ensued one of the greatest scenes of war, that can be conceived. If we look to the Right, Howe's corps ascending the Hill in the face of entrenchments, and a very disadvantageous ground warmly engaged to the left of the enemy, who kept pouring fresh troops by thousands over the land, and in the arm of the sea, our ships and floating batteries cannonadeing them. In a straight line before us a large noble town in one blaze, the church steeples being made of wood, were great pyramids of fire – and behind us the church steeples of Boston and the Heights of our Camp covered with spectators of the rest of our Army, all in anxious suspence. The roar of cannon, mortars and musquetry; the crash of churches, ships on the stocks and whole streets falling in ruin to fill the ear. The storm of the Redoubt, with the objects above described to fill the eye; and a reflection that a defeat was perhaps the loss of the British Empire in America to fill the mind, made the whole a picture, and a complication of horror and importance, beyond any, it ever came to my lot to be witness to.[5]

However dramatic the scene, the battle was not to be a walkover. One account balanced 'the lines advancing slowly, and giving time for the artillery to fire' with 'these orders were executed with perseverance under a heavy fire from the rebels', and alongside the unexpectedly heavy American fire there was considerable confusion on the British side, especially among the artillery, which failed to harm the American positions significantly.[6] Although an expert on light infantry and on amphibious operations, Howe moved ponderously, spending about two hours deploying his men and advancing in a traditional open-field formation. He probably hoped that his untrained opponents, described by Burgoyne as an 'undisciplined rabble', would crumble under a regular attack and saw no viable alternative to advancing across terrain that offered no cover. The entrenched Americans waited until the British were almost upon them, before shattering their first two assaults. Howe's attempt to turn the American flank was repelled. However, the Americans were running short of ammunition and a third British attack, in part by fresh troops, took the American redoubt, finally allowing Howe's men to use the bayonets with which they were more proficient than their opponents. The exhausted British, harassed by sharpshooters, were unable to stop the remaining Americans from retreating.

The battle was a disaster for the British, Major Sill writing several weeks later, 'the shocking carnage that day never will be out of my mind till the day of my death'. He attributed the high casualties to both sides behaving 'like veterans'.[7] The British lost 228 dead and 826 wounded, 42 per cent of their force engaged, and a number far larger than the American losses: 100 killed, 271 wounded and 30 prisoners. More serious than these heavy losses was the strategic consequence. Bunker Hill was followed by a year, up to the arrival of Howe's army in New York Harbour in June 1776, during which the major British force in North America did not act in an effective fashion against its opponents. Clinton observed on 20 June 1775, 'our army is very respectable but 6,000 men cannot conquer America', in mid-July 1775:

. . . little alteration in our affairs since I wrote . . . I fear the loss we sustained on the 17th of June (near 90 officers and 900 men killed and wounded) the number of the rebels, strength of their intrenchments, will prevent our attempting anything before the whole of the second embarkation arrives; even then I do not know that (without a great reinforcement is sent) anything *solid* can be done, however, no opportunity will be neglected; from the accounts we receive from all quarters, the spirit of revolt seems but too general, many things may be assigned why things are brought to the state in which they now are; but in my opinion none with more truth, than that infamous rapacity of some Scotch and Irish chiefs; whose tenants have been forced to quit their farms, and fly to this country, in far greater numbers, than is possible to conceive . . . The people of these provinces indisputably mean independence. Those of the southern provinces do not avow it, at least; I still flatter myself that something may be done with them by negotiation, which possibly might with propriety [be] contrived, after our sole advantage: but if nothing will do, and you determine upon war, there are but three things in my opinion to be done; try the temper of New York by sending a great force there; and if the majority there declare for you, see the effect that will have on the rest of the continent, another very considerable force must be sent to Canada, it will fix that province, and probably determine the home and distant Indians to join you; but if you do not resolve to reinforce us; there then remains either to withdraw great part of the present army, sending the remainder to Canada and the Floridas, to secure those provinces, and leave the rest to your fleet; their ports are all insultable, their ships may be burned, their harbours destroyed.

In short scenes too horrible to be described may be acted on their coasts; the other to leave them to themselves, in which case I have not the least doubt but you will be amply revenged, by the anarchy and confusion which must naturally be their lot; since I began this letter all the second embarkation is arrived, we must stretch our legs a little but . . . I rather wish there may, than expect there will arise any solid advantage to us from anything we can do; with our (comparatively) little army and in the present state of the provinces.

Ensign Jeremy Lister wrote to his father on 15 July 1775:

The rebels, almost every night, keep firing at our sentries, and sometimes continue firing till eleven or twelve o'clock in the day, but at such a distance they have not been able to do us any damage, except killing one man. We now look upon ourselves as besieged in Boston, as the rebels have a chain of fortifications all round us except towards the sea . . . we are now reduced to live upon salt pork and peas, as fresh provisions are not to be got for money.

On 12 August he envisaged no change unless the British were sent 15,000 or 20,000 reinforcements, 'as those we have here are hardly sufficient to garrison this place'. The lack of sufficient troops was to be a repeated theme in Clinton's correspondence during the war. In the autumn of 1775 he argued that without substantial reinforcements 'they had better leave the war to the fleet', but even if they were sent Clinton claimed 'he is a bold man who says we shall subdue these people in one campaign even then'. In 1775 the army remained in New England and acted there on the defensive, despite the fact that by mid-winter, when the poorly-equipped and ill-disciplined American army had fallen in number as men returned home, the British outnumbered their besiegers. Howe, who replaced Gage, remained affected by Bunker Hill. He only saw 10–20,000 troops positioned around him, not colonials who were in and out of camp with such frequency that Washington never knew how many men he had under his command. The British army was, of course, only blockaded on the landward side. It was possible for Burgoyne to urge a move to New York before the winter, and at the beginning of September Gage was ordered to do so or move to another port where the fleet could anchor safely. The failure to make such a move – Boston was not evacuated until 17 March – was to be very serious, ensuring that the British began their campaign in the middle colonies too late to take full advantage of the victories they were to gain in 1776.

Boston was to be one of the numerous might-have-been battles of the war. Each side had substantial forces there for nine months after Bunker Hill and both considered an attack, but no major engagement took place. The British position was a disagreeable one and revealed the problems that holding a port could entail, even when sea routes were under control. Short of food, especially fresh provisions, poorly covered against the long cold nights, affected by diarrhoea, scurvy, and smallpox, the British forces were also subject to cannonading and probing attacks by the Americans. These were not always successful, Percy writing on 29 October:

Nothing material has happened here since the 17th of June except the other night an experiment which the rebels tried with a piece of cannon or two in a flat bottomed boat. With these they fired 15 or 20 shot through our camp into the town, when alas one of the cannon burst, blew up the boat, and sent most of the crew to the devil. Our weather is now very rainy

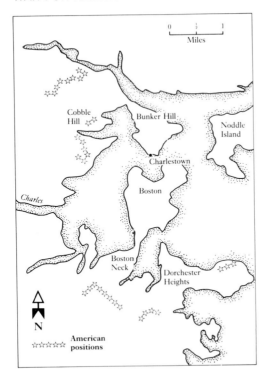

Siege of Boston

and cold . . . a tent is no very agreable habitation just now . . . The rebels have built barracks for their raggamuffins all round us, so that I suppose they intend to be our neighbours for *this* winter. I don't believe they will be very troublesome ones.[8]

However, though the Americans did not launch any major attack, the British achievement, retaining Boston, was only a negative one that offered no likelihood of defeating their opponents. By failing to attack the American army when it was most disorganized and least trained, the British lost an opportunity that might have brought both victory and the collapse of the rebellion. For his part, George Washington, the commander of the Continental army, proposed an attack on Boston in September, while Congress decided in December that if Washington and his officers thought that a successful attack could be made, it should be, but they were discouraged by the strength of the British position and by their own shortage of powder. Washington boldly tried to enlist his council of war to back his proposal for a winter assault on Boston across the ice, but he failed to win sufficient support. Charles Lee promised Franklin, 'Give us powder and Boston shall be yours', but the Americans benefited from having the British tied up in Boston. It was not until Colonel Henry Knox returned in January 1776 with the sledge-borne guns captured at Ticonderoga and the Americans erected a fortified battery on Dorchester Heights on the night of 4 March that the British anchorage became vulnerable. It only took one night to set up earth-filled gabions and emplace the artillery in the new position. Howe's

Early engraving of George Washington

Washington.

attempt to dislodge the Americans by attacking Dorchester Heights had to be cancelled when a spring gale wrecked his boats; an intervention ascribed to Providence by the Americans.

WASHINGTON AND THE CONTINENTAL ARMY

In the meantime, Washington had had considerable success in creating an organized and trained army out of the men that had besieged Boston, while these men had become accustomed to many of the tasks and experiences of war, ranging from digging trenches to enduring cannon-fire. Abigail Adams had written the previous July of encounters round Boston Bay, 'These little skirmishes seem trifling, but they serve to inure our men and harden them to danger', and the second half of 1775 was indeed a crucial learning period.[9] It was the period when the Continental army was organized. In June 1775 the Second Continental Congress transformed the New England force outside Boston into a national army. On 15 June George Washington of Virginia was selected as commander and the relationship between Congress and general was defined. Congress was to determine policy, Washington to follow orders. Other generals were appointed, and a relatively humanitarian military code drawn up.

Washington, a forty-three year old landowner and colonel of Virginian militia, had been in charge of Virginia's western defences against the French in 1755–8, learning how to cope with inadequate manpower and supplies. He had learnt from the British commanders fighting the French, and both General John Forbes and Henry Bouquet encouraged him to read and study the art of war. A believer in hierarchy and organization, Washington was determined to create a disciplined army, reflecting the united purpose of all the Thirteen Colonies. He wanted an army that could defeat the British in battle rather than simply harry it. Washington certainly found a formidable task outside Boston. The army was short of food, clothes, money, blankets and ammunition. The very determination to think for themselves and create their own arrangements that had led so many Americans to defy their king posed problems. It has been argued that the hard-core regulars of Washington's army 'acted out the essence of republican-ism and gave the concept concrete meaning in their era . . . Washington's small standing army, so serious a potential threat to liberty in the ideological terms of the times, was ironically the lifeblood of freedom and republican virtue. Such irony helps to explain why the origins of America cannot be treated separately from military concerns'. Many officers were elected. On 26 September 1775, for example, Washington had to confront the objections of the junior officers of the 2nd Connecticut Regiment to Ebenezer Huntington's appointment as lieutenant because he thus superseded men of longer service and higher rank. Wash-ington's response was more in keeping with the ethos of European armies than those of New England town meetings, although his stress on merit had social overtones, as in Europe:

> The decent representation of officers or even of common soldiers through the channel of their Colonel, or other superior officers I shall always encourage and attend to: But I must declare my disapprobation of this mode of associating and combining as subversive of all subordination, discipline and order . . . commissions should be ever the reward of merit not of age.[10]

Washington believed that the army could be improved by reforming the officer corps; he saw 'gentlemen' officers as crucial to the discipline and subordination he believed to be necessary. He was horrified to see a captain, a former barber, cutting his men's hair. Officers guilty of misconduct were removed. His attitude made a major difference to the army, but he had to confront a marked particularism that revealed itself in hostilty to serving in the same unit with men from another colony, a strong identification between men and their officers, and opposition to re-enlistment among men concerned about their farmsteads and families. Connecticut militiamen had to be prevented from returning home. As his army melted away towards the end of 1775, the expiry date of most enlistments, Washington had to rely on Massachusetts and New Hampshire militia units to maintain the blockade of Boston until freshly-enlisted troops arrived. Charles Lee, appointed 'second major-general' by Congress in June and a veteran of the Seven Years War, in which he had served as a British officer, advocated radical solutions amounting to a militarization of society and the creation of a national army under central control:

> 1st. A solemn league and covenant defensive and offensive to be taken by every man in America, particularly by those in or near the seaport towns; all those who refuse, to have their estates confiscated for the public use, and their persons removed to the interior part of the country with a small pension reserved for their subsistence.
>
> 2dly. New York to be well fortified and garrisoned or totally destroyed.

3dly. No regiments to be raised for any particular local purposes, but one general great Continental Army adequate to every purpose. South Carolina may be excepted from its distance . . .

4thly. The regiments to be exchanged. Those who are raised in one province to serve in another rather than in their own, viz. the New Englanders in New York the New Yorkers in New England and so on. This system will undoubtedly make them better soldiers.

5thly. A general militia to be established and the regular regiments to be formed by drafts from the militia or their substitutes.

6thly. A certain portion of lands to be assigned to every soldier who serves one campaign a double portion who serves two, and so on.[11]

Such notions obviously conflicted with the profoundly local nature of American political culture, a product of the separate and different governmental, political, social, religious and demographic development of the colonies. Local diversity along ethnic lines was very pronounced. Lee's ideas also clashed with the respect for the law and for individuals and property rights that was central to this culture, although with the obvious exceptions of Indians and Negroes, and that compromised any idea of a total mobilization of national resources. Such a mobilization was not to be achieved by legislation through the developing new political system: the individual colonies in effect achieved independence first and then cooperated on their own terms through a federal structure. However, initially this did not appear to be too serious because the British army was essentially confined to Boston and was not using that as a base from which to conduct significant amphibious operations, royal authority was collapsing elsewhere and the invasion of Canada was at first successful.

OVERTHROW OF ROYAL AUTHORITY

Lexington and Concord were followed by a widespread overthrow of royal authority that royal governors were powerless to resist. In New York:

. . . the news of the attack at Boston reached us on Sunday the 23rd and that very day the populace seized the City arms and unloaded two vessels bound with provisions to the troops of Boston. In course of the week they formed themselves into companies under officers of their own choosing, distributed the arms, called a provincial Congress, demanded the keys of the Custom House and shut up the port, trained their men publicly, convened the citizens by beat of drum, drew the cannon into the interior country and formed an association of defence in perfect league with the rest of the continent.

By 7 June over 2,000 men were reported to be training daily in New York and on 10 June it was claimed that 'if a stranger was to land here, he would be at a loss whether to pronounce this a city immersed in commerce, or a great garrisoned town'.[12] William Eddis, the Surveyor and Searcher of Customs in Baltimore, wrote six weeks later 'Government is now totally annihilated', and a Council of Safety was formed in Maryland in July. Lord Dunmore, the Governor of Virginia, moved the gunpowder out of the magazine at Williamsburg on 20 April, and, although there was no attempt to seize it, Patrick

Henry, at the head of an Independent Company, seized some of the royal revenues. On 8 June Dunmore left his Williamsburg seat to take up residence on HMS *Fowey* at Yorktown, and on 24 June the Virginia House of Burgesses adjourned their final session under George III's rule. In August the Virginia Convention ordered the recruiting of soldiers, the raising of militia units, the issue of paper money and the levying of taxes. Governor Josiah Martin of North Carolina had already fled to Fort Johnston on Cape Fear and, after that weak and poorly-defended position fell, remained off the coast on HMS *Cruiser*. A Carolina Loyalist, who was an Irish emigrant, left an account that made it clear that the decisiveness of the Revolutionaries was crucial, 'When the war broke out . . . the congress party early in 1775 were sending a quantity of ammunition and cloathing as presents to the Indians; on which the Loyalists who had not joined them assembled and went to Ninety-Six a wooden fort. After besieging the place for some days took it and the stores . . . both parties agreed to a cessation of arms for some weeks . . .', but the Revolutionaries broke the truce and sent a force which imprisoned the leading Loyalists and disarmed the rest.[13] Lord William Campbell, Governor of South Carolina, went on board HMS *Tamar* in September 1775, Sir James Wright of Georgia onto HMS *Scarborough* the following February. John Wentworth of New Hampshire had left for Boston in August 1775, William Tryon of New York took to the water, the Acting Governor of the island of St John was seized by American privateers

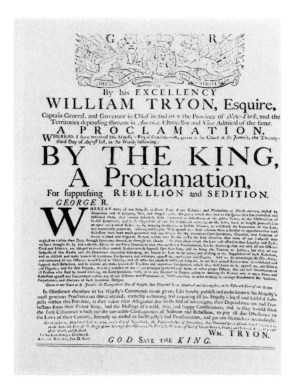

Proclamation 'for suppressing Rebellion and Sedition' by William Tryon, Governor of New York, 1775, ordering the citizens of the state to 'cease their rebellious actions'

in November and Benjamin Franklin's son William, the Governor of New Jersey, was arrested by the Americans the following June.

A mixture of popular zeal, the determination of the Revolutionaries and the weakness of their opponents decided the fate of most of the colonies. It was not only the radicals who were convinced that they enjoyed widespread support.[14] A British naval officer wrote from Boston after Concord and Lexington that 'The enthusiastic zeal with which these people have behaved must convince every reasonable man what a difficult and unpleasant task General Gage has before him'.[15] Those who held contrary opinions were intimidated. Eddis wrote from Annapolis on 3 May:

> The universal cry is *Liberty!* to support which an infinite number of petty tyrannies are established, under the appellation of committees, in every one of which a few despots lord it over the calm and moderate, inflame the passions of the mob, and pronounce those to be enemies to the general good who may presume any way to dissent from the creed they have thought proper to impose.

Two months later he added 'Speech is become dangerous; letters are intercepted'.[16] Loyalist publications were attacked. James Rivington, the printer of *Rivington's New York Gazetteer* who later became an agent in New York City

A reply to an address 'A Candid Examination of the Mutual Claims of Great Britain and her Colonies', by Joseph Galloway Esq of Philadelphia. Printed in New York, 1775

for Washington, was assaulted in May, his types seized when his printing shop was attacked in November. The disorientating experience of the agencies of law and authority being taken over by those who were willing to connive at or support violence affected many who were unhappy about developments. To resist this the royal governors had little to turn to apart from a few warships, although the potential for action was indicated by Dunmore who, with two warships, two companies of regulars from St Augustine in East Florida and some armed Loyalists and Negroes, seized the towns of Gosport and Norfolk. Virginia had a smaller percentage of active Loyalists than other states, but there were many in and near Norfolk and Dunmore was able to win their assistance. He issued a proclamation emancipating slaves who joined his force and launched a number of raids before being defeated at Great Bridge on 9 December 1775 and obliged to move his force afloat.[17]

Other governors felt that they could do more if they were given support. Admiral Graves and Gage said they could not provide any for Dunmore, although the amphibious force that destroyed Falmouth (now Portland, Maine) on 18 October 1775 would probably have been better employed helping Dunmore, and sustaining a second front in Virginia. The Revolutionaries were worried that this attack would lead soldiers in the army outside Boston into returning home to protect their families. Given the substantial reinforcements sent to Boston, it is worth noting such suggestions as that of Robert Eden, the Governor of Maryland, that one regiment would have quashed resistance there, or the pressure from Josiah Martin of North Carolina for assistance. The possibilities that amphibious power offered were indicated in Rhode Island and Georgia. The threat of naval gun-fire allowed the British to use Newport as a naval base until the squadron was withdrawn in March 1776, while, after attempts to purchase rice at Savannah for the Boston garrison had failed, a night raid there that month led to the seizure of eighteen merchantmen carrying rice.[18]

British generals and admirals did not like to disperse their strength, amphibious operations were difficult to execute successfully and units that were landed might have found it difficult to obtain supplies and would have risked defeat at the hands of larger American forces, the retreat from Concord being repeated up and down the eastern seaboard. It is not difficult, however, to feel that opportunities were missed and that the British failed to make adequate use of their sea power. An anonymous British pamphlet of 1776 complained that the Americans had been given 'the advantage of gaining time to form a union of counsels, to adjust plans of action, to turn their resources into the most convenient channels, to train their men in regular discipline, and to draw to their camp ammunition and stores, and all the necessary implements of war'. It is easy to understand why the Revolutionaries were concerned about the possibilities of British operations outside the Boston area. Lee's agenda for military success included mobile reserves near Hampton Roads and Annapolis and 'Charleston to be well watched and guarded' and he pressed Franklin in December to 'send some man who has the reputation of being a soldier to Virginia. I think Virginia is our weak vulnerable part . . . I must repeat that I think Virginia in danger and that you ought to take your precautions.'[19] The previous month Congress resolved that Charleston should be fortified 'immediately', although they left South Carolina to bear the burden.

Arguably the same problems that were to face the British in the south in 1780–1 would have affected earlier operations there: to make a sufficiently widespread impact it would have been necessary to dispatch substantial forces and thus the British army in America could have been defeated in detail. On the other hand, the Revolutionary position would have been far less consolidated than it was to become, while British control of the sea was not challenged effectively until French entry into the war in 1778. In 1775 the government did decide to mount a major expedition to challenge the Revolutionary successes in the south but the decision was not taken until mid-October, and the bulk of the force was to come from Britain not Boston. Disappointed in the hope of winning the support of Catherine the Great and thus obtaining the assistance of Russian troops, Lord North pressed for an expedition that would offer parliament some hope of a victory and thus lessen domestic criticism of the conduct of the war. The southern governors were pressing for action, arguing that a small force of British regulars would enable them to restore order, and North was confident of Loyalist strength in the south. He hoped to force the southern colonies to submit to royal authority and then to send the troops north to join Howe, thus reconquering America from south to north. If no such submission could be obtained, North, nevertheless, hoped that the governors might be left at the head of Loyalist forces able to 'keep the Rebels quiet'.

George III agreed. He argued that the expedition should aim first for North Carolina where the Scottish settlers were believed to be favourably inclined. It was planned that the expedition would sail from Cork for Cape Fear in early December, restore royal authority in North Carolina and then join Howe as early in the spring as was possible. The Earl of Dartmouth, who was soon to be replaced as Secretary of State for the American Department by the more resolute Lord George Germain, informed Howe that:

> ... the whole success of the measure His Majesty has adopted depends so much upon a considerable number of the inhabitants taking up arms in support of government, that nothing that can have a tendency to promote it ought to be omitted: I hope we are not deceived in the assurances that have been given, for if we are, and there should be no appearance of a disposition in the inhabitants of the southern colonies to join the king's armies, I fear little more will be effected than the gaining possession of some respectable post to the southward, where the officers and servants of government may find protection.

Clinton, who was to command the land forces, was sceptical from the outset, complaining that he had been ordered:

> ... on an expedition, not of his own planning; but formed on the representation of governors who I fear may have been too sanguine. Should that prove the case little can be expected for it must not be supposed that 2,000 men the utmost extent of my command, can awe one part of the continent, while above four times that number are besieged in a small town in another ... Governors are sanguine, the malady is catching and ministers sometimes infected.[20]

However, this expedition was seen as secondary. The plan was designed to be fulfilled before the 1776 campaign began in earnest in New York, not to be the campaign of that year. Control of New York was seen as the basis for a successful attack on New England, while the *Public Advertiser*, a London newspaper, of 16 September 1775 announced that 'From all accounts lately received by government from New York, there are great hopes, that, notwithstanding all the manoeuvres of the present ruling party there, in case that place becomes the head quarters of the main body of troops in America, the friends of government will come in, and join them in great numbers'.

The decision to transfer operations from Boston to New York was sensible, while there was considerable merit in the idea of linking up with the North Carolina Loyalists. However, both moves were to be seriously delayed in 1776, fatally so in the latter case, part of the heavy price Britain paid for not being prepared for a major war. Nevertheless, early setbacks did not lead to a fall in support for governmental policy within Britain. Typical of many protestations of loyalty was the address to George III drawn up by the Devon Justices of the Peace meeting at Quarter Sessions on 5 October 1775 which spoke of their 'unfeigned readiness to strengthen the hands of government' and of 'the miseries which our deluded fellow subjects in America have brought upon themselves by that daring abuse which they have made of your parental tenderness'. On 26 October George III, opening a new session of parliament, declared that it was necessary 'to put a speedy end to these disorders by the most decisive exertions', and that he would give his commanders on the spot powers 'to receive the submission of any province or colony which shall be disposed to return to its allegiance'. The government won majorities of 176 to 72 and 76 to 33 in the opening debates in the Commons and Lords and on 7 December the Commons rejected David Hartley's conciliatory proposal for the repeal of the Coercive Acts.[21]

INVASION OF CANADA

The American decision to invade Canada further demonstrated the danger of failing to restore the Thirteen Colonies to royal authority. Canada in British hands was seen as a strategic threat by the Americans while it was hoped that the preponderantly French population of Quebec, only conquered as recently as 1759–60, would assist in overthrowing the small British garrison. To a certain extent the Americans were guilty of wishful thinking. Although the bulk of the French population showed little support for George III, they were not outraged by the Quebec Act's denial of self-government, but rather accepted British rule with its support for the position of the Catholic Church. The wealthier members of the community tended to back George. Nevertheless, French Canadians only played a modest role in hostilities: the Americans and the British were forced to rely essentially on their own efforts. This spelled major difficulties for the Americans, who were accustomed to popular support. Canada would have to be conquered.

Successful attacks on garrisons on the shores of Lake Champlain in the spring of 1775 suggested that isolated British positions would fall readily. A force under Ethan Allen and Benedict Arnold easily captured Ticonderoga, whose unprepared garrison was only forty-five strong, on 10 May. Crown Point, with its garrison of less than a dozen, fell on the 12th. The way to Canada was now open, a route that was not vulnerable to the British navy. British forces in Canada had suffered as a result of the despatch of reinforcements to Boston.

Concerned about the prospect of the British stirring up the Indians, Congress on 27 June ordered Major-General Philip Schuyler, the commander of the Northern Department, to invade Canada. Schuyler could not draw on a developed logistical system and he found it very difficult to obtain the necessary supplies in a region that was distant from more fertile and wealthier areas. Complaining about 'that variety of difficulties which is ever attendant on a want of method and regularity',[22] he also suffered from poor health and indecision. While Schuyler was away, his second in command, Brigadier-General Richard Montgomery, moved north along Lake Champlain towards a rumoured British build-up at St Johns, a fort on the Richelieu River, seized by the Americans in May, but then recaptured by the British. Schuyler rejoined his command in time to order them back from St Johns, under the mistaken impression that it was strongly fortified, and then to launch an unsuccessful attack, but he finally left Montgomery in command and the fort was besieged on 16 September. The

Benedict Arnold

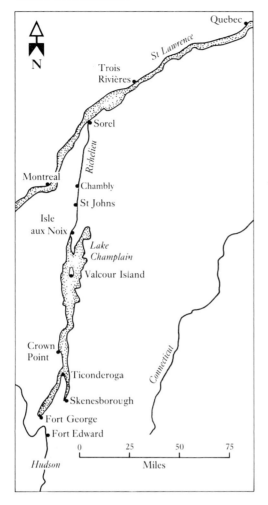

Invasion of Canada

British commander, Major Charles Preston, did not surrender until 2 November, when he had only three days' provisions left. The lengthy siege in cold and wet conditions had demoralized Montgomery's force, already affected by disease, and the delay was to be serious for an army facing the onset of winter and the expiry of enlistments.

In the meantime American forces had been operating further north. Ethan Allen, sent north to recruit Canadians, had tried to seize Montreal, but was defeated by Loyalist volunteers on 25 September. The poorly-fortified Fort Chambly, on the Richelieu, fell the following month after a forty-eight-hour cannonade from two cannons. The garrison, only seventy-eight strong, had had only small arms, while the American force had been aided by several hundred Canadians.[23] After the fall of St Johns, Montgomery marched on Montreal, and the outnumbered British commander in Canada, Major-General Guy Carleton,

'Old View of Quebec', from Popple's American Atlas, 1730

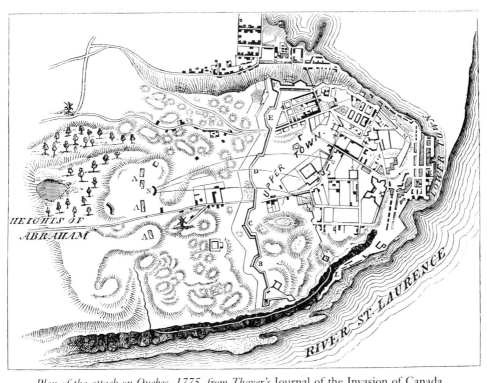

Plan of the attack on Quebec, 1775, from Thayer's Journal of the Invasion of Canada

Governor of Quebec, fled to Quebec, leaving Montreal to surrender on 12 November. Meanwhile a separate force of 1,050 men under Benedict Arnold had been sent by Washington in September from Newburyport in Massachusetts on an arduous advance through Maine to the St Lawrence. Landing at Gardinerstown on the Kennebec, Arnold was handicapped by rain, a shortage of food, strong currents on the rivers and rough trails across the intervening carrying places. Some men died, several hundred turned back, and only about 600 arrived opposite Quebec on 9 November.

Arnold crossed the St Lawrence by canoe on the 13th and was joined by Montgomery with about 300 men on 2 December. Although most of the few British regulars in Canada had already been taken prisoner, Carleton and Colonel Allen Maclean displayed talents at improvisation in Quebec that all too many British senior commanders were not to share during the war. A defending force composed of French Canadian militia, Loyalists, seamen and marines from British warships and merchantmen and about 100 regulars was organized. The British refused to sally out and risk defeat in the field, as the Americans had hoped. Bitter weather and terms of service due to end on 31 December, made the siege-works that were begun appear foolish and the Americans instead attempted to storm Quebec in the early hours of 31 December under cover of snowfall. The plan was betrayed by a deserter, though, in the darkness and the heavy snow, the defenders' confusion gave the outnumbered Americans a chance. However, Montgomery's death, the wounding of Arnold and a failure to follow the lead of Daniel Morgan robbed the Americans of the necessary decisiveness. Over 400 Americans, including the intrepid Morgan, outmanoeuvred by Carleton, surrendered.

Thus 1775 ended with the Americans defeated at Quebec, their best chance to conquer Canada lost. On the other hand, in the north, as more obviously in New England, the British had been forced onto the defensive. The revolution had not collapsed. The following year, 1776, would see if the British could be more successful with larger forces.

6   1776: The British Attack

Although the language of the French ministry to me is pacific . . . much will depend upon the continuance of success in America.

Viscount Stormont, British Ambassador in Paris, 18 November 1776[1]

The British government hoped that by mounting what was then the largest trans-oceanic expedition ever sent out from the British Isles, it would be possible to overawe the Americans. Convinced that the Revolution was the work of a few miscreants, who had rallied an armed rabble to their cause, they hoped that the Revolutionaries would be intimidated by the expeditionary force. Then the vast majority of Americans, who were loyal but cowed by the terroristic tactics of the Sons of Liberty and others of their ilk, would rise up, kick out the rebels, and restore loyal government in each colony. Ignoring the advice of General Gage, the initial general perception of the rebellion was more of a large-scale riot, or, at worst, a rebellion like that of the Jacobites. The concept of a massive popular rebellion and what was tantamount to a nation in arms was alien to them.

The British hoped in 1776 that one army would clear Canada and then advance via Lake Champlain to the Hudson, linking up with Howe's troops coming north from New York City. This would cut off that hotbed of disaffection and sedition, New England, from the more loyal middle and southern colonies. Based on various falsehoods, this strategy, none the less, could have succeeded if a Wolfe or Wellington could have been found to command the British army. Washington's army had dissolved in the late summer of 1775, and was reassembled, only to dissolve again that winter outside Boston. British strategy was relatively sound had there been an energetic commander. A successful quelling of the rebellion required rapidity of movement, flexibility of action and boldness of execution.

The year 1776 was to be one of British attacks. They can be divided into three: the southern expedition that culminated in the unsuccessful strike at Charleston; the relief of Quebec, the subsequent clearing of Canada and the advance along Lake Champlain; and Howe's capture of New York, followed by successful British operations nearby and the advance across New Jersey. The last two were significant achievements, but neither was as conclusive as had been hoped. The southern campaign revealed the difficulties of amphibious operations. For the Revolutionaries the year was militarily mostly one of setbacks, first in Canada and later around New York. On 30 December John Hancock, the President of Congress, announced in a circular that:

> . . . the strength and progress of the enemy . . . have rendered it not only necessary that the American force should be augmented beyond what Congress had heretofore designed, but that it should be brought into the field with all possible expedition.[2]

On the other hand, politically, the year had been bad for the British. American resolve had stiffened and independence had been declared on 4 July. The new government slowly became better prepared to wage war, a Board of War and Ordnance being instituted on 12 June, although this was to prove a considerable hindrance to Washington. The Revolutionaries strengthened their position in many states. In Pennsylvania, for example, a new constitution destroyed the political ascendancy of the Quakers, whose official position was that of loyalty to George III. Several were interned. The principal Loyalist initiative, the rising in North Carolina designed to cooperate with the southern expedition, was defeated by the North Carolina militia at the battle of Moore's Creek Bridge on 27 February. Elsewhere the militia was used to strengthen the new revolutionary establishment and harry or intimidate its opponents. In Maryland, for example, non-associators and non-enrollers were disarmed by the militia in the spring.[3] Dunmore's activities and the need to stabilize the political situation fostered Virginian support for a final break with Britain. In the early months of the year Lee, inspecting the defences of New York, Maryland and Virginia, sought to prevent their new governments from remaining in touch with their royal governors and to end the sort of compromises that had allowed British warships off New York to continue to receive provisions and to moor alongside wharves. Clinton's force on the way to attack North Carolina anchored in New York Harbour on 4 February, having promised not to attack the city. Lee entered New York City with several thousand men on 5 February 1776, the *modus vivendi* with the Royal Navy collapsed and by the end of April the warships had been forced to withdraw from the harbour and the narrows.

Had the British been well-prepared they would have been able to challenge this loss of New York Harbour. On 17 March the army in Boston under the command of William Howe, who had taken charge on Gage's departure in October 1775, had completed its evacuation of Boston, undisturbed thanks to a threat to destroy the town. Howe (1729–1814), the younger son of a viscount, had plenty of military experience. He had served in the Low Countries in 1747–8, taken part in the capture of Louisbourg in 1758, commanded a light infantry battalion that played a major role in the capture of Quebec in 1759, and took an important part in the successful attacks on Montreal (1760), Belle Isle (1761) and Havana (1762). Promoted to major-general in 1772, Howe was responsible in 1774 for the training of selected companies from line regiments in a new system of light drill and for the general introduction of light companies into such regiments. He was thus experienced in light infantry tactics, amphibious warfare and North American operations.

In March 1776, instead of proceeding to New York, Howe felt that the condition of his troops required rest and reorganization before he began offensive operations. Archibald Robertson, an officer in the Royal Engineers, wrote in 16 March of 'a vast deal of confusion in every department'.[4] Howe sailed to the British base of Halifax, Nova Scotia staying there until the second week of June. The British army did not land on Staten Island until 3 July 1776, by which time the Americans had had an opportunity to prepare New York for attack, although the mobile reserve established by Congress was below its anticipated strength and the preparations proved fruitless. The New York area was too large and, rather than concentrating his forces, Washington spread them out over the area.

FAILURE OFF CHARLESTON

The diversion of Howe's force to Halifax was a serious setback for the plans to attack New York, as was the decision to send 10,000 reinforcements to Canada, although neither was as spectacular a blow as the ill-fated southern expedition. Had it sailed from Cork on 1 December 1775, as intended, it might have reached Cape Fear by early February, which would have provided an opportunity for some action, before moving on against New York in the spring. Had the arrival of the force been coordinated with the rising by the North Carolina Loyalists, it might have proved a formidable challenge. The schedule was probably unrealistically tight, Clinton complaining from Cape Fear on 18 May that he had received instructions from Germain on the 3rd 'relative to a winter's expedition, and I find it is expected, that after I had (with less than 2,000 men), reinstated government in the four southern provinces, I was to join the commander in chief early in the spring, at the distance of 5,000 miles'. But war was and is often determined by bold strokes and expedients and the British enjoyed the naval superiority that enabled them to plan how best to employ the troops they were transporting to America. Bad weather and administrative deficiencies wrecked the plan. With reference to America in general, Germain told James Harris MP, a government supporter, on 1 May 1776 that 'he wished there had not been such delay', and he complained about incompetence in arranging for the despatch of reinforcements to Quebec.

Delay also affected the southern expedition. The admiral, Sir Peter Parker, did not sail from Cork until 13 February. On 7 March Lieutenant-General Earl Cornwallis, who had sailed on 10 February, reported to Germain:

> . . . our voyage hitherto has been very unsuccessful; the wind has been almost always contrary, and, till the first of this month, constant and most violent gales of wind . . . I fear there is no chance of our arrival on the American coast before the end of next month at soonest, and the assembling the fleet off Cape Fear, where there is no port, may be a work of some time.[5]

Although the first ships reached the anchorage on 18 April, Cornwallis did not do so until 3 May. The commander of the troops, Clinton, had already arrived from Boston on 12 March, too late to help the North Carolina Loyalists, defeated at Moore's Creek Bridge on 27 February, and unsure about how best to proceed. He had already been informed by Germain on 6 December 1775 that, in light of the strength of the Revolutionaries in North Carolina, he should attack elsewhere, but that he should then return in time to help Howe. Clinton decided that it would be best to seize some base that could be used for a campaign in the south. At first intent on the Chesapeake, he was persuaded by Parker and by Lord William Campbell, Governor of South Carolina, to attack Sullivan's Island, a sand-spit which protected the harbour of Charleston. Sailing at the end of May, the British did not attack until 28 June. Clinton had been already prevented from moving his men from Long to Sullivan's Island because the water between them was far deeper than reported. This was not the first serious intelligence failure of the campaign: the bar at Cape Fear had been found to block the entrance of ships of deep draught into the river. The difficulty in obtaining accurate information was to be a major problem for the British. It was a major hazard in fighting in a world that was poorly mapped and charted, and the situation was more serious in America than in better known Europe; though the Rochefort expedition of 1757 was but one European operation that failed because of inaccurate intelligence. Clinton explained the unexpected depth of the water off Sullivan's Island by noting that 'when many rivers fall into a sandy bay, new channels are formed every tide, and those which have 3 inches today may have thirteen feet tomorrow'. Delayed by contrary winds, Parker did not attack Sullivan's Island until 28 June. His relations with Clinton were poor, and he decided to act without the support of the army in order to destroy the unfinished fort by gun-fire. However, three ships ran aground, and one of them, which could not be refloated, had to be destroyed. The fort, commanded by Colonel William Moultrie, was not subdued. Its thick earth walls, faced by palmetto logs, were not badly damaged by the British cannonballs, but the warships suffered heavily from the well-aimed cannon in the fort. Clinton blamed the navy for the failure:

> The attack was advised on a supposition that there was water enough close to the . . . Fort . . . instead of going within 100 yards, as the pilot in my presence told them they might, they were by all accounts I have ever heard, not within 800 yards, no grape shot, no small arms, no fire from tops; in short they saw the scrape they were in, and would have drawn off, if the tide had permitted. The rebel fire was slackened a little for want of ammunition, but it was renewed again, and so hot, that the ships were glad to cut their cables and steer away to their former stations.

He claimed that had the frigates closed in and the army been able to attack the British might have succeeded. It was a humiliated and bloodied force that sailed north to New York, where Clinton's men were landed on 2 August.

This failure does not mean that the idea of a southern expedition was misjudged. The vigorous American response had owed much to the energy of Lee, who had among other things, forced whites to do work usually reserved for slaves, and to the respite before the British attacked. Had Lee and Schuyler exchanged expedition commands the fate of both the Canadian expedition and the defence of Charleston might well have been very different, although probably not. Lee had been helpful in setting up the defences, but played no part, whatever he said, in the actual defence. The British attack on New York was to demonstrate what a well-coordinated amphibious operation could achieve. However, it would have been better to send the troops directly to New York once it was clear that the fleet could not sail until February and that North Carolina was not such a good prospect, although the seriousness of this delay in building up troops for an attack on New York was diminished by Howe's decision to go first to Halifax. Nevertheless, given that the objective in sending such a massive force was to 'overawe' the Americans, the delay in the British attack on New York was less serious than it appears with hindsight.

Charleston was a humiliation for the British and it allowed the Revolutionaries to fight in the middle colonies without fearing for their position in the south, where their authority was further consolidated. Clinton regretted the failure to devote more resources to the south. In December 1776 he sought without success to persuade Howe to send him to the Chesapeake rather than to Rhode Island, complaining, 'I must still think great things might have been done in the southern provinces, and dread what the enemy may do, if we are not there to oppose them'.[6] Charleston was not to fall to the British until 1780.

THE CLEARING OF CANADA

After the failure of the attack on Quebec, the Americans, now under Arnold, continued their siege, although they had little prospect of success, and their force was affected by expiring enlistments, a shortage of provisions, powder and money and a lack of support from the local population. An account from the American headquarters outside Quebec on 28 March 1776 listed:

> . . . a catalogue of complaints. Indifferent physicians and surgeons . . . a few cannon without any quantity of powder or ball will never take a fortress if by a cannonade it is to be done three small mortars with a few shells will cut a despicable figure at a bomb battery and expose our weakness. Suppose you had a good train of ordinance with plenty of ammunition we have not an artillery man to serve them (there are here about twenty in all, drafted out of the different corps; the whole of whom seem to know very little about the matter) not an artificer for the making carcasses fire balls and many other necessary compositions for signals etc if the artificers came many articles necessary for the compositions are not to be had in the province or at least the quantity so extremely small as not to answer the purpose. No engineer nor any accounts of one . . . a well furnished military chest is the soul of an army . . . Without it nothing can be done for want of it inevitable ruin must attend us drove to the last extremity in want of almost every necessary.

Without hard cash, the Americans had been forced to issue a proclamation on 4 March declaring that those who would not receive their paper currency as an equivalent were enemies, a measure that lost them Canadian support, of which they had little to begin with. The army was also affected by smallpox:

> . . . every method that prudence could suggest has been attempted but in vain repeated orders given and as repeatedly disobeyed or neglected . . . the slowness of our operations is one

means of a great backwardness in the Canadians engaging . . . we were promised that cash should be sent after us none is yet arrived without [it] recruiting goes on badly all over the world and particularly in Canada . . . Bricks without straw we cannot make.[7]

The American garrison in Montreal was determined to return home as soon as the ice on the St Lawrence broke, while there were complaints about the priests stirring up the people against the Americans and about the difficulty of motivating the unpaid Canadians.[8] It was clear that as soon as the ice broke a British relieving force would reach Quebec. This occurred on 6 May and the Americans fell back in some disorder to Sorel. Reinforced and under a new commander, Major General John Sullivan, the Americans on 8 June attempted a surprise attack on the British camp at Trois Rivières (Three Rivers), but it was poorly executed and they were misled by local guides.

Lieutenant William Digby, whose 53rd regiment had recently joined Carleton's army, left an account of the engagement:

> About 4 in the morning an alarm was given by an outpiquet of the approach of a strong body of the enemy . . . soon after the alarm was given a few shots were heard from one of our armed vessels that was stationed a small way above the village who fired on part of the enemy advancing between the skirts of the wood and the river. In the mean time the troops on shore were ordered to line every avenue from the village to the wood, and take post in the best manner possible . . . . About 5 o 'clock strong advanced parties were sent towards the wood, where they discovered the enemy marching down in three columns, who immediately began a heavy fire with small arms, which was instantly returned. In the mean time a strong reinforcement of our troops with some field pieces arrived, which soon swept the woods, and broke their columns, the remains of which were pursued by us, as far as was prudent. The enemy from that time did nothing regular, but broken and dispersed, fired a few scattered shots, which did little execution.[9]

This battle, in which the Americans suffered heavy casualties, broke their will to remain in Canada. Sullivan wished to hold Sorel, but he was overruled and the demoralized army, short of food, retreated to Crown Point. The British were surprised by the extent of the American withdrawal. They reached Sorel on 14 June, expecting to have to fight, but found it deserted. Four days later they found Fort Chambly deserted and burnt. Davis recorded:

> . . . between the forts of Chambly and St Johns, about 12 miles, they destroyed all the bridges, which in such a wild country are not a few, for every rivulet must have something like a bridge to render it passable and this detained us some hours . . . The army marched in the greatest regularity, as from intelligence received the general had no doubt but he should be attacked on his march, our road leading through thick woods.

Far from blundering forward, as Braddock had done in 1755, the light infantry were deployed as an advanced guard. St Johns was found abandoned and on fire, Digby noting, 'Canada saved with much less trouble than was expected on our embarking from Great Britain'.[10] The British then moved on to Lake Champlain, finding signs of the American retreat. John Hayes wrote of the Isle-aux-Noix, 'The putrid effluvia from the corrupted bodies of the rebels who were buried here made it necessary for General Fraser, to order them to be burned and every such stench removed. They had the smallpox'.[11]

Thus ended the best American chance to conquer Canada. Fresh attempts were to be suggested[12] and concern was to be expressed by British generals,[13] but invasion plans drawn up in 1778, 1780 and 1781 were not followed through for a variety of reasons, including a lack of French support, more pressing opportunities and problems in the Thirteen Colonies and the logistical difficulties of operating in this largely barren region. Canadian emigrés, such as Moses Hazen, pressed unsuccessfully for action, but the military task was formidable. An invasion would have entailed sieges of strong positions by forces enjoying scant local support and dependant on distant sources of supply. The Americans in the long-run probably profited from being driven out of Canada. Such extended lines of communication and supply and the commitment of manpower required would have bled the Continental army dry and possibly led to mutinies. Washington reflected on the failure to take Quebec, 'hence I shall know the events of war are exceedingly doubtful, and that capricious fortune often blasts our most flattering hopes'. A British ballad, 'Captain Ephraim or the Yankee Entertainment', was more cutting:

> Brother Ephraim sold his Cow,
> And bought him a Commission,
> Then he went to *Canada*,
> To fight for the nation:
> But when Ephraim he came home,
> He prov'd an errant Coward,
> He wouldn't fight the Englishmen,
> For fear of being devoured.[14]

Washington's response reflected the impact of failure in Canada. On the one hand it was a serious blow to what had at times been a dangerous over-confidence in political circles about the military challenge posed by Britain. On the other Carleton failed to exploit the situation adequately and did not cut off his defeated enemy's retreat, although he had of course to avoid the risk of plunging his force into an ambush.

British strategy called for Carleton and Howe to join their forces along the axis of the Hudson and thus cut off New England, preparatory to attacking it. Mahan argued that:

> . . . it seems impossible to doubt that active and capable men wielding the great sea power of England could so have held that river and Lake Champlain with ships-of-war at intervals and accompanying galleys as to have supported a sufficient army moving between the head-waters of the Hudson and the lake, while themselves preventing any intercourse by water between New England and the states west of the river. This operation would have closely resembled that by which in the Civil War the United States fleets and armies gradually cut in twain the Southern Confederacy by mastering the course of the Mississippi.

This assessment was over optimistic about naval capabilities and failed to note the major differences between the two conflicts. Aside from the limitations of naval power, the British task was complicated by the difficulty of ensuring speedy communications between the two armies. Despite the substantial reinforcement that he had been sent, part of which would possibly have been used more effectively in the middle colonies, Carleton's performance was disappointing. He spent several months constructing from scratch a flotilla with which he could operate on Lake Champlain, a necessary preliminary to any advance south, but one that took longer than was required because he wished to ensure overwhelming superiority over the flotilla Arnold was building. In the meantime Carleton failed to reconnoitre or harry the American positions and he sent his Indian allies home. The Americans used the opportunity to reinforce and strengthen their position at Ticonderoga. Colonel William Phillips complained from Chambly on 10 July:

> We are here waiting the building of 600 or 700 boats to take the army upon Lake Champlain – it is a very tedious work – cruelly so – it prevents us from going forward -and from acting in favour of General Howe. Could this army have directly followed the rebels in their retreat I dare say the whole affair would have been decided for us – but they will now have time to recover and to fortify Crown Point and Ticonderoga.

Digby's account illustrates the hardships Carleton's army faced. On 14 August 1776 he moved to Isle-aux-Noix, 'our camp which was badly situated, being in a swamp and much troubled with snakes etc . . . the shore is such a swamp and so thick with wood that you can scarce land and those unbounded forests quite uninhabited except by Indians and other savage beasts'. Sixteen days later Digby noted:

> For some days past we had the most severe and constant rain; it poured through all our tents, and almost flooded the island, yet the days were very hot, with violent bursts of thunder, attended with frequent flashes of lightning. The idea of service to those who have not had an opportunity of seeing any, may induce them to believe the only hardship a soldier endures on a campaign is the danger attending an action; but there are many others, perhaps not so dangerous, yet in my opinion, very near as disagreeable: remaining out whole nights under rain and almost frozen with cold with very little covering perhaps without being able to light a fire fearing the enemies discovering the post, and not knowing the moment of an attack, but always in expectation of one.

Digby could hear wolves at night, and in September, having been on duty in very heavy rain, he became delirious due to a severe cold. Carleton's army was certainly better provided for than the American forces in Canada had been, Digby recording in early October:

> We were all provided for the cold weather we then soon expected in crossing the lake, with warm clothing, such as underwaistcoats, leggings, socks, etc. And smoking tobacco was counted a preservative of the health against dews, damps, etc. which arose from the many swamps and marshy drowned lands that surrounded the island.

Arnold had moved his fleet towards the British, leading to fears on the part of the latter that they would be attacked, but on 11 October Carleton's stronger squadron defeated the Americans off Valcour Island, destroying most of their vessels in the battle and subsequent pursuit. The British then occupied the deserted Crown Point, but Carleton failed to attack Ticonderoga, despite the advice of some of his officers. He believed it was too late in the season to begin a siege, and the American force was reputed to be large. Carleton's attitude contrasted markedly with that of Montgomery the previous year. Having failed to attack, Carleton was then persuaded by his engineers, who told him that they could not construct sufficient works to shelter the troops for the winter, that he could not stay on Lake Champlain. Crown Point was abandoned on the grounds that it was too late in the year to fortify it, 'Not a house or barrack left unconsumed by the rebels, the sawmills destroyed, by which we could not have a single board to build huts, and a want of assistance . . . totally cut off from any assistance we could give them on account of the ice etc'. Carleton retired to St Johns, ensuring that when Burgoyne marched south from Canada the following year he had first to advance to and then seize Ticonderoga. Had Ticonderoga been Burgoyne's jumping off point in 1777, he would have been much closer to Albany and the Hudson at the start of the campaign, and Howe probably would have had little choice but to cooperate with him.

George III responded to the retreat by suggesting that Carleton was possibly 'too cold and not so active as might be wished'.[15] Carleton's decision can be criticized on strategic grounds, although the army was in no state to winter beside Lake Champlain, and the fate of other forces wintering in adverse circumstances during the war should be noted. Possibly some troops should have been left to hold Crown Point, although such a detachment would have been vulnerable to nearby Ticonderoga and a long way from assistance. Without taking Ticonderoga a British position on the lake would have been exposed, and the fortress appeared a difficult proposition: too strong to storm and too late in the year to blockade. The British did not know that their opponents had almost run out of provisions. The following July Burgoyne was to take the position in less than a month, by exploiting its vulnerability to artillery from a commanding mountain. Carleton had not seen this possibility, and it is easy to understand why he decided to withdraw. Such cautious generalship would make it difficult to destroy American armies, although it also helped to avoid British defeats. Carleton was not defeated, unlike the bolder Burgoyne.

THE NEW YORK CAMPAIGN

Howe was to be more successful than Carleton. Having arrived at Staten Island, the valuable base near New York that naval cover provided, he decided not to attack until his army was completed by 'the arrival of the troops from Europe, and from the expedition against South Carolina. That intermediate time . . . from the violent heat of the weather, little active service could have been done . . . such service would probably have been attended with much sickness to the troops'. Howe thought that 'the enemy is numerous, and strongly entrenched . . . with a respectable artillery'. Clinton, who had arrived at Staten Island on 31 July, wrote on 2 August:

> The rebels are in some force, and as their whole attention since Howe quitted Boston, has naturally fallen upon New York, that city and island is covered with works, I suppose nothing

will therefore be attempted till our whole assembles. My idea is comprehended in a few words, that recollecting they are in such force in New York Island such a stroke ought if possible to be made as added to the noble efforts I am convinced the northern army will make, may break the heart of this war.[16]

In the meantime Howe and his elder brother Vice-Admiral Richard, Viscount Howe, who had been appointed naval commander-in-chief in American waters in February 1776, sought to use their powers as Peace Commissioners in order to negotiate with the Americans. In light of the Declaration of Independence this was belated and over-optimistic and the approach was rejected. On 22 August Howe made an unopposed landing at Gravesend Bay, Long Island. Naval strength gave him the ability to choose where he should launch amphibious attacks. Washington's forces were scattered throughout the area. Against his better judgement and never to do this again, Washington allowed political considerations to dictate his operations. New York City was impossible to hold with the forces Washington had, and facing the power of the British navy, who quickly proved that they could sail and land troops at will. Rather than concentrating his forces, he placed them all over the harbour area, each section too small to do anything other than hinder a British landing. If the winds had been favourable, the navy could have swept up the East River and controlled the narrows between the Bronx and Long Island, and much of Washington's force

Richard, Viscount Howe, naval comman-der in American waters 1776–8, by Henry Singleton, 1790

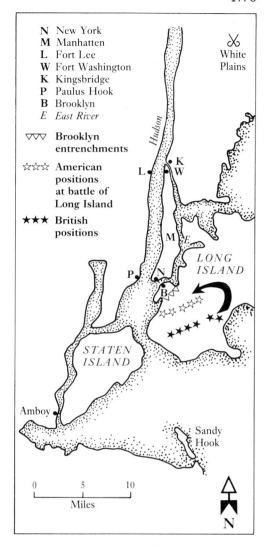

N New York
M Manhatten
L Fort Lee
W Fort Washington
K Kingsbridge
P Paulus Hook
B Brooklyn
E *East River*

⌄⌄⌄ **Brooklyn entrenchments**

☆☆☆ **American positions at battle of Long Island**

★★★ **British positions**

New York operations

would have been cut off. Energetic commanders would have found a way to attempt this, but the Howes did not, despite the fact that the wind and tide were not always against them. Much of the American army was on Manhattan, but the Americans on Long Island were divided between entrenchments at Brooklyn and a force strung out along the Heights of Guan, a ridge in advance of this position. The American troops guarded the coastal flanks of the Heights on Gowanus Bay, and Flatbush and Bedford passes, but a failure to guard Jamaica Pass on the left of the American line was exploited by the British, who outflanked the outnumbered Americans and defeated them in the battle of Long Island on 27 August. Captain William Leslie, who was on the left of the British line, and thus part of the force designed to engage the American front while its left flank was turned, recorded:[17]

At 5 o'clock we began our march again, and about 7 perceived the Rebels within musket shot drawn up to a great extent at the top of a rising ground with every advantage they could wish; their right extended to a marsh over which they could retreat under some cannon, their left was covered with a very thick wood in which were innumerable riflemen; it is supposed there were two lines in the rear to support their main body; in their front were two field pieces, and all the bushes, hedges, trees and hollows were lined with riflers. Our disposition was very soon made . . . some grape shot dislodged them from the bushes near our front and from which they fired at our regiment at a few yards distance . . . the advanced guard, who were much incommoded by riflers from behind the hedges; during all this time showers of grape were tumbling among us which wounded some of our men . . . A few minutes after I joined the advanced guard I was told Sir Alexander Murray was killed and Lieutenant Morgan wounded, my two most intimate friends! I was never so shocked in my life . . . a little after poor Murray's fate the fire ceased by degrees and the Rebels began to retreat in pretty good order across the marsh on their right, at last a company of grenadiers appearing in their rear a panic seized them and they took to a precipitate retreat without the least order.

Leslie had prefaced the account he sent to his father with a reflection that the contradictory nature of contemporary battle accounts amply bears out, 'a private officer has so little opportunity of knowing the particulars of any action that does not happen under his own eye that I shall mention nothing but what I saw'. Howe failed to press on and attack the American positions on Brooklyn Heights at once, although that would not have mattered had the Royal Navy been in place. Washington's response can also be criticized. Instead of ordering a withdrawal from Brooklyn, a position that could be cut off by the navy, he reinforced it on the 28th. Howe decided on 'regular approaches', rather than storming, in order to lessen casualties, and opened trenches on the night of the 28th; while Washington, finally appreciating the exposed nature of his position, retreated successfully to Manhattan, under cover of a thick fog, on the night of the 29th.

The battle of Brooklyn was a great might-have-been. Victory might have brought Howe the crushing defeat of the main American army, an achievement that would have enabled him to act less cautiously in his subsequent operations round New York and therefore to advance on Philadelphia before the end of the year. Washington was foolish to divide his force in the face of a superior enemy which might be able to employ its naval power. The American entrenchments at Brooklyn could probably have been overrun by the victorious British on the 27th. Bunker Hill offered a warning about the defensive strength of the Americans, and Leslie thought the American lines strong, but by the time the British reached Brooklyn their opponents had already been defeated. Franklin suggested that a British defeat would have been decisive, 'for they can hardly produce such another armament for another campaign: But our growing country can bear considerable losses, and recover them so that a defeat on our part will not by any means occasion our giving up the cause'.[18] He possibly exaggerated American resilience, by neglecting the potential for Loyalist action and sentiment, such as was demonstrated on Long Island after the battle, but he was largely correct about the British. Howe bore the burden of knowing that defeat would be difficult to reverse, losses hard to replace, while his army had few places to withdraw to. Howe subsequently told the House of Commons that:

... the most essential duty I had to observe was not wantonly to commit his Majesty's troops, where the object was inadequate. I knew well that any considerable loss sustained by the army could not speedily, nor easily be repaired. I also knew that one great point towards gaining the confidence of an army (and a general without it, is upon the most dangerous ground) is never to expose the troops, where . . . . the object is inadequate. In this instance, from the certainty of being in possession of the lines in a very few days, by breaking ground, to have permitted the attack in question, would have been inconsiderate, and even criminal. The loss of 1,000, or perhaps 1,500 British troops, in carrying those lines, would have been but ill repaid by double that number of the enemy, could it have been supposed they would have suffered in that proportion.[19]

This defence ignored the value of inflicting a serious defeat on the Americans, both in terms of their morale and in order to facilitate British operations. Howe was only correct for the wrong reasons: there was little reason to attack when naval control of the East River could have led to a sweeping triumph. While Leslie and his men slept for a fortnight 'on the ground wrapt in our blankets' near the village of Bedford, Admiral Howe approached Congress, and on 11 September the sole meeting between officially appointed representatives of the two sides before the final peace negotiations took place. The Declaration of Independence proved to be the stumbling block. Howe declared that it prevented him from negotiating and that he could not acknowledge Congress as it was not recognized by the king. The American delegates stressed the importance of independence, Edward Rutledge arguing that Britain would receive greater advantages by an alliance with an independent America that she had hitherto done from the colonies. His perspicacious observation underlined the emptiness of Howe's negotiating position. As with most states dealing with rebellions, it was difficult to put aside past relationships and the constitutional perspective, and the British did not rise to this challenge.

Instead, Sir William Howe resumed operations. American forces had been reduced significantly. Having seen what war and battle were like, many deserted, while much of the militia returned home for the harvest. The American position on Manhattan Island was exposed to the threat of an amphibious British flanking attack, although Howe rejected Clinton's bold proposal for a landing in the South Bronx, followed by an advance to cut off Washington's escape route. The Howes never made full use of British control of the water. They had a tendency to land their amphibious forces in front or at the flank of American positions, rather than behind them. The Americans were reluctant to abandon New York City, unwilling either to burn it down or to allow the British to seize such an excellent naval base, but on 15 September 4,000 British troops landed at Kips Bay, half-way up eastern Manhattan, near to the site where the United Nations building now stands. Leslie reported:

We landed under cover of the shipping, without opposition, although the Rebels might have made a very great defence as they had high grounds, woods, and strong breastworks to cover them, but they scoured off in thousands when the ships began to fire; indeed they are so outgeneraled that it is impossible for them to know where to prepare for defence . . . the rogues have not learnt manners yet, they cannot look gentlemen in the face.

Leslie's contempt was characteristic of many British officers, but it was not to save his life. Within four months Leslie was shot dead near Princeton.

'The entry of royal troops into New York', contemporary line engraving, c. 1776

The American defenders, mostly Connecticut militia, fled in panic, but the slow-moving Howe failed to cut off the retreat of the troops still in lower Manhattan. Abandoning their heavy guns, the Americans retreated up the west side of Manhattan. The following day at Harlem Heights an advancing body of Hessians and British light infantry that was failing to take proper precautions was checked. This check restored the morale of the American troops. They had met and fought British soldiers in the open and seen their backs. Larger triumphs were to spring from such small successes. This discouraged Howe from attacking the American concentration at the northern end of the island, centred on Fort Washington. The American army was affected by irregular pay, inadequate provisions and desertion. Clinton reported on 20 September that the Americans 'desert to us fast officers as well as men', while Leslie claimed that 'the poor infatuated wretches we took were most all drunk, even the officers'. However, the American defensive position was stronger than it had been hitherto. Howe decided to outflank it, but did not launch his attack until 12 October, yet another of the crucial delays that was to lessen the impact of British successes. He subsequently defended the delay by citing the need to dig entrenchments to protect New York while the main force was absent and the difficulty of obtaining accurate information:

> The country is so covered with wood, swamps and creeks, that it is not open in the least degree to be known, but from post to post, or from accounts to be collected from the inhabitants entirely ignorant of military description .... I found the Americans not so well disposed to join us, and to serve, as I had been taught to expect; that I thought our farther progress for the present precarious, and that I saw no prospect of finishing the war that campaign.[20]

Howe's initial unopposed landing at Throg's Neck was poorly advised, as the

Battle of Harlem Heights, 16 September 1776

Americans were able to demolish the bridge that linked it to the mainland. Nevertheless, the Harlem Heights had been outflanked and on 18 October Washington began to evacuate them. Re-embarking, the British landed at Pell's Point on the 18th. Instead of seeking to cross the Bronx River and cut off Washington's retreat, Howe moved slowly north, in part because of the check received at the hands of an American detachment under Colonel John Glover firing from behind stone walls, the 'battle' of Pelham Bay on 18 October. Washington retreated to a defensive position at White Plains. On 28 October British and Hessian troops attacked Chatterton's Hill on the right of the American position. The initial attack was unsuccessful, but the position was finally carried, the Hessians having to advance through a field that had been set alight. This success was not, however, followed up by an attack on the main American entrenchments. The opportunity of the 28th was lost and a subsequent plan was thwarted by heavy rain on 31 October, Leslie recording, 'it rained excessive hard the whole night so that we who lay in the open air had most of our ammunition spoiled and ourselves dripping wet, notwithstanding which the men were in high spirits eager for attack', only to be thwarted by the American retreat.

Howe, instead of following the retreating Washington, turned south to cut off and attack Fort Washington, with its garrison of 2,900. It threatened New York and a deserter had revealed the plans of the fortress. Nathanael Greene had persuaded Washington that the position could be defended successfully and the garrison withdrawn across the Hudson whenever required, but he was to be proved wrong. The Anglo-Hessian assault was delayed until 16 November by heavy rains, but the American lines around Fort Washington was then attacked successfully, despite heavy fire from their defenders. Leslie suggested that had Fort Washington been 'properly defended' it must have 'cost the lives of thousands'. He was impressed by the Hessians who 'advanced in two columns and kept the same order although three six-pounders with grape fired upon them while they scrambled up the rock'. Leslie recorded, 'The Rebels kept a constant fire with grape and musquetry from behind rocks and trees in spite of which our troops gained the top of the hill and drove all the rebels into the fort', which then surrendered. The size of the surrendering American force, 2,818 men, was not to be surpassed until the fall of Charleston in 1780. The Americans had hoped that the British would find themselves as hemmed in in New York by American fortifications as they had been at Boston, but the disaster at Fort Washington was a shattering blow. It had been foolish to divide their forces and to leave so many men in a vulnerable position, and Washington's reactive generalship had only been saved from worse disaster by Howe's caution and by heavy rain. The failure of the hemming in strategy had already been demonstrated by the success of the British navy in running up the Hudson on 12 July and 9 October, despite the American defences at Forts Washington and Lee. This lessened the value of the forts to the Americans.

Howe followed up this victory by sending a force under Cornwallis across the Hudson on 20 November to attack Fort Lee, which, with the facing Fort Washington, guarded the passage up the river. The garrison under Greene abandoned the fort hastily, leaving much valuable equipment and munitions behind. Another force under Clinton was sent to Rhode Island. Clinton was worried that the Americans there might have fortified themselves in an entrenched camp, and the British find it too late in the year 'for breaking ground, the country covered with snow, no possibility of making huts, no straw, and scarce any wood for firing'. In fact, as he noted, the Americans had failed to do what they might throughout the campaign, and Newport was seized without resistance on 8 December; and thus a base, called by Clinton 'the noblest harbour in America', secured for the fleet. Cornwallis set off in pursuit of Washington, who had crossed the Hudson at Peekskill after White Plains. Washington left Lee and about 3,500 men in the Highlands, and his own force had fallen to under 3,000. On 28 November Cornwallis entered Newark, as Washington's rearguard was leaving, and on 1 December reached New Brunswick. Howe ordered Cornwallis to halt there and wait for reinforcements, a widely-criticized step, but the pursuit was resumed, the British reaching the Delaware at Trenton on 8 December. The Americans had seized or destroyed all the boats to prevent their opponents from crossing, but New Jersey had been lost, the way to Philadelphia appeared open, when the river froze or rafts or pontoons could be built, and the American army was demoralized, short of supplies and threatened by expiring enlistments. Leslie, who was with the advancing force, wrote to his mother that the Americans:

> . . . cut down the bridges and gave us all the molestation they could (except fighting), notwithstanding which we were within two hours of coming up with the rear of their army, crossing the Delaware at Trenton . . . the Delaware stopped our course, for we had not one boat nor was there one on our side for eight miles up or down . . . it is the general opinion that

as soon as the river is froze up we shall proceed to Philadelphia . . . for all the lateness and coldness of the season, I believe there is not an officer or soldier who is not sorry and much disappointed at not passing the Delaware . . . the desolation that this unhappy country has suffered, must distress every feeling heart, although the inhabitants deserved it as much as any set of people who ever rebelled against their sovereign . . . great numbers are come in.

As with the unexpectedly easy clearing of Canada, this success exposed a lack of British planning and adaptability. Clinton proposed to go on to Philadelphia, as did some of the Hessian commanders. Clinton had certainly not been disillusioned about the prospect of amphibious operations by the failure at Charleston. He suggested:

. . . 10,000 men to march upon the Delaware, the fleet up that river with such a number of troops, as may be necessary to clear their way, and the little corps I command . . . to go up the Chesapeak as far as the head of it, within 40 miles of Philadelphia.

Howe was to be attacked in parliament for the failure to press on, but he was

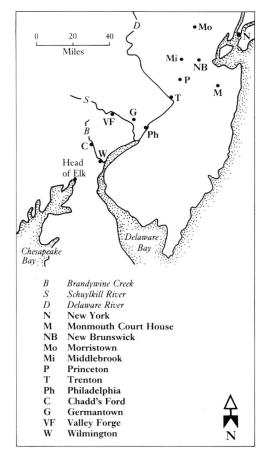

B	Brandywine Creek
S	Schuylkill River
D	Delaware River
N	New York
M	Monmouth Court House
NB	New Brunswick
Mo	Morristown
Mi	Middlebrook
P	Princeton
T	Trenton
Ph	Philadelphia
C	Chadd's Ford
G	Germantown
VF	Valley Forge
W	Wilmington

New Jersey and Pennsylvania

concerned about winter quarters. Initially, Howe intended to have restricted these to north of the Raritan, but he was impressed by Loyalist support in New Jersey and wished to offer protection, writing on 20 December:

> The chain, I own, is rather too extensive, but I was induced to occupy Burlington to cover the county of Monmouth, in which there are many loyal inhabitants, and trusting to the almost general submission of the country to the southward of this chain, and to the strength of the corps placed in the advanced posts, I conclude the troops will be in perfect security.

Clinton thought the chain too extended. Howe praised Cornwallis, especially 'the ability and conduct he displayed in the pursuit of the enemy from Fort Lee to Trenton, a distance exceeding eighty miles, in which he was well supported by the ardour of his corps, who cheerfully quitted their tents and heavy baggage as impediments to their march'.[21] That advance showed what the British were capable of and formed an obvious contrast to Howe's slower and somewhat indirect methods. However, they were in pursuit of a defeated enemy, across generally favourable terrain and not far from supporting forces and their base. Furthermore, the rapid advance did create supply difficulties, especially in the vital sphere of footwear. Widespread looting by the British troops owed something to a shortage of supplies, but it had a detrimental effect upon local opinion at a critical moment. Every American was perceived by the British and German troops as a rebel, and pillaging and rape were rampant, particularly in northern East Jersey. Many Americans who had hitherto been lukewarm towards the Revolutionaries turned against Britain. The same situation was to occur in the south later in the war.[22] The British decision to go into winter quarters can be defended, but a case can also be made for having pressed on, especially if the American position is considered. Although Washington had been reinforced by Pennsylvania militia and the Philadelphia Associators, a volunteer force, the inadequate response of the New Jersey militia was discouraging, while acute supply problems were being exacerbated by widespread demoralization. Congress itself adjourned from Philadelphia to Baltimore.

The European response was bad for the Revolutionary cause. In Paris Silas Deane found that defeats made it difficult to obtain credit, while the British government's success in parliament was attributed to victories in America. The Bavarian envoy in Vienna greeted the fall of New York with the reflection that the colonies would doubtless submit and that the war was over.[23] The British were hopeful that many Americans would accept the offer of pardon that Howe made on 30 November, with a sixty-day limit. The British press carried reports of American Loyalism, 'two-thirds' of Rhode Island and 'vast numbers' coming in daily in New Jersey.[24]

TRENTON AND PRINCETON

British hopes were to be challenged by Washington's riposte at the end of December. After a difficult night crossing of the icy Delaware, a surprise Christmas attack on the Hessian outpost at Trenton led to the surrender of nearly 1,000 Hessians at the cost of only four American wounded. The Americans had been helped by the defeated Colonel Rall's failure to heed reports of a forthcoming attack and his refusal to construct defensive positions, for which he was later criticized by Howe; by the out-gunning of the Hessians, whose wet muskets would not fire, by the Americans, who were supported by well-sited cannon brought across the river with some difficulty; and by the Hessian lack of tactical flexibility. The Hessians were tired, some drunk, after their Christmas celebrations. The assault was also a triumph for bold general-ship, while the successful simultaneous attack by two columns revealed the American ability to mount well-conducted operations.[25]

The attack was part of a wider plan that included another on the Hessian garrison at Bordentown. That was abandoned because of a failure to get the artillery across the Delaware and, as a result, Washington recrossed the river on the 25th, instead of pressing on to attack Princeton. However, as a consequence of a Hessian withdrawal from Bordentown, Washington crossed the river again on the 27th. Meanwhile, Cornwallis and 8,000 troops had been sent to deal with the American advance, entering Trenton after American delaying action on 2 January 1777. Washington's outnumbered force was drawn up on the other side of Assunpink Creek, vulnerable, if defeated, because they were on the eastern side of the Delaware. Washington's bold response was a night march towards the British position at Princeton. He left his camp-fires burning and a detachment that made a lot of noise and totally fooled Cornwallis. The following morning one of Washington's detachments clashed with a British force southwest of Princeton. The Americans were scattered by a bayonet charge, but Continental reinforcements under Washington's personal command reversed the situation. Most of the British escaped, but over 200 were captured. A British army surgeon who was present reported:

. . . the 17th and 56th [regiments] were on their march from Princeton to join a detachment of the army at Trenton. When they were about a mile and a half from the former the advanced guard discovered a body of Americans which though superior in number Colonel Mawhood had no doubt of defeating, however, he went himself to reconnoitre them and discovered their vast superiority in numbers which made him wish to retreat to the town from whence he had come but this he found impossible as the enemy were so near. There was a rising ground which commanded the country about half a mile back and about a quarter of a mile off the road. This he wished to gain and drew up the two regiments with 50 light-horse on one flank and 50, who were dismounted, on the other. The Americans endeavoured also to gain this rising ground and their first column reached the one side of it rather before the two regiments got to the other, so that just when the 17th reached the top they received the fire of this column composed of about 2,000 men by which all the mischief was done. The 56 (who would not advance in line with the 17th in spite of Colonel Mawhood frequently calling out to Capt. [—] who commanded them to mind his orders and come up) as soon as they saw such a slaughter among the first rank of the 17th, immediately ran off, on their commanding officer saying it was all over with the others. The 17th returned a very well-levelled fire against the provincial column and instantly leaped over some rails which were [tear on page] them and charged them with their bayonets [tear on page] though ten times their number almost, they ran off and retreated to the other columns of the rebels . . . when the provincials first fired they were about 25 paces he thinks from the 17th and is certain they were not above 30. Upon the whole rebel army advancing the 17th regiment and the 50 light-horse who were mounted (and who behaved very well) retreated as fast as possible leaving their killed and wounded . . .

The battle of Princeton by William Mercer. It appears that Mercer copied this painting c. 1786–90, in Charles Wilson Peale's studio from an original by James Peale. The American troops occupy the left of the scene, and in the middle distance the body of General Hugh Mercer, the father of the artist, can be seen

The 56th ran off in the greatest confusion to Princeton. The 40th who were left to guard Princeton never came up with the 17th, although Colonel Mawhood sent for them.

Washington was unable to follow up this victory by attacking New Brunswick, because of expiring enlistments, the tiredness of his troops and Cornwallis' advance, and he retired to the hilly country around Morristown, to camp for the remainder of the winter.

In just over a week the British army had lost over 1,250 men and hopes of an easy and rapid advance on Philadelphia had been quashed. Most of New Jersey was abandoned by Howe, who pulled back to New Brunswick, Amboy and the line of the Raritan, and, having lost the initiative, the British adopted a defensive posture. As with the retreat from Crown Point, this put the British in a worse situation for the start of the 1777 campaigning season. Equally important was the evidence of American resilience. The reviving effect the victories had on Washington's army, Congress and the Revolution as a whole was never fully appreciated by the British. They spoiled the Howes' conciliatory efforts, their offer of pardon. Washington's ability to create a new army should have been a warning to Burgoyne, confidently advancing after the fall of Ticonderoga in 1777. The battles around New York had suggested that American forces could not face regulars with confidence, but the operations in New Jersey had revealed British vulnerability when in units of less than army size. The Secretary of State,

Lord Germain, failed to take Trenton and Princeton seriously, writing to Howe 'I cannot help flattering myself that these winter efforts of the rebels are rather the effects of despair than of courage, and that they are symptoms of weakness, not marks of strength'.[26] It seemed reasonable to predict that Howe would be able to seize Philadelphia in 1777, but the prospect of conquering America with his army was remote. Small forces of regulars could not count on victory, and the British were to have to hope first for a decisive defeat of Washington's army, a concentration of the strength of both parties preparatory to a major battle seeming the best prospect, and secondly for the supplementing of their army by Loyalist forces. The campaign of 1777 was to indicate the strategic importance of a major victory, but it was to be one won by the Revolutionaries.

7 1777: Philadelphia and Saratoga

The rebels stood their ground till our troops charged them with fixed bayonets, upon which they immediately decamped with great precipitation, and I fancy that hour would have put an end to the Yankee empire, if the darkness of the night and the fatigue of our troops had not rendered any longer pursuit impossible.

Lord Lindsay on Brandywine[1]

The hopes of the people at large, as well as of the Rebel army, are greatly raised from this event [Saratoga] ... I do not apprehend a successful termination to the war from the advantages His Majesty's troops can gain while the enemy is able to avoid, or unwilling to hazard a decisive action, which might reduce the leaders in rebellion to make an overture for peace; or, that this is to be expected, unless a respectable addition to the army is sent from Europe to act early in the ensuing year ... If this measure is judged to be inexpedient, or cannot be carried into execution, the event of the war will be very doubtful.

Were any one of the three principal objects viz: New York, Rhode Island or Philadelphia given up to strengthen the defence of the other two one corps to act offensively might be found, in the meantime such a cession would operate on the minds of the people strongly against His Majesty's interests ... in the apparent temper of the Americans a considerable addition to the present force will be requisite for effecting any essential change in their disposition and the re-establishment of the King's authority.

Howe to Germain, 30 November 1777[2]

BRITISH PLANS

The year 1777 was to be one in which British generals mismanaged the war, while the Americans fought with more success than the previous year. It marked arguably the last real chance the British had, if indeed one had ever existed, to conquer America. 1777 was the last year in which the British fought only the

Revolutionaries and did not have to worry about French naval power. It was a year in which British forces were well-supplied. Their position was considerably better on 1 January 1777 than it had been a year earlier. Canada had been cleared and the British army based there had been able to operate as far forward as Crown Point. Boston had been evacuated successfully, New York City captured and the main American army defeated. Arguably, the principal setback had been not the failure to exploit these successes, but rather the continued inability to make any real military impact south of New Jersey and the sustained consolidation of the Revolution there.

This remained the case in 1777, a year in which there was to be no equivalent of the abortive Charleston expedition of 1776. Clinton warned of the danger of losing support through 'severity on one part and neglect on the other'. In Maryland, for example, where there was considerable Loyalist disaffection near the Chesapeake, there was no British intervention, while the militia was used to deal with Tory (Loyalist) risings, and the creation of the post of County Lieutenant helped to merge the militia with the revolutionary political system.[3] The British hoped to counteract this loss of the south. Howe's initial plans for 1777, sent to Germain on 30 November 1776, envisaged an autumn attack on Philadelphia and Virginia, followed by a winter campaign in Georgia and South Carolina. The south took at best a minor role in Howe's successive plans, however, while his repeated calls for more troops ensured that there were none to spare for separate operations there. Germain was left to hope that it would be possible to engage the Revolutionaries in the south by using Indians.[4] As Howe believed that it was necessary to defeat the Revolutionaries in a decisive battle, a concentration of British strength was obviously called for. It is easy to understand why British troops were not sent to the south, and yet, in light of the damaging consequences, it is difficult not to feel that more could have been done by troops based in Florida operating alone or in conjunction with a small amphibious force. By leaving crucial decisions to his field commanders, Howe, and Burgoyne who took command of the army invading from Canada, Germain ensured that the range of British operations was restricted.

Nevertheless, the British still had the initiative and numerous options. As with 1776, 1777 was to be a year in which the Americans essentially responded to British moves. Although Washington hovered around New York and considered launching a major attack, these Americans plans had as little effect as British plans to use New York as a base for major operations in New England. The American dream of conquering Canada was postponed, and the Americans concentrated on thwarting the apparent intentions of Burgoyne and Howe, unaware of the plans of either and largely unable to mount offensive operations. British positions in New Jersey were harassed in the spring, but no more was done. While Howe was on his lengthy voyage to the Chesapeake Washington, trying to separate fact from rumour about sightings of the British fleet, could not act decisively.

Although the Americans, faced with serious manpower and supply problems, did not take the initiative, that did not free the British from concern about them. Garrisons had to be left in Canada, Rhode Island and New York, the whole amounting to a considerable force. And yet a striking feature of the year's

The war in 1777

campaign is the extent to which the British did not consider the possibility of American initiatives, only of American responses, and then not sufficiently. In part this was a matter of arrogance, a failing that the self-confident Burgoyne appears to have been especially subject to,[5] and a natural consequence of the largely successful 1776 campaign. The latter can also be held partly responsible for a central feature of British operations in 1777: the fatal failure to coordinate the campaigns of Burgoyne and Howe.

In 1776 it had mattered little that there had been no such coordination, because both Carleton's and Howe's armies had been successful, although Germain had been able to trace a connection between the two spheres of operations. In March 1777 he informed Carleton that when the latter had fallen back from Ticonderoga, the Americans were able to detach troops from there to join their compatriots in the middle colonies, a measure Germain blamed inaccurately for Washington's attack on Trenton. The Americans were thus able to move troops between their armies, although their communications had been disrupted by Howe's capture of New York and the subsequent British advance. However, the British failed to exploit the possibilities of their new situation. A Hudson river strategy would have required much closer collaboration with the upriver Loyalists than the Howe brothers were willing to consider. Washington was concerned that British naval penetration past Fort Washington would lead to significant collaboration with local Loyalists. He and the New York Convention thought that the upriver Loyalists were numerous and, if not armed, armable. However, no serious collaboration between the navy and the Loyalists was attempted in 1776, and the New York militia was able to control the shoreline, though not without difficulty.

In 1777 the Americans were again to benefit from moving units between their armies, sending troops from Washington's to that of Gates' in the Hudson valley, and then back again. However, the British failure to coordinate operations was far more serious than it had been in 1776, because one of their armies was destroyed, forced to surrender at Saratoga on 17 October. Before surrendering, its commander, Burgoyne, had expected a supporting advance from the south by British troops based on New York, through the Highlands, the hills about forty miles north of the city, and along the Hudson to Albany. Clinton, the commander at New York, felt that he lacked sufficient troops to do so, and it had not been intended that he should mount such an offensive, although he did conduct a successful advance into the Highlands in early October, capturing Forts Clinton, Montgomery and Constitution. As Washington was in Pennsylvania and Gates, with the only other significant American force, was facing Burgoyne, it is probable that Clinton could have launched a bolder offensive earlier, and his lack of decisiveness at this critical juncture remains a question mark against his reputation. The bulk of Howe's army was in Pennsylvania, unable to assist in any way.

Germain had instructed Howe to cooperate with Burgoyne, although he had left both generals considerable latitude in their plans. This can be seen as an understandable decision in light of the unexpected developments of the previous campaign. In 1755 Cathcart wrote of American operations, 'considering how ill we are informed, I think particular orders could not be well concerted and a

General   Sir   William   Howe,
by J. Chapman

latitude very necessary to those intrusted'. Alternatively, Germain's instructions can be presented as resulting in a total absence of a clearly defined objective. On 18 May 1777 Germain wrote to Howe:

> As you must from your situation and military skill be a competent judge of the propriety of every plan, His Majesty does not hesitate to approve the alterations which you propose; trusting, however, that whatever you may meditate, it will be executed in time for you to cooperate with the army ordered to proceed from Canada, and put itself under your command.[6]

By that stage Howe's shifting plans made such cooperation implausible. The notion of Howe moving quickly suggests that Germain was out of touch and revealing that he could do little more than hope. Germain's failure to provide adequate strategic direction[7] was already having its baleful effects. Howe's initial plan, sent to Germain on 30 November (it reached London on 30 December), was compatible with a march to the Hudson by Burgoyne. He had envisaged a force of 10,000 advancing from New York to Albany, one of 5,000 to defend New York City, another of 10,000 to seize Providence and then march on Boston, one of 2,000, based on Rhode Island, to attack Connecticut and an army of 8,000 in eastern New Jersey to threaten Philadelphia. Assuming success elsewhere, troops would be shifted to permit an autumn attack on Philadelphia and Virginia, followed by a winter campaign in the south. Howe's plan required

35,000 men, and he called for 15,000 reinforcements, which would have easily given him such a force, as he had 27,000 effectives.[8]

By 20 December 1776, however, Howe had changed his mind. In response to the apparently collapsing American position in the middle colonies, Howe believed capturing Philadelphia offered a better prospect of success than the idea of a march from Rhode Island toward Boston, a proposal that might have resulted in a disaster to match Saratoga. This new plan envisaged no such march. Instead 2,000 men were to stay in Rhode Island, 4,000 in New York, 3,000 on the lower Hudson 'to cover Jersey on that side, as well as to facilitate in some degree the approach of the army from Canada', while Philadelphia was to be attacked with 10,000 troops.[9]

This plan was a response not only to the more specific opportunities presented by the American retreat, but also to the problem of indicating how an offensive could be conducted if no reinforcements were sent. It did not reach London until 23 February 1777. Five days later Burgoyne, then in London, sent Germain a memorandum in which he proposed an advance from Canada to Ticonderoga and then on, either to the Hudson, or east through the Green Mountains to the Connecticut River to link up with a force from Rhode Island. In the instructions sent by Germain to Carleton on 26 March the latter option was ignored, a result of Howe's decision not to base an offensive army on Rhode Island. Instead, an advance to Albany was stipulated, supported by a diversion from Oswego on Lake Ontario down the Mohawk. General William Phillips, who served under Burgoyne, was to complain in July 1777, 'I cannot help repining that our march is directed to Hudsons River, the whole country of New England northward and the Connecticut open to us – plans of war made in a Cabinet at several thousand miles distant from the scene of action are not always good'.[10] As Germain had also approved Howe's projected invasion of Pennsylvania, he was aware that Burgoyne could not receive significant support until late in his advance. The fate of delayed operations, such as Clinton's southern expedition of 1776, might have induced caution on this head, as might Howe's unexpected request of 20 January for 20,000 reinforcements, which could not be provided. However, the Pennsylvania plan did not appear to require a lengthy campaign, while, despite the checks at Trenton and Princeton, it was believed that Howe would be able to succeed with only 5,500 fresh troops.

Nevertheless, Howe felt that he could not undertake to support the advance from Canada. On 2 April he wrote to Germain complaining about a lack of reinforcements. Three days later Howe informed Carleton that:

. . . having little expectation that I shall be able, from the want of sufficient strength in this army, to detach a corps in the beginning of the campaign to act upon the Hudson's River consistent with the operations already determined upon, the force your Excellency may deem expedient to advance beyond your frontiers after taking Ticonderoga will, I fear, have little assistance from hence to facilitate their approach, and as I shall probably be in Pennsylvania when that corps is ready to advance into this province . . . the officer commanding it . . . must therefore pursue such measures as may from circumstances be judged most conducive to the advancement of his Majesty's service consistent with your orders.[11]

Howe promised to leave a force to clear the Highlands and then possibly to help the northern army, but it was clear that he did not feel bound to assist its operations. On 20 April he wrote to Germain expressing his doubts that he would be able to complete his Pennsylvania campaign in time to help Burgoyne. Howe's decision, communicated in his letter of 2 April, which reached London on 8 May, to advance on Philadelphia by sea, rather than across New Jersey, ensured that this would indeed be the case.

The decisions of each of the three principals can be criticized: Germain for failing to reconcile the plans of the two generals; Howe for neglecting the problems of the northern army; Burgoyne for failing to appreciate the strength of the opposition. Clinton argued in July that Howe should cooperate with the operations of Burgoyne's army and move north and that 'Burgoyne's army ought never to join ours'. Even had Burgoyne fought his way through to Albany, the value of such an advance could be queried. Alexander Hamilton, one of Washington's aides, argued on 5 April 1777:

> . . . as to the notion of forming a junction with the northern army, and cutting off the communication between the Northern and Southern states, I apprehend it will do better in speculation than in practice . . . would require a chain of posts and such a number of men at each as would never be practicable or maintainable but to an immense army.[12]

Such criticisms are justified, but it would have been inappropriate for Germain to formulate too rigid a plan, while, however much the operations of two independent armies might assist each other, their fate ultimately depended on their separate campaigns. Advances south from Ticonderoga and north through the Highlands would not have been easy under more favourable circumstances. Howe could defend both his decision to invade Pennsylvania and his chosen approach, via the Chesapeake, instead of the Delaware, or across New Jersey. His goals were unsettled: a decisive battle but also manoeuvres to seize major centres,[13] yet he obtained both Philadelphia and two major battles: Brandywine and Germantown. Had Germain wanted to secure Howe's assistance for Burgoyne he should have sent clearer and firmer orders earlier. Even this, however, would not necessarily have prevented Burgoyne from a Saratoga-type fate, although had Burgoyne been certain of a major advance from New York he might both have not felt it necessary to send a detachment to Bennington and have held on for a few more days at Saratoga.

Such a discussion is dangerously abstract, not least because it neglects the imponderables of American moves, although these were largely reactive. Any campaign conducted under such circumstances by two independently-operating forces faced difficulties, and scholars can be remorseless in their judgements. Had both British armies operated on the axis of the Hudson, then Germain and Howe might have been criticized for neglecting the opportunity to seize Philadelphia, while a successful march south by Burgoyne might have left British positions in his rear vulnerable to attack. To have been successful, Burgoyne would have had to have defeated Gates decisively. Flexibility in conception when planning a campaign from across the Atlantic seems desirable, and it is possibly more appropriate to criticize the individual commanders, while accepting that had they succeeded – Howe in winning his decisive battle, Burgoyne in reaching Albany – judgments might have been very different.

General 'Gentleman Johnny' John Burgoyne, by Sir Joshua Reynolds

On the other hand, it could be argued that there was not a British campaign of 1777; rather, there were two totally uncoordinated campaigns. Operating in conjunction with each other, Howe and Burgoyne might have been able to wreck the two American armies, to gain total control of the Hudson valley, to separate New England from the middle and southern states and to initiate a state-by-state pacification of New England, while the coast was controlled by the Royal Navy.

Operating, however, as two roving columns, and commanded by two lack-lustre generals, with no overall unity of command and no clearly defined master strategy or guidance from Germain, the two armies could not have achieved the potential successes outlined, even had the American forces been defeated. Even well-planned and well-coordinated operations fail, often due to laggardly behaviour, but the absence of unity in command was certainly felt in the British planning. Howe and Burgoyne acted with a complete lack of coordination; but, in addition, the situation challenged Euro-centric military thinking, centred as it was on a well-known topography with roads, strategic rivers and towns. In part, this was irrelevant in the New World, as was the concept of operating on interior lines. The latter notion was of limited value in America, where in large part the conflict was a war without fronts. New World geography, recruitment and logistics all created a hybrid Euro-American style of war similar on the surface to European warfare, yet at the same time very different.

OPERATIONS IN NEW JERSEY

For the first months of the year the military situation centred on Howe's army in north-eastern New Jersey. The northern 'front' towards Canada was shrouded in snow, the rivers and lakes blocked by ice. Howe's men around Brunswick and Amboy found it difficult to obtain supplies as a result of American harassment, but they were reinforced at the end of January with troops from Rhode Island (an early indicator of Howe's decision to prefer Pennsylvania to a northern strategy), in preparation for an attack on the Americans as soon as the weather improved. Washington's small army wintered around Morristown, poorly fed, clothed and housed and suffering from smallpox, the general commandeering supplies. The American force was barely holding together: it took a plea from Washington on 1 January to keep enough troops to form an army. Washington was unsure about Howe's intentions, but when the weather improved and his army was reinforced by new enlistments, albeit raw recruits, Washington moved south to Middlebrook, west of New Brunswick, to block any British advance on Philadelphia. His army increased from less than 3,000 men in March to nearly 9,000 by the end of May. The way therefore appeared clear for the decisive battle that Howe needed, and had he secured one and defeated the Americans in the spring the fate of the entire campaign in 1777 would have been very different. Washington, though, had already decided to eschew battle unless political circumstances or a chance of success loomed large. He very much wished to take the initiative but a lack of men and supplies kept him from doing so. The short-term militia that had joined Washington's army were of little value except for increasing his numbers and for eating his supplies.

Howe was delayed first by the weather, a serious impediment to operations, as it was difficult to transport supplies on bad roads, while encampments in winter temperatures were detrimental to the health and morale of an army. The Americans thought Howe likely to attempt Philadelphia, though they expressed increasing confidence that his force was too small to ensure success and that Howe would suffer from a shortage of baggage horses. Middlebrook was a strong position. Washington could always pull back behind the strong defensive position of the Watchung Mountains. Washington put Howe under the necessity of fighting if he wanted to advance to Philadelphia without leaving a powerful enemy army nearby, while denying him the opportunity of determining the terms of the engagement. By the beginning of April Howe had anyway decided to invade Pennsylvania by sea, so that it would not be necessary to fight his way across New Jersey. Howe, however, was not to sail for several months and in the meanwhile he did try to engage Washington. He subsequently told the House of Commons:

> I have been blamed for not marching, before I left Jersey, to attack general Washington, posted at Middlebrook ... To have attacked general Washington in that strong post I must necessarily have made a considerable circuit of the country; and having no prospect of forcing him, I did not think it advisable to lose so much time as must have been employed upon that march, during the intense heat of the season. Exclusive of this consideration, our return must have been through a very difficult and exhausted country, where there was no possibility of keeping up the communication with Brunswick, from whence alone we could draw our

provisions; and the force with me at that time, amounting only to about 11,000 men, it would not admit of sufficient detachments to preserve the communication. The movement which I did make in two columns was with a view of drawing on an action, if the enemy should have descended from his post, and been tempted towards the Delaware, in order to defend the passage of the river, on a supposition that I intended to cross it.[14]

This, however, did not succeed. The Americans avoided Howe's attempts in the second half of June to lure them into battle.[15] His failure can be seen as yet another of the missed opportunities of the year, although possibly more serious was his delay in preparing to sail, once he had decided to go by sea. Howe did not appreciate how weak the force facing him was, nor the advantage of striking before it was substantially reinforced, properly fed and trained. Had he crossed the Delaware he might well have obtained the battle he sought, but he told the Commons in 1779 that he had insufficient troops and:

... that, from a want of sufficient means to pass so large a river, I judged the difficulties and the risk too great, more especially as the enemy had a corps ready for the defence of it, exclusive of their main army in my rear ... The communication for provisions through such an extent of country, could not possibly be maintained with the force then at my command.[16]

In fact, the corps Howe referred to consisted of militia, whose morale was low, and a few cavalry pickets. The difficulties that the British were to face when withdrawing overland from Philadelphia in 1778 lend weight to Howe's fears, but the British were nevertheless successful in doing so. Had Howe wanted a battle foremost he probably should have sought to march overland, possibly supported by diversionary amphibious forces in the Chesapeake and Delaware, and by a demonstration by the force based on New York City. His stress on the need for reinforcements reflected a sense that he did not have sufficient men to guarantee success, and his resort to the sea indicated a desire for the assured security provided by the navy. It also illustrates Howe's overall insecurity and lack of enthusiasm. Howe also began pulling in his New Jersey detachments that spring, abandoning New Jersey to his opponents and leaving the Loyalists to their less than tender mercies.

The ability to turn readily to the navy was one of several factors that distinguished Howe's advance from that of Burgoyne, who was not interested in the maritime option offered: transportation of the Canadian army by sea so that it could operate on the New England coast. Such a course would have entailed delays even greater than those Howe faced, and could not have been reconciled with the use of so many transports by Howe. Howe missed another opportunity by his fruitless manoeuvres in New Jersey, that of clearing the Highlands. Clinton was to succeed there with a far smaller force, and had Howe sought to cover such an operation earlier it might well have paid enormous dividends. On the other hand, the capture and retention of the Highlands would have required cooperation with both Burgoyne and the navy. Holding a few strong points alone, without the navy, would have been of limited value, and garrisoning the positions in the Highlands would have required quite a number of troops.

Having decided to move his army by sea, Howe did not sail until late July. His troops embarked between 9 and 11 July, but Howe held back until he received an optimistic letter from Burgoyne on the 16th and he was then further delayed by contrary winds. A journal of an officer on the voyage helps to explain why it was so uncomfortable. Having sailed on 23 July, the fleet was becalmed on the 24th and 25th and affected by fog and thunder on the 28th. The Virginia Capes were not weathered until 17 August, after which it was intensely hot. The troops landed at Head of Elk (modern Elkton, Maryland) on the 25th 'without any opposition or a shot fired', although they then enjoyed 'rain all night and without tents'. Instead of the Delaware, Howe had decided to sail up the Chesapeake, the lengthier of his two maritime options. He was informed erroneously by Captain Hamond, the commander of the squadron blockading Delaware Bay, that Washington had crossed the Delaware, was marching on Wilmington and would be able to contest a landing, a situation no commander of an amphibious force risked readily. The British could, in fact, have landed in the Delaware in August 1777 provided that they had done so below Newcastle.[17] Thus Howe did not open his campaign against Philadelphia until late August and then after having failed to engage Washington earlier in the year. This ensured that no matter how successful Howe was, he could not exploit his victory with winter approaching. In addition, if Washington had been engaged earlier he could not have released the troops that eventually made all the difference at Saratoga, and, by their absence, in the Philadelphia campaign.

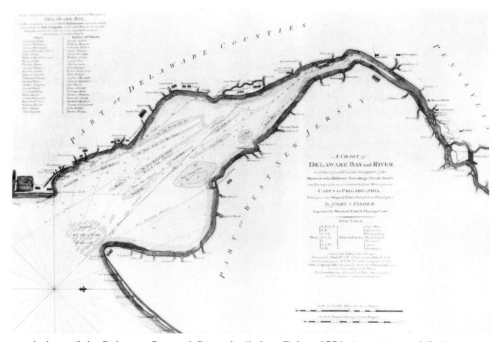

A chart of the Delaware Bay and River, by Joshua Fisher, 1776, 'containing a full & exact description of the shores, creeks, harbours, soundings, shoals, sands ... from the Capes to Philadelphia.'

THE SARATOGA CAMPAIGN

I will now return from that dreary barren waste, where the spectator sickens at the indolence, indecision and error, that everywhere catch his eye, to a different, but not more cheerful clime; to a region teeming with rash projects, visionary enterprises, and disastrous events.

Remarks on General Burgoyne's State of the Expedition from Canada
(London, 1780) p. 42

As Howe's troops disembarked on the Maryland shore, Burgoyne had already reached Fort Edward on the Hudson, while a detachment sent to Bennington had been defeated. The northern campaign was so far-advanced because Ticonderoga had not offered the expected resistance, although that also deprived the British of a likely victory. Burgoyne had reached Quebec on 6 May to find Carleton unhappy at losing command of the troops to be sent south, and far fewer Canadians and Indians to assist his army than he had expected, a serious problem, as the Canadians had been seen as essential for clearing a route through the forest. Assembling at St Johns in mid-June, the British reached Ticonderoga on 1 July to find an outnumbered garrison under Arthur St Clair. The Americans had failed to fortify Mount Defiance, which commanded their positions, because they believed that it was impossible to get artillery up its slopes. Burgoyne, appreciating its value, moved artillery onto the mountain, a tough engineering challenge that was solved successfully, leading the Americans to abandon Ticonderoga on the night of the 5th. Five days later General Phillips wrote, 'The success we have had is great, but it would have been much greater if the rebels had held at Ticonderoga as we should assuredly have cut them off . . . as it is there is infinite labour and fatigue to encounter . . . the country engenders rebels, and as we pursue them in front they arise afresh in the rear'.[18] On the 7th the American rear guard under Colonel Seth Warner was surprised near Hubbardton, but 'they soon betook themselves to their breastworks, which is a mode of the defence they have adopted . . . almost every shot took effect'. The breastworks, field fortifications constructed of logs, were an ideal cover for defensive fire. Though the Americans were outflanked and forced to disperse, the British had 'greatly suffered from their first fire', and their wounded were in an especially unfortunate position 'as assistance by either land or water could not be procured less than 25 miles, and that no cart road'.[19]

Instead of advancing to the Hudson via Lake George, whence there was a waggon road to the Hudson, Burgoyne chose to continue in the direction in which he had been pursuing the Americans, moving via Fort Ann, a decision that forced his men to cut a route through a wilderness, so that, as he wrote on 30 July from Fort Edward which he had just entered:

> . . . the toil of the march was great, the enemy having broke up the roads and cut down the trees, laid them across all the passes and rendered the passage very difficult through a perfect desart . . . the troops had above 40 bridges to construct, and others to repair, one of which was a logwood over a morass two miles in extent.[20]

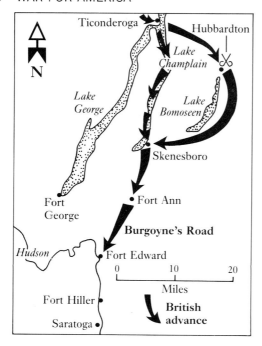

Burgoyne's advance to the Hudson

Employing a method used in this area by the Indians in the Seven Years War, the Americans felled trees in order to block the creeks. The already wet soil was turned into swamps as the side creeks backed up. Burgoyne took a long time to build bridges and a plank road across the resulting morass. Burgoyne argued that had he taken the other route that also would have been blocked.

If the British troops were tired, their opponents were also in a poor state, affected by low morale and desertion and uncertain how best to respond to Burgoyne's advance. The Americans, instead of resisting Burgoyne's advance, fell back to near the confluence of the Hudson and the Mohawk. Indeed, one of the most insistent themes in the correspondence of the generals on both sides in 1777 was the weakness of their forces, a theme that was to grow stronger as the war progressed, being joined on the British side from 1778 by a strong note of naval inadequacy. This sense of weakness could be crippling, discouraging generals from acting, even when their opponents were in no real position to obstruct them. Possibly Burgoyne should have pressed on at once after reaching Fort Edward, but he felt constrained by the need to accumulate supplies and open the Lake George route. He was to be criticized for burdening his force excessively, especially with too much artillery and an enormous amount of personal baggage, and he certainly did not act as if he realized the need to move decisively before the Americans reinforced their forces. As with Carleton on Lake Champlain the previous year, there was a clear determination to prepare his force but a failure to appreciate the strategic context, although, unlike Carleton, who he had criticized for evacuating Crown Point, Burgoyne was in an exposed position.

'Provincial General Buttons marching to Saratoga with plunder', by John Kay, Series of Original Portraits and Caricature Etchings, *1786*

Unable to obtain adequate supplies from Ticonderoga, Burgoyne decided to seize them from the Americans. As he subsequently told the Commons, 'It was soon found that in the situation of the transport system at that time, the army could barely be victualled from day to day, and that there was no prospect of establishing a magazine in due time'. An American magazine at Bennington appeared to offer a solution, especially as Burgoyne had been assured that the area was full of Loyalists. There had been similar assurances about Albany, whose Loyalists were allegedly asking for help 'to free them from those bonds of slavery, which these villainous rascals hourly impose on them.'[22] Burgoyne, however, was to be disappointed in all his expectations. Although about 300 Loyalists joined the force under the command of the Brunswicker Lieutenant-Colonel Frederick Baum sent to seize Bennington, the Loyalists did not make a decisive military impact either in the north or in Pennsylvania. It was only in areas already pacified that they were important, Clinton's force of 6,000 men based on New York being half composed of Loyalist units.

Unexpectedly, Bennington was protected by a New Hampshire militia force under Brigadier-General John Stark and Baum's outnumbered force, enveloped by the Americans on 16 August, found their Loyalist and Indian allies unequal to the struggle. The Indians abandoned Baum, who had mistaken the Americans in his rear for Loyalists. Never one to avoid the chance of damning others, Burgoyne subsequently blamed the dead Baum in the printed debate over the campaign that his own attempt to justify his actions inspired. He claimed that when the Americans were:

... discovered to be greater, the ill-consequences would have been avoided had not Colonel Baum deviated from his instructions, by committing his regular force in the woods instead of fortifying a post in the open country, and exploring the woods only with the Indians, Canadians and Provincials [Loyalists], supported by Captain Fraser's corps [light infantry], who were complete masters of such business.[23]

Burgoyne thus ignored the question of the wisdom of sending slow-moving dismounted dragoons on such an expedition. After their ammunition ran out, the Germans tried to fight their way out with their swords, but with scant success. Baum died and most of his men were captured. A relief force under Lieutenant-Colonel Heinrich Breymann sent by Burgoyne was defeated nearby later that day.

Bennington was a disaster for Burgoyne. He had lost 900 men, 696 captured and about 200 killed, and that from an army already denuded by the need to provide a garrison for Ticonderoga, because Carleton, who was still in command in Canada, refused to do so. British operations were inhibited by the confused command structure which exacerbated the effects of personal animosities between the generals.

Furthermore, the supporting thrust down the Mohawk had failed. Lieutenant-Colonel Barry St Leger landed at Oswego on 25 July, with a mixed force of regulars, Loyalists and Indians, and reached Fort Stanwix, which guarded the approach to the Mohawk, on 2 August. Far from being virtually abandoned, as St Leger had been informed, it had a garrison, under Colonel Peter Gansevoort, that was nearly as large as St Leger's force. Weak in artillery, St Leger decided on a siege. A militia relief column, under Brigadier-General Nicholas Herkimer, was checked at the battle of Oriskany on 6 August, but St Leger's Indian allies were unhappy at the lack of progress, and decamped when a relief force of Continentals under Benedict Arnold approached, obliging St Leger to follow. Burgoyne blamed the absence of local support, an ominous note in 1780 when he published his account, given British hopes then from the southern Loyalists: 'by the false intelligence respecting the strength of Fort Stanwix, the infamous behaviour of the Indians, and the want of the promised cooperation of the loyal inhabitants, Lieutenant-Colonel St Leger had been obliged to retreat'.[24] In addition, Burgoyne had no reason to look for help from Clinton, who had complained on 15 July about having too few troops, claiming that unless he was heavily reinforced he could not divide his force, and adding that Burgoyne's 'army cannot, ought not ever to join ours'. On 16 September Clinton stated that he dared not stir without reinforcements, asking 'what can I do a great extent of country to cover, and a most important place' to defend.[25]

Burgoyne was also faced by a growing American force. Washington had sent a large force including Daniel Morgan and his riflemen, Arnold had returned from the Mohawk and the American army, now under the command of General Horatio Gates, who had replaced Schuyler as commander of the Northern Department in August, was over 6,000 men strong, and growing every day as militia units arrived to fight Burgoyne. Burgoyne could not obtain sufficient supplies to remain on the upper Hudson and he had the choice of advancing or retiring. Optimism, over-confidence and conceit led him to the former, his army crossing the Hudson on a bridge of rafts on 13 and 14 September.

This decision was subsequently to be savaged in a pamphlet literature that is worth citing because it reveals the extent to which British military policy was debated publicly, to a degree that would have been unthinkable in major twentieth-century conflicts. In addition, this debate helped to provide a context within which decisions taken later in the war could be and can be judged. It is reasonable to judge Cornwallis and Clinton in light of the contemporary discussion of Burgoyne and Howe, and these generals appreciated that their conduct would be thus discussed in parliament and the press, and that their every action would give rise to debate. Burgoyne, Clinton, Howe and Admiral Howe were MPs, Cornwallis a member of the House of Lords. A pamphleteer of 1779 announced that he was:

> ... at a loss when I attempt to discover the prudence of passing the North River, or the expediency of pushing on to Albany. By the first you threw the impediments of a rapid, broad, unfordable river, to the retreat of an army, unwieldy with the baggage of necessaries and luxury, and hampered in an intended forced march with a train of artillery equal (in number at least) to what would be required for a succession of Flemish sieges ... the second ... could not be to raise men, or conciliate friends, for the whole march, as far as they went, was through uncultivated wood, except a few ill inhabited narrow slips of cultivation, which scattered upon the banks of the North River, threw just light enough upon the piece to mark the dreary darkness of the general design. Was it their intention merely to support their friends at Albany, and encourage them to declare themselves? Still their measures appear to me, ill concerted for the execution of their purposes:– An army, harassed by opposition, reduced by the fatigues and diseases incidental to a comfortless march through deserts, where the indulgence of fresh provisions could hardly ever be procured to gratify the active and relieve the exhausted or sickly soldier; whose marches became every day more difficult and less expeditious, from the failure of horses (whose provendor frequently consisted of leaves alone) in a country which afforded no recruit of them.[26]

The criticism was more pointed in a pamphlet of the following year:

> Knowing that every collateral operation had failed; with only a month's provision; having an enemy in front confessedly superior; and assured of a large body taking place immediately behind him, General Burgoyne crossed the Hudson, and abandoned his communication with Canada and his magazines, without any prospect of one being opened with New York.[27]

A defence can be made of Burgoyne's conduct until his crossing of the Hudson. To have not pressed on after having taken Ticonderoga so easily and when in command of one of the only three British forces able to mount an offensive would have been to make no contribution to what appeared likely to be a decisive campaign. The alternatives suggested – an advance into New England or maritime transportation to New York and a subsequent campaign – were not practical; and yet by early September neither was a march on Albany. Burgoyne complained about the difficulty in obtaining accurate information, and it is understandable that he should have underestimated the strengthening of Gates' army, but he also neglected the risks of advancing, risks that Baum's fate demonstrated. In spite of poor intelligence, Burgoyne, nevertheless, pressed on. Meanwhile, Gates had moved his forces north from Albany.

On 19 September Burgoyne approached Gates' position, fortified by breastworks and redoubts, on Bemis Heights, a heavily wooded area north of Stillwater on the western side of the Hudson. The advance was a disaster. Americans under Arnold and Morgan advanced to meet the British centre at Freeman's Farm, about a mile north of Bemis Heights, and Morgan's riflemen inflicted serious casualties. Every time the British advanced, the Americans withdrew, sniping from 200 yards, killing officers especially. Fortunately for

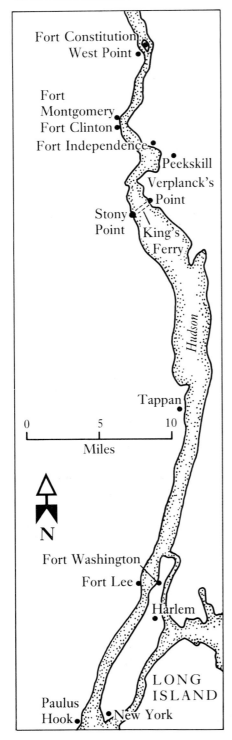

The Highlands forts

Burgoyne, Gates, an over-rated general, refused to leave his entrenchments in order to support Morgan and Arnold, while the British were assisted by an advance by the Germans under Riedesel, which eventually turned the American right flank. The British were left in command of the battlefield, but Burgoyne's army had lost about 600 men, compared to 300 Americans, while Gates still blocked the route south. Burgoyne later wrote:

> Few actions have been characterized by more obstinacy in attack or defence. The British bayonet was repeatedly tried ineffectually. Eleven hundred British soldiers, foiled in these trials, bore incessant fire from a succession of fresh troops in superior numbers, for above four hours; and after a loss of above a third of their members (and in one of the regiments above two thirds) forced the enemy at last.[28]

The British had indeed fought bravely but they had not even reached Gates' entrenchments. Burgoyne was at fault for exposing them in an engagement in which they lost the initiative without possessing a strong defensive position to fall back on, and for failing to coordinate his three advancing units. Burgoyne decided to try again, but he then postponed his attack in order to see what impact Clinton's expected move into the Highlands would have. On 6 August Burgoyne had written to Clinton expecting to reach Albany about the 23rd and not asking for any help. However, the arrival of 1,700 men from Britain on 24 September led Clinton to plan a diversionary attack on Fort Montgomery in the Highlands, designed to reduce the pressure on Burgoyne. Five days later Clinton received news from Burgoyne that he was cut off from Canada and hoped to join up with the New York army. In response, Clinton with 3,000 men moved up the Hudson on 3 October, the first suitable tide. The small garrison at Verplanck's Point fled without firing a shot when the expedition appeared on the 5th, but while there Clinton received a note from Burgoyne, sent on 28 September, informing him that he was outnumbered, cut off from Canada and had provisions only until the 20th, and seeking to transfer responsibility to Clinton, by asking for his instructions and stressing the importance of Clinton's operations. In light of his earlier letter to Burgoyne, Clinton was surprised that he:

> ... should seem to entertain hopes of my being able to force my way to Albany with only 2,000 men, which, being the most I had promised him, was all that he could count upon; and of course they ought not to have excited much hopes of my being able even to seize the forts in the Highlands. For without proper artillery or the possibility of dragging them over mountains of difficult ascent (the passes through which would have been impracticable if defended) no great success could have been expected, from the handful of troops which prudence permitted me to draw from New York, against fortifications defended by ... cannon, fully garrisoned, and as strong as art and nature and the most difficult approaches could make them.
>
> Yet, had the reinforcement from Europe arrived in time to have enabled me to make the move sooner, I had little doubt that even the attempt might have so alarmed the enemy as to have called off some part of the multitude opposed to our northern army, and have thereby perhaps eased its retreat.

Clinton argued that Burgoyne's critical situation demanded that he attempt the impossible. He did not delay matters by besieging the principal fortresses in the

Highlands, whose garrisons had been weakened by detachments to the armies of Gates and Washington. On 6 October Clinton marched his infantry through the hills to the west of the Hudson and stormed Fort Montgomery and Fort Clinton. Despite British losses to the musket fire of the defenders, primarily militia or raw Continental recruits, the latter's fixed positions exposed them to the force of the British bayonet charge. The boom blocking the river was then destroyed and the Americans obliged to set fire to their squadron on the Hudson. On the 7th Fort Constitution fell when its garrison fled, leaving their cannon unspiked, at the approach of a British force.

On that day, however, Burgoyne had been defeated again. Since the engagement of 19 September his army had been affected by falling morale, decreasing supplies and desertions; 'not a night passed without firing . . . no foraging party could be made without great detachments to cover it'. At a Council of War on the 5th his officers pressed Burgoyne to retreat while there remained a chance, but he obdurately replied by calling for a full-scale attack on Gates whose army had increased to 11,469 effectives, compared to 6,617 in Burgoyne's force. When it was pointed out that the thick woods made it impossible to obtain accurate information, Burgoyne proposed a reconnaissance in force that could be broadened into a full attack to turn the American flank. Attempted on the 7th, this was repelled by the Americans at the battle of Bemis Heights, although Gates' refusal to commit all his troops limited the extent of the disaster. Nevertheless, two British redoubts had been overrun in the American attack and they had lost 600 men and several important officers. There were about 130 American casualties. The battle destroyed the morale of Burgoyne's army and on the 8th the British began to retreat, leaving their wounded. However, the Americans had already fortified the opposite bank of the Hudson to prevent a crossing. Burgoyne was persuaded to agree to abandon the guns and baggage and retreat by forced marches in order to cross the Hudson above Fort Edward, but when he discovered that the route was also blocked he countermanded the march. Encamped at Saratoga, Burgoyne's army was reduced to waiting for Clinton, while exposed to constant fire.[29]

Clinton had replied to Burgoyne's letter of 28 September by informing him that he was not in a position to issue orders:

. . . 'but if, in consequence of my unexpected success, as the river was now open between us, he should have decided to attack the rebel army, and could get to Albany, I would do my utmost to communicate with him, and give him a supply of provisions.' In my situation, not having heard from General Howe for six weeks, not knowing where Washington was, having left a small force in New York, with a communication of 140 miles between Albany and New York to open and keep, and the important post we had taken, to garrison, it was rather too greatly daring to attempt it, but I determined to venture 1,700 men under General Vaughan, to proceed up the river, under convoy of Sir James Wallace and the gallies, and, if possible, to assist his operations. I had likewise ready, in small vessels, such as could go within a few miles of Albany, provisions sufficient to supply General Burgoyne's army for six months: all this I had done, when I received a letter from the Commander-in-Chief, acquainting me, 'that his victories had been by no means decisive; and that notwithstanding I may have gone up the river (which I told him I proposed doing) if my object was not of the greatest importance, with a probability of fulfilling it in a few days I was to give it up and send him full 4,000 men . . .'

which he wrote on 13 October:

> I am now doing – Good God! what a fair prospect blasted! If Burgoyne has retreated, as he seemed under no apprehension of difficulties in his retreat, I dread none; but I wish, if he is gone, to hear that he is safe over the lakes having left a garrison in Ticonderoga.[30]

By 15 October, 2,000 men in Clinton's army under General Vaughan had reached Kingston, but the pilots, intimidated by the American soldiers on both banks, refused to take the transports on towards Albany. It did not matter. Clinton was mistaken in writing that his operations in the Highlands having succeeded 'beyond my utmost hope: the communication with Albany is now open', but he was correct in his fear that Burgoyne would not be 'there to avail himself of it'. On the 14th Burgoyne began negotiating with Gates. Keen to settle because he was concerned about Clinton's advance, Gates agreed to terms under which Burgoyne's troops were to return to Britain on condition that they did not serve again in America. This type of parole was natural to European combatants and Gates, an ex-major in the British army, believed that he was acting according to normal conventions, 5,895 men surrendered. Worried that they would simply replace other soldiers who could be sent to fight, Congress, however, was to disavow the convention and keep the soldiers as prisoners of

The surrender of General Burgoyne to Horatio Gates, at Saratoga, 17 November 1777

war. The British troops ended up in Virginia, marching all around the backcountry till late in the war.

Burgoyne's army, which marched out on 17 October, had discovered the folly of underestimating their opponents and Burgoyne admitted this when writing to Germain on the 20th. His approach to forest operations had been insufficiently flexible, the heavy baggage train a particular mistake, while the army had too few light infantry and discovered that reliance on the Indians was foolish, something that Amherst or any veteran of the Seven Years War in America could have told him. Most of the fighting on the American side was done by men detached from Washington's army under Arnold, who was probably the best operational combat commander in either army. Arnold, a heroic commander in the fore of his men, was wounded at the battle of Bemis Heights, shot in the same leg that had been hit in the attack on Quebec in 1775. The notion that the militia won the battle is a hoary old tradition no longer accepted by modern scholars. Gates' role should not be exaggerated. Arnold's boldness, and men and supplies forwarded by Schuyler in Albany turned the tide as, of course, did Burgoyne's folly. The British general, Simon Fraser, shot down by Morgan's marksmen at the battle of Bemis Heights, or his German counterpart, Frederick Riedesel might have succeeded in defeating the Americans, but with Burgoyne in command the British suffered seriously from poor leadership. To be 'Burgoyned', surrounded and captured, became a common term.[31]

In strategic terms Saratoga was a warning of the folly of thinking that the Americans had really only one important field army, and consequently that its defeat would signal the effective end of the conflict. When Burgoyne's advance had first been considered, it had been assumed that the sole significant risk would be if Washington moved against him. This was Germain's hope; that Washington would be crushed between Burgoyne and Howe. Instead Burgoyne had been defeated while Washington's army had been deployed against Howe, a point that Cornwallis would have done well to heed when he campaigned in the south. Saratoga had a serious impact in America and Europe. In America it raised the morale of the Revolutionaries, offsetting the effect of Howe's capture of Philadelphia. It also ensured that thereafter forces based in Canada would be no more than a modest diversion to the American war-effort. Howe noted that after Saratoga Washington was reinforced by men returning to his army from Gates' force.[32] This was in response to Washington's hope that such re-inforcements would enable him to treat Howe as Burgoyne had been treated, and despite Gates' fear that Clinton would press on to Albany.[33] However, Gates' reluctance in returning the troops Washington had sent him, troops that had been so important in the defeat of Burgoyne, prevented Washington from following up on Germantown and the vigorous defence of the Delaware River forts. Nevertheless, it is unclear how far the results of Brandywine, Germantown and the Delaware forts operations would have been different had Washington never sent the troops in the first place.

In the longer-term the strategic situation had altered greatly. The prospect of a successful British advance into the Hudson valley or New England had largely disappeared, while the British bases in Rhode Island and New York could be covered without the need to detach men from the main Continental army.

Saratoga also marked the end of any serious prospect of cutting off New England from the rest of America. The plan had not been without value as American anxieties about communications across the Hudson reveal.[34] British pressure on the upper Hudson threatened the crucial nexus of the Revolution, which was the Highlands. American forces in Pennsylvania depended in part on supplies from New England, especially Connecticut. New England sent live-stock, while Pennsylvania provided grain to New England. The possibility of isolating New England was thrown away in 1777. Had Burgoyne retreated he would have been in a position to threaten the upper Hudson again, possibly backed up by a larger force on the Mohawk. British garrisons in the Highlands, supported by a squadron on the river, would have been able to challenge the American position below Albany.

Howe, however, was so concerned about Pennsylvania that he ordered Clinton to send reinforcements and to evacuate Fort Clinton, obliging him to abandon the Highlands. Clinton complained, 'I imagine our chief meditates some blow of consequence as he has drawn everything to him' and left Clinton 'with much too slender a corps for the defence of a very extensive and important command'. He was later to claim that the loss of Burgoyne's army might have been accepted 'as a necessary sacrifice' had he been able to retain the Highlands.[35] Washington made a similar suggestion.[36] In military terms they were possibly correct, although it would have been more difficult to exploit such a success had Britain had an army less; but in political terms Clinton was wrong. Aside from the tonic effects in America and the demoralizing consequences within Britain, Saratoga, by helping to demonstrate American resilience, encouraged French intervention, and that was to alter the war totally. British politicians and diplomats were already assessing the progress of the war in large part in terms of its international consequences.[37] On 4 December the news of Saratoga reached Paris. Two days later the American commissioners were asked to resubmit their proposal for an alliance, a measure that would make war with Britain inevitable. The previous March Hans Stanley, a government MP, had pointed out that 'success had always depended much upon opinion.'[38] Saratoga was seen as a major triumph, the major event and consequence of the campaign of 1777.

BRANDYWINE AND GERMANTOWN

If we should be able to oppose General Howe with success in the field, the works will be unnecessary. If not, and he should force us from hence, he will certainly possess himself of them.

Washington, 13 September 1777, concerning the works on the Delaware[39]

Having rested his troops, and his horses, many of whom were near to death, at Head of Elk after their long voyage, Howe did not have far to go to Philadelphia, but Washington was determined to be more successful than he had been when covering New York. Washington's position was easier. His army was not divided

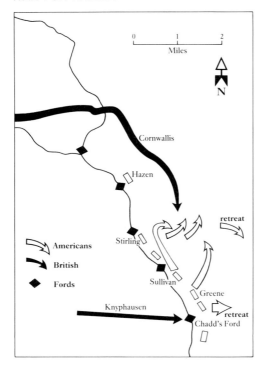

Brandywine

as among the islands of the New York area, nor vulnerable to amphibious attack, and was less likely to be defeated in detail. Still few in number, his Continentals were better trained. There were fewer shortages of munitions, in part thanks to French supplies, though the Maryland and Pennsylvania militia who constituted a major portion of his army were short of guns.[40] Washington decided to block Howe at Brandywine Creek, about halfway to Philadelphia. Advanced units skirmished with the British en route, not without some success, 'as some of our parties, composed of expert marksmen had opportunities of giving them several close well directed fires',[41] but on 11 September Howe attacked Washington's army. As the Creek could only be forded at a few places, it was a good defensive position, but Howe executed a successful flanking move while also feinting against the American centre. The flanking force under Cornwallis crossed the Creek at two undefended fords unobserved, benefiting from the failure of the American right wing under John Sullivan to patrol properly. An officer sent to reconnoitre Washington's right did not go far enough to detect Cornwallis' flanking move. Washington recorded the consequences at midnight:

> . . . the intelligence received of the enemy's advancing up the Brandywine and crossing at a ford about six miles above us, was uncertain and contradictory, notwithstanding all my pains to get the best [information]. This prevented my making a disposition adequate to the force with which the enemy attacked us on our right; in consequence of which the troops first engaged were obliged to retire before they could be reinforced. In the midst of the attack on the right, that body of the enemy which remained on the other side of Chadd's ford [opposite his centre], crossed it and attacked.[42]

The battle of Brandywine by an unknown artist, c. 1780s

Cornwallis' men, tired by an 18 mile march, did not press their opportunity home at once and this allowed Sullivan to turn his units to face the threat. Under fire from regular troops, this was a very tricky manoeuvre. When the attack came, Sullivan's men broke, the British exploiting a gap in their line, but they were helped by Greene's division which had been rushed over from the American centre. However, Greene's men were forced to withdraw under heavy British pressure, while the American centre, weakened by Greene's move, was beaten back by Knyphausen's men who crossed Chadd's Ford. British bayonet charges were decisive, but the British troops were 'much fatigued with a long march and a rapid pursuit . . . the weariness of the troops and the night coming on prevented any further pursuit'. The Americans retreated in relatively good order, surprising everyone. The tiredness of the British troops, their lack of cavalry and the arrival of evening prevented the pursuit from being pressed home, but the Americans had about a thousand casualties, compared with 500 British casualties. Nevertheless, Howe had not obtained his decisive victory, and that after a campaign in which he had earlier failed to force Washington to fight. Howe subsequently felt obliged to defend himself from criticism on this head. He told the Commons of 'the impracticability of a vigorous pursuit in a hostile country . . . more particular in America than in any other country I have seen . . . the inutility of attempting it farther than was done, in the peculiar state of the army at that time', a much more sound reason than his excuse of the need to consider the wounded and prisoners.[43]

Brandywine quenched neither Washington's desire to stop Howe reaching Philadelphia, nor his willingness to risk battle. Some of the militia left the army, but the core of Washington's force remained in decent fighting order and he was soon ready to do battle again. On 16 September the two armies clashed at Warren Tavern between Lancaster and Philadelphia, at what came to be known

'An East Prospect of the City of Philadelphia', taken by George Heap from the Jersey shore under the direction of Nicholas Scull, Surveyor General of the Province of Pennsylvania. Printed for and sold by Carington Bowles, London, 1778

as the battle of the Clouds, but heavy rain terminated the confrontation, ruining the American ammunition. Washington withdrew to replenish his army, leaving Wayne to harass Howe, but on the night of 20–21 September the British succeeded in surprising Wayne's camp in the Paoli Massacre. Wayne, a somewhat over-rated general, had failed to post proper guards. The Americans suffered 400 casualties to British soldiers who had had the flints removed from their muskets in order to ensure surprise, and, instead, relied on their bayonets. Washington covered the likely crossing points over the Schuylkill River, which lay between Howe and Philadelphia, but, by feinting to the west and counter-marching at night, the British were able to cross the river safely. on 23 September Washington reported, 'They had so far got the start before I received certain intelligence that any considerable number had crossed, that I found it in vain to think of overtaking their rear with troops harassed as ours have been with constant marching since the battle of Brandywine'. The Americans were also affected by desertion, their army also being short of clothing, blankets and shoes.[44] On the 26th Howe entered Philadelphia.

Capturing the capital of rebellion appeared a major triumph, but the Revolutionaries were hopeful that it would create serious difficulties for Howe. As American forts blocked the route up the Delaware to Philadelphia, he faced major supply problems, but, more generally, the Revolutionaries were hopeful that the major commitments represented by the new British position would stretch their opponents' resources and make them vulnerable. They were swiftly presented with an opportunity. Howe, believing the Americans to be thoroughly defeated, sent large detachments to clear the Delaware and convoy supplies, and encamped with less than 9,000 men in a poorly-defended position at German-

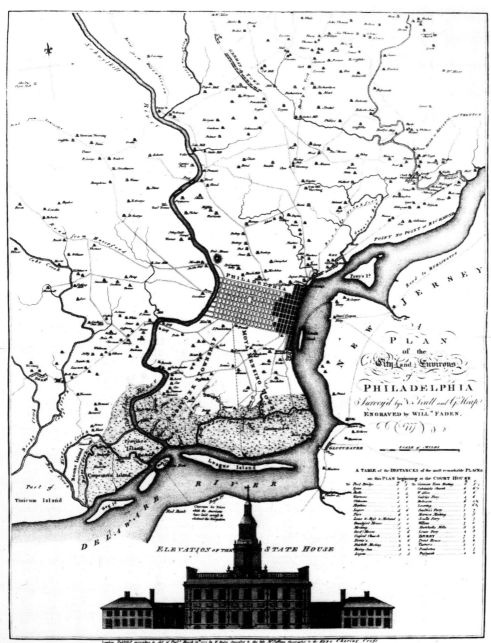

Plan of Philadelphia, engraved by William Faden, 1777

town to the north of Philadelphia. Washington planned to attack in the early morning of 4 October after a night march by four converging columns, a scheme that was easier to formulate than to execute. It would have been difficult enough for well-trained troops; for Washington's men this attempt to mount a larger version of the attack on Trenton could not be executed as planned. The two militia columns contributed little, and the two Continental columns failed to coordinate their advance, to the extent that, in the heavy fog of that morning, one, delayed as a result of having taken the wrong road, opened fire on the troops of the other. The Americans achieved surprise and pushed the British advance units back, but in the confusion of the morning were unable to exploit their advantage, while the British rallied quickly. A British counter-attack drove the Americans back with losses of 152 killed, 500 wounded and 438 captured to the British of just over 500. Nevertheless, Germantown revealed that the Americans could take the initiative without requiring the cover of the forests, while they were encouraged by the belief that they had come close to victory. Howe's army had, indeed, come close to being beaten. A British participant recorded 'this attack was the most spirited I believe they ever made on the British troops'. Washington reported on the 7th that he had been obliged to abandon the action when near victory and that 'the tumult, disorder, and even despair, which it seems had taken place in the British army, were scarcely to be paralleled'.[45] The battle was arguably more important than Saratoga in gaining French military cooperation. It showed that Washington, who had suffered a substantial defeat at Brandywine, remained pugnacious and ready to attack. The plans might have been over-ambitious, but the decision to attack was not foolish.

Germantown also demonstrated that Brandywine and the capture of Philadelphia had not delivered Pennsylvania to Howe, that there was to be no equivalent to the latter stages of the New York campaign the previous year with its rapid British advance across New Jersey. Unlike then, Washington's army was still very much in being and was not in flight. The limited value of capturing Philadelphia without a decisive battle was therefore demonstrated. On 19 October Howe evacuated Germantown in order to shorten his defensive circuit round the city. The British now had another important position to defend and supply in the face of an enemy army, and naval control was less helpful in the case of Philadelphia, which was not on the coast, than in that of New York.

In the meantime there was still the Delaware to clear and the possibility of another battle with Washington before the armies went into winter quarters. The Delaware was blocked by obstacles in the river, *chevaux de frise*, covered by American warships and two forts, Mifflin and Mercer, known as Red Bank. British works were hindered by rain. Having begun a bombardment of the former on 11 October, Howe sent Colonel Karl von Donop and a Hessian force to attack the latter on the 22nd. The strength of Fort Mercer's fortifications had been underestimated, but Donop, aware that it would be foolish to attack without heavy artillery, which he lacked, felt that his honour would be compromised if he withdrew. The attack was stopped, with nearly 400 casualties including Donop, by heavy fire from the fort and its covering gallies. These heavy casualties shattered Hessian morale. The following day two British warships engaging the batteries at Fort Mifflin were set ablaze. It was not until

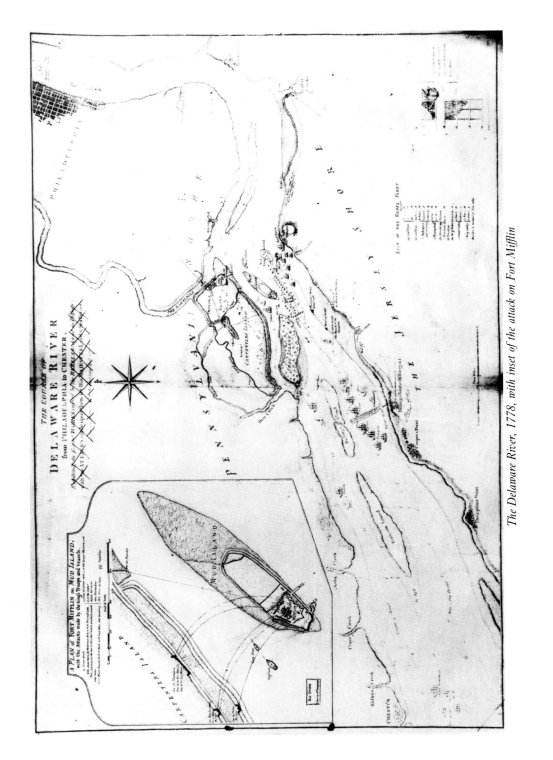

The Delaware River, 1778, with inset of the attack on Fort Mifflin

mid-November that both forts were abandoned in the face of heavier British fire-power. The British had been delayed by 'violent rains . . . filling the trenches and sapping the foundations of the batteries'.[46]

Washington had not been able to prevent Howe from consolidating his position in Philadelphia. After Germantown he had decided to wait for reinforcements and then act according to circumstances, but the American army was still faced with many of the problems of expiring enlistments and inadequate supplies that had dogged it from the outset. There were also serious command problems and important rivalries, including between Commodore Hazlewood of the Continental navy and the army, the Continental and the Pennsylvania navies, and Continental army and militia officers. Major General Dickinson ignored Washington's request to bring his militia force from northern New Jersey because he feared the state would be invaded from Staten Island.[47] All generals complain of insufficient manpower and supplies, but Washington's letters are worth quoting in order to underline the particular seriousness of his position, which is an important answer to the criticism of lack of vigour often advanced against his generalship, both by contemporaries, such as John Adams, and subsequently. On 7 October he was concerned about the state of the squadron on the Delaware:

> . . . many of the officers and seamen on board the gallies have manifested a disposition that does them little honour. Looking upon their situation as desperate, or probably from worst motives, they have been guilty of the most alarming desertions.

Three days later Washington reported of the Virginia militia, 'many of their arms are indifferent, and almost the whole are destitute of pouches and other accoutrements'. On the 11th he wrote, 'our distress for want of shoes and stockings is amazingly great, particularly so for want of the former. On this account we have a great many men who cannot do duty and several detained at the hospitals for no other cause', and on the 15th of, 'the wants of the army . . . every mode hitherto adopted for supplying them has proved inadequate'.

On 1 November Washington explained why he had not been able to attack Howe after Germantown, as he had hoped:

> The severe rain on the 16th of September, the action on the 4th, the removal of our stores and having to form a new elaboratory [for the manufacture of powder], added to the small number of hands engaged in the business of it, laid us under difficulties in the capital and essential article of ammunition that could not be surmounted. Every exertion was directed to obtain supplies but notwithstanding, they were inadequate, too scanty and insufficient to attempt anything on a large and general scale . . . The distress of the soldiers for want of shoes was also a powerful obstacle to the measure. I could wish that our circumstances were now such as to authorise a general attack for dislodging them from the city, but . . . they are not. This is also the opinion of my general officers.[48] The superiority of numbers on the part of the enemy in respect to regular troops, their superior discipline and the redoubts and lines which they have thrown up between the two rivers and about the city, the happy state of our affairs to the northward, and the practicability of drawing succours from thence, the consequences of a defeat, these were all motives which led to a decision against an attack at

'A view in America in 1778', a caricature by Darly, published in Darly's Comic Prints of Characters, Caricatures and Macaroonies, *1778. The well-clothed officers and member of Congress contrast with the cold and poorly-attired soldiers and the wounded negro in the foreground*

this time . . . by continuing the campaign, perhaps many salutary if not decisive advantages may be derived. But it appears to me, that this must depend upon the supplies of cloathing which the men receive.

Most of the Maryland militia had already left for home, and the Virginia militia was due to follow soon. Washington replied on 17 November to criticism that he had not been 'more active and enterprising', by referring to the lack of clothing for the troops and the delay in receiving reinforcements from Gates, without which he had not felt able to intervene on the Delaware. On the 23rd he returned to the issue of clothing, noting that he had been told that the lack 'has arisen from the difficulty of importing on account of the numerous fleet, which lines our coast. However, I am persuaded that considerable relief might be drawn from the different states were they to exert themselves properly'; and on 1 December Washington commented that the troops found it difficult to purchase clothes with depreciated paper money. Washington's troops were truly in a terrible condition, in European terms unfit for service. Many, without clothes or shoes, were simply wrapped in blankets.

Due to his problems, Washington did not wish to risk another attack, and thus Howe was to be denied the decisive battle he sought. On the night of

4 December Howe advanced to attack Washington's camp at Whitemarsh, 12 miles west of Philadelphia, but he found the position too strong and abandoned the idea, possibly a mistake in light of the decreasing strength of the American force. Washington commented on the 10th, 'reason, prudence and every principle of policy forbade us quitting our post to attack them. Nothing but success would have justified the measure, and this could not be expected from their position'.[49] This was a refrain that Washington used from September 1776 onwards.

The armies turned to their winter quarters, Howe's at Philadelphia, Washington's the cold comfort of Valley Forge, which it reached on 21 December. The campaign had closed without the decisive victory that both had sought. Howe had captured Philadelphia but without this having the dramatic consequences that he had anticipated, in part because his success was overshadowed by Saratoga, but also because the notion that the capture would necessarily have such consequences was flawed. Had Philadelphia fallen a year earlier, against the background of the collapse of the American position in the middle colonies, the situation might have been very different, but in 1777 the fall of Philadelphia could have been decisive only had it been accompanied by a repetition of the position a year earlier: the collapse of the major American force in the field. Philadelphia was an important city, but as a capital it was held in no regard by the Americans. In Europe, the capture of a capital would have ended many wars; although Maria Theresa had been prepared to fight on had she lost Vienna in 1741, while Frederick the Great survived the temporary loss of Berlin in 1760, and Alexander I that of Moscow in 1812. In America the loss of Philadelphia was far less serious. The Revolution was primarily fought to uphold ideas and ideals and, therefore, European standards were not applicable. This was demonstrated in 1814 when Admiral Cockburn burnt Washington, a source of embarrassment but not crucial to the course of the Anglo-American war of 1812.

Thanks to Washington's caution and the fighting skills and spirit of the American soldiers there had been no decisive British victory in 1777. Washington chose to fight only when in a good defensive position at Brandywine and when at Germantown an attack seemed propitious. Neither encounter lived up to expectations, and Washington was forced from the field, just as elsewhere the Americans had revealed deficiencies: in the defence of Ticonderoga and the Highland forts, in the failure to organize a successful attack on Rhode Island and the more serious inability to supply Washington's army. However, in both battles, as at Freeman's Farm and Bemis Heights, the fighting spirit and skills of the American soldiers had been complemented by enough leadership under pressure and tactical flexibility to create a formidable military challenge to the British. By the Hudson, the terrain, Burgoyne's folly and American numerical superiority had brought a clear victory. Near Philadelphia the outcome had been less happy for the Americans, but they had fought well enough to deny Howe what he needed, a clearly successful conclusion to the Pennsylvania campaign, one that could not only justify his strategy, but also convince opinion in America, Britain and the Continent that Britain was winning and would triumph. Germantown, as John Adams reported from Paris, had as much of an impact on

Congress voting for Independence. (American Museum in Britain)

Minutemen on Lexington Green by H.B. Wollen. (National Army Museum, London)

'The Marches of Lord Cornwallis', by William Faden, 1785. (North Carolina Department of Cultural Resources)

George Washington in the uniform of colonel of the Virginia Militia, by Charles Willson Peale. (Peter Newark's Historical Pictures)

Henry Lee, by William L. Shepherd. (Virginia State Library)

The American submarine Turtle, *designed by David Bushnell, approaching HMS* Eagle *in New York Harbour, 1776. (Peter Newark's Historical Pictures)*

Right: A sergeant of the Coldstream Guards, 1775, by Lieutenant Nevile R. Wilkinson. (Peter Newark's Historical Pictures)

Below: 14th Light Dragoons, 1776, by Richard Simkin. (Peter Newark's Historical Pictures)

The death of General Warren at the battle of Bunker Hill, by John Trumbull, 1786. (Peter Newark's Historical Pictures)

Battle off Virginia Capes, 1781. From a painting by V. Zveg. (Peter Newark's Historical Pictures)

Officers of the Continental army, 1779–83: commander-in-chief, aide de camp and line officers. From a painting by H.A. Ogden. (Peter Newark's Historical Pictures)

Infantry of the Continental army, 1779–83. From a painting by H.A. Ogden. (Peter Newark's Historical Pictures)

The surrender of Yorktown, 1781, by Louis Nicolael van Blarenberghe, c. 1790. (Painting in Chateau de Versailles, photograph: Bridgeman Art Library)

the French as did the more glorified Saratoga. British politicians were already discussing the abandonment of offensive operations in America in favour of amphibious attacks and a blockade, a course that appeared necessary to some if, as seemed likely, the French intervened.[50] On 15 December Basil Feilding, Earl of Denbigh, a supporter of the ministry, wrote of a recent visit to:

> London where I left all the King's friends and well wishers to their country in very low spirits indeed; not only on account of the very extraordinary misfortune that has happened to General Burgoyne, but also on what may happen in consequence . . . The Cabinet seems very irresolute whether to raise new corps and to carry on the war by land (which in our present situation I think impossible) or to stand upon the defensive in the few places we have got in our hands, or prosecute it vigorously by sea. There is not a foreign soldier more to be got for love or money . . . We have hitherto kept up our great majority in both houses of Parliament but what will happen when we'll next meet God only knows.[51]

8   1778: France Enters the War

Washington is too wise to risk anything when he believes we are preparing to quit the continent. In that he is however mistaken, for notwithstanding I shall be much weakened when the detachments ordered by government are made I am determined to keep what we have this winter in hopes next spring of being reinforced or recalled. One must happen for I cannot submit to remain Governor of New York.

Clinton, 24 September 1778

The French interference gives a new colour to everything that relates to the American contest.

Earl of Carlisle, one of the Peace Commissioners and head of British Intelligence, 29 September 1778[1]

The entry of France into the conflict followed from the signing on 6 February 1778 of a treaty of alliance and another of amity and commerce between France and the United States, although Anglo-French hostilities did not begin until 16 June. The French Foreign Minister Vergennes sought war in order to humble Britain's colonial and maritime position and thus restore France's international influence.[2] The Franco-American alliance completely altered the war for the British and the Americans, pushed naval considerations to the forefront and brought about a shift of geographical focus to encompass the West Indies and even India. The war in North America took a second place for the British, below the struggle with France, which centred on the security of the British Isles and the fate of the profitable British and French colonies in the West Indies. This shift in strategy was marked most clearly in the North American colonies by the fact that the British troops largely stopped coming. Since Lexington and Concord British forces in North America had been reinforced with fresh recruits to replenish existing units and with new units, albeit not always to the satisfaction of the generals. As a result bold offensives could be proposed: British generals felt that they had a choice of offensive options. From 1778 this flow was drastically cut, while the army in North America was expected to serve as the source for forces to be sent to the West

Indies and the Caribbean, to confront, first, France and, from 1779, Spain, which entered the war as a result of the Franco-Spanish treaty of 12 April 1779.

BRITISH PLANS

Even before French entry appeared inevitable – France acknowledged her new treaty of commerce with the Americans on 13 March, a deliberate challenge to George III – it was already clear, however, that a major change was required in British military policy in North America. The plans of 1777 had clearly failed, not only at Saratoga, but also in Pennsylvania, where the British position was now exposed to an increasingly stronger American army. At the beginning of 1778 the British controlled more of America than they had done at any stage since the beginning of the revolution, but the fall of Philadelphia had not been followed by an explosion of Loyalist military activity, and the presence of Howe and much of the army near the city suggested that it could only be retained if such large forces were deployed that Britain's offensive capability elsewhere would be drastically reduced. Such a strategy could have worked only if American morale and resistance had collapsed after the fall of major cities or if there had been a Loyalist resurgence capable of taking over the defence of such cities, but neither had occurred. Although Loyalist troops could be brave,[3] there had been insufficient time to raise and train a substantial army of them. Aside from the particular failings of the plans adopted in 1777, there was a more general sense both that the overall strategy of converging advances along the Hudson axis to cut off New England had failed and that the senior commanders had to be replaced. In fact, the 'Hudson' strategy had never been properly attempted. In 1776 Carleton had not attacked Ticonderoga, while Howe's forces had advanced into New Jersey, not the Highlands; in 1777 Howe had both concentrated on Pennsylvania and left insufficient forces in New York to encourage Clinton to advance into the Highlands, a situation further exacerbated by his decision to move by sea, rather than advance across New Jersey and thus cover New York.

Nevertheless, there was to be no attempt to revive the strategy. Canada was no longer to be the base for substantial invading forces, while the British were to move onto the defensive in the middle and New England colonies except for some coastal raiding. Given the need to retain a large force for the defence of New York, this might be considered a mistake, although the abandonment of the Highlands at the end of 1777 had already weakened the British position. Washington was aware of the importance of these positions. On 20 March 1778 he wrote, 'my solicitude for the communication of the North river gives me very uneasy sensations on account of our posts there . . . A respectable force at those posts would awe New York and divide General Howe's force – or expose the city'.

The best use of his troops for offensive purposes was not Howe's priority at the start of 1778. He was most concerned about maintaining his position in Philadelphia, not an arduous task since Washington had gone into winter quarters at Valley Forge, and considering how to defend his reputation in the face of growing criticism of his conduct in 1777. Carleton resigned in 1777, because of poor relations with Germain, although, as his replacement, the Swiss-born General Frederick Haldimand, a veteran of the Seven Years War in America, could not take up his position until the following summer, he remained in his post till then. Howe offered his resignation on 22 October 1777, and pressure from Germain was ultimately responsible for his being replaced by Clinton. On 4 February 1778 Germain wrote to Howe announcing that he could come home, and on 8 May Clinton arrived in Philadelphia to replace him. This protracted period of change-over was partly responsible for the absence of British military initiatives in America in early 1778, a marked contrast to Clinton's desire for action and to the new ideas circulating in London. Clinton wrote from New York City on 22 March:

> These people are certainly hard pushed whether from the little appearance of support from France, or from the great and spirited preparations making by us they are certainly drove to try dangerous experiments, now is the time to press them hard, and offer them terms and if something is not now done, I shall have still greater reason to lament that the commander in chief took from me last November 4,000 men at the greatest risk to this place.

There was revived interest in London in the idea of a campaign in the south, support for amphibious attacks on New England and a willingness to consider a complete change in military priorities, including an abandonment of Britain's position in the middle colonies. Interest in a southern campaign had not disappeared after the 1776 failure at Charleston, although it had been considered as secondary and subsequent to success in the middle colonies. The southern governors who had taken refuge in Britain, particularly Lord William Campbell and Sir James Wright, continued to press Germain on the possibility and significance of such a campaign. On 3 September 1777 Germain wrote to Howe hoping that he would fulfil his plan for the conquest of the south that coming winter. Howe replied on 16 January:

> . . . supposing a sufficient force could be spared from hence upon their plan, which is by no means the case, and admitting of the promised success of His Majesty's arms, still no solid advantages could be expected unless the acquisitions were held by a considerable force. If on the contrary the troops should be withdrawn to other objects, the rebels would not fail to wreak their vengeance upon such of His Majesty's faithful subjects, relying upon a continuance of support, as should fly to the royal standards. For I am so far from subscribing to the opinion those gentlemen entertain of the power or influence of the well affected inhabitants, however well armed they may be, to maintain a superiority in their respective provinces that I should with much more readiness assert His Majesty's forces would have nothing better to expect than an equivocal neutrality, excepting in a few instances not to be considered in the opposition to the body of the people.
>
> Experience has proved this to be the case in every province, and in some instances where assurances have been given, equal to those in the memorial now before me, not only of the wishes, but of the determination of the inhabitants, to cast off the usurped power of their new rulers and return to their allegiance.

Howe also drew attention to 'the expediency of keeping the troops collected that they may be in a situation to act against the enemy's main army when the season permits'.[4] He had indeed highlighted the problem of relying on the

Loyalists, who were reported to be numerous but lacking arms and ammunition,[5] but his reply was too inflexible. The 1777 campaign had revealed not only the difficulty of acting successfully against Washington's army, but also his ability to replenish his forces during the campaigning season. There was no real prospect that 1778 would be more fortunate in this respect, while the need to defend Philadelphia and its supply lines would have added a major restriction on Howe's room for manoeuvre. The army in Philadelphia faced considerable supply problems. Lieutenant-Colonel Sir John Wrottesley MP subsequently referred to 'the distresses of the army' there, adding 'he had often experienced the greatest difficulty to obtain even the necessaries of life'. The easy capture of Savannah in December 1778 suggests that Howe could have been more active earlier in the year, and sought to capture ports in the south, even if he had not sent a major force to operate in the interior. Unlike Philadelphia, posts in Savannah or Charleston would be readily accessible to the sea and would not have to confront the main American army, while they would also prevent attacks on East Florida, such as the unsuccessful invasion mounted by Major-General Robert Howe, the commander of the American Southern Department, in 1778. Sir William Howe, however, gave little thought to the south. Clinton was more interested, although after his experience at Charleston in 1776 he was not particularly sanguine about launching another southern initiative. Germain was clearly not impressed by the arguments against a southern strategy, for he outlined one in his instructions to Clinton on 8 March 1778.

Howe was also unwilling to heed the idea of amphibious attacks on New

Lord George Germain, Secretary of State for the Colonies 1775–82, by Nathaniel Hone, 1760

England. On 18 February 1778 Germain instructed him to attack the New England ports, in order to destroy their warships and privateers, and thus hit American trade.[6] Not only would this complement the British blockade, which had been less than completely successful, but it might also help to counteract criticism in Britain about the failure to prevent American privateering. Howe replied on 19 April:

> Your Lordship is pleased to direct that these troops should be detached consistent with the defensive plan I have proposed . . . to send a considerable force from hence does not appear to me advisable; considering that the remainder would not be able so far to improve any successful operation in the field, or other favourable circumstances that may occur, as to change the defensive into an offensive plan, which I presume is an idea that an army, though acting on the defensive, should always entertain . . . less than 4,000 would be insufficient for the proposed service, being fully persuaded a smaller number making a descent on the coast of New England, where there may be an object in view, would very soon be opposed by a great superiority of force . . . and the difficult navigation upon these coasts, with a fleet, the frequent fogs that prevail, the want of a convenient port of rendezvous, the flatness of a great part of the coast, which must impede the receiving of necessary assistances from the shipping, as well in landing, as in the reimbarkation of the troops, will, I fear, render any effectual service extremely hazardous.[7]

There was considerable force in Howe's observations. Amphibious operations against France during the Seven Years War, in which Howe had been involved, had not always been successful in their execution or significant in their consequence, and later in 1778 Clinton was to be thwarted by the weather when mounting amphibious expeditions in New England.[8] Yet, Howe's reply was inadequate. Successful attacks had been mounted, as against Danbury in 1777, and Clinton's forces were to be successful against New Bedford and Fairhaven. There already was a British base at Newport, and in New England British operations would be unconstrained by the need to consider the ambivalent prospect of Loyalist support and expectations. Raiding coastal New England and even fairly substantial incursions were to be a regular feature of the war from 1777, particularly in Connecticut. Amphibious operations were always hazardous, but Howe's protestations were indicative of his overall lassitude towards the offensive. He lacked the drive of his elder brothers, George, revered by the colonists and killed fighting the French at Ticonderoga in 1758, and Admiral Richard Howe. As with the south, Howe offered no suggestion as to how to improve the British position short of a decisive victory that he was unlikely to obtain. On 19 April 1778 he had also written to Germain:

> The enemy's position continues to be at Valley Forge and Wilmington: Their force has been diminished during the course of the winter by desertion, and by detachments to the back settlements, where the Indians make constant inroads; but the want of green forage does not yet permit me to take the field, and their situation is too strong to hazard an attack with a prospect of success, which might put an end to the rebellion; whereas a check at this period would probably counteract His Majesty's intentions of preparing the way for the return of peace by the Bills proposed . . . When I mentioned my idea of a defensive plan . . . I meant it in a general sense that your Lordship might not be deceived into the hope of very essential conquests, from the force then under my command, but without any design to exclude the prospect of seizing every advantage that might arise from the vicissitude of military operations.

The stress on the danger of a check was especially appropriate in light of Saratoga, but it also reflected Howe's general attitude. So did his hope that a negotiated peace could be obtained, and that he should operate in a fashion that made that more probable, rather than seek to make it unnecessary by risking all on bold strokes. The British government had responded to the failure of the 1777 campaign by reviving the attempt to negotiate, last made in 1776. In February 1778 parliament agreed to renounce the right to tax America except for the regulation of trade, and a commission, headed by the Earl of Carlisle, was appointed to negotiate the end of the war. They were to be allowed to address the Revolutionaries 'by any style or title which may describe them', a concession not made in 1776, and to accept as part of the peace settlement the withdrawal of all British forces from the colonies, but 'open and avowed independence' was unacceptable. America was to be granted direct representation in the House of Commons.[9] The French envoy in London reported that the ministry were determined to make peace with America.[10] The concessions offered were radical, representing the complete recasting of the imperial system, and they were accepted gloomily by parliament and grudgingly by George III. They were now no longer sufficient. Charles Mellish told the Commons in March 1778:

> ... that no more than one-fifth of the people were ever in any revolution, and consequently, though the quiet men might have been silenced by the army, it was no proof that this country had not friends in America; that the Conciliatory Bills would make us more friends, and we should have still more, when the Americans found their governors were giving them up to France.

A British memorandum preserved in the papers of Lord Amherst, who was effectively appointed commander-in-chief of the army in March 1778, argued that the failure to protect the Loyalists had had serious consequences and must be reversed:

> No posts have been taken, nor works erected at proper stations to secure the possession of the ground we had gained while the army proceeded to make new acquisitions; and the finest European army that ever was or ever will be in America with a general series of successes, has not only failed in effecting anything, but actually brought the affairs of Great Britain in the revolted colonies to a state of almost desperation ... the Congress and their retainers in the different provinces, are possessed of the government, and of the sword, and all who upon any consideration disapprove of their measures or wish to overturn their government are obliged to disguise their sentiments, and never will venture to declare for Britain till they see a prospect of being placed in security against their enemies. It is probable then that in order to render military operations however successful, effectual to the re-establishment of the British interest in America we must wherever we prevail counteract the Congress in their own way, that is, we must put our friends in the possession of forfeited lands, and punish our irreclaimable enemies agreeably to the forms of civil justice. For this purpose the idea of indiscriminate war is to be disclaimed in America. We ought to declare ourselves the protectors of the pacific ... as it may be of use to hasten the natural progress of an aristocracy on that Continent in order to correct the levelling spirit of the people, and form an interest connected with monarchy and with Great Britain, the Council of State should be empowered to dispose of honours and establish family distinction in America corresponding to that of the peerage.

In place of total war, including a blockade, there should be civil government

'The Commissioners', a cartoon by Darly published in Darly's Comic Prints of Characters, Caricatures and Macaroonies, *1778. A prosperous America is appealed to by Admiral Viscount Howe, Sir William Howe, the Earl of Carlisle, William Eden and George Johnstone. The Howes, in fact, refused to serve under Carlisle*

through a Council of State.[11] However, a conciliatory policy might indeed win friends, but it was not going to impress the Revolutionary leaders, other than as a sign of weakness. Also, if such a policy failed as a basis for negotiation, it could only encourage a Loyalist upsurge if supported by a significant military presence. To that extent, Howe was correct about the need to retain his army undefeated, but he failed to appreciate both the effect of his lack of activity and the fact that French intervention would lead to the dissipation of his force. The dispatch of the Peace Commissioners marked a new stage in the conflict. The ministry, and more crucially George III, had been forced to accept both that the war would be ended by negotiation – that a war of conquest, a decisive victory followed by an American collapse, was unlikely – and that the imperial relationship would be substantially altered. Though there was still a determination to keep America in the empire, not least in order to separate her from France, this was now a lesser priority than the war with France. It was not so much that the American conflict was seen as dependent on the fate of that war, although that was clearly crucial in the naval sphere; rather, that war with France was seen as more important. A desire for revenge, a hope of gain, a sense of the intractability of the American conflict and of the greater strategic and commercial importance of the West Indies led to a shift of attention towards the Caribbean. Mellish argued:

> . . . that it should be considered whether the army in America can make any decisive stroke; if

not, I think it should be drawn off not for the defence of the Newfoundland fishery, Nova Scotia, or our West India islands, but to attack and storm the settlements of France in the West Indies.[12]

On 8 March 1778 Germain had sent instructions to Clinton. If he could not defeat Washington at the beginning of the campaign he was to stop offensive operations in the middle colonies and, instead, adopt a more dispersed strategy. The New England coast was to be attacked, if necessary at the cost of evacuating Philadelphia, and in October the long-delayed invasion of Georgia and South Carolina was to be mounted. As this would result in a permanent commitment in the south and only an episodic one on the New England coast, the net result would be a southward shift in the centre of British activity. This reflected a sense of opportunity there, a feeling that the war in the middle colonies had entered an impasse and an inability to send Clinton substantial reinforcements. As success in the south would presumably affect the war further north, a southern expedition also offered the prospect of putting pressure on the Americans. In addition, if the primary British offensive operations were in the south, it would be easier for the Royal Navy to support both those operations and those in the Caribbean, Georgia being about 1,000 miles closer to the Caribbean than New York.

This plan can be seen as the blueprint of the strategy eventually adopted, but it was different in one important respect. Germain's plan assumed control of the

4th Earl of Sandwich, First Lord of the Admiralty 1771–82, after Zoffany c. 1763

Atlantic and the consequent ability to move units readily, but that control was to be challenged by French entry, which made any reliance on a strategy of dispersed effort more vulnerable. Had the strategy outlined on 8 March 1778 been attempted earlier, with the additional support of a powerful army based in Canada, then the progress of the war might well have been very different, but this strategy was no more given its chance than the Hudson axis plan had been.

The French acknowledgement of their new alliance led Germain to send Clinton new instructions on 21 March. They followed a sustained debate in governmental circles that matched, in its willingness to consider new options, the discussions about a reconstituted ministry, possibly including Chatham, that had been held. George III had already on 31 January proposed a withdrawal of forces from the Thirteen Colonies, an offensive war in the Caribbean and a naval war against the Americans, 'destroying the Trade and Ports of the Rebellious Colonies', and thus bringing them to terms.[14] Sandwich, the First Lord of the Admiralty, supported such an idea, but Lord Amherst warned that this would allow the Americans to attack the West Indies. It was therefore decided to evacuate Philadelphia, a city that would not be important in any naval war, but retain New York. Clinton was also instructed to send 5,000 men to attack the French West Indian island of St Lucia, 3,000 to reinforce the Floridas, which took on a more central strategic role as war with the Bourbons became more likely, and, after he had reached New York, he was to send reinforcements to Halifax, newly vulnerable as a consequence of French entry into the conflict. Clinton was also offered the option of evacuating New York. He complained on 23 May that he would 'have wished to avoid the arduous task of attempting to retrieve a game so unfortunately circumstanced' and that he had hoped to receive a command 'not . . . tied down with instructions'.

The prospect of French entry had not led the British ministry to adopt a defensive strategy. Their plans and aspirations for the Caribbean were clearly aggressive, but to support these it was necessary to weaken the army at Philadelphia and thus to lessen the prospect of successful operations in America. Throughout his period of command, Clinton was to complain about having insufficient forces, but this was an obvious consequence of the French war. When Germain informed Clinton on 4 May, 'the reinforcement to be sent from hence will not exceed 1,200 men, and as a French war appears to be inevitable, no more troops can be spared', he was also warned to be ready to send reinforcements to Canada, which was expected, albeit wrongly, to be the focus of American and French ambitions.[15] Clinton's army, the largest British force outside Great Britain, was to be the source for operations in the western hemisphere (rather as troops from India had been employed in the Manila expedition of 1762); and Sir Henry had been informed that at any time he might be instructed to dispatch substantial detachments. A substantial part of the North American squadron was also to be redeployed. In the short-term the southern expedition was delayed and curtailed; in the longer-term Clinton found that he lacked sufficient troops to undertake a sustained offensive against Washington in the middle colonies, but could not guarantee the naval superiority necessary to ensure the security of his dispersed operations.

RETREAT FROM PHILADELPHIA

Since the earliest return of spring a succession of detachments from hence, has ranged the country for many miles round this city, and in the province of Jersey, to open the communication for bringing in supplies, to relieve the peaceable inhabitants from the persecution of their oppressors, and to collect forage for the army. These detachments have without exception succeeded to my expectations.

Sir William Howe, Philadelphia, 11 May 1778[16]

Washington's army had wintered at Valley Forge, 18 miles north-west of Philadelphia. Washington selected the position for several reasons. He had hoped, following Germantown, to launch another attack on Howe. Secondly, he wished to remain close to Philadelphia, to prevent British incursions and to shadow any possible British movements. Thirdly, he hoped that the rich Pennsylvania countryside would provide his men with food and forage, since what passed as Continental army logistics were weak at best, and New Jersey was bare. As over previous winters, Washington's army largely dissolved in the winter of 1777/8, leaving only a hardcore of officers and men who were, by now, attaining the status of veterans; learning war through war. They had an arduous time, cold and short of supplies, but it was important for the training of the Continentals so that they could confront the British on the battlefield without having to rely on defensive positions, as on Long Island and at Brandywine, or on surprise, as at Germantown. Under the self-styled Baron von Steuben, a German soldier of fortune who had served in the army of Frederick the Great, though not at the high rank he claimed, they were drilled in bayonet practice and in battlefield manoeuvres. Most European officers tried to impose their training on Americans, but Steuben, appointed acting Inspector General, realizing that Americans were not Prussians, reworked Frederickian drill to fit American needs. He was prepared to explain manoeuvres, and to answer questions. Drill was important, but the key factor was that by the spring of 1778, Washington had an, albeit small, corps of junior-grade officers, NCOs and men who had been blooded in combat and toughened by strenuous toil. According to Patrick Henry in January 1778, the army was, however, handicapped by a supply system in 'a state of uncertainty and confusion . . . this country abounds with the provisions for which the army is said to be almost starving'. From Valley Forge Hamilton criticized Congress the following month:

> By injudicious changes and arrangements in the Commissary's department, in the middle of a campaign, they have exposed the army frequently to temporary want and to the danger of a dissolution, from absolute famine. At this very day there are complaints from the whole line, of having been three or four days without provisions; desertions have been immense, and strong features of mutiny begin to show themselves.[17]

The army also faced manpower problems. It had to be largely recreated in order to put any sort of force in the field that spring. Washington was unwilling to see militiamen as a substitute. The American ideological – political preference for militia over a trained army continued throughout the war, creating numerous problems for Washington. 'To depend too much upon militia, is in my opinion putting everything to hazard', he wrote in March 1778, while he responded to the decision of Congress on 4 April to empower him to call 5,000 militiamen from Maryland, Pennsylvania and New Jersey, by arguing that:

> ... granted the practicability of collecting such a number it would prove a work of time, difficulty and expence; to evince which, I need only recur to the experience of last campaign on similar occasions – and to remind you that it was not possible to obtain 1,000 men, nor sometimes even one hundred from this state, although the former number was required and promised, for the purpose of covering, during the winter, the country between Schuylkill and Delaware.

It would also hinder the completion of the Continental regiments. Washington therefore proposed to call for a small part only of the allocated militia, suggesting also that the militia could be most useful if they freed the Continental troops from serving as 'remote guards', garrison units distant from the centre of operations. He predicted 'our campaign will not be as the sanguine' expect and referred to the problem of filling the Continental regiments:

> Pennsylvania and Maryland have tried the effect of voluntary enlistments to little purpose, and the first in direct contradiction to the most pointed injunctions laid on the officers, have their recruits composed chiefly of deserters who will embrace the first opportunity of escaping with our arms.

Virginia had employed a draft, but the numbers raised were inadequate and had been lessened by desertion.[18] These problems were partly responsible for the cautious American stance in the early stages of the campaigning season. James Lovell summed up the reactive nature of American strategy on 16 April 1778:

> I find it impossible to convey to you anything of a plan of operations for this campaign. The enemy, having the sea open to them, must have the lead in military matters; we must oppose or follow them, just as they think fit, either to attempt an advance or to retire.[19]

Four days later, at the same time as the garrison in Philadelphia was faced with a rumoured American plot to blow up the playhouse and then benefit from the confusion in order to attack the city, Washington asked his leading officers whether they advised an attack on Philadelphia, an attack on New York or remaining in camp while the army was prepared for a later confrontation. The response was divided: Wayne argued that any attack was better than remaining on the defensive and allowing the British to implement their plans, and he proposed an attack on Howe, but Washington decided to remain at Valley Forge and await developments.[20]

Neither army, therefore, undertook major offensive operations in the late spring, but in the summer the impasse was broken. At the same time it became clear that the peace commissioners would be unsuccesful. Like the Loyalists, Germain was hopeful that American war-weariness and British military success would lead the Americans to accept negotiations, 'as we understand several of the general officers in Mr Washington's army and the people of the country were disposed to peace'. He believed that a successful attack on American shipping and stores along the Delaware in early May that led to the destruction of forty-two American ships had shown how effectively the British could ruin American commerce and shipping.[21] However, these assumptions were wildly over-optimistic, and the denial of American independence wrecked the negotiations, the Americans insisting that a British withdrawal or acknowledgement of independence was a pre-condition. Clinton, therefore, faced the prospect of a contested withdrawal from Philadelphia. As a large number of Loyalists wished to accompany the force, he decided that he lacked sufficient shipping to leave by water. Such a course would have also exposed his army to attack while embarking, one of the most vulnerable positions in which an army could be caught, and while the army was at sea it would be unable to cover New York from assault. Having decided to return by land across New Jersey, Clinton appreciated the danger of weakening his force and determined not to send the expeditions to St Lucia and the Floridas until after he had reached New York.

Clinton left Philadelphia at 3 a.m. on 18 June and crossed the Delaware safely that day, but the march across New Jersey was difficult. The Americans had destroyed the bridges and Clinton reported:

> ... as the country is much intersected with marshy rivulets, the obstructions we met with were frequent, and the excessive heat of the season rendered the labour of repairing the bridges severely felt ... encumbered as I was by an enormous provision train etc ... a train which, as the country admitted but of one route for carriages, extended near 12 miles.

He subsequently wrote:

> Respecting the evacuation of Philadelphia. I can say very little more than that it was done by order. As to the manner of doing it; had I obeyed the orders I received for that purpose, all would probably have been lost.
>
> In my march through Jersey I met with every obstruction, every indication of annoyance, but not the least reason to suppose the enemy intended a general action: no possibility of taking any steps towards one myself, without I could make offence necessary to defence, which was the case at Monmouth, where, if I had not attacked them, they would in my opinion have broke in upon my baggage.
>
> With respect to provisions, we were obliged to carry a great quantity, as our march lay through a devoured country inimical almost to a man. And as to baggage I must say it was wantonly enormous. To leave it behind would have been disgraceful. To burn it, indicated an intended flight, but fortunately we did not lose a waggon, nor suffer the least insult.[22]

The Americans were undecided as to how best to respond. A Council of War on 17 June considered an immediate attack on Clinton who was clearly about to march. Although Wayne favoured such a course, most of the officers agreed with Washington that it was best to await more precise information about Clinton's plans. When on the 18th news arrived that Clinton had set off, Washington was concerned that he should be shadowed, in part to prevent a British advance to the Highlands. His officers were undecided whether to provoke a general action. Charles Lee, who had been captured in December 1776 and recently

*The capture of General Charles Lee, by
J.S. Templeton*

exchanged, asserted that it would be dangerous to risk battle unless success was certain, and in a Council of War on the 24th argued that Clinton's retreat should not be obstructed, as it would be convenient if his army was shut up in New York City. Although he had lost considerable favour and Washington distrusted him, Lee still commanded a certain amount of respect among the amateur American generals. It is possible that Lee may have re-entered British service during his captivity. The contrary view for an attack on the British army while it was in motion was advanced by Greene, von Steuben, Wayne and a French volunteer the Marquis de Lafayette, who had been commissioned as a major-general by Congress.

Washington decided to send 1,500 men to harass the British, while the rest of the army remained ready to intervene, although he subsequently resolved to act more forcefully. Clinton's force was greatly slowed by its extensive baggage train, which included about 1,500 waggons, but their pursuers were not without their problems. Hamilton, who was with them, reported on 26 June:

> Our reason for halting is the extreme distress of the troops for want of provisions. General Wayne's detachment is almost starving and seem both unwilling and unable to march further till they are supplied. If we do not receive an immediate supply, the whole purpose of our detachment must be frustrated.

He added of the British:

Their march today has been very judiciously conducted – their baggage in front and their flying army in the rear, with a rear guard of 1,000 men about 400 paces from the main body. To attack them in this situation without being supported by the whole army would be folly in the extreme.[23]

Washington ordered Lee, who was placed in command of the 5,000 men nearest Clinton, to attack the British rear on the 28th, although Lee had no information concerning the size or disposition of the British army and received no specific instructions as to how to proceed with the assault. On the 28th a confused engagement took place near Monmouth Court House. Lee has been criticized for losing control of the situation and not developing a clear plan of attack, but the British rearguard, under Cornwallis, was stronger than anticipated and Lee was probably correct to withdraw his men. On the other hand, Lee was not behind Washington's order to attack, he did not push the assault and Washington recognized him, correctly, as an intriguer. An angry Washington reprimanded Lee and drew up his army on a ridge beyond the last of a series of ravines. Washington had a volcanic temper which he kept in check only through tight self-control. A student of the theatre, who followed Frederick the Great's dictum that a general must always be on stage, Washington's venting of his spleen on Lee must be considered as equal portions of histrionics, morale-building and anger at Lee's reluctance to attack. Clinton reported:

Battle of Monmouth Court House

With regard to the affair of Monmouth I knew Washington could have passed the defiles with nothing but his avant garde. I knew Lord Cornwallis's division was equal to that, and therefore I attacked. I saw that attack must operate on the troops sent round my flanks, which accordingly happened, and Lee wisely quitted, and when I had secured the first defile, which I might have held against the world, I tried the experiment a little further for had Washington been blockhead enough to sustain Lee, I should have catched him between two defiles, and it is easy to see what must have happened.

Washington was not to be drawn at this stage; but, in his account, neither was Clinton eager to expose his forces:

. . . it was not for me to give him the advantage I had lately taken by attacking him so posted, nor indeed could I have done it, as the troops were fairly spent. Having fulfilled my first and great object, given time for my baggage to move into safety, the troops retired to the first defile, and the rebels repassed the second and took post on advantageous ground. The 33rd Regiment, and 1st Battalion of Grenadiers attacked handsomely. The rebels quitted in confusion, and thus ended the fray, for though it was two hours before the 33rd Regiment (making the rearguard) joined us at the defile, not a shot was fired during that time.

The weather was not helpful to the British. It was around 98° to 100°F. Clinton noted, 'the heat of the weather was intense, and our men already suffered severely from fatigue . . . our men were so overpowered with fatigue' that they could not press our advantage, 'a great part of those we lost fell dead as they advanced without a wound'.[24] The American stress was somewhat different: on Washington's success in bringing order to Lee's retreating force, and on the ability of the American army to hold their final position. Cornwallis' attack was repelled. Thus American regulars could be regarded as seeing off British regulars, not retreating in disorder as in previous engagements. Indeed at the end of the battle Washington ordered an advance against Clinton's retiring force, but his men were too tired and hot to comply, while Clinton's position was reasonably strong. Battles in the summer brought longer evenings for fighting, but the heat and humidity affected the soldiers.

The battle ended Lee's military career. He was court-martialled for failing to attack and for retreating, and suspended from command, a questionable verdict. The Americans had, however, been thwarted in their hope of having 'a second edition of Burgoyne'.[25] Wayne wanted to pursue Clinton the next day, but Washington decided that the army was too exhausted, and indeed Clinton was prepared to fight again if necessary. However, the British could not manoeuvre in New Jersey as they were running short of supplies and 'had not a day's provision left' when they reached Sandy Hook on 1 July. Clinton's army was then ferried to New York City, just before the arrival of a French fleet under d'Estaing.[26]

THE FRENCH ENTER THE WAR

The arrival of the French in American waters – d'Estaing was spotted by the British off the entrance to the Chesapeake on 5 July – reflected the failure to keep the French fleet in European waters. There were two principal French naval bases, Brest on the Atlantic and Toulon on the Mediterranean. In the Seven Years War both had been blockaded, although in 1756 a French invasion force had succeeded in landing on Minorca, a British-ruled island in the Mediterranean, when Toulon was not blockaded. An analogous situation occurred in 1778. Then the desirability of blockading the French ports, and thus of preventing the French from intervening in the western hemisphere, pressed by Germain, clashed with the argument, strongly advanced by Sandwich, that British naval strength should be concentrated in defence of home waters. By thus failing to blockade Toulon or block the Straits of Gibraltar, the Toulon fleet would be free to sail to North America. If the French made such an attempt, however, a matching squadron could theoretically be sent in pursuit, although it was possible that the French fleet might inflict serious damage before the British arrived. A fierce governmental dispute over strategy,[27] exacerbated by concern over the general level of British naval preparedness, which swiftly

A summary of the main events of the War of Independence

became a political issue, was not eased by naval success. There was to be no famous triumph until Rodney's victory at the battle of the Saints in 1782. Proposing on 22 March 1779 a motion of censure on the government for not sending reinforcements to Admiral Lord Howe at New York the previous year, Charles James Fox claimed that:

> ... if Lord Howe had been reinforced, or the Streights of Gibraltar watched, in either event the effect would be similar; that of securing to Lord Howe the full advantage of the force under his command, or giving him a superiority in case the Toulon squadron was permitted to cross the ocean.[28]

However, Admiral Keppel had failed to destroy the outnumbered and evasive Brest fleet off Ushant on 27 July 1778,[29] while d'Estaing, who had sailed from Toulon on 11 April, was able to reach American waters. The crucial question was where he would go and whether the British response would be adequate. The British were vulnerable in three respects. First, their forces were based on ports, New York and Newport, and if these were cut off from maritime supplies they might well be forced to surrender. Secondly, army movements were by water, and in 1778 a number of important moves had to be made, both short distance in the case of the last stage of Clinton's retreat, and long range, in the case of the projected detachments for St Lucia, the Floridas and, eventually, Georgia. Thirdly, if a superior French fleet defeated a smaller British one it would alter permanently not only the balance of naval advantage in American waters, but also the Anglo-French maritime balance of power, with possibly fatal consequences for the defence of home waters.

On the morning of 11 July Lord Howe, still commander of the fleet in American waters, was informed that d'Estaing was nearing Sandy Hook, which covered the approach to New York Harbour. Howe was to claim:

> ... that had the French fleet got to Sandy Hook, all the naval force that England could send out, could not have saved the army, who must have been starved, as the victuallers could not in that case have reached the port of New York.[30]

Outnumbered, Howe nevertheless anchored his ships so that they would be able to cannonade the French warships as they were obliged to enter the channel individually. The unwelcoming nature of the position was compounded by the shallowness of the bar at Sandy Hook on which the French might run aground, the French lack of adequate pilots and information, and the deployment of British troops and cannon on Sandy Hook. Having, understandably, failed to attack, d'Estaing finally sailed away on 22 July. Although New York had been saved, it was now necessary for the British to consider how best to thwart whatever d'Estaing might do next. In marked contrast to the situation since the defeat of the American attempt on Quebec, the British had now lost the initiative, as Clinton's uncertainty in July over French intentions and the arrival of British naval reinforcements indicated. This loss of the initiative related to the American colonies only, and arose in part because the British were making a bid for the initiative in the Caribbean. In America both sides could now attempt amphibious operations.

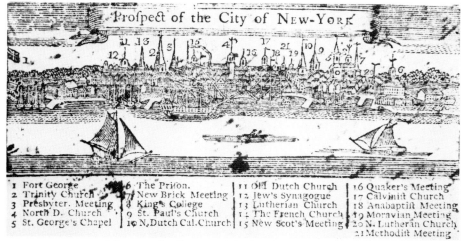

A line-cut of a 'Prospect of the City of New-York', 1771

The French and Americans struck at Newport, where d'Estaing, his fleet and 4,000 troops appeared on 29 July. The local American commander Major-General John Sullivan was reinforced by troops from Washington's army and on 9 August landed on the north east of Rhode Island, with a force of about 10,000 men. However, Sullivan made no allowances for the special problems of naval operations and did not appreciate that d'Estaing was both unwilling to be treated as a subordinate and was not totally committed to the expedition. Franco-American military cooperation in the early years of the alliance was very limited. So few Americans spoke French that the officers in Rochambeau's army, which arrived in 1780, were to have greater success employing Latin. Until Rochambeau and Washington met to coordinate plans, the alliance was basically one failure after another.

When a British fleet under Lord Howe approached Rhode Island on 9 August 1778 d'Estaing sailed to engage him. Having manoeuvred to gain the weather gauge, Howe was prevented from attacking by a storm on 11 August that damaged both fleets. The need to repair his ships led d'Estaing to abandon Rhode Island, to the fury of Sullivan whose siege of Newport was thereby weakened. The siege was also undermined by militia desertions, so that Sullivan abandoned it on 27 August. The British under Sir Robert Pigot attacked the withdrawing Americans on the next two days, but initial success on the 28th was followed by a strong American defence and the Americans were able to evacuate the island successfully, in advance of Clinton's relief force which had been delayed for a week by the weather and therefore 'missed a great stroke', in Clinton's estimation.[31] Howe failed to cut off the retreating American force, because he had instead tried to intercept d'Estaing, before he reached Boston, but he was unsuccessful. The British used their command of the sea to raid New Bedford and Martha's Vineyard successfully in early September, Clinton writing on the 21st:

General John Sullivan

... had Lord Howe's endeavour to intercept the French fleet in their retreat to Boston, and mine to cut off Sullivan's retreat from Rhode Island succeeded I really believe the war in America would have finished, but the winds said *no*. General Grey's expeditions since will have good effect, I hope convince these people that although a war of devastation is not yet carried on (nor I hope never will be under my command) that should Great Britain ever be forced into it she can ruin the colonies.

Howe, however, rejected Clinton's pressure for an amphibious attack on Boston in order to destroy the French fleet, a measure supported by Carlisle.[32] Clinton had 6,000 men to spare for an attack on Boston. Whether it would have succeeded is unclear, but it indicates that he was not as unwilling to take risks when in command as is sometimes argued. The prospect of success was probably greater than that of d'Estaing at Sandy Hook, but, as then, the obvious note was of a naval reluctance to take chances. Howe thought that Boston was too strong to risk an attack. Warships took years to construct and were expensive and trained crews were difficult to obtain. It was understandable that admirals generally preferred not to risk defeat, especially in partly-unknown inshore waters, although on 12 July 1776 British warships ran what were supposed to be strong American batteries at the entrance of the Hudson, threatening the western flank of the American troops on Manhattan. One of the most important features of the war was the absence, until the battle of the Saints in April 1782, of a decisive naval battle that could have determined which power would enjoy lasting superiority in North American waters. The action of 5 September 1781 confirmed French tactical control of the Chesapeake and paved the way for

Yorktown. The temporary and localized French superiority that it reflected and sustained was not, however, the consequence or cause of a climatic battle in which one fleet destroyed the other and, as a result, it did not lead to a decisive shift in naval superiority. Still less was there any such battle in American or Caribbean waters in 1778–80.

The relief of Newport did not end operations in 1778, although little was to happen near New York. Carlisle observed:

> Washington's army was strong at the White Plains ... an extreme mountainous country. There was no object within our attempt that could draw him to an action. If we marched out against him, he had nothing to do but to retire into the strongest country possible, where it was in vain to think of following him. In the mean time the country we should possess afforded no provision, or at least by no means sufficient, for the army.

Clinton had decided to:

> ... make a move into Jersey, and endeavour to draw Washington to an action in ground favourable for us. He quitted his position near Kingsbridge before I made this move (alarmed, as I have reason to believe, at the new system of war), he was too wise to meet me on my own terms, and therefore did not stir in consequence of my moving into Jersey.

This expedition in late September served to bring in some much-needed forage,[33] but, thanks to the caution of Washington, as earlier of Lord Howe, Clinton was not able to make victorious use of the campaigning months that remained after his withdrawal from Philadelphia or of his forces before they were partly dispersed to the West Indies and the south. Washington retired behind the Watchung Mountains. If the British wanted to fight, Washington, following the dictums enunciated by Marshal Saxe, avoided battle. Only when he was ready would he launch an attack on the ground of his choice. Clinton had been very depressed by the need to send troops to the West Indies and Florida and feared that he would have to send more to Canada. In July and August Clinton argued that he would probably be forced to abandon New York. Citing the lack of reinforcements, Clinton on 20 August declared his wish to resign and on 21 September he complained of:

> ... half the army and by far the best half taken from me, liable to still further requisition ... in our present state ... any move of ours can mean nothing of consequence, but if anything offers we shall not neglect it, in short let Great Britain either resolve to push the war with vigour or garrison certain points and carry on that sort of war through Canada which the French (though inferior at sea) were able to do against the united force of Britain and her colonies.

On 8 October Clinton sought his recall, claiming that the detachments had destroyed 'the very nerve of this army' and left him unable to achieve anything important. Germain was less pessimistic. On 5 August 1778 he wrote to Clinton ordering him to pursue the strategy outlined in the instructions of 8 March, of attacks on New England ports and a winter expedition to the south. The following month Germain added that if an evacuation was necessary, Newport, not New York, should be abandoned.[34]

Meanwhile, the situation in the Caribbean had become pressing. On 7 September the French successfully invaded Dominica , exposing the British weakness in the West Indies. It was not until 3 November that the British force of over 5,000 troops sailed from Sandy Hook to attack St Lucia, while 1,000 men left for Pensacola in West Florida. Four days later 2,000 men sailed to invade Georgia. Fortunately for the British, d'Estaing was unaware of these moves and, after leaving Boston on 3 November, he sailed for the West Indies on a parallel course to the British force heading for St Lucia. The British landed there on 13 December and repelled the larger French army brought by d'Estaing on 16 December.

FALL OF SAVANNAH

The British were also fortunate in the south. On 2 November 1778 Congress instructed Benjamin Lincoln, who had been appointed commander in the south in September, to invade East Florida (essentially the modern state of Florida) if possible, in order to destroy the threat posed by the British garrison in the capital St Augustine under General Augustine Prevost. However, he was provided with little support and was dependent on help from the states. This was insuffcient. On 16 November Henry Laurens, the President of Congress, asked the Governor of Virginia to send 1,000 militia to Charleston to strengthen American forces in the south, but on 28 November the Virginian Council of State decided that it was impracticable to march because the troops lacked tents and kettles. On 23 December Lieutenant-Colonel Archibald Campbell, who had served with Wolfe at the capture of Quebec, landed near Savannah. The outnumbered defenders under the unimpressive Major-General Robert Howe were unable to prevent Campbell from taking Savannah with only four killed and five wounded, compared with their losses of about 550. Campbell was led by a slave through a swamp to a weak point in the defences. He boasted:

> . . . the rebel army was beat, and hurried out of the province in six days after the landing . . . shoals flock to the royal standard daily; and I have got the country in arms against the Congress . . . I have taken a stripe and star from the rebel flag of America.

This strenghtened the pressure for a southern initiative and showed the value of strategic movement by sea followed by coastal operations.[35]

At the end of 1778 both optimistic and pessimistic notes were struck by British leaders. On 4 November Germain replied to a letter from Clinton, Carlisle and Eden, sent on 21 September:

> I agree entirely with you, that if any decisive stroke had been given to the French squadron or to the forces of the rebels which attacked Rhode Island, it must have had the most happy consequences, with respect to this country not only in America but in Europe. However we must hope that the rebels not having reaped that advantage from their new allies which they were taught to expect, and our superiority at sea being again restored, may incline many people to return to their allegiance . . .

Germain feared correctly that Spain would enter the war, adding 'I sincerely wish that the resources of this country could afford such reinforcements as might enable Sir Henry Clinton to carry on an offensive war in the most extensive manner', but France's entry into the war made this impossible:

> The forces which are now in America, I trust will be sufficient to maintain our present possessions, and when recruited, I should hope, with increasing as much as possible the provincials, that sufficient detachments may be spared for carrying on expeditions . . . the rebels will severely feel the effects of a war which will keep their coast in perpetual alarm, and by taking or destroying their ships and stores whilst we prevent their growing into a maritime power, our own commerce may be freed from the insults of their privateers . . . The breaking up of Mr Washington's army proves how little dependence he can have on the militia, for any continued service, and the small number of regulars which he has been able in this last campaign to bring into the field, convinces me that the Congress will meet with innumerable difficulties hereafter, in raising or supporting a respectable body of regular troops, and that they will not be able to continue the war in any other method than by occasionally calling out the militia.

Germain expressed his wish for a glorious end to the campaign,[36] but his analysis was weakened by his failure to consider adequately British vulnerability to a return by d'Estaing's fleet, his over-optimistic portrayal of American weakness and demoralization and his failure to appreciate Clinton's reluctance to accept that his army could be reduced without destroying his ability to act. Clinton thought it impossible to drive the Americans to negotiations without a substantially greater force, and he complained bitterly about 'the state of the army . . . before June we shall be reduced to a most strict defensive, and at no time shall be able to risk from us above 1,000 men, and those not further than Nantucket Shoals or Cape Hatteras . . . I cannot stay'.[37]

On the other hand, the American position was not without severe difficulties. Washington's army had serious weaknesses and, after the failure at Newport, it was not clear how he could operate most effectively. Poor pay and inadequate supplies continued to hit enlistments and many units were below strength: in September 1778 the fifteen Virginia regiments in Continental service were consolidated into eleven. British intelligence reported that the garrisons in the Highlands were below strength and that due to expiring enlistments Washington's army would be only 5 or 6,000 strong by the spring of 1779.[38] However, in the winter of 1778–9 Washington was able to keep the largest American force-in-being of any winter of the war thanks to improvements in the supply system the previous year,[39] a development doubtless helped by the abandonment of inland offensive operations by the British which might have threatened the newly-created system of magazines along the main lines of communications. Jeremiah Wadsworth improved the commissariat, Greene the quartermaster's department. Washington was keen to keep his army together in order not to have to face the problem of re-enlistments. Nevertheless the extension of the war to the south revealed new problems. Lincoln faced militia desertion and ill-discipline when he marched towards Savannah. Loyalists argued that the Revolution was about to collapse and that this could be precipitated by British pressure.[40]

Despite the problems the American forces faced, there was a growing confidence on the American side about the likely military outcome of the war, which can be seen in the letters of Delegates to Congress. This owed much to international recognition. The French alliance was likely to be followed by that of Spain; British control of the sea had been challenged successfully.[41] It also reflected the changing fortunes of the war on land. Whatever the consequences in terms of detachments sent elsewhere, the withdrawal from Philadelphia represented a retreat from the high-water mark of British advance, while if New York had not yet been attacked by the Americans and Newport had resisted successfully they were both now clearly far more vulnerable.

Nevertheless, reports of American vulnerability circulated in Britain. A letter from New York of 21 October published in the British press claimed:

> You may rely on it, that the rebellion is much weaker now than it was this time twelve month; and nothing but a little wisdom in planning her schemes, on the part of Great Britain and vigour in their execution is wanting to crush it. The French alliance is greatly disliked by many of the violent rebels . . . Taxation is now grievously felt, The credit of the Congress money is irretrievably sunk . . . Men can scarcely be prevailed upon to take up arms, either by compulsion or for money. Washington has not 10,000 men, and these are divided into different parties. His method is, in any emergency when the King's army appears, to force the militia to join him; but what dependence there is to be placed in these, and what resistance they make to regular troops, repeated experience has shown.[42]

John Hayes, who had been captured at Saratoga, reported from New York at the end of 1778 on his time on New England, which he presented as demoralized:

> . . . the approach of their not being able to feed their army – New England that supplied it with beef is near exhausted – The carriage of the country difficult; the demands so exorbitant for every article as well as necessary of life, that a revolt from the tyrannical system must be the consequence – their money so much depreciated, that the farmers almost refuse it . . . They cannot recruit.

Similar reports were received by the British government. Hayes recommended bringing 'desolation' to the Americans in order to bring them to terms,[43] but Clinton argued that 'a war of buccaneer is not becoming a great nation and at this period would be ineffectual', a comment on the impact of French naval power. Angry that the army was not being kept adequately supplied with food, he was also sorry that the peace commissioners had to return to Britain, but he asked, 'how could it be expected they should [operate], with the army in retreat'. Nevertheless, Clinton was not without hopes that if the men sent to St Lucia returned, Washington was defeated and there was no French interference, the war might be ended in 1779. Patrick Tonyn, the Governor of East Florida, claimed in November 1778 that the Revolutionaries were too divided to maintain the struggle for another year, that the British could win if they adopted 'a vigorous plan of action', and that 'the four southern provinces are incapable of making any very formidable resistance', were unprepared for war and would therefore surrender quickly.[44]

The themes of widespread Loyalism and American weakness were repeated by governmental supporters in parliament,[45] but, in light of commitments elsewhere, Germain on 4 November only felt able to allocate 3,000 recruits as reinforcements for Clinton, a force that indicated that America was not at the forefront of the ministry's mind. As governmental supporters placed hopes on Indians,[46] Loyalists, the devastation of the American coastline and the internal collapse of the Revolutionaries, they indicated their appreciation of the fact that the pursuit of victory in the middle colonies had both failed hitherto and been abandoned by a government that was more concerned about France. As *Sarah Farley's Bristol Journal* pointed out on 2 January 1779, the army, after two campaigns, had returned to its old quarters in New York. Possibly the alternatives outlined should have been attempted earlier with greater urgency, although they confronted a range of problems, including the state of the British navy, after over a decade of peacetime economies, the difficulty of sustaining a blockade given the capabilities of eighteenth-century warships, and political opposition to a war of devastation, which was voiced in parliament in December 1778.[47] Nevertheless, a sense that an offensive war in the middle colonies was no longer possible was to encourage a greater stress on the south. This was the product of expediency, rather than reflecting any acceptance of criticism of the conduct of the war. Having finished his service in America, Wrottesley told the Commons on 16 December 1778, 'our posts were too many, our troops too much detached on various services to be timely collected for any effective operations . . . the chain of communication was too far extended', but these problems were to be exacerbated by operations in the south. However, it would have been thought foolish not to follow up the success at Savannah, and it is all too easy to criticize ministers for failing to have a clearly-conceived strategy. There were too many imponderables to permit the execution of any rigid plan, and, although the British now ran the risk of losing control of American waters, that would have been fatal had their strategy been defensive or offensive. 'We should never have less than six months supplies in advance', Clinton had argued,[48] but that was a counsel of perfection. Without them any trans-oceanic operations faced serious risks, but those were ever-present in eighteenth-century conflict.

9 1779: Georgia and the Highlands

. . . the late arrival of the reinforcement from England, its insufficiency, its sickness, the sickness of the army in general, my having been obliged to send near 2,000 men to Canada all this had determined me to give up all thoughts of operation in this part of the continent, and prepare to send a considerable expedition to South Carolina.

Clinton, New York, 10 October 1779[1]

For both sides 1779 was a year of disappointment; with no decisive events or encounters occurring, it would be a mistake, however, to regard it as a year without consequence. The failure of the Bourbon attempt to invade England ensured that Britain would be able to fight on in the New World. It also had an important effect upon the naval forces available in American and Caribbean waters in 1779, as did Spain's entry into the war in June. There were also significant developments in America. Clinton's assessment of the failure of the Franco-American attempt to storm Savannah on 9 October, 'I think this is the greatest event that has happened this whole war',[2] was the product of euphoria rather than reflection, but the battle was a crucial one, and had the town fallen, British plans for the south would have suffered a major, possibly fatal, setback. The strategies of both sides in 1779 can be faulted. D'Estaing did not bring his fleet from the West Indies until late in the year and was unwilling to remain long at Savannah, the assault on which was a costly failure, greater than that of the British at Sullivan's Island off Charleston in 1776. Washington appeared to be able to do little more than avoid battle with Clinton and wait for the French, a strategy that left the initiative for most of the year with the British. They, in turn, can be faulted for failing to follow up the capture of Savannah, by sending more troops to the south, and for devoting too much time to an unsuccessful attempt to force Washington into a decisive battle.[3]

Yet, these disappointments were not strategically unsound. Washington was wise to avoid such a battle; the French had much at stake in the West Indies; and Clinton did not receive, for reasons that could not be predicted, reinforcements from Britain until later than expected. He also had to take note of the new, more hazardous naval situation and, in seeking a decisive battle with Washington, sought both to make use of his largest force, that based on New York, and to create a context within which civil government could be restored in New York and the surrounding area. Such a restoration was regarded as crucial to creating the nexus of Loyalist support that was increasingly seen at the very least as an option to be tried, if not a panacea for Britain's manpower problems. The policy, although designed in large part to serve military ends, was itself dependent on the creation of secure areas through military means. In place of the peace and victory duality that had characterized, and possibly confused, British policy in 1776 and 1778 there was to be a new duality: the securing and protection of areas within which civil government could develop and a war of movement. This was linked to what has been fairly seen as the slow and hesitant manner in which the British moved to implement a fully-fledged southern strategy between 1778 and 1780.

BRITISH PLANS

In 1779 hopes for civil government centred on Georgia and the area around New York. Archibald Campbell favoured the re-establishment of legal government in Georgia with a civilian governor, writing on 19 January:

> Its effects at this juncture, whilst the mind of the people in the neighbouring provinces are worn out by persecutions, extortions, and apprehensions; must operate more powerfully than twenty thousand men.

*Rt. Hon William Eden. Engraved by
T. Holloway, 1786*

On 3 January Campbell and Hyde Parker, the commander of the naval force at Savannah, issued a proclamation announcing the reinstatement of British government and calling on Loyalists to 'rescue their friends from oppression, themselves from slavery'. Campbell explained what he saw as the advantage of associating himself with Parker, a commodore 'in a country where Lieutenant-Colonels and cobblers sprout up like mushrooms', a comment that reflected the heirarchical and ordered notions of British officers.[4] Augusta fell to his forces later in the month.

There were also hopes for civil government and an upsurge of Loyalism in New York. General James Robertson and Joseph Galloway, who had served in the First Continental Congress before joining the British, both argued that most Americans opposed the revolution. This attitude, they stated, could be encouraged and exploited by creating a civil government around New York City. Carlisle and his influential co-peace commissioner, William Eden, supported the idea and, like Robertson, claimed that the crucial military preliminary must be the seizure of the Highlands. This was seen as having the additional benefit of wrecking the American war-effort by hindering their communications. The crucial American line of communications into New England ran via Newburgh and Danbury to Hartford. Hayes stated that:

> ... the North river ought to be our object ... it would open resources, nay it would effectually end the rebellion. The possession of the North river would separate New England from the southern provinces. New England could not support its inhabitants; and must fall without a blow. The Indians would effectually secure the westward, and northward would be open from Canada. Flour, horses and men would come in in abundance and every assistance be given for any future military operations.[6]

Robertson was less euphoric, but he still argued that American communications could be cut and that British forces could be supplied locally, a crucial consideration. Indeed, Long Island Loyalists and Connecticut farmers kept a steady supply of produce going into New York City. Robertson also claimed that the government of New York would soon be able to support itself. These ideas inspired Germain's instructions to Clinton of 23 January 1779. Clinton was to receive 1,000 men from Halifax and 6,600 from Britain, bringing his strength in New York and Rhode Island, exclusive of Loyalist units, to 29,000, sufficient for garrisons of 9,000, a field army of 12,000 and amphibious raiding forces of 8,000. Germain wrote:

> It is most earnestly to be wished that you may be able to bring Mr. Washington to a general and decisive action at the opening of the campaign, but if that cannot be effected it is imagined that with an army of about 12,000 men in the field under your immediate command you may force him to seek for safety in the Highlands of New York or the Jerseys, and leave the inhabitants of the open country at liberty to follow what the Commissioners represent to be their inclinations, and renounce the authority of the Congress and return to their allegiance to His Majesty which would obviate the chief objection to the re-establishment of civil government in New York, as a majority of the counties in the province could then send members to the Assembly and the ancient constitution could be restored in its due form.

Arguing that this would remove American fears that they would be under military law if they submitted to the government, Germain added that:

... the operations proposed to be carried on in other parts would be greatly facilitated by your obliging General Washington to keep the whole of his regular troops together to oppose your army; and on the other hand those operations could not fail to prevent his receiving succours from the countries attacked. It is therefore intended that two corps of about 4,000 each assisted by a naval force should also be employed upon the sea coasts of the revolted provinces, the one to act on the side of New England and New Hampshire, and the other in the Chesapeak Bay and by entering the rivers and inlets wherever it was found practicable, seize or destroy their shipping and shores and deprive them of every means of fitting out privateers or carrying on foreign commerce.

A considerable diversion will also be directed to be made on the side of Canada by a succession of parties of Indians supported by detachments of the troops there alarming and harassing the frontiers and making incursions into the settlements.

Germain hoped that it would be possible to raise sufficient Loyalists to:

... enable you to strengthen the corps you appoint to attack Virginia and Maryland so as to give protection to the loyal inhabitants of Jersey or the lower counties on the Delaware in any attempts they may be disposed to make in the absence of the rebel army to deliver themselves from the tyranny and oppression of the rebel committees and to form a force sufficient to withstand any efforts of the Congress to continue them under its authority.

The south was not therefore at the centre of Germain's plans at the beginning of 1779, but the desire to exploit Loyalist support was. As Clinton planned a summer attack on South Carolina and it was hoped that Campbell would be able to invade that state from Georgia, there was a prospect of British activity and success throughout America. Clinton wrote on 2 March:

... should it be determined to send Grant back to me [from St Lucia], he may fall most providentially at Charleston any time before June, or even later. If the secret is kept it cannot fail, and if we get possession of Charleston these people are ruined.

He suggested an outflanking attack:

Grant goes to Port Royal, whence by a rapid move he will get behind Charleston and I think that must fall . . . should this happen before July, I will assist with all I can spare from hence . . . I know no place where that corps can act with more probability of solid advantage at this time than at South Carolina. A garrison will keep it after it is taken, and the remainder of his corps might be employed in a healthy climate instead of a burying ground, and the winter may be employed in a formidable expedition either to the West Indies, or to complete the business to the southward . . . I am not apt to be too sanguine . . . this first part would succeed.

Clinton was to write in August, 'Georgia runs great risk if we don't take South Carolina and the only chance we have of taking it is by going early and in *great* force'. These hopes were to be thwarted, in part due to unpredictable factors: storms and adverse winds delayed reinforcements from Britain; American and French activities, principally French naval moves, but also American resilience in South Carolina and Washington's ability to avoid battle while continuing to challenge Clinton's hold in the middle colonies; and in part to problems inherent in the plan itself. These ranged from the over-optimistic assessments of the possibilities of reinforcing Clinton speedily and the likelihood of obtaining substantial Loyalist support, to the fundamental ambivalence felt by British generals about restoring civilian authority. Clinton warned Germain in May that Loyalist units had to be handled with care:

> The Provincial Corps when scarcely half their number has been raised, have always been led into the field, and exposed to all the casualties of service. It is hardly to be expected that these battalions should even be completed whilst they are subjected to a continual drain almost as copious as their resources. I need only instance the Queen's Rangers: that corps had enlisted at least a thousand men; their present strength is 378 rank and file.[7]

The Queen's Rangers were one of the best units in either army. Loyalist troops had been used as shock troops and pioneers and for counter-insurgency operations. If there was difficult work to be done, they tended to be the ones to do it. In general, Loyalists sought the confidence of military cover as a pre-condition to offering support, an attitude shared by many of their opponents, as the collapse of local resistance in New Jersey in December 1776 in the face of Cornwallis' advance indicated.

OPERATIONS IN THE SOUTH

The British failed to live up to expectations in this respect in 1779. They had the bad habit of moving into an area, rallying Loyalist support, and then leaving them on their own. After the British proclamation at Savannah on 3 January, the Georgia militia leaders issued a counter-proclamation, giving the Loyalists three days to join the resistance or be treated as enemies.[8] The Rebels were unable to prevent Campbell taking Augusta, but the arrival of a North Carolina force on the opposite side of the Savannah river, falsely reported to be 11,000 strong, led him to fall back, exposing the Loyalists in Augusta to reprisals.[9] The only substantial force of backcountry Loyalists that had risen, 800 Carolina Loyalists under Colonel James Boyd, were surprised on their way to join Campbell at Augusta, and defeated by backcountry militia at Kettle Creek on 14 February. A force of Creek Indians led by David Tait was defeated by the Georgia militia on the Ogeechee.

Elsewhere the Loyalists were also disappointed. Clinton abandoned both Rhode Island and his gains in the Highlands in late 1779. Although a British civilian government was restored in Georgia, with an assembly and the return of the governor, less progress was made in New York, while British conduct did not always inspire support. Clinton was unhappy about limiting his authority and created nothing stronger than an advisory council with a civilian majority. He remained the sole commissioner for issuing pardons, restoring territories to the King's peace and granting exemptions from the Prohibitory Act of 1775. In Georgia, however, tension was more acute. Campbell had a low opinion of Thomas Brown's East Florida Rangers, a Loyalist force, but he was popular in Georgia, unlike Prevost. Described by Campbell as 'too old and unactive for this service',[10] Prevost looted widely on his advance from East Florida and had no interest in the restoration of civilian government. Plundering and forced requisitioning by British forces in Georgia turned many Loyalists into enemies. Campbell returned to Britain in disgust when his measures for raising a loyal militia were not put into effect.

Noting that 'besides Indians, blacks, etc Government has many friends' in Georgia, Clinton wanted to see if developments there would affect South Carolina. Prevost argued that operations in Georgia should be supported by an 'impression' at Charleston or Beaufort, claiming 'it would be a blow to the rebellious colonies which they could not recover and which might reduce them to reason, much sooner than anything that can be effected to the northward.'[11] Prevost sent a small unit to Beaufort, but that was defeated by a larger force of South Carolina militia on 3 February and had to be evacuated by sea. However, on 3 March Prevost routed a North Carolina force under John Ashe at Briar Creek by attacking it from the rear. This defeat was followed by the return of many Carolina militiamen to their homes when their enlistments expired. Nevertheless, Lincoln outnumbered Prevost, and on 23 April he crossed the Savannah in order to challenge the British position in Georgia.

Prevost boldly countered by invading South Carolina on 29 April. However, instead of marching at once for vulnerable Charleston, he delayed to loot the plantations, and when he reached Charleston Neck on 9 May Prevost found hastily erected earthworks. Summoning the town, he was offered its occupation by John Rutledge, Governor of South Carolina, in return for a guarantee of the neutrality of the harbour and the remainder of the state for the rest of the war, proposals that scarcely suggested a bellicose spirit, and that indicate what bold advances in other circumstances might have achieved. Prevost was only prepared to accept unconditional surrender, an unwise attitude in a world of loyalties made ambivalent by shifting military fortunes. Before he could attack the city, he discovered that Lincoln was marching to its relief and withdrew on 12 May to John's Island, whence he planned to retire by sea. While the expedition was being evacuated, a detachment left at Stono Ferry to cover it was attacked by Lincoln's force on 20 June. Poor intelligence led the Americans to attack redoubts that were stronger than anticipated, and they were repulsed with 165 casualties compared to 129 from the British 71st Regiment. The British force then retired to Beaufort on Port Royal Island, summer heat and humidity being the most effective of all truces.

Prevost's advance revealed the vulnerability of coastal South Carolina, while Stono Ferry indicated that an outnumbered British force which had not had long to entrench itself and which was operating without support from the locality could maintain its position. This was, however, dependent on two considerations that were not stressed sufficiently in British discussion of a southern strategy. Success along the coast would not determine the fate of the backcountry, while this success was itself largely dependant on control of the sea. Washington was aware that stronger American forces were required in the south, although he was unable to provide either men or advice.[12] Nevertheless, if the British were to gain further successes they would need to send reinforcements. Lyttelton told parliament on 23 April:

> It is now said there is good news – what is it? Colonel Campbell is arrived from Georgia with the news of a victory, and in the same breath requires a reinforcement . . . Georgia is ours, Boston was ours, Philadelphia was ours, but after five years contest we are reduced to, little more than half a province.[13]

STONY POINT AND CASTINE

Further north Clinton had had no success in forcing Washington to a battle. He wanted a decisive engagement, but he believed that it depended on reinforcements. Clinton subsequently wrote:

> Had the promised reinforcements arrived in any reasonable time, my opening the campaign this early had given me every advantage over the enemy I could wish. For the different states had not yet sent in their respective quotas of men; and their magazines of flour, corn, and dry forage were nearly exhausted, so that they could not venture to take the field in any numbers, as the vegetation of the earth was not yet sufficiently advanced to furnish a substitute for either . . . I have not the smallest doubt but I might have availed myself with the fullest success of the then very critical circumstances and situation of the enemy.

This assessment of American difficulties' actually understated them. On 22 May Washington outlined his problems in a circular to the states: the weakness of his army, the depreciation of the currency, and disaffection and lethargy among the population. He warned against 'an expectation of peace and an opinion of the enemy's inability to send more troops to this country'. Clinton, however, failed to appreciate the other commitments the British government had to consider and the difficulty of sending adequate reinforcements speedily. Unhappy about the size of his force,[14] Clinton felt that it would be better not to advance on Washington, who had wintered in New Jersey, but rather to move into the Highlands. This would protect New York City and, by threatening American communications, might force Washington to risk battle.

In the meantime a major coastal raid had been launched to destroy American supplies and prevent reinforcements from joining Washington. On 5 May a force of 1,800 men under Brigadier-General Edward Mathew escorted by Commodore Collier left Sandy Hook for the Chesapeake. This was far less than the 4,000 men designated in Germain's plan, and Mathew was instructed to return as soon as possible in order to help the projected attack of the Highlands. Thus, the idea of establishing a base from which Loyalist activity could be inspired and supported was abandoned in favour of a large-scale cutting-out operation.

The British force landed near Portsmouth, the small garrison of the fort there abandoning its post. Forts Nelson, Norfolk, Suffolk and Gosport were also seized and extensive damage was done: ships, timber, pitch, tar, turpentine and tobacco being destroyed, as was the important shipyard at Gosport.[15] Washington responded by pressing for the removal of stores from coasts and navigable rivers,[16] a comment on American vulnerability to amphibious operations after the French entry into the war. Collier wished to establish a post at Portsmouth from which the Chesapeake could be controlled. He was encouraged by the attitude of the local population and hopeful of establishing a new naval base. Mathew, however, insisted on abiding by his orders and the troops were re-embarked on 24 May.[17] Collier's idea has been criticized on the grounds that such a lightly-held base would have been vulnerable,[18] although the fate of British operations in Georgia and South Carolina in 1779 suggests that the situation was more complex.

On 28 May Clinton advanced towards the Highlands and on 1 June, under naval cover, seized Stony Point and Verplanck's Point on the Hudson at their southern end, thus gaining control over King's Ferry. The Americans abandoned Stony Point without fighting and their small garrison in the other post surrendered after a bombardment. Washington did not advance to dispute this move, while Clinton did not receive the expected reinforcements from Britain that he hoped would enable him to exploit the situation. Hoping to draw Washington away from West Point into a position where he could be readily attacked and to repeat the recent success on the Chesapeake, Clinton sent Collier and Major-General William Tryon to attack the Connecticut coast. Raiding by both sides was a regular feature of the war along Long Island Sound. Between 5 and 11 July New Haven, Fairfield and Norwalk were captured and destroyed, but, before New London could be attacked, the Americans seized Stony Point in a daring night attack mounted by Wayne's brigade of light infantry on 15 July. Total surprise was lost as the attackers moved through a nearby swamp, but the speed and unexpectedness of the assault enabled the Americans to enter the British works and in the consequent mêlée the outnumbered British garrison was defeated in hand-to-hand fighting. General James Pattison observed that Stony Point, 'considered to be safe against any *coup de main* and capable of resisting almost any open attack that could be made against it', had fallen in less than twenty minutes. However, Verplanck's Point successfully resisted an American attack, and the British reacted swiftly, sending Tryon's force from Long Island up the Hudson. Washington ordered Stony Point's works destroyed and the position abandoned. The British reoccupied it, Washington having revealed again his unwillingness to fight even in defence of an important entrenched post.[19]

A less successful American attack on another British outpost led to an amphibious response in August. In June a British force from Nova Scotia had established a post at Castine, on Penobscot Bay, on the coast of what was then Massachusetts and is now Maine. It was designed to deny the Americans both a naval base from which they might threaten Halifax and timber supplies from the area. The General Court of Massachusetts, acting unilaterally without Congressional assent or assistance, decided on a swift response, and a force of 1,000 militia under Brigadier-General Solomon Lovell supported by a fleet under Commodore Dudley Saltonstall reached the bay on 24 July. American attempts on 25 July to force the entrance of Castine Harbour and to land nearby were both unsuccessful, though the Americans managed to land on the 28th. Although they outnumbered the British force, whose fort was very weak, the Americans did not press their advantage, but instead began slow siege operations, while Lovell and Saltonstall sought to shift the burden of the attack onto the other. Sir John Moore, later a distinguished British general during the French Revolutionary and Napoleonic Wars, received his baptism of fire during the American attack. On 13 August a British squadron under Collier arrived. Rather than fighting, all but two of the far larger American fleet fled up the Penobscot river, where the ships were beached and set alight. The other two ships did not escape. The American soldiers and sailors fled into the woods.[20]

Castine was held by the British for the remainder of the war. The American debacle, which effectively knocked Massachusetts out of the war financially and for which Saltonstall was court-martialled and summarily dismissed from the service, indicated both that the Americans were not as successful at amphibious operations as the more experienced British could be and that in offensive operations their militia was not necessarily an impressive force. The British garrison had been exposed by temporary American control of the sea, but, as at Savannah later in the year, that did not have to entail defeat. Although a strategy of dispersed forces without the backing of secure control of the sea was not without risks, the same is true of war in general, and hitherto isolated British fortresses had succeeded in holding out, as at Newport the previous year. Relief from the sea was important, but, as the French had commitments of their own in the West Indies, it was unlikely that their forces would remain in American waters for long.

SIEGE OF SAVANNAH

This was to be the case with d'Estaing's intervention in 1779. Washington had rejected the admiral's proposal for a joint attack on Halifax or Newfoundland in the spring. D'Estaing remained in the Caribbean during the summer, capturing Grenada on 3 July, while St Vincent fell to another French force. Washington wanted French naval assistance for attacks on New York or Rhode Island, a bold proposal that might well have led to a decisive encounter,[21] but d'Estaing sailed north, instead, in response to a request for help in removing the British threat to South Carolina. He arrived on the Georgia coast on 1 September with twenty ships of the line and 5,000 troops. D'Estaing's original plan was to disrupt the British at Savannah before sailing for Newfoundland, but a damaging storm on 2 September led him to decide instead to remain on the coast and besiege Savannah until the hurricane season ended.[22] General Lincoln was aware that d'Estaing would not remain for long and he rushed south from Charleston, but his march was slowed by broken bridges and poor roads.[23]

On 12 September the French landed near Savannah and on the 16th Lincoln arrived. Prevost, reinforced by the force from Port Royal and by cannon from the ships in the harbour, rejected a summons to surrender, and regular siege operations began, although they were hindered by bad weather, which made it difficult to move the cannon. In addition, as Lincoln noted, d'Estaing's 'cannon not being mounted on travelling carriages, and he having but one pair of wheels to transport them occasions much delay being obliged to substitute wheels taken from timber cutters and to make trucks of the bodies of large trees'. These delays allowed the British to make a weak position much stronger. On 5 October the bombardment of the town finally began, with thirty-three cannon and nine mortars, and it continued until the 8th, but without obtaining a surrender. Lincoln noted, 'The Count being informed by his engineers that to reduce the garrison by regular approaches would be a work of considerable time'[24] now resolved to storm Savannah. The army officers in his force opposed the idea, as did Lincoln, but d'Estaing was adamant.

The attack on the morning of 9 October was a disaster. Thanks to a deserter, the British were forewarned, the attacking columns did not coordinate their operations and, despite the bravery of the South Carolina Continentals and the French, who planted their flags on the British ramparts, they were repulsed with heavy losses. Almost one-fifth of the men engaged were killed or wounded, compared to minor British losses. About 800 American and French troops and sixteen British soldiers died. Lincoln wanted to continue the siege, but d'Estaing refused and on the 18th it was lifted.[25]

The attack on Savannah was the last major encounter of the year, but in the closing months of 1779 a number of moves took place that were to be of considerable consequence for subsequent operations. Clinton had expected substantial reinforcements, the return of the force sent to St Lucia and 6,600 men from Britain. He was to be disappointed. Delays on the part of the transports, unfavourable winds and the need to wait for escorts ensured that the reinforcements, a sickly 3,800 rank and file, did not arrive at New York until 25 August, with over a thousand following on 21 September. Sickness spread among the troops in New York and on 25 September Pattison noted, 'We have at present upwards of 5,000 men of this army unfit for duty'. Meanwhile Grant's force in the West Indies had been decimated by illness and when reinforcements from France led to the French regaining naval superiority in the Caribbean in June the regiments destined for America were dispersed in order to guard the principal islands. Clinton had hoped to use them to assist in an attack on South Carolina, a direction in which he was increasingly looking as he abandoned hopes of engaging Washington. Wayne's storming of Stony Point had greatly depressed Clinton, who became pessimistic about the possibility of achieving anything against Washington. His spirits were lowered still further on 19 August when a small American force under 'Light-Horse Harry', Major Henry Lee, surprised the British garrison at Paulus Hook (modern Jersey City), on the New Jersey shore opposite New York and overran most of the fortress. The following day Clinton again asked to be replaced. He had already had to send 2,000 men to reinforce Canada and the prospect of any successful operations around New York now seemed remote.

Attention shifted to the south. In early September Cornwallis and 3,000 men were prepared for an expedition to South Carolina, to be supported by a naval diversion in the Potomac, but on 15 September Clinton received an appeal for help from the commanders on Jamaica, the largest British possession in the West Indies. The Carolina scheme was abandoned and Cornwallis and 4,000 men were embarked for Jamaica, when news arrived on the 24th that d'Estaing was off Georgia.[26] The expedition was abandoned and, under the pressure of an apparently forthcoming French attack on New York, Rhode Island or Halifax, the British position was reassessed, although the decision to abandon Rhode

Island also owed much to the need to reorganize British forces in order, in the absence of substantial reinforcements, to create a force for the Carolina expedition. New York was hastily prepared to resist attack, batteries being constructed for the artillery. On 6 October Admiral Marriot Arbuthnot, who had positioned his ships at Sandy Hook as Howe had done the previous year, wrote to Clinton about:

> ...the several conversations we have had, respecting the evacuating of Rhode Island, originated in the idea of strengthening the corps that might be employed to the southward: in the course of which I gave it as my opinion that a powerful diversion might be made for their assistance, by more entering the Chesapeak, and attacking Virginia, with the whole of the King's ships and a small number of troops, and that the troops at Rhode Island, in my opinion, might be employed better on this service, than remaining at that place, which hitherto had never been of the smallest use to the navy; and in that idea I still remain; for if Count d'Estaing was to render me so unhappy as to take this place [New York], everything will fall with it, all the ships stores, provisions and magazines of all sorts ...

Clinton observed on the same day, 'the occupying that place is of no advantage to land operations in the present stage of the war, nor to judge from appearances can became of any in the prosecution of it', although he asked Arbuthnot whether it might not be necessary to retain Newport in case d'Estaing entered New York. Fearing that d'Estaing had taken Halifax, Arbuthnot wrote that, if so, it would be necessary to hold onto Rhode Island 'because New York is not a place for large ships', although if the British retained Halifax he did not think it worth blocking up 'such a number of troops' in Newport:

> ... The ships of the line cannot winter in the port of New York, much less can they come upon the coast near it, being of all others the most dangerous for large ships ... the line of battle ships will be as soon with you from Halifax and in better order than they could be from any other port on this continent.[27]

Clinton wrote of Rhode Island:

> ... if d'Estaing goes there it cannot hold out 48 hours, that till we are superior at sea we are never sure of keeping it, and when we are superior, nobody else can.

Rhode Island was abandoned and the French were able to use it as a base in 1780–1. Since the French entry, commanders had increasingly become concerned with naval bases, one reason for the growing importance of the Chesapeake, and thus the loss of Newport could be regarded as a major blow, but it freed 5,000 British troops and a number of warships at a time when both were in short supply and when coastal operations in New England were a decreasing priority, while an advance on Boston or into the interior was no longer a possibility.

Clinton also blamed unforeseen developments for his failure to attack Washington towards the end of the year. He had received encouraging news about the sympathies of the Vermonters and, in addition, felt it necessary to forestall a reported planned Franco-American attack on New York. However, from there Clinton wrote on 10 October:

> . . . I am going to attack Washington. I can promise nothing but an opportunity shall not be missed, but while d'Estaing threatens our port, I dare not move up in great force, nor could I indeed at this moment if he was out of the question as we have near 5,000 sick. Many regiments have not 100 men fit for duty; some much less.

Nevertheless, Clinton's attention was really directed towards the south and he did not advance against Washington, who was out of reach, as he noted on 10 November:

> . . . he still keeps at a great distance from us and so near the [Watchung] mountains that a few hours puts him into them out of our reach indeed the greatest part of his army is still behind the mountains.

Often a man for might-have-beens, Clinton harped on what he could have achieved had he only been reinforced as originally intended and had d'Estaing not arrived,[28] but he was already thinking ahead towards the capture of Charleston in 1780. The Highlands strategy, whether for provoking battle with Washington, cutting American communications or providing the basis for a revival of civil government, had been discarded and in order to free troops for a southern offensive Stony Point and Verplanck's Point were abandoned as well as Rhode Island.

Earlier in the year Clinton had decided on a winter campaign in South Carolina, supported by the establishment of a base on the Chesapeake. He was encouraged by reports of the number of Loyalists in South Carolina and fearful that if he did not act Georgia would fall. Loyalists pressed for action. One complained to Amherst in October 1779 that too little had been done that summer, that there was 'a strange fatality attending all our military operations' and that:

> . . . an inglorious campaign has given great spirits to the rebels, and depressed the friends to government, both within and without the lines; that there are yet a great number of those can not be doubted when it is known what sufferings thousands still undergo rather than take part in rebellion.

On 22 October Clinton wrote to Arbuthnot:

> . . . whilst I am sensible how great an influence the operations of an enemy may and should have upon our plans for defensive war, so as to thwart our measures or to divert our attention from them; I think it becomes us still to keep in view the general line from which we are obliged to swerve and which if pursued we had considered as most directly tending to the detriment of the enemy. Our expedition to South Carolina was a principal object and one having reference to that (or indeed of importance enough in itself), to the Chesapeak was another . . . Georgia and Pensacola chiefly claim our attention as requiring succour Charleston and New Orleans as points where by well timed exertions we may possibly reap some brilliant advantage . . . relieving Georgia will . . . go in hand with the attacking Carolina.

Arbuthnot pointed out that 'the north-west winds which blow with the utmost violence upon all the American coasts after the beginning of December, must render any sea expedition that may be undertaken after that time exceedingly precarious', as was to be demonstrated, but Clinton was not discouraged; if Georgia was lost he was prepared to invade the Chesapeake instead of South Carolina.[29] The stage was therefore set for a major change of scene, one in which Washington's army was to be of little consequence and the war would centre on Charleston, not the Highlands. Informed at last that Savannah was still British and that d'Estaing had left for Europe, Arbuthnot and Clinton sailed from Sandy Hook for South Carolina with 7,600 troops on 26 December. The war in the south was about to begin in earnest.

10   1780: The Siege of Charleston; Impasse in the North

When will this war be over? I think it bids for a conclusion.

John Hayes, 22 August 1780

Lord Cornwallis can now make rapid strides towards the subduing of North Carolina and draw the line in Virginia, for the protection of the Southern Colonies.

John Hayes, 31 December 1780[1]

The British attack on Charleston was the only major planned operation of 1780 that was executed and, as a result, the siege and its consequences have dominated the military history of the year. Had any of the major blows intended further north been attempted – Washington's plans for a Franco-American attack on New York, Clinton's for a blow against the French expeditionary force once it had arrived at Newport or his hopes of exploiting Benedict Arnold's willingness to betray West Point – the war in 1780 would not have had such a pronounced southern orientation. This is also true, although to a far lesser extent, of the consequences of the delay until the very end of the year of the British dispatch to the Chesapeake of a force instructed to establish a post there. Had such an expedition been mounted earlier in the year, as was projected, then it is probable that fewer Continental soldiers would have been sent south to face the British in the Carolinas. This might well have ensured that Cornwallis was provided with a better opportunity to disperse his forces in order to 'pacify' the south, organize Loyalist forces and thus fulfil the expectations originally focussed on the southern campaign. Clinton claimed in August that 'for want of cooperation in Chesapeake, the rebel force in North Carolina is great'. British hopes of a successful war in the south sustained by Loyalist troops and supplies

The South

from securely-held areas were to be dashed. By the end of 1780 it was clear that the optimism inspired by the fall of Charleston and the surrender of the largest American force to capitulate during the war had to be qualified by a realization that this would not mean an uncontested triumph in the Carolinas.

For Britain's enemies, 1780 was also a year of disappointment. The French expeditionary force which arrived in Newport achieved nothing, while Washington was unable to shake British control of New York. His troops were increasingly demoralized and were to mutiny early in the new year. The British still controlled the sea, and if their impact in the interior was limited they revealed at Charleston and around the Chesapeake an ability to use their amphibious forces to considerable effect, taking the initiative, harrying their opponents and disrupting the American economy. Nevertheless, this achievement was precarious. 'Naval victory may, however, recover all, but how to obtain it', Clinton had asked in October 1779.[2] There was to be no such victory in 1780 and, without it, British generals continued anxiously to scan the oceans.

THE FALL OF CHARLESTON

The fall of Savannah and Prevost's successful advance on Charleston had demonstrated the vulnerability of the south. A greater British effort had been anticipated and in September 1779 Washington had advised a building up of American defences in the region.[3] However, this course was not pressed sufficiently and Congress preferred to call for an expedition by Benjamin Lincoln's army against St Augustine. On 18 November 1779 the North Carolina Continentals had been ordered to march south to join Lincoln, but the sometime superiority of amphibious operations was demonstrated by the greater

General Benjamin Lincoln

speed of the British fleet which cleared Sandy Hook on 26 December and mostly reached Tybee Island off Savannah on 30 January. The voyage also illustrated the drawback of such operations, because on 28 December a terrible storm struck the fleet off Cape Hatteras. Much of it was dispersed by storm and current, one transport ending up off Cornwall, while most of the horses and much of the supplies, especially ordnance stores and entrenching tools, were lost. Hayes suffered '. . . full forty days beating the boisterous ocean'.[4] As a result the fleet did not anchor off North Edisto Inlet, 30 miles south of Charleston, the original destination, but instead went to Savannah for recuperation and repair. The delay this caused should induce some caution in advancing claims, as has been done, that the British could have made a better effort from 1778 in moving forces between America and the West Indies in order to achieve seasonally propitious annual campaigns in both. It was not simply organizational conventions and weaknesses that made such operations difficult.

The fleet sailed again on 10 February and on the 11th troops were disembarked on Simmon's Island on North Edisto Inlet. Over the following days Clinton's force consolidated their position on James Island. Lincoln neither obstructed their advance nor moved his army away from Charleston, unlike Washington's conduct at Philadelphia in 1777 and New York in 1776 respectively. There was considerable political pressure to hold Charleston and this plays a key role in explaining how Lincoln came to be trapped in the city. In addition, the ambivalent and neutralist response in the city the previous year

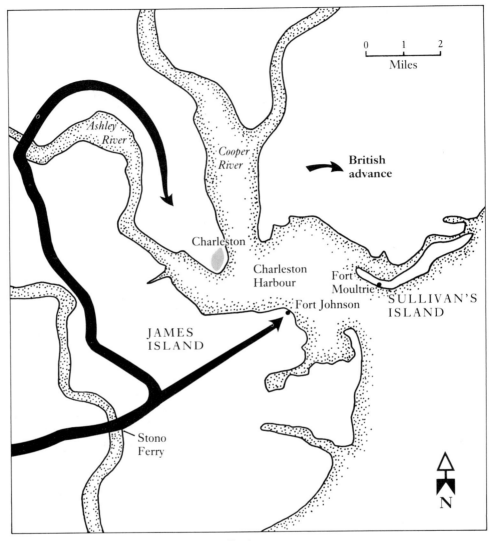

Charleston

towards Prevost's advance suggested the danger of abandoning it. There would also be logistical problems for the Americans were Lincoln to do so; and if the British occupied the city, there was the danger that they might create a strong defensive base, as Prevost had at Savannah, and press on to operate elsewhere, possibly in the Chesapeake.

The British advance was delayed by a lack of horses, which obliged the soldiers to drag cannon and carry ammunition.[5] By mid-March the southern side of Charleston Harbour had been overrun, Fort Johnson being taken on 6 March. The Americans were entrenched at Charleston and on the other side

Colonel Banastre Tarleton by Sir Joshua Reynolds

of the harbour. Lincoln unrealistically expected large numbers of re-inforcements from further north. On 29 March Clinton's advance-force crossed the Ashley river at Drayton's Landing 12 miles above Charleston, the enterprise being accomplished with considerable skill and speed, while the Americans offered no resistance.[6] Gradually the British drew the net round poorly-fortified Charleston. On 30 March the British camped near the city between the Ashley and the Cooper rivers and on 1 April began digging siege entrenchments. A week later Arbuthnot and seven warships forced their way past American fortifications on the north side of the harbour, a Hessian quartermaster recording, 'we could see nothing of the ships except the flashes of their guns because of the smoke. The majesty of this sight can hardly be described'.[7]

On 13 April the British siege guns began firing. The disruption of the siege train in the storm meant that cannon and artillerymen had to be supplied by the fleet. The following day in a surprise attack the British Legion, a Loyalist unit of cavalry and light infantry under Lieutenant-Colonel Banastre Tarleton, routed an American cavalry force under Brigadier-General Isaac Huger that controlled a possible withdrawal route, through Monck's Corner on the Cooper. Clinton recorded in May:

> . . . a variety of difficulties and some misfortunes had delayed our operations to the month of March. These had tempted the rebels to assemble their whole force and risk the fate of the two Carolinas on the siege of Charleston which they fortified by all that could be done with water, impassable swamp, wood, sand and labour; the rebels had likewise a very superior cavalry which gave them command of the country . . . there was no possibility of forming a complete investiture of the place without passing the Cooper river, and though I was convinced that the admiral would make every exertion to get a naval force into it . . . I always doubted the practicability while the enemy had Sullivan's Island. I was therefore determined to attempt the passage higher up the river which could only be done by suprise. This Colonel Tarleton . . . effected.

On 16 April Lincoln allowed the civil authorities to dissuade him from accepting advice to evacuate his men across the Cooper. On 29 April a cutting-out party of marines and seamen seized the American works at Mount Pleasant and in early May Sullivan's Island and Fort Moultrie fell similarly, the American defenders fleeing. Under increasingly heavy artillery bombardment, that included hot shot designed to cause fires, morale and resolve in Charleston crumbled. British reinforcements from New York arrived on 19 April. Lincoln's offer on 21 April to surrender the town as long as the army was allowed to march away was rejected, as were the terms offered on 8 May: surrender with full honours of war and permission for the militia to go home. By now the population, their wooden homes aflame as a result of British shelling, was in favour of peace on any terms, while the British siegeworks were very close. On 6 May Tarleton demonstrated the strength of the British investiture of Charleston, by defeating an American cavalry force attempting to cross the Santee at Lenud's Ferry. On the 12th the American force, about 5,500 Continental soldiers, militia and armed citizens, surrendered. The Americans also lost most of what was left of the Continental navy, which had been foolishly left there and employed only in static defence.[8]

The Americans had been less successful than the besieged British at Savannah in 1779, but Clinton was stronger, had more time and was supported by a more active naval force than the besiegers of Savannah. Clinton finally achieved the decisive battle he had sought so fruitlessly around New York, but that was because Lincoln was unwilling until too late, and then unable, to withdraw from a position where he was at a serious disadvantage: surrounded and constantly hammered by a British force supported by naval fire-power and supplies. The difficulties of defending a city were also exemplified by the pressure Lincoln was placed under from the civilian population. State-level political interference in military operations was at its worse in the south in 1779 and 1780, and Lincoln faced serious problems, not unlike those of his predecessor General Robert Howe. Accepting that the American position at Charleston was, like Long Island in 1776, a poor one, it was nevertheless the case that they fought very badly. The failure to defend outlying forts was serious and helped to allow the British to concentrate their army and navy against Charleston. Though the forts were in a poor condition, bold defences had been mounted from such positions before, as by the Americans on Sullivan's Island in

1776 and the British at Castine in 1779. Lincoln had spent a day working on the fortifications in order to lift American morale (Clinton similarly 'was the most indefatiguable officer in the [British] lines'),[9] but he was an unenergetic general, and the defence was irresolute, unimaginative and, on the whole, lacking the brave fighting spirit that the Americans displayed on so many occasions during the war. The exceptions, such as the sortie on 23 April, were rare.

The surrender of Charleston was followed by the speedy spread of British control over most of South Carolina, especially the Tidewater. Clinton wrote on 12 May, 'if the French and Spaniards do not interfere and our reports from our friends in the country are founded I hope we shall soon have hereby conquered both Carolinas'. A small force of Virginia Continentals under Colonel Abraham Burford marching to help Charleston had turned back on news of its fall but were overtaken by Tarleton at the Waxhaws on 29 May. He reported that his men had travelled 105 miles in 54 hours, the infantry on horseback. The Americans, who were offered terms, refused to surrender, and the outnumbered Tarleton attacked 'cavalry and infantry blended', the woodland of the southern Piedmont being easier to attack in than the denser forests of the Hudson valley. Tarleton praised 'the bravery' of his men, but his opponents had a different view. A considerable number of the surrendering Americans were slaughtered after laying down their arms and the cry 'Tarleton's Quarter' was soon to be used to justify similar American atrocities.[10]

In Tidewater South Carolina British authority was swiftly recognized. On 5 June more than 200 of the more prominent citizens of Charleston congratulated the British commanders on the restoration of the political connection with the Crown. A loyal address came from Georgetown the following month, while several of the leading politicians of the state returned to Charleston to accept British rule.[11] This appeared to be a vindication of the British policy of combining military force with a conciliatory policy, offering a new imperial relationship that granted most of the American demands made at the outbreak of the war. It is scarcely surprising that northern politicians, such as Ezekiel Cornell of Rhode Island, came to doubt the determination of their southern counterparts.

British hopes of pacification through conciliation were to be compromised by Clinton's attitude. He rejected Arbuthnot's pressure for publishing the terms of the future political settlement and ending the rule of military law. Instead, Clinton pressed Germain 'to restore the civil establishment partially and by degrees', arguing that the 'violent commotions which have so long prevailed, will not admit of the instant return of that regular and gentle flow by which formerly justice was distributed and government conducted'. On 1 June Clinton and Arbuthnot issued a proclamation offering full pardons to those who would take an oath of allegiance, but on 3 June Clinton issued a second releasing all those on parole, but requiring them to take an oath to support British measures; those who refused, to be treated as rebels. Clinton's foolish refusal to accept the apathetic and neutral sentiments of much of the southern population and his insistence that they pledge themselves to provide active support aroused hostility. On 29 June Cornwallis wrote to Arbuthnot:

. . . the Proclamation of the Commissioners, of the 1st, and that of the General, of the 3rd, did not at all contribute to the success of my operations. Nothing can in my opinion be so prejudicial to the affairs of Great Britain as a want of discrimination. You will certainly lose your friends by it, and as certainly not gain over your enemies. There is but one way of inducing the violent rebels to become our friends, and that is by convincing them it is their interest to be so.[12]

The steps that Cornwallis criticized were to undermine the logic of the British strategy in the south, a symbiosis of reconciliation and military superiority. Instead, the generals were forced to rely on small regular forces, unable to control more than a fraction of the area, and on Loyalists, who were increasingly defeated in a savage civil war by their opponents. Clinton's revocation of the parole agreement was controversial and can be seen as his most foolish move. Many Americans had come in on the offer of parole, but then Clinton changed the terms of reconciliation. Parole was no longer sufficient. Instead the Americans had to join in the fight against their former compatriots. Many felt themselves no longer bound by their parole. Having issued the new proclamation, Clinton departed for New York on 8 June with 4,000 troops, leaving Cornwallis in a more vulnerable position. Many of the Rebels who fought alongside Greene in 1781 were former parolees who believed that Clinton's attempt to make them fight their former compatriots abrogated any agreement of parole.

The limitations of pacification had already been displayed in Georgia where in the summer of 1780 Augusta was attacked by irregular American forces under Elijah Clark. John Pringle, a pro-government MP, had warned in May 1780:

Government say they have great reason to think an accommodation might take place with all the Southern colonies. I wish they may not flatter themselves too much and be deceived as heretofore, for an enthusiastic, rancorous spirit prevails much in that country against this heightened by many crueltys wantonly committed by the military and their despair by being many of them totally ruined.

CAMDEN

Yet the military situation appeared propitious. Cornwallis, who was to be left in command on Clinton's return to New York to deal with the threat posed by a French expeditionary force, wrote from Camden on 2 June:

Appearances in this province are certainly very favourable . . . I have no doubt of being able to subsist a body of troops here this summer, without bringing anything from Charleston but rum and salt.

Cornwallis' optimism extended to backcountry South Carolina, whose inhabitants he thought 'sincerely happy' to return to their union with Britain.[13] The short-term challenge to the British position in South Carolina was easily overcome. Major-General Horatio Gates was appointed by Congress to succeed Lincoln as commander of the Southern Department in June 1780, although Washington had recommended Nathanael Greene. On 25 July at Coxe's Mill on

General Horatio Gates

the Deep River in North Carolina he took command of the Southern army, a variable force that comprised those who had escaped capture at Charleston, as well as those who had not arrived in time to relieve it. Among them were 1,400 Delaware and Maryland Continentals, hardened veteran soldiers many of whom had seen combat from the battle of Long Island on, under a good officer and veteran of European wars, the self-styled 'Baron' Johann de Kalb who had been sent by Washington. The army was short of supplies and required time for organisation into an effective fighting force. Kalb had planned a cautious advance via Salisbury and Charlotte, where the people were sympathetic and supplies plentiful, followed, if possible, by an attack on the British post at Camden.

Gates foolishly rejected such caution. He instead ordered a direct march on Camden through a largely infertile region, most of whose population was Loyalist, and he dismissed warnings about the supply situation. Gates believed it necessary to advance before the British could move into North Carolina and was aware that it was important to repair the effects of Charleston and counter the recent drop of morale. He was under pressure to act from local military and political leaders. Food for Gates' army was collected by the use of threats and violence, but sufficient supplies did not arrive and the troops who marched on 27 July were forced to eat green corn and peaches. It was extremely hot and some of the starving militia went home. Gates did not seek a major battle, and believed wrongly that Cornwallis had withdrawn troops from Camden. Instead, despite the sickness of his force in Charleston, Cornwallis, worried about the British position at Camden,[14] had arrived there with reinforcements on 13 August. He decided that it was best to launch a pre-emptive stroke against Gates, and on the night of 15 August he set out for a dawn attack. The British

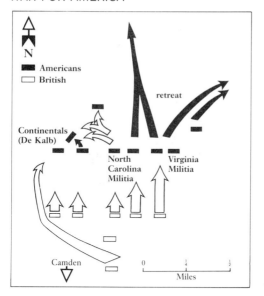

Camden

force, 2,043 effectives, including 1,226 Loyalists, stumbled into the advancing Americans, about 3,100 men, in the darkness and, having regrouped, fought the next day. Gates put his Virginia and North Carolina militia on the left, unsupported by any Continental troops, and they collapsed when the regulars, placed on the right of the British line, advanced. The Virginians themselves advanced, but most soon fled in the face of the British. Their panic spread to the North Carolinians. Many fled without firing a shot, discarding their arms and equipment. Their panicky retreat unravelled the American front, although the Delaware and Maryland Continentals on the right fought bravely, and nearly broke the British left. They were, however, exposed by the flight of the militia, enveloped by the British and attacked in the flank by Tarleton's cavalry. The Continentals broke under the fearsome pressure. Colonel Otho Williams of the 6th Maryland Regiment wrote of how the army was:

> . . . completely routed. The infamous cowardice of the militia of Virginia and North Carolina gave the enemy every advantage over our regular troops . . . Our retreat was the most mortifying that could have happened. Those who escaped the dangers of the field knew not where to find protection. The wounded found no relief from the inhabitants who were immediately in arms against us, and many of our fugitive officers and men were disarmed by those faithless villains who had flattered us with promises of joining us against the enemy. The Tories are now assembling in different parts of the country, and there is actually a sort of partisan war waged between them and the Whigs of this country. The greatest part of our baggage was plundered by those who first left the field. The enemy took a part and much of what escaped them has been pillaged by the inhabitants on the retreat. The waggon horses have been stolen and frequently taken from the drivers . . . An unfortunate general usually loses the confidence of his army, and this is much the case with us at present.

De Kalb, who would not flee, was one of the many killed in the battle, the Americans suffering about 800 dead and wounded, as well as having 1,000

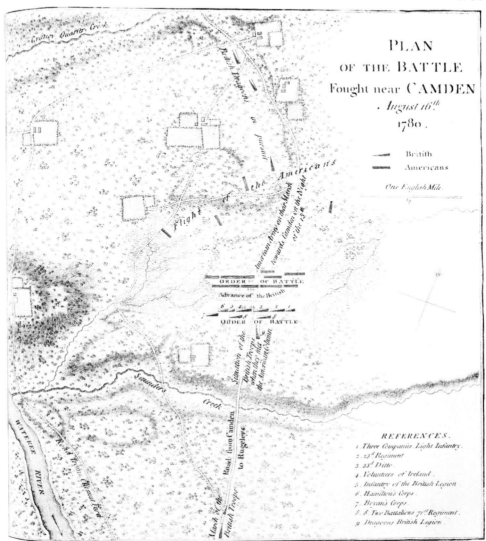

Plan of the battle of Camden, 16 August 1780. Engraved for Stedman's History of the American War

prisoners taken and the loss of their supplies. A terrified Gates fled the field, riding nearly 70 miles non-stop to safety. When the Continentals re-assembled at Hillsborough ten days later there were only 700 of them. For his 300 casualties, Cornwallis had gained 'a most complete victory', blocked the challenge to Camden, cleared South Carolina of Continentals and left North Carolina exposed.[15]

THE UNPACIFIED SOUTH

Despite these events the task of consolidation was far from easy. Cornwallis faced the familiar problems of insufficient troops and precarious supplies, but in the south the uncertainty over crucial local support was a worrying and unpredictable exacerbating factor. Prior to Camden, Cornwallis already had become aware that the situation was less promising than it might look to Clinton in Charleston, that it might be difficult to assist the Loyalists and that the attempt to help them might complicate British strategy. On 2 June he wrote of North Carolina:

> . . . the back part of that province is in a want of provisions nearly approaching to famine, so that it will be impossible to establish any post there until after the harvest; I have sent emissaries to our friends in that country to state my situation . . . and to submit to them whether it would not be prudent for them to remain quiet until I can give them effectual support, which could only be done by a force remaining in the country, at the same time I assured them, that if they thought themselves a match for their enemies without any regular force, and were determined to rise at all events, I would give them every assistance in my power by incursions of light troops, furnishing ammunition etc.

Cornwallis wished to prevent 'a premature rising' which might 'ruin all our plans for the reduction of North Carolina'.[16] However, 1,300 Loyalists rose under John Moore, only to be defeated at Ramsour's Mill on 20 June. A number of bitter engagements between Loyalists and Rebels, such as Williamson's Plantation (12 July), Rocky Mount (1 August) and Hanging Rock (6 August), revealed that the South Carolina backcountry was far from pacified, although on 18 August at Fishing Creek Tarleton defeated Thomas Sumter, one of the American leaders in the backcountry war. Cornwallis was frustrated. He found the Loyalist militia that Clinton had organized limited: its 'infidelity', absence of subordination and low morale he felt would make a force of regulars necessary for the defence of South Carolina until North Carolina had been subjected. Germain was informed of the drawbacks of militia:

> . . . can be of little use for distant military operations, as they will not stir without an horse, and on that account your Lordship will easily conceive the impossibility of keeping a number of them together without destroying the country.[17]

The militiamen had their own complaints, one Loyalist recording:

> A dissatisfaction prevailed at this moment amongst the militia founded on general Clinton's hand-bill which required every man having but three children, and every single man to do six months duty out of their own province when required. This appeared like compulsion, instead of acting voluntarily as they conceived they were doing and they were in consequence ready to give up the cause . . .

But they were dissuaded by the efforts of their officers.[18] Cornwallis' conclusion was that he should conquer North Carolina in order to cover the southern states and he argued that the whole might be retained with a force no larger than that needed to defend South Carolina and Georgia.[19] However, he made no effort to advance rapidly after Camden. The British army was debilitated and required rest, while Cornwallis hoped for supporting action in the Chesapeake. On 10 August he had already written to Clinton:

> If we succeed at present and are able to penetrate into North Carolina, without which it is impossible to hold this province, Your Excellency will see the absolute necessity of a diversion in the Chesapeake and it must be made early.

Cornwallis returned to the theme on the 23rd:

> The diversion in the Chesapeake will be of the utmost importance. The troops here have gained reputation but they have lost numbers . . . Our sickness is great and truly alarming. The officers are particularly affected. Doctor Hayes and almost all the hospital surgeons are laid up. Every person of my family and every public officer of the army is now incapable of doing his duty.

He also suggested that the Loyalists were so terrified that they would only rise if the army advanced into North Carolina.[20] Believing that it would be useful to advance, Cornwallis was delayed by sick troops, the enervating summer heat and partisan attacks on his supply lines. The British uniform with its wool and high stock was ill-suited for the high humidity and deadly heat of fever-ridden coastal Carolina. Finally moving north on 9 September, Cornwallis did not reach Charlotte until 26 September. His advance was flanked to the west by a column of Loyalist militia under Patrick Ferguson, designed to counter any activity on the part of the frontiersmen. The measure failed, Ferguson's entire force being killed or captured at King's Mountain on 7 October when attacked by frontiersmen able to exploit the wooded cover to harry Ferguson's men, who resorted to bayonet charges but were unable to break the encirclement. The wounded and those who sought to surrender were killed to the shouts of 'Tarleton's Quarter'. Clinton was to blame Cornwallis for this disaster. He wrote on 1 November:

> Rebel reports mention a check that Colonel Ferguson has met with. I can not credit it as I am persuaded Lord Cornwallis will not permit detachments from his army without sustaining them, Bennington and Trenton are too fresh in our memory . . .

Then again ten days later that he did not credit the reports, as Cornwallis would not 'trust such a corps unsupported'.[21] Against this criticism it might be suggested that the situation had not seemed so threatening, that detachments and small forces had succeeded earlier, Tarleton at the Waxhaws and Prevost on the march to Charleston in 1779 for example, and that if Cornwallis wanted to cover his flank the measure does not seem unreasonable. The British in the south used detached forces, setting up a series of outpost forts, Augusta, Granby, Orangeburg, Motte, Watson and Ninety-Six, in a war of posts. Ferguson had underestimated the mobility of the frontiersmen. He was withdrawing towards Cornwallis' force when attacked, although it has also been argued that he sought a battle. The southern militia and frontiersmen rode, while their northern counterparts walked; the frontiersmen also carried rifles.

As a result of King's Mountain, Cornwallis lost a substantial part of his supporting forces and he therefore decided to abandon his invasion of North Carolina and retreat to Winnsborough, South Carolina, which he reached on 29 October. Fortunately for Cornwallis, the Americans were not in a position to exploit this setback. Gates' position was undermined by intrigues by some southern politicians, but after Camden there was clearly need for a fresh face in the south, and Congress dismissed Gates on 5 October. Delayed by the quest for supplies, his successor, the Quartermaster-General, Nathanael Greene, did not reach Charlotte and take command of his force until 2 December. Greene, a Rhode Island anchorsmith and ex-Quaker, who had read widely in military history and theory and been appointed a general by Congress in June 1775, had been considerably influenced by Washington, who nominated him to Congress and to whom he was close. He was disheartened by the state of his army and by the military situation, writing of the British on 6 December:

> I am more afraid they will carry on a war of posts than make long and sudden marches into the country. Should this be their plan, as I am persuaded it will from its being evidently their interest and agreable to their former mode, and, if their collective strength is much superior to ours, they can establish a post almost where they please, and by laying in a large stock of provision can easily hold them. For we have no heavy cannon to dislodge them, nor have we strength enough to set ourselves down before a work with security or confidence of obliging a garrison to surrender. And the idea of storming works which many speak of with as much familiarity and confidence as they would talk of gathering a basket of fruit, unless it can be effected by suprise affords but a poor prospect of success. Nor would a fort be an object unless we had a force sufficient to hold it after possessing ourselves of it. And to make an attempt and not succeed will bring not only disgrace but will be attended with the loss of our best troops besides which while so much depends upon the opinion of the world both as to time and money, as little should be put to the hazard as possible. Neither the army nor the country want enterprise, and if both are employed in the partisan way until we have a more permanent force to appear before the enemy with confidence, happily we may regain all our losses. But if we put things to the hazard in our infant state before we have gathered sufficient strength to act with spirit and activity and meet a second misfortune, all may be lost, and the tide of sentiment among the people turn.[22]

As so often in this, as in other conflicts, it is instructive to read the correspondence of generals on both sides and appreciate that they all faced serious problems. With the army in a poor state and his leading subordinates opposed to a surprise attack upon Cornwallis,[23] Greene, who believed it vital to keep his force in being, found it in his 'power to carry on nothing but a kind of fugitive war'. He felt that Cornwallis did not need to invade North Carolina, but could instead consolidate his position in South Carolina and that this had to be challenged. Daniel Morgan, recently promoted to brigadier-general, was given command of a section of the southern army which was detatched and ordered to the Broad river to, 'spirit up the people' in upper South Carolina, hinder the collection of supplies by the British and attack their flank or rear if they advanced into North Carolina.[24] Aware anyway of the value of cavalry,[25] Greene found himself obliged to rely heavily on the activities of partisan bands under such leaders as Thomas Sumter and Francis Marion. The use of partisans was an obvious response to the defeats of Charleston and Camden, the uncontrollable vastness of the south and the need to counter Loyalist activity. Appointed a brigadier-general in the South Carolina militia in October 1780, Sumter was instructed to harass and attack the British and those officials who served them throughout the state.[26] The consequence was a vicious and confused local war. Unlike Marion and Andrew Pickens, Sumter refused to coordinate his personal war with Greene. Greene reported on 7 December that Sumter and Marion's militia were:

> . . . composed of men whose cases are desperate being driven from their dwellings and others who are allured by the hopes of plunder. The first are the best of citizens and the best of soldiers; the last are the dregs of the community and can be kept no longer than there is a prospect of gain.

Three weeks later he added:

> . . . the spirit of plundering which prevails among the inhabitants adds not a little to our difficulties. The whole country is in danger of being laid waste by the Whigs and Tories who pursue each other with as much relentless fury as beasts of prey. People . . . are frequently murdered as they ride along the . . . road . . . great numbers of Tories are waylaying the roads. However they are now coming in, in many parts; being tired of such a wretched life, and not finding that support, respect and attention which they expected from the British army.[27]

Far from the British bringing a new peaceful order, they had brought chaos, a chaos Cornwallis blamed in part on the 'supineness and pusillanimity' of the Loyalist militia.[28] The Loyalists found that British military control was insufficiently extensive, while British officers were increasingly frustrated by their limited control over their supply lines. Mastery in the south had slipped from British hands, although it did not come into American keeping. Instead, it was anarchy, a true civil war with all the awfulness such a war entails. Greene was shocked by the savagery. It was more and more tempting for the British to feel that if only operations were extended further north, and consequently American supplies cut and their regular forces driven back, that this would lead to the settlement of the south. This attitude, combined with the feeling that something had to be done, and that it would be best to leave South Carolina and its debilitating environment, led Cornwallis to look north, although, before he is blamed for unsound judgment, it is worth bearing in mind that the south had been invaded as a stage on the route to a denouement in the middle colonies.

CHESAPEAKE AND WEST POINT

As Cornwallis looked north the focus of attention within the south switched from South to North Carolina, while the Chesapeake emerged into increased prominence, not only as a crucial staging post between New York and British forces in the south, but also as an eventual goal of British operations. Clinton pointed out on 4 July that operations in the Chesapeake would depend on naval superiority:

> I can not flatter myself with any brilliant offensive operation till I am reinforced – Chesapeak must be our next object; but we must go in sufficient force to give the experiment a fair trial,

and that cannot be till we see what France and Spain do. For if we are catched there by a superior fleet or Washington's army is reinforced I shall have [word obscure] to meet him . . . if the French and Spaniards are kept at home and I am reinforced by next June we shall probably have all the southern provinces; if . . . a superior enemy's fleet awes this coast I shall be reduced to a strict defensive here [New York] not to say worse, and all our detached corps will be beat en detail.[29]

Yorktown was to bear out his warning. The unexpected arrival at Sandy Hook on 14 September of Admiral Sir George Rodney and ten ships of the line from the West Indies encouraged Clinton to think afresh about the Chesapeake. Cornwallis' growing problems, the likelihood that Washington would yet again deny Clinton a decisive battle in the middle colonies, his lack of interest in Rodney's proposal for a joint attack on the French at Rhode Island and the failure of Arnold's conspiracy to betray West Point all encouraged this step. On 16 October Major-General Alexander Leslie and 2,500 men left New York for the Chesapeake with orders to destroy American supply depots at Petersburg and Richmond, which Clinton believed would handicap their forces in the south, and thus assist Cornwallis. Leslie was also ordered to establish a post on the Elizabeth river and to follow Cornwallis' orders. However, the desire to help operations in the south more directly led to the curtailing of the plans for the Chesapeake. Leslie was ordered instead first to Cape Fear, to assist Cornwallis in North Carolina, and then to Charleston, where he arrived on 14 December. The disaster at King's Mountain had led Cornwallis to seek reinforcements. Leslie's force reached Camden on 4 January 1781 and was then incorporated into Cornwallis' army, although the earl was very disparaging about the quality of most of the soldiers. Many were to be among the heavy casualties at Guilford Court House.

West Point viewed from the north, as it appeared at the close of the war, c. 1786

Further north the campaign of 1780 was indecisive. Bold moves were planned, including a Franco-American attack on New York, the betrayal of West Point, the leading fortress in the Highlands, to the British by its bitter and discouraged commander Benedict Arnold, and a British attack on Rhode Island, but none were realized, no more than Clinton's long-desired decisive battle. The year opened with Washington's army wintering at Morristown, cold, hungry and dissatisfied, the number of soldiers and officers on actual service far less than those listed. Clinton and a substantial part of the British army was in South Carolina until June. Aware that money and foreign aid were required for a decisive offensive campaign, Washington felt it necessary to remain on the defensive, although that did not preclude bold steps such as Lord Stirling's unsuccessful raid on Staten Island in January.[32] Throughout the year Washington was pressed to send troops to the south, to a far greater extent than Clinton, who did not suffer from the same measure of political interference. Hamilton replied to one such request in March 1780:

> We are very weak and from the embarrassments in the Quarter Master's department, for want of money in the early period of the season, we cannot concentrate our force . . . our distress is so great that if there were no objection to parting with the men it would be almost impossible to convey them to you.[33]

In fact, the Maryland Continentals went south the following month, but Washington's parlous situation explains both why he was so needful of French support if he was to mount a major operation and why he did not seek battle without such assistance. Washington wished the French to act against New York, not the south, and thus to ensure that the largest American force would be able to attack its British counterpart. In June a British move into New Jersey from New York did not lead to a battle. Washington used the shelter of 'his fastnesses in the Highlands'[34] during the summer to threaten New York without risking battle. A French expeditionary force of 5,200 men under the Count de Rochambeau, accompanied by seven ships of the line, anchored at Newport on 11 July. Clinton pressed Arbuthnot, a difficult man with whom his relations were increasingly poor, for a joint attack designed to destroy the French force, which he hoped would end the French threat, and, failing that, for naval cover for raids on coastal Connecticut. Obstruction on the part of the admiral prevented the mounting of an attack during the crucial period before the French could fortify Newport, Arbuthnot, for example, refusing to lend naval guns. Having failed to mount an attack, Clinton felt that with the arrival of French troops he could act only if sent reinforcements. He wrote from New York City on 14 August:

> Washington will now raise an army, and should his object be this post, he may easily increase it to 30,000, which with 6,000 French in addition will make him formidable indeed; but while we remain superior at sea, I shall be under no apprehension, however, you must expect nothing offensive from us. This French armament arrives most unfortunately. With reinforcements such as government will of course send me on hearing of my success to the southward, I had every reason to suppose that this winter's operations would have placed Washington over the Hudson: As it is, without very considerable reinforcements come, I wish

FAC-SIMILE OF MAJOR ANDRE'S MINIATURE,

DRAWN BY HIMSELF, OCTOBER 1, 1780, THE DAY PRECEDING HIS EXECUTION.

Taken from the original in Trumbull Gallery, Yale College.

CERTIFICATE.

The above copy of the original portrait of Major Andre, by himself, and now in the Trumbull Gallery, appears to me to have been correctly made.   B. SILLIMAN.

Yale College, August 9th, 1834.

CORRESPONDENCE.

NEW HAVEN, August 8th, 1832.

To Jeremiah Day, D. D., President of Yale College.

DEAR SIR,—It affords me pleasure, as the agent of Jabez L. Tomlinson, Esq., of Stratford, (the father of our late Governor,) and of Nathan Beers, Esq. of this city, to request your acceptance of the accompanying miniature of Major *John Andre*, Adjutant General of the British army during the revolutionary war. The melancholy fate of that accomplished gentleman excited such universal grief in the hearts of his countrymen, and such undisguised sympathy in the breasts of his foes, that it is presumed this memorial may be viewed with interest, and be deemed worthy of preservation among the historical collections of the college. Although the gift, without some explanation, might appear to be trivial, yet it possesses an *incidental value* that renders it truly interesting.

It is the likeness of Major Andre, seated at a table in his guard room, drawn by himself with a pen, on the morning of the day fixed for his execution. Mr. Tomlinson informs me that a respite was granted until the next day, and that this miniature was in the mean time presented to him, (then acting as officer of the guard,) by Major Andre himself. Mr. Tomlinson was present when the sketch was made, and says it was drawn without the aid of a glass.

The sketch subsequently passed into the hands of Deacon Beers, a fellow officer of Mr. Tomlinson on the station, and from thence was transferred to me. It has been in my possession several years.

While the high character of the officers who have preserved since the revolution this interesting memorial of a lamented victim to the necessary usages of war, places its genuineness beyond doubt, it may be remarked that its accuracy as a likeness is rendered probable, from the circumstance that Major Andre was accustomed to delineate, as an amusement, the outlines of his face and person.

The London edition of Joshua Smith's narrative of Arnold's treason, and of his personal connection with Andre in his attempt to escape, has a frontispiece, exhibiting the likeness of Major Andre. It is noted by the engraver as a copy from a portrait by Major Andre himself, now (or then) in the possession of his relatives in England. I have compared the sketch with that engraving, and thought that I could discern in the outlines a striking similarity.

Mr. Tomlinson and Mr. Beers were officers in the regular line of the army at the time of Major Andre's execution. I believe they severally held the rank of lieutenant.

With great respect,

Your friend and obedient servant,

EBENEZER BALDWIN.

YALE COLLEGE, August 10th, 1832.

Dear Sir,—Permit me, for myself and the guardians of the college, to express to you, and to the venerable revolutionary officers, J. L. Tomlinson, Esq., and N. Beers, Esq., my grateful acknowledgments for the miniature of Major J. Andre, generously presented to the institution. A memorial of one whose melancholy fate has long been contemplated with tender emotion, derives an additional interest from the fact that his name is associated with one of the most critical periods in the history of our glorious struggle for independence. Our possession of it at the present time will perhaps be the more highly appreciated, from the circumstance that the college is just now making arrangements for the preservation and exhibition of other monuments of revolutionary characters and events.

With affectionate regard,

Your friend and servant,

JEREMIAH DAY.

Ebenezer Baldwin, Esq.

Facsimile of a miniature of Major André, drawn by himself on 1 October 1780, the day before his execution we may be able to keep what we have, and I shall tremble for Canada next year . . . Why that number of troops in the West Indies? If superior at sea you need them not, if inferior of no avail. Had my old ten regiments been returned to me and enabled by sea to have followed our blow in Chesapeak, what might not have been expected . . . For God's sake send us money, men and provisions or expect nothing but complaints.

Clinton wanted Arbuthnot replaced and the transports put under the command of the army commander so as to end crippling disputes between the army and naval commanders in chief and to facilitate expeditions. William Dalrymple, the Quartermaster General, was sent to London to demand these changes and at least 10,000 reinforcements, with the threat that otherwise Clinton would resign.[35] Washington meanwhile warned that his army must disband or subsist by plunder unless its supplies were improved. American morale fell as it became clear that the French would not cooperate and that there would be no attack on New York. In September both sides encountered difficulties in ensuring cooperation within their forces. The French resisted Washington's proposal that their armies join, stating that they were ordered to keep their army and navy together, and rejected the idea of a winter expedition against Canada. At the same time, by offering too few troops, Clinton blocked Rodney's proposal for a joint attack on Rhode Island.[36] Instead, he relied on the prospect of Arnold betraying West Point, with the consequent collapse of the American position in the Highlands. Such a move would have blocked any likely attack on New York and would have made Washington's position very difficult. However, the details of the conspiracy were exposed when the intermediary Major John André, Clinton's adjutant-general, was captured, dressed in mufti, on 23 September. Arnold fled from West Point, escaping to the British camp, but André was hanged, to the great distress of Clinton. 'A long meditated and most important stroke has failed', the general wrote, but, as important as the failure to take West Point, was the extent to which Clinton's hopes for this project had led him to reject the opportunity for an attack on Newport offered by Rodney's presence. In many respects the fate of the war after 1778 depended on which side would make the best use of temporary naval superiority to secure a permanent advantage in the war on land. Had the French expeditionary force been defeated in 1780 then there would have been fewer trained troops available to take advantage of Cornwallis' advance into Virginia the following year. The destruction of the French warships at Newport would also have altered the naval balance throughout the western hemisphere, with important consequences for the campaign the following year.

Disappointed of French support, Washington still hoped for one blow against the British before winter. Instead of the long hoped for attack on New York City, he decided to surprise the posts at Kingsbridge and on northern Manhattan, but this was abandoned as a result of British naval moves on the Hudson. Clinton, fearful of the consequences of the French arrival, was, however, concerned about the security of New York, and, as a result, called for reinforcements and stressed the danger of sending troops south.[37]

The year closed with Benedict Arnold, now a British officer, setting sail with another expedition for the Chesapeake. Rodney had argued the need to hold a base there, Portsmouth or Norfolk, for the navy,[38] and the expedition expressed the desire to help Cornwallis without irretrievably committing too many men to his army and southern operations. The close of 1780 saw the central themes of the 1781 campaign already clear: the need for Franco-American cooperation if a major blow was to be struck against the British; Cornwallis' problems in the south; the rising importance of the Chesapeake; and the crucial role of naval power. However, the contrasting results of the campaigns of 1780 and 1781 indicate that these circumstances and problems made nothing inevitable.

11   1781: Yorktown

Although I never dared promise myself that any exertions of mine, with my very reduced force (nearly one-third less than that of my predecessor) could bring the war to a happy conclusion; yet I confess that the campaign of 1781 terminated very differently from what I once flattered myself it would.

The Narrative of Lieutenant-General Sir Henry Clinton (London, 1783) p. 5

... one maxim appears to me to be absolutely necessary for the safe and honourable conduct of the war, which is, that we should have as few posts as possible, and that wherever the king's troops are, they should be in respectable force ... In regard to taking possession of Philadelphia by an incursion, (even if practicable) without an intention of keeping or burning it (neither of which appear to be adviseable) I should apprehend it would do more harm than good to the cause of Britain ... if offensive war is intended, Virginia appears to me to be the only province in which it can be carried on, and in which there is a stake, but to reduce the province and keep possession of the country a considerable army would be necessary, for with a small force, the business would probably terminate unfavourably, though the beginning might be successful ... instead of thinking it possible to do anything in North Carolina, I am of the opinion, that it is doubtful whether we can keep the posts in the back part of South Carolina ... the infinite difficulty in protecting a frontier of three hundred miles against a persevering enemy, in a country where we have no water communication and where few of the inhabitants are active or useful friends.

Cornwallis to Clinton, 26 May 1781

War is a crucial business and the fate of the day after every possible precaution depends upon the most trifling incident.

Nathanael Greene, 2 May 1781[1]

Thanks to Cornwallis' surrender at Yorktown, 1781 witnessed the last real campaign of the war in America. Until then the war had not been as disastrous as had been feared and anticipated by some British participants and observers. Despite the anxieties expressed in 1778, French entry did not oblige the British to abandon New York, nor had it led to another attack on Canada nor to the permanent postponing of operations in the south. Similarly, the British position did not collapse outside America. She weathered the threat posed by Spanish entry on the side of France in 1779 and the Bourbon attempt to invade southern England that year had failed, due to poor leadership, disease and inadequate supplies, rather than the British navy. The fears aroused by the attempted invasion help to explain hesitation about weakening home defences for the sake of America. By the beginning of 1781 Britain had lost few possessions outside North America. She still retained Gibraltar, Minorca and most of her Caribbean colonies. Isolated in Europe by the Armed Neutrality, an alliance of Denmark, Sweden and Russia organized in 1780 by Catherine the Great to oppose the British claim to search neutral shipping, Britain had added the Dutch to her enemies in 1780. Rising tension over the British claim to search Dutch shipping led the British government to order hostilities on 20 December 1780. This added to the list of Britain's naval and colonial enemies. Nevertheless, thanks to her well-established system of public credit, which was far better than that of France, Britain was able to finance massive expenditure on the war substantially by borrowing. In 1780 military expenditure rose to £12.2 million, in 1783 to £13.7 million. The national debt rose from £131 million in 1775 to £245 million in 1783. This enabled the British to increase their naval strength faster than their opponents, so that by 1782 British maritime superiority was established.[2] In addition, Lord North's government won the general election of 1780, in part thanks to the reaction against scenes of anarchy in London and elsewhere during the anti-Catholic Gordon Riots. At that point also the war seemed to be going well, Charleston having fallen. The election results meant that a negotiated end of the war was unlikely unless the military situation altered greatly, and this was appreciated by Americans.[3]

In America there were hopeful auguries for the British, with the conspicuous exception of West Florida. Despite the vigorous efforts of the British governor, Peter Chester, Bernardo de Galvez, the Spanish governor of Louisiana, captured the British forts at Manchac, Natchez and Baton Rouge in September 1779 and Mobile in March 1780. In May 1781 Pensacola fell to a far larger Spanish force. The defeated British commander attributed the defeat 'to the notorious omission or neglect, in affording Pensacola a sufficient naval protection and aid', a warning about the danger to the British position elsewhere. The Spanish navy had grown considerably in strength since 1763 and the Spaniards exploited their naval strength in the Gulf of Mexico, moving troops from their base at Havana and employing amphibious operations.[4] The war in West Florida was largely distinct from that on the eastern seaboard, however, and Spanish success owed something to its minor place in British priorities. Whereas real and supposed threats to Jamaica, the largest British island in the Caribbean, could move British commanders to take major steps, there was no such response in the case of Pensacola which was regarded as too distant or insignificant.

At the beginning of 1781 British control in inland South Carolina and Georgia was obviously limited, but Gates' defeat at Camden suggested that the Americans would not be able to operate successfully in army size, as opposed to partisan groups, unless Cornwallis left the region. He had been able to advance unchallenged to Charlotte. The Chesapeake was clearly open to British

The taking of Pensacola, Florida, 9 May 1781

amphibious attack, while a British amphibious expedition from Charleston took Wilmington, North Carolina without resistance on 28 January 1781. Washington's hopes of an advance on New York City continued fruitless. As yet little lasting benefit had been obtained from French military intervention. At the same time, the American army was poorly supplied, still affected by recruitment problems, and in the winter of 1780–1 its morale was very poor. The correspondence of delegates to Congress continued to be full of the crippling financial problems that the new state faced. Clinton had been thwarted, not defeated. It was therefore reasonable for British generals to hope that they would make some progress in the campaign of 1781, although the expectation that something could and should be achieved was in large part responsible for the disaster that was to ensue.

Given the weak state of the armies of Greene and Washington and French concern with the West Indies, it is probable that Clinton and Cornwallis could essentially have preserved their positions and waited on the defensive while Britain pursued her maritime war outside America. This would not have brought victory, but might have resulted in negotiations with the Bourbons and the consequent collapse of the anti-British coalition. The principal political problem with this strategy was that the cost of the conflict led to domestic political pressure in Britain for its end, while going onto the defensive in America would have led to the collapse of the southern strategy. Without necessarily arguing that the pacification of South Carolina required the subjugation of North Carolina and this in turn the conquest of Virginia, it seems likely that had Cornwallis remained on the defensive, his position in South Carolina would have worsened. He would have had to concentrate his forces, as Greene built up his army, to repel an attack from North Carolina and yet that would have exposed the Loyalists and isolated British posts to partisan attack.

By, moving north, however, Cornwallis exposed the British force in South Carolina under Lord Rawdon to Greene's advance and did so without being clear what his move to the Chesapeake was supposed to achieve. In the printed controversy between Clinton and Cornwallis that followed British defeat, Cornwallis explained his advance into North Carolina by reference to the need to defend South Carolina and blamed his failure to consolidate his position there on the lack of Loyalist support. He began with a characteristic stress on the need for action:

> I was principally induced to decide in favour of its expediency from a clear conviction, that the men and treasures of Britain would be lavished in vain upon the American war, without the most active exertions of the troops allotted for that service; and that, while the enemy could draw their supplies from North Carolina and Virginia, the defence of the frontier of South Carolina, even against an inferior army, would be from its extent, the nature of the climate, and the disposition of the inhabitants, utterly impracticable. The many untoward circumstances, which accrued during the four months succeeding the complete victory of Camden, had entirely confirmed me in this opinion. Our hopes of success, in offensive operations, were not founded only upon the efforts of the corps under my immediate command, which did not much exceed three thousand men; but principally, upon the most positive assurances, given by apparently credible deputies and emissaries, that, upon the appearance of a British army in North Carolina, a great body of the inhabitants were ready to join and cooperate with it, in endeavouring to restore his Majesty's government . . . The unexpected failure of our friends rendered the victory of Guilford of little value. I know that it has been asserted or insinuated that they were not sufficiently tried upon this occasion : But can any dispassionate person believe, that I did not give every encouragement to people of all descriptions to join and assist us, when my own reputation, the safety of the army and the interests of my country were deeply concerned . . . the accounts of our emissaries had greatly exaggerated the number of those who professed friendship for us.[5]

Cornwallis indeed had operated in difficult circumstances in North Carolina, especially in so far as supplies were concerned. He wrote of the Carolinas in June 1781, 'the want of navigation rendering it impossible to maintain a sufficient army in either of those provinces, at a considerable distance from the coast'.[6] However, his criticism of the Loyalists was unreasonable. Cornwallis' brief appearances in North Carolina did not offer the Loyalists, who had been harried and intimidated since 1775, any real guarantee of support. It is understandable that so few acted or had time to act.

It is easy to stress Cornwallis' mistakes, but he alone was not responsible for the British disaster and he was aware of the dangers of a post on the Chesapeake, asking Clinton on 30 June:

> . . . whether it is worth while to hold a sickly defensive post in this Bay, which will always be exposed to a sudden French attack and which experience has now shown, makes no diversion in favour of the Southern Army.[7]

Clinton conversely supported the idea of a base there and was less concerned about its vulnerability than about the apparent threat to New York. He assured Cornwallis on 15 July that he did not think there was any chance of the French 'having a naval superiority in these seas for any length of time, much less for so long a one as two or three months'.[8]

Clinton was to be proved wrong. His moves since 1778 revealed his awareness of the crucial role of naval power, but in 1781 he miscalculated the likely strength of French naval forces in American waters. Had this mistake not been made then possibly Cornwallis would have been pressed hard to leave the Chesapeake and cooperate with all his army in Clinton's projected invasion of Pennsylvania, but, had the French not had Cornwallis as their target then they might have been willing to fulfil Washington's long-held plans for an attack on New York. On the other hand, New York was a tougher proposition than Yorktown, more akin to Boston, which Washington had not dared attack in 1775–6. Thus in 1781 the British army proved to be the victim of a naval strategy that could not ensure a close blockade of French ports. De Grasse was able to leave Brest for Martinique with twenty ships of the line in March 1781, just as d'Estaing had been able to leave the Mediterranean in 1778. In August 1781 de Grasse and 3,000 troops sailed from Saint Domingue (Haiti) for the Chesapeake, intent upon staying there until 13 October. It was this fleet that was to give the French superiority in American waters. Without it there would have been no capitulation at Yorktown. Cornwallis probably would have been obliged to withdraw, but in circumstances possibly similar to those of Clinton's withdrawal from New Jersey at the end of his retreat from Philadelphia in 1778, although, unlike Clinton in 1778, Cornwallis had no nearby strongly-held base into which he could retreat.

Thomas Jefferson, a print from the original by R. Peales c. 1800

THE CHESAPEAKE: EARLY 1781

At the outset of 1781 Washington was in no position to challenge Clinton. The French were so worried by the mutinies in his army that de Grasse was given the option of evacuating the French forces at Newport if the situation continued to deteriorate. The mutinies gave Clinton renewed confidence,[9] and he was also encouraged by the success of Benedict Arnold's expedition to the Chesapeake. Arnold had left Sandy Hook on 20 December 1780, been characteristically disrupted by a winter storm and had reached Hampton Roads on 30 December. Moving up the James river, he landed at Westover on 4 January, the British entering Richmond on the 5th. Having destroyed much of the town and nearby American supply bases, they left the Virginia capital on the 6th, retiring, largely unopposed, to Portsmouth, where they established a base. The vulnerability of Virginia to British amphibious attack had been demonstrated amply. On the 6th Steuben informed Thomas Jefferson, the Governor of Virginia, that he had 'not heard of a single gun being fired at them either on their march from Westover or during their stay at Richmond',[10] and the American war-effort in Virginia in early 1781 was to fall short of expectations. Arnold, however, felt that he required reinforcements if he was to hold Portsmouth against a likely attack.

The threat posed by the French navy was to be shown in January and March. Arnold was challenged at Portsmouth first by three French warships who escaped the British blockade of Newport in January; and then, more seriously, two months later when the entire French squadron in Newport sailed. They were able to sail because the British blockading squadron had been badly damaged by a storm but, fortunately for the British at Portsmouth, the French were engaged by Arbuthnot off the Virginia Capes on 16 March. Arbuthnot was outmanoeuvred and several of his ships badly battered, but the French did not press their advantage to gain control of the Chesapeake.

The Chesapeake was thus becoming the focus of the war in the middle colonies, though this seemed to be as much due to unrelated and unexpected actions and reactions as to definite plans. The strategy that was to lead to Yorktown was already clear, though it was to be a remarkable combination of luck and planning that brought two French fleets, a French army and Lafayette's Virginia force together at Yorktown in September and October 1781. In February Washington decided to reinforce American units in the area in order to take advantage of the sailing of the French Newport fleet. He sent 1,200 men under the Marquis de Lafayette to cooperate with the French squadron, which was itself carrying troops, and the local militia. Washington was well aware of the crucial role of naval power, instructing Lafayette on 20 February that if the French fleet was unable to cooperate 'you will return with the detachment under your command, as the enemy cannot be effected by it while they have the command of the water'. Delayed by heavy rain and bad roads, Lafayette reached the Chesapeake in early March, only to find first that the French squadron had not arrived and later that the British fleet still dominated the bay after the battle of the Virginia Capes, 'a circumstance which destroys every prospect of an operation against Arnold'.[11] Later in the month Arnold was reinforced by over 2,000 troops under Major-General William Phillips, who assumed command of the entire force. Clinton had been able to send them only because naval control of the Chesapeake had been assured. Thus, the campaign in March underlined a number of strategic lessons that were to be demonstrated again that autumn when Cornwallis surrendered at Yorktown. The vulnerability of a British position in the Chesapeake had been indicated, but so also had been the possibility of saving it and rendering a build up of opposing forces on land abortive if only naval superiority could be maintained or regained.

COWPENS AND GUILFORD COURT HOUSE

In the meantime Cornwallis was finding the pacification of the south an increasingly intractable task. Greene arrived in Charlotte in early December 1780. Having hanged a few deserters, he succeeded in bringing some order to his army. As food and forage were in very short supply, Greene sent Morgan and about 700 men (experienced Continentals, Continental cavalry under Colonel William Washington and some Maryland and Virginia militia) westward. They were to seek food and to threaten Augusta. Greene then sent Henry Lee's well-trained, veteran Legion (300 mixed cavalry and infantry) to coordinate activities and guerrilla attacks on the British on the South Carolina coast with Francis Marion. Greene moved the remainder of his army to Cheraw on the Pee Dee.

General Daniel Morgan

Without firing a shot, Greene had stolen the initiative from Cornwallis. If Cornwallis moved after Morgan, Greene could join Marion and Lee and threaten Camden or even Charleston. If Cornwallis moved after Marion and Lee, Greene could help Morgan and threaten Augusta. If Cornwallis moved against Greene, Morgan and Lee could rapidly march to join the retiring Greene who could then retreat, as Washington had in New Jersey in December 1776, all the while seeking an opportunity to attack Cornwallis, who would be advancing deep into the hinterland, far from his lines of communication and away from the protective guns of prepared and defensive positions and the Royal Navy. South Carolina irregulars were already snapping up messengers and foraging parties in Cornwallis' rear. Greene thus demonstrated a real strategic grasp at the operational level. Cornwallis took the bait.

The danger for the British of operating in detachments in order to catch the mobile bands of Americans, already shown at King's Mountain, was illustrated again at Cowpens on 17 January. At the start of January Cornwallis sent Tarleton to attack the American force under Morgan, which threatened the western flank of any advance into North Carolina. Morgan retreated before turning to fight in a defensive position at Hannah's Cowpens. Determined to defeat Morgan and concerned about the possibility that his opponent would receive militia reinforcements, Tarleton decided to attack, hoping to surprise Morgan or force him to fight before properly deploying his force. Tarleton was a raider, not a field officer, or, rather, he was a typical cavalryman. He pushed his men hard; they arrived at the open field at Cowpens exhausted, but Tarleton barely formed them up before sending them crashing into Morgan's force.

Morgan drew up his men in three lines: a skirmishing line of sharpshooters, a second line of South Carolina militia and a third of Continentals and Virginia militia, with the cavalry in reserve. Aware of the propensity of the militia to break under attack, Morgan ordered the South Carolina force to fire three volleys and then withdraw to the left. Tarleton's advance, affected by the sharpshooters, was encouraged by the withdrawal of the second line in the face of British bayonet charges, but fell victim to the Continentals and to the cavalry. An American stratagem, a feigned retreat by the Continentals, led the pursuing British infantry to break formation and they fell victim when the Americans faced-about, fired and charged. The British infantry fled, throwing the cavalry into confusion. Tarleton's attempt to rally his troops was largely unsuccessful, and those who did rally were forced to flee after a sharp but brief struggle. The British losses were 110 dead and 702 taken prisoner, 200 of whom were wounded, out of about 1,150 men. This compares with 12 American dead and 60 wounded. A Loyalist participant recorded:

... we suffered a total defeat by some dreadful bad management. The Americans were posted behind a rivulet with riflemen as a front line and cavalry in the rear so as to make a third line; Colonel Tarleton charged at the head of his regiment of cavalry called the British Legion which was filled up from the prisoners taken at the battle of Camden. The cavalry supported by a detachment of the 71st Regiment under Major McArthur broke the riflemen without difficulty, but the prisoners on seeing their own regiment opposed to them in the rear would not proceed against it and broke: The remainder charged but were repulsed. This gave time to the front line to rally and form in the rear of their cavalry which immediately charged

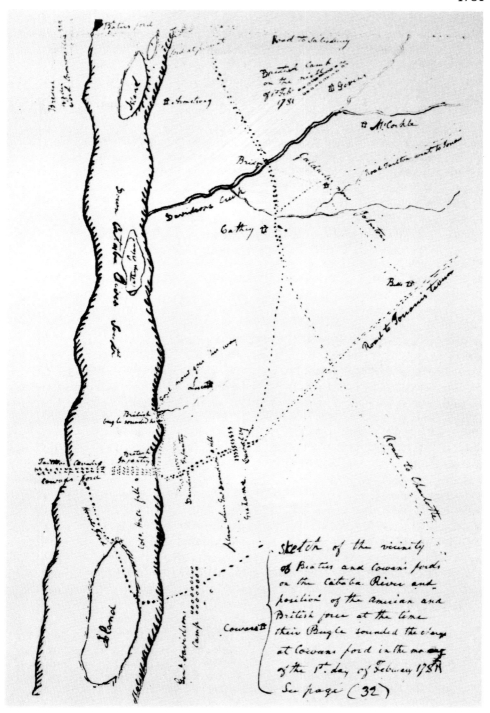

Sketch map of the vicinity of Cowan's Ford, by General Joseph Graham, 1 February 1781

and broke the 71st (then unsupported) making many prisoners: the rout was almost total. I was with Tarleton in the charge who behaved bravely but imprudently. The consequence was his force was dispersed in all directions. The guns and many prisoners fell into the hands of the Americans.

Cornwallis was more generous though less accurate, writing that April that Tarleton:

> . . . was once unfortunate, but by no fault of his. He never showed more ability than in the manoeuvres, which compelled General Morgan to fight him, and his disposition was unexceptionable. The fate of that unfortunate day was one of the events to which war has been ever liable.

However, the British had lost a crucial mobile force of light troops that was essential in their operations in the south.[13] Cornwallis, depressed by the news, reacted by setting off in pursuit of Morgan, but was delayed by inaccurate information about Morgan's movements, his own baggage and guns and by the effects of rain on the roads. He therefore decided on 21 January to burn most of the baggage, and at Ramsour's Mill the army was shod in repaired shoes, a crucial preliminary to the gruelling march across North Carolina. Greene meanwhile had decided to reunite his force with that of Morgan, in order to be able to respond to Cornwallis' moves more successfully. Henry Lee's veterans also quit the coast and rejoined Greene, Lee's infantry riding double with the cavalry.

A successful British feint led to the crossing of the brimming Catawba at Cowan's Ford on 1 February, the American defending force of North Carolina militia under General William Davidson being pushed back, although Cornwallis had his horse shot from under him.[14] Davidson was killed. The Americans retreated towards the Yadkin, Cornwallis reaching it at Trading Ford on 4 February, only to find that the Americans had crossed it by boat and that it was in flood. Eventually crossing the river at Shallow Ford, Cornwallis resumed the pursuit, determined to cut off Greene and Morgan, whose forces had been reunited, before they could cross the Dan (or Roanoke) and reach the supplies and reinforcements of Virginia, the Race to the Dan. Greene's army was too weak to enable him to face Cornwallis with enthusiasm. On 30 January he had written to Sumter:

> The question is what is to be done with Lord Cornwallis : He seems to be pushing into the country with great confidence. Methinks if the militia could be generally brought out in aid of the Continental Army he might be ruined . . .

but on 9 February he wrote:

> The enemy are penetrating this country with great rapidity, nor do I see anything to stop their progress. There are few or no militia with us, nor are there many in the enemies rear . . . If I should risk a general action in our present situation, we stand ten chances to one of getting defeated, and if defeated all the southern states must fall. I shall avoid it if possible, but I am afraid it will be out of my power. Our force is so small and in such distress that I have little to hope and everything to fear. The Tories [Loyalists] in this quarter are collecting very fast.[15]

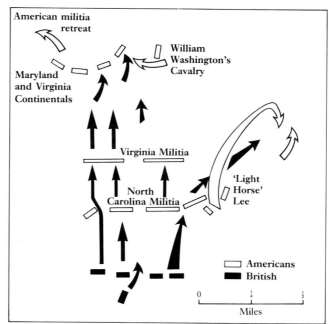

American militia
retreat

William
Washington's
Cavalry

Maryland
and Virginia
Continentals

Virginia Militia

North
Carolina Militia

'Light
Horse'
Lee

□ Americans
■ British

0 ¼ ½
Miles

Guilford Court House

However, Greene's army won the race, in part by misleading the British about their likely crossing place. The Americans crossed the Dan by boat on 13 February. They had left North Carolina, but Cornwallis did not pursue them. Both sides were totally spent. Greene has been criticized by some American historians for not burning his baggage as Cornwallis had done. For Greene, however, his pitiful stores and what passed as baggage were all that separated his army from a total lack of supplies. The rivers in this area ran west–east, and were rocky and unnavigable for long stretches. Greene depended upon inadequate local forage and supplies, supplemented by what could be brought by waggon.

Cornwallis felt it necessary to turn south in order to supply his tired and hungry men and to elicit Loyalist support. On 22 February Cornwallis erected the royal standard in Hillsborough, then capital of North Carolina, and called on the people to take up arms in the royal cause. The response was poor, and one of the few Loyalist forces, led by Colonel John Pyle, was slaughtered by 'Light-Horse' Lee in 'Pyle's Massacre' or 'Hacking Party'. Lee's men, dressed as if from Tarleton's Legion, totally surprised the Loyalists. Loyalist morale fell further when Greene recrossed the Dan on 23 February and Cornwallis left Hillsborough on 25 February. Greene's army was reinforced in early March, and he avoided the battle Cornwallis sought until the middle of the month, by which time the American force was twice as large and the enlistments of many of the militia were due to expire. Greene waited until he could face Cornwallis on a field of his own choosing.

The battle was fought on 15 March near Guilford Court House. Green had 4,400 men, drawn up in three lines, the formation employed at Cowpens, a defence in depth. There was, however, one glaring difference: no Daniel Morgan to inspire the militia. He had left the army due to poor health. In addition, Greene placed his men too far apart. At Cowpens Morgan kept his lines 150 yards apart to allow for the militia to fall back in an orderly fashion when pressed. Greene placed them 400 yards apart. In the first line were Greene's weakest troops, 1,000 North Carolina militia, although they were supported on their flanks by Virginia riflemen, Delaware Continentals, and cavalry, both William Washington's force of about 800 and Lee's Legion. In the second line, a quarter-mile further back, were the Virginia militia; in the third about 1,400 Virginia and Maryland Continentals, but there was no reserve and the lines were not within supporting distance of each other. While some among the Continentals were many of the best and most seasoned troops in the American army, Greene also had numerous newcomers who were Continentals in name only. The defensive position was a good one, while Cornwallis suffered from a lack of information about American dispositions.

The militia in the first line brought down many of their attackers with two volleys, but most fled the British bayonet charge, as expected. The engagement with the second line was more confused, not least because the left of the American front line still resisted, while the British in the woods suffered from American rifle fire. Cornwallis had another horse shot from under him. The Virginians fired, then retreated: in panic on the right and stubbornly and in good order on the left. They were slowly pushed back. The Continentals in the third line repelled the advancing British, taking the Guards in rear and flank. To block their attack Cornwallis ordered two cannon to fire grapeshot into the mêlée, which led both sides to disengage with casualties. As the British reformed and resumed the attack, Greene retreated. Cornwallis was unable to pursue because his men were exhausted and his light troops had been lost at Cowpens. Greene's official casualty figures were 263 killed and wounded, although Cornwallis estimated them to be far higher. Over one-quarter of the earl's force, 532 men, were dead, wounded or missing. After the heavy casualties at King's Mountain and Cowpens, and the death-toll during his punishing, yet unsuccessful, pursuit of Greene, Cornwallis could not afford his losses at Guilford.

Cornwallis had won the field of battle, but that was all: Guilford Court House was no second Camden. The Americans had fought well, and not all the militia had justified Greene's earlier strictures on their value. There had been no final engagement between the Continentals and the reformed British line, but it was clear that American regulars had conquered their fear of the bayonet and that, well-led in defensive positions, they were formidable soldiers. Yet it is also reasonable to note the bravery, discipline and determination of the British soldiers and officers who had faced the successive challenges posed by the American position. Greene was impressed by the discipline of the British. Had their force been equal in size to that of the Americans, they would probably have won a major victory, although, arguably, separating militia from Continentals left Greene with far fewer troops of value than Cornwallis. British generals had to win with smaller armies and in 1781 a convincing victory in the south eluded Cornwallis.

NORTH TO VIRGINIA

The British army was in a weak position after Guilford Court House. Without food and with many wounded to care for, they remained on the battlefield until 18 March, when they marched towards Cross Creek at the head of the Cape Fear river, leaving those who were badly wounded to become Greene's prisoners. Cornwallis, now with only 1,360 effectives, hoped both to obtain supplies in a settlement reputedly inhabited by Loyalist Scots and to prevent an American attack on his army. He issued a proclamation on 18 March calling on rebels to surrender and Loyalists to act, but the latter were demoralized by the obvious British inability to protect them. Cross Creek was also a disappointment, the locals not offering support, while the river proved unnavigable. As a result, Cornwallis set off for British-held Wilmington, North Carolina, devastating the countryside as he retreated.

He arrived there on 9 April. Greene, meanwhile, had decided to advance into South Carolina. He informed Sumter on 30 March that Cornwallis had left the battlefield:

> ... with such precipitation as to leave their dead unburied ... The greater part of our militia's term of service being out will prevent our farther pursuit; especially as the difficulty is very great in procuring provisions. Indeed it would be impossible to subsist the army in the pine barrens ... nor can we fight them upon equal terms after our militia leave us. All these considerations have determined me to change my route, and push directly into South Carolina. This will oblige the enemy to give up their prospects in this state, or their posts in South Carolina, and if our army can be subsisted there we can fight them upon as good terms with your aid as we can here ... I am in hopes by sending forward our horse and some small detachments of light infantry to join your militia, you will be able to possess yourself of all their little outposts before the army arrives. Take measures to collect all the provisions you can : for on this our whole operations will depend.

Greene wrote again on 7 April:

> If we can get provisions and you can raise a considerable force to cooperate with us, I think we shall perplex the enemy not a little, and perhaps do them an irreparable injury. The enemy might give up their posts or leave North Carolina to come and support them – in either case we shall reap an advantage and this is the only manoeuvre that promises any.[16]

Cornwallis faced a choice: either moving south to help Rawdon hold South Carolina or marching to the Chesapeake in order both to seek the decisive battle in Virginia and to cover the Carolinas.[17] He preferred the latter option. South Carolina had been tried and found wanting as a field of operations: the Loyalists disappointing because of poor handling, lack of support and too many broken British promises and defeats, provisions lacking, the rivers difficult to cross. Cornwallis' correspondence and his move to Virginia, leaving the Carolinas unpacified and Georgia threatened, suggest that he was a beaten man. On 24 April Cornwallis wrote to Phillips:

> My situation here is very distressing. Greene took the advantage of my being obliged to come to this place and has marched to South Carolina; My expresses to Lord Rawdon on my leaving Cross Creek warning him of the possibilities of such a movement, have all failed;

mountaineers and militia have poured into the back part of that province, and I much fear that Lord Rawdon's posts will be so distant from each other and his troops so scattered as to put him into the greatest danger of being beat in detail, and that the worst of consequences may happen to most of the troops out of Charleston. By a direct move towards Camden, I cannot get time enough to relieve Lord Rawdon, and should he have fallen, my army would be exposed to the utmost danger from the great rivers I should have to pass; the exhausted state of the country, the numerous militia, the almost universal spirit of revolt which prevails in South Carolina, and the strength of Greene's army, whose Continentals alone are at least as numerous as I am.

His estimation of American strength suggests that Cornwallis saw enemies where there were none. Justifying his decision in July, Cornwallis claimed that, '. . . from Wilmington to the Waggamaw is a perfect desert; and indeed in all that low country it is impossible to subsist in the summer for want of water to turn the mills.'

Cornwallis therefore, decided to move towards Hillsborough, in the hope that this would lead Greene to return north. He would then cross the Roanoke on the lowest ford 'because in a hostile country, ferries cannot be depended upon'.[18] Cornwallis was still willing to return to South Carolina if Greene defeated Rawdon and on 24 April he ordered Lieutenant-Colonel Nesbitt Balfour, commander at Charleston, to send transports accordingly. The following day he left Wilmington with 1,435 rank and file, leaving the sick and wounded behind, but the march north was not easy. On 3 May Cornwallis informed Balfour:

The difficulties I allude to are principally the troops becoming sickly and many of the mills being useless by the dryness of the season, which prevents my keeping up my stock of provisions, so as to enable me to return, if necessary, from any point of the march to Wilmington. Dispatch transports and provisions. Perhaps it will be proper for you to lay an embargo on provisions, to turn out of town all parole men and disaffected people, with their friends and many Negroes, and to shut your gates against many of the poor country people and all Negroes that your stock of provisions may hold out . . .[19]

A necessary step, but one that was unlikely to make the British more popular. At Halifax on 12 May Cornwallis heard that Greene had been defeated at Hobkirk's Hill, and he therefore decided to march north. The following day he crossed the Roanoke. Cornwallis reached Petersburg on 20 May. Within five months he was to have his decisive encounter.

THE WAR IN THE SOUTH

The conflict in the Carolinas in the summer of 1781 was not to decide the fate of the war, but it was nevertheless of considerable importance. It helped to underline the extent to which the pacification strategy had failed and Loyalist support had been a disappointment, and highlighted the confusion about British strategy. In the absence of Cornwallis' force, Greene was able to move south. He aimed to drive the British from the outposts in order to undermine the pacification plan. As earlier with Gates, Camden was Greene's goal, and he was hopeful that it would deliver control of Piedmont, South Carolina. In mid-April he wrote to Sumter:

> . . . our force when collected is very small; and therefore you should not lose sight of a junction should Lord Cornwallis move this way. If he should not, and the garrison at Camden is not well supplied with provision, it must fall in a few days. I have little hopes of the garrisons falling in any other way, as we have no battering cannon, and too few troops to warrant a storm . . . If the Virginia militia come up I think we shall fight the enemy to great advantage; but if not we shall be weak . . . although I am a great enemy to plundering, yet I think the horses belonging to the inhabitants within the enemy's lines should be taken from them; especially such as are either fit for the wagon or dragoon service. If we are superior in cavalry, and can prevent the enemy from equipping a number of teams it will be almost impossible for them to hold their posts and utterly impossible to pursue us, if we should find a retreat necessary.

On 19 April Greene's army of 1,500 took up position on Hobkirk's Hill near Camden, but he was both short of supplies and found Camden stronger than he had anticipated. He realized that his army was too small to allow a siege and that it would be exposed to attack, which he hoped would provide an opportunity for defeating the British. Rawdon had only 900 men in Camden and on 25 April he advanced on Greene's camp hoping to surprise it. The American pickets gave warning and Greene sought to outflank Rawdon. However, the First Maryland regiment had to regroup, as the result of the breaking under fire of part of the regiment. The American advance having faltered, their troops were driven from the field by the British. Greene wrote on 5 May:

> Nothing could be more unfortunate than our repulse the other day, which was entirely owing to an order . . . ordering the First Maryland Regiment to take a new position in the rear. This impressed the regiment with an idea of a retreat, and drew off the Second Regiment with it. The enemy were all in confusion and retiring at the same time. Victory was ours if the troops had stood their ground one minutes longer.

In fact, the Americans were pursued from the field, and only narrowly saved their artillery. Greene was determined that this check should not alter his plans. While he sought more food, arms, ammunition and horses, the outnumbered Rawdon, far from giving battle again, decided to retire from Camden, which was abandoned on 10 May. Thus, tactically Rawdon had won the battle of Hobkirk's Hill, for which he was greatly praised by Cornwallis, but strategically it was a British failure. Rawdon fell back on Charleston, while other British posts were captured, Orangeburg falling to Sumter on 10 May, Fort Motte to Lee and Marion on 11 May and Augusta to Pickens on 5 June. The Loyalist Chesney recorded 'there were daily skirmishes at this period, the Americans constantly contracting our posts in every direction'.

Greene settled down to besiege Fort Ninety-Six, the principal British post left in the interior, which was 96 miles from the North Carolina border. He hoped that he would be able to besiege Charleston if a French fleet arrived. Instead of that, Rawdon received three regiments from Britain with which he was able to relieve Ninety-Six, Greene finding that the militia were unable to prevent Rawdon's advance. Quite a number of the British troops fell out and died on the

Battle of Eutaw Springs, North Carolina, 8 September 1781

forced march to Ninety-Six, showing the problems faced by unacclimatized troops in the steaming South Carolina summer. Greene remained determined to drive the British 'into the lower country'. He believed correctly that if he kept his force united the British would not dare make the detachments necessary for the establishing of fresh positions. Rawdon's pursuit of Greene in the summer heat after the relief of Ninety-Six was unsuccessful and he abandoned the fortress.

The British retired to coastal Carolina, while Rawdon, his health broken by the campaign, left for Britain, only to be captured at sea by the French. On 8 September Greene, with about 2,200 men, attacked the same number of British, under Lieutenant-Colonel Alexander Stewart, in their camp at Eutaw Springs, on the south bank of the Santee river 30 miles north-west of Charleston. The Americans were again drawn up in three lines and although the militia in the first gave way before a British bayonet charge they fought better than their counterparts at Guilford. The North Carolina Continentals sent forward from the second line to fill the gap were similarly broken but the British were beaten back by their Maryland and Virginia counterparts using the bayonet. However, the pursuit collapsed in disorder as the hungry Americans looted the British camp, especially for food. This threw Greene's advance into disarray, allowed the British to rally and enabled them to drive the Americans back, forcing Greene to retreat. Although the British held the field and suffered fewer casualties, their losses were nevertheless serious and they decided to fall back on Charleston, which, apart from Savannah, was the only major British base left in the south. As the Americans were not strong enough to besiege either port, the war in the south became less volatile, while Greene made strenuous efforts to persuade the Loyalists to abandon their cause. Given Cornwallis' complaints about a lack of Loyalist support, it is interesting to note that on 23 June Greene wrote from near Ninety-Six that Loyalists 'are as thick as the trees and we can neither get provisions or forage without large guards to protect them. They even steal our horses within the limits of our camp'. Ninety-Six was deep in Loyalist country. Many followed Rawdon back to Charleston. In addition, the British garrison in Wilmington helped to sustain active and successful Loyalist resistance in North Carolina during the summer and autumn of 1781. This suggests that Cornwallis' claims that there were few Loyalists in the state were inaccurate, and instead that Clinton was correct to argue that the occupation of secure bases by British garrisons would inspire Loyalist activity.

However, by the summer of 1781 such Loyalist activity was too late. Cornwallis had in effect abandoned North Carolina when he advanced into Virginia. The earl had ordered Major James Craig, the British commander, to evacuate Wilmington when he joined Phillips in the Chesapeake, and too few British troops had been left in the Carolinas to protect the Loyalists.[20] Had Craig sailed for Charleston as instructed there would have been more troops available to help Rawdon's manoeuvres in the interior of South Carolina, but the Loyalists of North Carolina would have been completely abandoned.

Whatever the strength of the Loyalists, the British position over much of the south had collapsed by the time of Yorktown, despite a creditable performance in the two battles, the successful relief of Ninety-Six, and the retention of Wilmington. British manpower was limited and the Loyalists were unable to hold the interior with the limited assistance they were given. As with other wartime strategies, that of pacification was not given sufficient time and not attempted under ideal circumstances, but it had clearly failed prior to Yorktown and this was indeed a prelude to the British defeat. Cornwallis dismissed the strategy on 20 May, the day on which he joined Phillips' force at Petersburg. He wrote to Rawdon:

> The perpetual instances of the weakness and treachery of our friends in South Carolina and the impossibility of getting any military assistance from them, makes the possession of any part of the country of very little use, except in supplying provisions for Charleston. The situation of the province renders it impossible for us to avail ourselves of its rich produce, and a strong garrison in Charleston with a small corps in the country, will prevent the enemy from reaping any advantage from it, unless they keep a considerable body of Continentals in the country for that purpose.[21]

The earl clearly had no time for pacification, as his later actions in India and Ireland were to show. Instead he continued to seek the decisive battle. Pacification could not be combined with the destruction of regular American forces, which could look north for reinforcements and supplies, and, without that, was unsuccessful. Cornwallis' return south would probably have left the British able to retain their inland posts, but, short of a decisive defeat of

Greene's army, these posts and their supply-lines would have remained exposed and pacification would have been limited.

THE YORKTOWN CAMPAIGN

Cornwallis' advance into Virginia obliged the British to reconsider their plans for 1781. Clinton saw the Chesapeake as a diversion and wrote to Cornwallis on 30 April, 'the operations of the summer . . . must in great measure depend upon your Lordship's successes in Carolina, the certainty and numbers of the expected reinforcements from Europe, and likewise of your Lordship's sending back to me', Leslie's corps, adding 'I fear no solid operation can be carried on to the northward of Chesapeak, before those to the southward of it are totally at an end, either from success or the season'.[22] Clinton had sent reinforcements to the Chesapeake, and the British forces there under Phillips and Arnold mounted damaging raids which Lafayette was unable to counter. On 20 April Phillips landed at Williamsburg. Having defeated local militia near Petersburg and forced the Americans to scuttle their armed vessels on the James River, Phillips entered Manchester on 30 April, destroying a large quantity of stores. Phillips, however, fell ill of fever, dying at Petersburg on 13 May.

Lafayette complained about the quality and arms of the Virginia militia, British numerical superiority and the difficulty of obtaining accurate information. However, Clinton did not share Germain's confidence in the value of

Marie Joseph Paul Yves Roch Gilbert du
Motier, Marquis de Lafayette

operations in Virginia. He considered making an attack on the Hudson Highlands, but that depended on 10,000 reinforcements from Britain and the return of troops sent to Cornwallis. Clinton showed more interest in the idea of operating at the northern end of the Chesapeake towards Philadelphia, where he felt that there was likely to be more Loyalist support than in Virginia. However, this plan also depended upon major reinforcements, including detachments that Cornwallis was in no position to provide.[23]

Germain, in contrast, wanted to see Virginia conquered.[24] The British invasion of the state had led to demoralization and chaos among the Americans. Cornwallis, writing to Clinton on 26 May, proposed dislodging Lafayette from Richmond and then to move to Williamsburg 'which is represented as healthy and where some subsistence may be procured and keep myself unengaged from operations which might interfere with your plan for the campaign'. He sought 'a proper harbour and place of arms'.[25] Clinton continued to favour the Pennsylvania option and, if Cornwallis would not support this, wanted him to adopt a defensive position and send a detachment to New York. On 29 May he informed Cornwallis that the force he had sent to the Chesapeake was 'fully sufficient for all operations there', adding that naval control was crucial, 'a circumstance, which I am ever aware of in carrying on operations in the Chesapeake, which is, that they can be no longer secure than whilst we are superior at sea . . . nor have I any reason to suspect we shall not' remain so. Clinton had pressed Arbuthnot to consider this, 'having repeatedly told him, that should the enemy possess it even for 48 hours your Lordship's operations there may be exposed to most imminent danger'. Arbuthnot was more concerned about the situation at Newport, though he promised to guard the Chesapeake.[26]

Clinton was more worried about New York City. Washington and Rochambeau had met at Wethersfield, Connecticut on 21–3 May. There it was decided that Rochambeau's force should unite with Washington's before New York City. Details of the meeting had been gained from intercepted letters and Clinton appreciated the danger that this united army, especially acting in conjunction with a French squadron, posed to New York City. On 8 June he informed Cornwallis of the danger that New York would be besieged and asked him to send the howitzers and artillery men he lacked. The following day Clinton wrote to Germain about his dangerous position, and on 11 June he again pressed Cornwallis to send troops. Assessing his effective force as only 10,931, Clinton argued that he was outnumbered, adding that he recommended:

> . . . to you as soon as you have finished the active operations you may be now engaged in, to take a defensive station in any healthy situation you choose (be it at Williamsburg or Yorktown). And I would wish in that case that after reserving to yourself such troops as you may judge necessary for an ample defensive, and desultory movements by water for the purpose of annoying the enemy's communications, destroying magazines etc . . .

that he should send troops. Clinton added:

> Until the arrival of the expected reinforcements from Europe, it will be impossible for me to judge what future operations may be within my power, under my present circumstances . . . experience ought to convince us that there is no possibility of re-establishing order in any

rebellious province on this continent without the hearty assistance of numerous friends. These are not I think to be found in Virginia, nor dare I positively assert that under our present circumstances they are to be found in great numbers anywhere else; or that their exertions when found will answer our expectations. I believe there is a greater probability of finding them in Pennsylvania than in any except the southern provinces.

He proposed an advance on the American magazines at Philadelphia, which he hoped would 'overset their schemes and break up their public credit', and was encouraged by a belief that the officers of the Pennsylvania Line didn't trust their men. Although Clinton thought there were few Loyalists in Virginia, Jefferson had been very concerned about the position the previous October. Draft riots also scared Jefferson, who was not a particularly effective wartime governor.[27] Yet in May 1781 Cornwallis abandoned his ill-conceived plan for conquering Virginia in large part because of the lack of Loyalist support. Clinton, on the other hand, believed that the Maryland and Pennsylvania Loyalists might be of strategic importance, that the elusive Loyalist counter-revolution might be realized in part. Discussing the situation with Arbuthnot on 17 June 1781 Clinton was more fearful of an attack on New York City than one on Cornwallis; in fact, he failed to consider the prospect of the latter sufficiently seriously. Two days later he wrote to Cornwallis expressing his fear that New York City would be besieged and that when de Grasse:

> ... hears that your Lordship has taken possession of York river before him, I think it most likely he will come to Rhode Island ... I am however under no great apprehensions: as Sir George Rodney seems to have the same suspicions of de Grasse's intention that we have, and will of course follow him hither. For I think our situation cannot become very critical, unless the enemy by having the command of the Sound should possess themselves of Long Island; which can never be the case, whilst we are superior at sea.

Cornwallis was asked to spare 3,000 troops and told that Arbuthnot had agreed that if he failed to intercept the French fleet he would 'take his station between the Nantucket Shoals and Delaware, where his fleet is to cruise for the protection of this harbour and our communications with the Chesapeake'.[28] On 28 June Clinton wrote to Rodney pressing him to send sufficient ships to counter de Grasse's expected arrival.[29] Meanwhile Washington had been informed by Rochambeau that de Grasse would probably arrive about 15 July. Rochambeau suggested to the admiral that he make first for the Chesapeake in order to attack Cornwallis before sailing on for New York. On 10 June Rochambeau's force of 3,000 men, guided by beautiful maps drawn by Lieutenant Berthier, later to be Napoleon's chief of staff, left Newport to join Washington's army, nearly 6,000 strong, which it did at Phillipsburg, New York. Washington planned a joint night attack on the British posts around New York City, but surprise was lost and the British were able to move across the Harlem river to unassailable positions. Although the forces facing him were no larger than his own, Clinton felt under pressure and renewed his requests to Cornwallis to send troops. On 28 June, the threat to New York, having apparently abated, he asked for extra troops in order to attack Philadelphia. On 8 July Clinton suggested that the earl was not faced by substantial forces and on

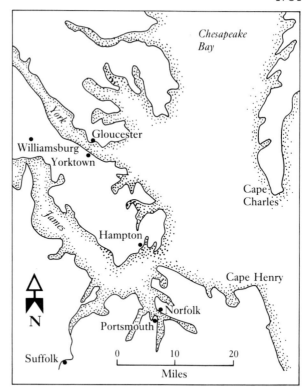

Yorktown

the 11th repeated his demand.[30] Cornwallis, meanwhile, had reconnoitred the positions recommended by Clinton, Williamsburg and Yorktown, and found them wanting. On 30 June he wrote to ask:

> . . . whether it is worth while to hold a sickly defensive post in this bay, which will always be exposed to a sudden French attack and which experience has now shown, makes no diversion in favour of the Southern Army.

He stated that he would attack Lafayette if he had an opportunity and 'attempt water expeditions', but he asked for permission to return to Charleston if Clinton was determined to have a naval base on the Chesapeake.[31] Cornwallis abandoned the Williamsburg peninsula in order to establish himself at Portsmouth from where he planned to send Clinton the troops he requested. On 6 July at Green Spring beside the James River he sprang an ambush on Lafayette's force, but only caught the van under Wayne, which was routed. The engagement demonstrated the risks senior officers ran and the brave leadership that they were expected to display. A bullet took the plume from Wayne's hat, Lafayette had two horses shot from under him and Cornwallis personally led the British charge.[32]

After this success the British launched raids on American stores while Cornwallis prepared to embark his troops for Clinton's Philadelphia expedition.

However, on 20 July he received Clinton's message of 11 July in which he was informed:

> I am just returned from having a conference with Rear Admiral Graves . . . we are both clearly of opinion that it is absolutely necessary we should hold a station in Chesapeak for ships of the line, as well as frigates.[33]

To protect this it was necessary for Cornwallis to retain control of the Williamsburg peninsula, and especially Old Point Comfort, which controlled Hampton Roads. Cornwallis was also instructed not to detach any troops from his force. This letter crossed with one of the 8th from Cornwallis in which he expressed his strong doubts about the value of a base in the Chesapeake, although, characteristically, he was writing of the army, not the navy:

> . . . the utility of a defensive post in this country, which cannot have the smallest influence on the war in Carolina and which only gives us some acres of an unhealthy swamp, and is forever liable to become a prey to a foreign enemy with a temporary superiority at sea: desultory expeditions in the Chesapeake may be undertaken from New York with as much ease and more safety, whenever there is reason to suppose, that our naval force is likely to be superior for two or three months.[34]

There was considerable force in the earl's observations. If the British simply wanted to raid the Chesapeake they could do so from New York, as they had already demonstrated. If a conquest of Virginia was intended then it would obviously be important to have a base on the Chesapeake, but Clinton did not see such a step as a necessary corollary to British security in the south, while Cornwallis was no longer pressing the idea. However, Graves, who officially replaced Arbuthnot on 4 July, did not think that Gardiner's Island at the eastern end of Long Island, from which Newport had been watched, and New York City were suitable winter anchorages. As Newport had been lost, the Chesapeake appeared the only alternative to distant Halifax and Clinton did not want the naval base too far from New York City. He wrote to Cornwallis again on 15 July stressing the value of a Chesapeake base and the vulnerability of his position in New York and stating that he did not think there was any chance of the French 'having a naval superiority in these seas for any length of time, much less for so long a one as two or three months'.[35] The highly-strung Clinton was increasingly frustrated by Cornwallis' reluctance to heed his wishes, and he was also depressed by the general strategic situation, particularly the danger of a Franco-American attack on New York City.

The variety of Clinton's ideas during the summer, with his fluctuating views on the threat to New York City, the desirability of an advance on Philadelphia and the use to be made of Cornwallis' force and of the Chesapeake, was well demonstrated in the second half of July. On the 18th he expressed a healthy scepticism about the possibility of making permanent gains without Loyalist support when he wrote to Germain:

> Though I am strongly impressed with the importance of recovering Virginia, I fear the entire reduction of so populous a province is not to be expected from an operation solely there;

unless our friends in it were more numerous, and were heartily inclined to assist us not only in conquering, but in keeping it.[36]

Six days later Clinton wrote:

As I am of opinion it is of the greatest importance to hold Chesapeak, and that could not be well done by the sickly station of Portsmouth (at least such is Admiral Graves's opinion) I thought it right for the present to give up every other object, and order his Lordship to return to his old station of Williamsburg and York, for if the enemy should possess them, as I am determined to prosecute operations in Chesapeak as soon as the season will admit, I should be concerned to begin with a siege.[37]

Thus the flexibility that had characterized British operations in Virginia was to be lost, the offensive possibilities offered by the Chesapeake to be postponed. Instead Cornwallis was to fortify a base and thus surrender the initiative. This was serious, not only because of the potential vulnerability of his position, but also because the French and Americans were preparing to act. Old Point Comfort was rejected in late July as hard to fortify and offering insufficient protection for ships. Instead, Cornwallis decided upon Yorktown, a defensive position that had little to commend it, being unfortified, low-lying and commanding no ground, although it did have an anchorage suitable for ships of the line. Beginning to fortify the position on 2 August, he wrote twenty days later:

My experience . . . of the fatigue and difficulty of constructing works in this warm season convinces me that all the labour that the troops here will be capable of, without ruining their health, will be required at least for six weeks to put the intended works at this place in a tolerable state of defence.

The earl complained about a lack of heavy artillery and ordnance and engineers stores and about pressure on his provisions.[38] He was not to have the six weeks for, as he reported on 2 September:

Comte de Grasse's fleet is within the Capes of the Chesapeak. Forty boats with troops went up James river yesterday, and four ships lie at the entrance of this river.[39]

Washington had hoped to utilize the French army and fleet, both the ships at Newport under Admiral Comte de Barras and the larger force under de Grasse, in order to attack New York City. Its fall would be a fateful blow to the British military position in North America and might well lead to the effective end of the war, a step the Americans desperately required. The loss of New York would certainly leave the British without a secure anchorage for their fleet south of Halifax, and it was difficult to believe that their position on the Chesapeake would not collapse. The Americans could then turn south to besiege Charleston and Savannah. Thus America could be reconquered from north to south.

However, Washington was sufficiently flexible to appreciate that such an attack might not be possible, but that instead it might be practical to cooperate with the French against Cornwallis. The relatively smooth cooperation between

Washington and Rochambeau in 1781 was to be a major contributory role in their success and contrasted markedly with the tension and shifting of the blame that characterized so much of the British command. The French were keen to cooperate, although their priorities were indicated by the fact that de Grasse did not sail directly to America, but went first to the West Indies where Tobago was forced to surrender on 2 June. In addition, no reinforcements were sent to Rochambeau. Although de Grasse was informed that Washington wanted him to sail for Sandy Hook, Rochambeau and the French envoy, La Luzerne, advised going for the Chesapeake and it was on the basis of this advice that de Grasse decided to do so. Washington learned this on 14 August, and at once took steps to dispatch Rochambeau's force and 2,500 American troops to Virginia. He would have preferred to send them by sea, but de Barras, the commander of the Newport squadron, was unwilling to escort them, a prudent decision given the risk of encountering a British squadron.[40]

It is easy to present the capitulation at Yorktown as somehow inevitable, but the naval situation was very unpredictable. De Barras, who did not relish the idea of serving under de Grasse, had been dissuaded with difficulty from sailing to attack Newfoundland, de Grasse might be recalled or Rodney might defeat or preempt him.[41] Cornwallis might evacuate Yorktown[42] or Clinton might attack the force marching for Virginia. Washington depended in large part on French cooperation and British complacency, but his own skill and determination were also important. On 15 August he instructed Lafayette to prevent Cornwallis from marching south into North Carolina. De Barras was persuaded to convoy the French siege train to the Chesapeake; on 25 August he left Newport on a circuitous course designed to avoid British interception, reaching the Chesapeake on 10 September. The siege guns he brought were scarcely mobile for any distance inland; yet another indication of the importance of river and sea transport and the inability to operate with a sizeable force at any distance from a navigable river or the coast, which was an important dimension of the operational problem for European armies in America.

On 19 August troops from Washington's army destined for Virginia began crossing the Hudson. In order to mislead Clinton, the Americans and French moved until 29 August on a route that would suggest they were heading for Staten Island or Sandy Hook. On 27 August Clinton wrote to Cornwallis that Washington might be moving against either of them, that therefore he couldn't spare Cornwallis many troops, although he would send some in late September, after the effects of the equinox were over, 'for I am persuaded the Admiral will not approve of any water movement till then'.[43] The following morning the British squadron from the West Indies, of ten of the line and four smaller ships, under Admiral Sir Samuel Hood, which had looked into the Chesapeake en route, anchored off Sandy Hook. An indecisive and apparently ailing Rodney had sailed for Britain, escorting prizes back to England.

The British naval response was inadequate, being both insufficient and belated. Graves and Clinton were considering an attack on Rhode Island when Hood arrived. Had they been prepared to do so, they might have been able to assist Cornwallis instead, but Graves' ships were in New York harbour, not over the bar at Sandy Hook, and several of them were unfit for service. Hood persuaded his fellow commanders of the seriousness of the situation, and on 31 August the combined British fleet, under the senior admiral Graves, sailed for the Chesapeake. De Grasse had sailed from Cape François on Saint Domingue with twenty-eight ships of the line on 5 August, anchoring off the Chesapeake on 30 August.[44] Two days later, 3,000 French troops landed near the entrance of the James river. Rochambeau and Washington had not yet arrived: they were not to reach the Williamsburg peninsula until 14 September, much to de Grasse's annoyance.[45] Thus, Cornwallis had an opportunity to try to fight his way out and retreat to North Carolina. It is understandable, however, that he should have hesitated; the opposing force was superior, and hope of naval relief remained strong. In addition, Clinton's letters offered scant warning of Washington's march south. On 30 August Clinton wrote that there was no sign of such a move and instead expressed his concern that Cornwallis was using his troops, rather than Negroes, for fortification work. On 2 September the message was very different, although Clinton again offered reassurance. He reported that Washington was moving south but promised reinforcements or a diversion, adding that Graves had sailed and that Cornwallis would therefore have little to fear from the French fleet.[46]

However, the British navy was not to bring help. Graves was outnumbered, twenty-four to nineteen in ships of the line, and, although the British ships had copper bottoms and were therefore faster, it was subsequently to be argued that the ships Hood had brought were 'in want of everything and almost unfit for service'. Several certainly required repairs. On 5 September Graves, instead of taking the risky course of ordering a general chase on the French van as it sailed in disordered haste from the Chesapeake, manoeuvred so as to bring all his ships opposite to the French line of battle, which was given time to form. The engagement lasted for just over two hours, neither side having any ships sunk, but both suffering considerable damage. De Grasse failed to use his numerical superiority in order to inflict a defeat that might have ended all British hopes of relieving Cornwallis, maybe even threatening their position in New York City and possibly affecting the course of the whole Anglo-French struggle. He both retained his superiority and still blocked the entrance to the Chesapeake, however, and the battle must therefore rank as a British defeat. Graves' fleet was badly damaged and he did not feel able to engage de Grasse again. The alternative course of sailing to the Chesapeake before the French and blocking the entrance, suggested by Hood, appeared too risky. Unaware of the route of de Barras' squadron, he failed to intercept it, a serious failure as it made de Grasse almost unassailable and the chance of a lengthy defence of Yorktown less likely. In the end Graves decided to sail to New York for repairs after which the fleet would be able to challenge de Grasse again, but, instead of doing so on the 6th, the ships did not begin their journey until the 13th, arriving off Sandy Hook on the 20th.[47]

On 6 September Clinton had written to Cornwallis promising naval relief and reinforcements. This led the earl to reply on 16 September:

If I had no hopes of relief I would rather risk an action, than defend my half-finished works, but as you say [Admiral] Digby is hourly expected, and promise every exertion to assist me, I do not think myself justified in putting the fate of the war on so desperate an attempt . . . since the Rhode Island squadron has joined, they have thirty six sail of the line. This place is in no state of defence. If you cannot relieve me very soon you must be prepared to hear the worst . . . [48]

a message that reached Clinton on 23 September. Attacking Lafayette appeared too risky, a move that would exchange a position where he could hold out for a while ('provisions for six weeks'[49] he reported on 8 September), for an engagement with a superior force. Even if Cornwallis was victorious, a retreat into the Carolinas, without provisions and abandoning the wounded, and on which he would probably be harried by the militia, was an unpleasant prospect.

Both sides were working against the clock. Aside from the threat posed by the besiegers, Cornwallis had only limited supplies, while de Grasse planned to leave at the end of October. Clinton had decided to send 4,000 men to reinforce Cornwallis, but he could not do so until de Grasse was defeated. On 24 September a council of war at New York decided that, once refitted, Graves would return to the Chesapeake, carrying over 5,000 troops, and that they would relieve Cornwallis. A message, accordingly dispatched to the earl and reaching him on the 29th, stated that it was hoped to sail on 5 October. Rear-Admiral Robert Digby and three ships of the line reached New York from England on the 24th, but the repairs to Graves' ships took longer than anticipated, Graves informing Clinton on the 30th that he would not be ready to sail until 12 October,[51] whereas two days earlier he had promised 'sooner than the 8th'. Graves was worried about the danger of attacking a superior force, understand-ably so, as the risky plan advocated by Clinton and Hood endangered the largest British naval force in the western hemisphere and the continued viability of the New York garrison. The respective junctures of de Barras' and Digby's squadrons with those of de Grasse and Graves had given the French an even greater superiority than they had had on 5 September.

Rochambeau troops and Washington's army, about 16,000 men in all, took up positions round Yorktown on the night of 28 September and on the 29th. Encouraged by Clinton's promise of relief, Cornwallis abandoned his outer works on the night of the 29th, in order to tighten his position in the face of the more numerous besiegers. Washington's men occupied the outer works on the 30th, though they had to cope with heavy fire from Cornwallis' cannon until, on 6 October, the besiegers' artillery arrived. They were then able to begin conventional siege-works against what was, by the standards of the period, a weakly-fortified position. On the night of the 6th the besiegers began to dig the first parallel, a trench parallel to the fortifications and a crucial part of normal siege-works. They completed it on the 9th and that afternoon they began the bombardment with a larger and heavier artillery force than that of Cornwallis, causing heavy casualties and damage and badly affecting the morale of the defenders. Cornwallis' headquarters was heavily damaged, forcing him to use a cave for staff meetings. On 11 October, as his opponents dug a second and closer parallel, the earl wrote to Clinton, repeating what he had said on the 3rd:

. . . that nothing but a direct move to York River, which includes a successful naval action can

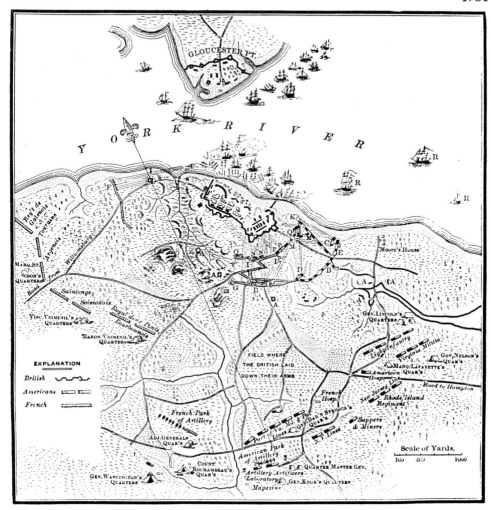

Plan of the siege of Yorktown

save me. The enemy made their first parallel on the night of the 6th at the distance of 600 yards, and have perfected it, and constructed places of arms and batteries, with great regularity and caution. On the evening of the 9th their batteries opened and have since continued firing, without intermission with about 40 pieces of cannon, mostly heavy, and 16 mortars . . . many of our works are considerably damaged; with such works on disadvantageous ground, against so powerful an attack we cannot hope to make a very long resistance.

On the 12th he added a postscript, 'Last night the enemy made their second parallel at the distance of 300 yards. We continue to lose men very fast'.[52]

Many of the earl's cannon had been silenced by the bombardment, while a lot of his troops were wounded or ill. On the night of 14 October the besiegers bravely stormed the two redoubts that obstructed the path of the second parallel to the river. Cornwallis wrote the next day:

> Experience has shown that our fresh earthen works do not resist their powerful artillery . . . The safety of the place is therefore so precarious that I cannot recommend that the fleet and army should run great risk in endeavouring to save us.[53]

This realization should have come sooner. If Clinton had reached the Chesapeake, his arrival might have precipitated a disaster surpassing Yorktown, with the French fleet destroying the British force. Cornwallis can be faulted for failing to appreciate the vulnerability of his position earlier. Clinton had instructed him to take up a position on the Williamsburg peninsula, but Cornwallis had already shown a willingness to disregard his commander's intentions when it suited him. He had been misled by Clinton as to the likelihood of a French force both appearing and remaining in the Chesapeake, but the history of the past few years should have warned Cornwallis that naval operations were unpredictable. Clinton, however, felt it important to try to relieve the earl. He wrote on 15 October to the Duke of Newcastle, a relative and political contact:

> This is not my Dear Lord a move of choice, 'Tis of necessity. If Lord Cornwallis's army falls I shall have little hope of seeing British dominion re-established in America, as our country cannot replace that army. If I succeed in a junction with Lord Cornwallis and there is a possibility of attacking Washington afterwards I shall certainly attempt it.

Clinton, nevertheless, was already preparing the justification that he realized would be necessary in the controversy that would follow the campaign, whether successful or not. He continued, 'I informed the minister that if the enemy should hold a naval superiority for only a few weeks we should in our insular and detached state, run the greatest risks . . .' and he noted that he had been informed that Rodney would be ordered to follow de Grasse. This was to be a theme to which Clinton was to return, on 29 October attributing Cornwallis' capitulation to the lack of a fleet and warning 'such will be the fate of every post we hold if the enemy remain superior at sea', and on 28 December blaming only those who had failed to send a fleet from the West Indies to match that of de Grasse and claiming that the lack of 'naval force to cover our operations' was the sole cause of the disaster.[54]

Had the fleet been repaired as originally scheduled, Clinton would have reached the Chesapeake before Cornwallis capitulated. This did not prove possible. New York did not have a naval dockyard, there was a shortage of naval stores and food and a number of accidents delayed matters. It was not until 17 October that the refitted ships moved to Sandy Hook, till the 18th that 7,149 troops were embarked and till the 19th that Graves' fleet, twenty-five ships of the line and eleven other warships, sailed. That day Clinton wrote to Germain that according to Cornwallis on the 11th:

> . . . the enemy are advancing fast in their approaches; However as all the ships have passed the bar, and we are now under sail with a fair wind, I still flatter myself that notwithstanding

No. V.

York, in Virginia, 18th Oct. 1781.

SIR,

I AGREE to open a treaty of capitulation, upon the bafis of the garrifons of York and Gloucefter, including feamen, being prifoners of war without annexing the condition of their being fent to Europe; but I expect to receive a compenfation in arranging the articles of capitulation for the furrender of York-Town in its prefent ftate of defence. I fhall in particular, defire that the Bonetta floop of war may be left entirely at my difpofal from the hour the capitulation is figned; to receive an aid-de-camp to carry my difpatches to Sir Henry Clinton, and fuch foldiers as I may think proper to fend as paffengers in her, to be manned with 50 men of her own crew, and to be permitted to fail without examination, when my difpatches are ready; engaging on my part, that the fhip fhall be brought back and delivered to you, if fhe efcapes the dangers of the fea; that the crew and foldiers fent as paffengers fhall be accounted for in future exchanges as prifoners; that fhe fhall carry off no officer without your confent, nor public property of any kind: and I fhall likewife defire that the traders and inhabitants may preferve their property, and that no perfon may be punifhed for having joined the Britifh troops.

If you chufe to proceed to negociation on thefe grounds, I fhall appoint two field officers of my army to meet two officers from you, at any time and place that you think proper, to digeft the articles of capitulation.

I have the honour to be, Sir,

Your moft obedient

And moft humble Servant.

CORNWALLIS.

His Excellency Gen. Wafhington, commanding, &c.

[*Here followed the Articles of Capitulation agreed on between the two Commanders.*]

Letter from Cornwallis to Washington concerning the surrender of Yorktown and the Treaty of Capitulation, 18 October 1781. The letter was printed in New York in 1796

the rapidity of the enemy's progress and our having been delayed by the necessary repairs of the fleet so far beyond the expected time, it may yet be in the power of our joint exertions to relieve his Lordship.[55]

That very day Cornwallis surrendered. On the 16th a sortie designed to spike the besiegers' guns had had only a limited and temporary effect. Cornwallis therefore decided to try to cross the York River to the British outpost at Gloucester by night and then to attack the French force blockading that position. The first detachment crossed the river successfully late on the 16th, but 'a most violent storm of wind and rain' prevented the boats from crossing a second time, and by the time the weather improved it was too late to mount an attack and Cornwallis had to recall the first wave. Under a ferocious bombardment that could not be countered, Cornwallis decided to treat and on 17 October, the fourth anniversary of Burgoyne's surrender at Saratoga, he proposed an armistice in order to settle terms for his surrender. Commissioners negotiated on the 18th and Washington offered reasonable terms, although he refused to accept Cornwallis' attempt to protect Loyalists in his force. On the

The surrender of Lord Cornwallis' army at Yorktown, 19 October 1781, engraved for l'Academie Imperiale et Royale de Vienne, 1783

19th the British troops marched out of their ruined positions to the tune of 'The World Turned Upside Down' and grounded arms, some weeping, some swearing.[56]

* * *

Five days later Clinton's expedition picked up three men off the Virginia Capes who brought news of the surrender. The fleet still sailed to the mouth of the Chesapeake, whence the general reported to Germain that the capitulation might have been prevented 'could the fleet have been able to sail at or within a few days of the time we first expected', and complained about Hood's numerical inferiority to de Grasse, writing 'to this alone, is our present misfortune to be imputed'. Clinton was to return to these themes later, writing in 1782 'I was forced by Lord Cornwallis and the minister into solid operations in Chesapeake. I repeatedly represented the danger of it if not covered by a fleet', and telling George III that summer that Germain:

> . . . had most positively and repeatedly promised that covering fleet that Hood on the 25th of August informed me by letter, and on the 28th informed Council that he had brought an adequate fleet, and which had convinced me that Washington would never dare move into

Chesapeak, that it was not till the 26th of September that I had reason to suppose His Majesty's fleet was inferior.

Clinton's complaints were not without force. In December 1780 he had complained about the 14 September order of the Cabinet to dispatch at least five ships of the line to the West Indies when the winter season began, and warned that it would wreck operations in the Chesapeake and expose both the British position in the south and Long Island Sound, and therefore New York City. Clinton was well aware of the importance of naval superiority.

In November 1781 Clinton was, however, also thinking about how best to respond to the disaster. He sent Lieutenant-General Leslie to defend Charleston, although he felt that holding that would also depend on naval power:

> The enemy may perhaps attempt Charleston. It has a good garrison, its works complete, and I hope the last supplies from Europe got in, in which case it can stand a long siege, but this fortress also must finally fall if not timely succoured by a naval superiority.

Clinton also claimed that 'from the position the French fleet took to cover the siege our naval chiefs are of opinion they could have forced them and succoured his Lordship, but the delays of the fleet prevented our arriving in time'.[57] This is questionable as it is unclear what Clinton could have done with his troops had he reached the Chesapeake. A diversionary landing was the best option, since Yorktown was commanded by enemy artillery, but such landings with enemy forces nearby were dangerous.

Yorktown has been seen as the 'logical outcome' of a strategy of scattering troops along the seaboard without adequate naval cover,[58] but that is possibly being wise after the event. Cornwallis' position was terrible, the earl claiming:

> A successful defence in our position was perhaps impossible; for the place could only be reckoned an entrenched camp, subject in most places to enfilade; and the ground in general so disadvantageous, that nothing but the necessity of fortifying it as a post to protect the navy could have induced any person to erect works upon it.[59]

Had a better site been chosen then Cornwallis might have resisted to better effect. The Franco-American strategy was not without its faults, including the dangerous though understandable decision to entrust the siege train to de Barras' squadron, which could have been intercepted by Graves' larger fleet. De Grasse's time in American waters was limited, as d'Estaing's time off Savannah had been. Had de Grasse left with Cornwallis undefeated then the campaign of 1781 might have illustrated two problems, both found very frequently in eighteenth-century warfare: those of combining army and naval operations successfully and of achieving cooperation between allies.

As it was, Yorktown was lost not because the naval dimension was ignored, as a demonstration of its importance was hardly necessary, but because the British got it wrong, for which Rodney must bear much of the blame thanks to his failure to send sufficient ships from the West Indies.

12 Epilogue

A German officer, who has served in America of high rank, has assured the King that if the coast of America, ten miles from the sea was burnt, and reduced to desert, a thing entirely practicable, the war would soon be over.

Morning Herald, 24 August 1782

About one hundred of the first regiment of cavalry mutinied and marched . . . for Virginia taking all the best horses belonging to the corps. They give out they are coming to lay their complaints before the Legislature and to demand their pay . . . If an example is not made to deter soldiers from practices of this sort it will be impossible in future ever to keep an army from mutiny.

Nathanael Greene, 20 May 1783

MILITARY CONCLUSIONS

The British defeat at Yorktown did not necessarily mean the end of the war. They still had substantial forces in America, while the Americans remained dependent upon allies who had their own very different agenda. The immediate aftermath of the surrender did not see the collapse of the British position in America. Washington appreciated that his success at Yorktown was largely due to French assistance, and he hoped to persuade de Grasse to cooperate in a speedy attack on Charleston or, failing that, Wilmington, North Carolina. Such a development had indeed been anticipated by the British. General Cuthbert Ellison wrote on 7 December that Cornwallis' surrender would:

> . . . occasion the loss of all the southern colonies very speedily. From the great superiority of the enemy's force, naval and military, in the West Indies, I apprehend the Leeward Islands, if not Jamaica also, to be in imminent danger.[1]

De Grasse was, however, unwilling to cooperate in an attack on Charleston. As he planned to remain in American waters for little longer there was simply not enough time and a hurried expedition risked a repetition of d'Estaing's failure at Savannah in 1779, especially as Clinton had been able to send reinforcements under Leslie to Charleston. Instead, de Grasse promised to convoy an expedition to Wilmington. Nonetheless, he was delayed in the

Chesapeake by the appearance of Graves and Clinton, and he then decided that there was no time for Wilmington, despite Washington's attempts to persuade him to the contrary. On 4 November 1781 de Grasse sailed directly for the West Indies from the Chesapeake.

It was therefore clear that there would be no major blow before the end of the year. Benjamin Lincoln confirmed Washington's view that an attack on Charleston without naval support was unlikely to succeed. It was well-fortified and had a large and well-supplied garrison. Washington decided to send a force overland under Arthur St Clair to reinforce Greene, while he himself returned north to shadow Clinton in New York. He was hopeful that the French would return the following May, permitting an attack on New York in June 1782.

This plan was to meet with disappointment. The campaign of 1782 indicated how little the Americans could achieve offensively when deprived of naval support and faced by British forces that were unwilling to leave fortified positions. St Clair did not need to attack Wilmington, as the British had evacuated it on 14 November 1781, the garrison, accompanied by about 1,000 Loyalist troops sailing to Charleston in order to avoid attack by a much larger American force. However, Virginia troops came close to mutiny when ordered to march to South Carolina. Nevertheless, if the French fleet had reappeared Washington would have had the choice of attacking New York or convoying troops and heavy artillery for an attack on Charleston. On 16 July 1782 he told Rochambeau that if the French came early, New York should be the target, if late, Charleston, and that if the French offered financial and military support it would be possible to invade Canada. However, on 12 April off the Iles des Saintes south of Guadeloupe the outnumbered de Grasse was soundly defeated by Rodney, who captured five ships of the line and de Grasse. Admiral Vaudreuil with thirteen ships of the line sailed for Boston from Saint Dominigue on 4 July to obtain provisions and repairs. The idea of an attack on New York had been discussed by the French only to be rejected on the grounds that Washington was not ready, while it was decided that it was the wrong season for operations in the south.[2] Whether Washington was judged ready or not, the aftermath of the 'battle of the Saints' was not the moment to plan operations that required naval superiority. The French and Spaniards had abandoned their plan for a joint attack on Jamaica, and they were clearly losing the initiative in the western hemisphere. Just as French naval power had cost Cornwallis his army, so the recovery of the British naval position helped to keep New York for George III for another year.

In the south the British were increasingly hemmed in around Charleston and Savannah, but they were secure in both towns. Strengthened by troops from Washington's army, Greene sent Wayne into Georgia in January 1782 in order to drive the British back to Savannah. Wayne's force was hindered by the expiry of terms of enlistment and had to face widespread Loyalism and Indian activity on the part of the British. He complained to Greene in February:

> The duty we have performed in Georgia was much more difficult than that of the Children of Israel, they had only to make brick without straw, but we had provision, forage and almost every article of war, to provide without money . . . [3]

Wayne's operations were hindered by the systematic British seizure of supplies in the area around Savannah, while he had to try to control Loyalist–Patriot violence in order to win Loyalists to the Revolutionary cause. In spite of this, in early February, Wayne established his headquarters at Ebenezer, about 25 miles from Savannah. Despite the size of the British force in the town, they lost control of the state, while the Loyalist militia crumbled through desertion. Skirmishes continued, but the Americans continued to be too weak to attack Savannah, while the British were aware that they would abandon it soon. Throughout the south guerrilla action continued, becoming even more nasty, as revenge became the primary motive.

Germain had responded to the news of Yorktown, which reached London on 25 November 1781, by producing a plan for fighting on, holding onto existing positions with a force of 28,000 men, mounting amphibious expeditions along the coast, regaining Rhode Island if possible and exploiting Loyalist support in the lower counties of the Delaware. Germain argued that by retaining New York, Charleston and Savannah, British trade would be secured and bases maintained from which winter operations could be mounted in the Caribbean. Combined with action by British troops based in Canada, this was a variation of the plans advanced since French entry into the war, seeking to exploit naval strength and Loyalist sentiment, rather than focussing on the quest for a decisive battle. Militarily the strategy was plausible, more so if Rodney's success at the Saintes could be anticipated. James Robertson, the Governor of New York, wrote thence to Amherst on 27 December, that there were nearly 13,000 men in the garrison and that:

> . . . we can arm four thousand very well disposed militia, this force I should think able to beat any Washington can collect, as he has now only 4,000 French.
> But an army confined to a defensive in posts, is not only useless but ruinous, an army without the hope of getting back America, should not stay in it – A reinforcement at least of 4,000 well conducted might revive the hopes of our friends and turn the tide of opinion, and peoples actions are governed by their belief about what government is to take place – the assistance or resistance we are to meet with depends on this opinion, and that on the measures His Majesty may be pleased to direct – If the war is to be carryed on, even an assurance of this will prevent the growth of the rebel army, which the most sanguine hopes cannot collect – nor bring against this place till the middle of May – an army cannot lie on the ground – or horses find pasture sooner – our succours in place of arriving in August should be here by the first of May.

However, such ideas were no longer politically viable. Willingness to battle on in America was disappearing and in Britain there was increasing pressure for a change of ministry. One MP wrote on 30 November:

> There was a strong opposition to the Address in both houses on the ground of their pledging themselves by it to continue the ruinous American war . . . It seems to be pretty generally allowed that the prosecution of it internally is no longer possible.[4]

The government faced growing pressure from its supporters for a change of policy. On 8 December 1781 the Cabinet decided to send only recruits, not new units, to America. On 23 December they agreed to accept Clinton's desire to

No 1. Movements Relative to the Enemy that Landed at Beaufort on the morning of the 5th April 1782 —

[Apr. 19, 1782]

Wednesday April 3 the Enemy Landed a boat on Hagleford's banks with five men as Friends, they where met as Friends by the whalemen they Inform'd them the privateer belong'd to New England & the Ship & Schooner where prizes which they had taken & wanted to git into the Inlet —

Thursday 4th the Ship & two Schooners appear'd off the Barr haveing onboard two pilots which they had taken onboard from Cape Hatteras — the pilots of this place went off & took Charge of them as Friends & in the Afternoon brought them to Anchor under Bordens Bank's fronting the Town the principal part of the Inhabitants went onboard no Boats Returning occasion'd a Suspicion in Major Dennis who was in Town who sent off Capt Ded[n] Gibble with a Flagg they not returning a Messenger was dispatch'd to me informing of the several Circumstances I Repair'd Immediately to Town & Collected what men their was got the Centry's properly posted at 2 AM was patroleing the Shore heard the Centry's at Taylors Creek hole advance that way discover'd a Number of boats at the mouth to the Creek and the Officer which prov'd to be the Major who Command'd makeing use of every artfull Insinuation to delude our Centry I soon discover'd the deception Order'd our men to fier about 8 in Number on which they pour'd in a very heavey fier from them

Revolutionary correspondance concerning a British landing at Beaufort, South Carolina, 5 April 1782

resign. He was to be replaced by Sir Guy Carleton. George III and Germain were unwilling to abandon America, but political pressure was mounting. The country gentlemen who usually supported the government in the House of Commons were no longer willing to continue supporting the cost of an unsuccessful war. On 7 February 1782 the ministry's majority fell to only twenty-two on a motion of censure. On 22 February an address against continuing the American war was only narrowly blocked and on the 27th the government was defeated on the issue. The motion encapsulated the opposition view on policy towards America:

> . . . that the further prosecution of offensive warfare on the continent of North America, for the purpose of reducing the revolted colonies to obedience by force, will be the means of weakening the efforts of this country against her European enemies, tends under the present circumstances dangerously to increase the mutual enmity, so fatal to the interests both of Great Britain and America, and, by preventing an happy reconciliation with that country, to frustrate the earnest desire graciously expressed by His Majesty to restore the blessings of public tranquillity.[5]

This view had been advanced from the outset by critics of the conflict. Before 1778 they warned that war with America would weaken Britain in the face of likely Bourbon revenge for the defeats of the Seven Years War (1756–63). When their warnings were justified and France entered the war they argued that Britain should concentrate her efforts on her ancient enemy and settle with America or, failing that, go onto the defensive in North America. Ministerial thinking was not too different, as the Carlisle Commission and the instructions to Clinton in 1778 to send troops to the West Indies indicate, but George III was unwilling to concede independence and the government not prepared to abandon hopes of success in North America.

After Yorktown both strategy and ministry collapsed. At a council of war in New York on 17 December 1781 Leslie was given discretion to evacuate Georgia if the American force gathering against it seemed likely to overrun Savannah. The Cabinet was not interested in Germain's schemes for continuing the war and before Christmas he pressed the king to allow him to resign. Attention shifted to the West Indies and to the naval situation, Yorktown having emphasized its obvious importance. Nevertheless, there continued to be calls for action in America, especially from Loyalists. One London newspaper, the *Morning Chronicle*, in its issue of 11 January 1782, urged the government to 'carry fire, sword, and a depredatory war' to New England, adding:

> . . . it is the effect of their own ill-judged, fantastic and iniquitous ambition, and but a just punishment for their wickedness, obstinacy, rebellion and notorious guilt . . . reduce them to submission as absolute and abject as their revolt was proven wanton and insolent.

John Hayes, still at Charleston, was in favour of evacuating New York and moving the army south in order to secure South Carolina and Georgia. 'We should get possession of a country rich in produce and put a total stop to the great aim of the French nation'. In July 1782 the London press contained reports 'that America may yet be conquered' if sufficient forces were sent:

George III c. *1767, from the studio of A. Ramsay*

50,000 men and twenty ships of the line would deliver the colonies back in two campaigns.[6]

Such hopes seemed increasingly outdated. Press commentators turned to other targets, though some still kept America in their sights. A 'Plebean', writing in the *Morning Chronicle* of 4 September 1782, suggested that the government exploit discontent in Spanish America:

> . . . withdraw all troops from America, except those necessary to maintain New York, to aid the insurgents against Spain . . . Spain being thus employed by her subjects, we, leaving the rebel colonies awhile to themselves, with the rest of our forces attack the insidious Gauls and insulting Mynheers [Dutch], who cannot long withstand the bravery of British courage. Thus, recovering our former dignity and superiority over our most inveterate enemies, let the whole power of Great Britain be turned upon the rebellious colonies.

Such ideas were as fanciful politically as they were militarily. Germain resigned as Secretary of State for America on 10 February 1782. North, increasingly abandoned by the country gentlemen, announced the government's resignation to the Commons on 20 March. George III was forced to turn to the Opposition whom he detested and on 27 March the government of the Marquis of Rockingham took office. A new political wind blew. The ministry was changed, the government reorganized, the American Department being abolished. The new government wanted peace and, in so far as the war continued, a concentration of forces against the Bourbons in the West Indies. Carleton was instructed to evacuate New York, Charleston, Savannah and, if circumstances justified, St Augustine, to reinforce the West Indies, and to inform the Americans of his intentions.

These instructions were carried out, although the process of disengagement took longer than had been anticipated. Washington was sceptical about British intentions. On 5 May Carleton reached New York; four days later Washington received a letter from him announcing that he and Admiral Digby were joined 'in the commission of peace' and wished to reduce the needless severities of war. The pugnacious Washington, on the contrary, still hoped to deliver, in cooperation with the French, a mortal blow to the British cause in America, against either New York or Charleston. There were also hopes of a French-supported invasion of Canada. Washington drew up a plan for one on 1 May. The general was, however, to be disappointed by the French response, and it became increasingly clear that the British did indeed intend to evacuate. Vaudreuil's force, of only thirteen of the line and 2,300 troops, was smaller than Washington had hoped and seemed too small to be of much help, and when the news reached France in late August that the British were moving troops from America to the West Indies, Rochambeau was authorized to embark part or all of his force, while Vaudreuil was instructed to return to the Caribbean.[7]

The British meanwhile were disengaging. On 22 April the Earl of Shelburne, the new Secretary of State for Home and Colonial Affairs, wrote to General Haldimand, the commander in Canada, informing him that the ministry had decided to abandon offensive action as well as any measures suggesting an intention of regaining America by force. On 20 June Carleton wrote to Haldimand stating that, in view of the possibility of peace, only defensive military measures could be taken.[8] Wilmington had been abandoned at the end of 1781. On 14 June 1782 evacuation orders reached Savannah to the astonishment of the Loyalists, who considered the position a strong one. Sir James Wright, the last royal Governor of Georgia, argued that if 500 re-inforcements were sent it would be possible to drive Wayne from Georgia, the sort of argument so often made in these circumstances.[9] Nonetheless, on 11 July Savannah was evacuated and the city entered by Wayne's forces. The British troops left Tybee Island, at the mouth of the Savannah River, later in the month.

Greene was in no position to attack Charleston, despite the fact that in May 1782 1,300 troops had been sent thence to the West Indies, which was increasingly the pivot of the Anglo-French struggle. His army, forced to rely on inadequate state supplies and impressment,[10] was smaller than the garrison and suffered from expiring enlistments. The Americans were, however, able to limit British foraging seriously and to cut links between Loyalists and Charleston. Charleston and New York were not to be taken by assault. They were evacuated on 18 December 1782 and 25 November 1783 respectively, tasks complicated and delayed by the tremendous administrative and transportation burdens that were faced.[11]

These departures wrecked the Loyalist cause and helped to embitter them greatly. Many fled to Britain or other British dominions, especially Nova Scotia. From Charleston, many fled to the Bahamas. Chesney, his property raided and his wife dead, sailed in April 1782 from Charleston for Ireland, where he settled and remarried.[12] Others compromised with the new order, leading Nathanael Greene, for example, to issue a certificate in August 1782 that 'Colonel Fenwick in the British army has agreed to send me intelligence from time to time of all the military operations which the enemy may concert to the prejudice of the United States', had indeed done so for some months and that Greene promised 'to use all my influence with the state of South Carolina to restore him to all his fortunes and the rights and privileges of a citizen'.[13] Many Loyalists complained. Patrick Tonyn, the Governor of East Florida, joined the Houses of Assembly of the colony in protesting about its abandonment to Spain at the peace. In June 1784, however, the new Spanish governor arrived at St Augustine.

PEACE AND THE POST-WAR WORLD

Some British newspapers carried articles warning about the dangers of granting independence to America. The *Public Advertiser* of 15 January 1783 carried a letter from a Bostonian claiming that 'the French and our states will rear such a navy in America, that England will not hold an inch of territory on the face of the earth in a very few years'.

Nevertheless, for British politicians the sole remaining question was the terms that should be granted. The ministries that replaced the North government, the

The Peace Treaty, signed at Versailles on 3 September 1783, by which Britain gave independence to the Thirteen Colonies, ceded Minorca and the Floridas to Spain and Tabago and Senegal to France. The pictures depict some of the main incidents of the conflict including the battle of Trenton (top left) and the battle of Monmouth Court House (top right). Engraved in 1783

Second Rockingham administration formed in March 1782 and the Shelburne ministry which replaced it in July, after Rockingham's death, were motivated by a desire to divide the opposing coalition in order to concentrate their efforts against the Bourbons, and a hope that it might somehow be possible to create a new harmonious Anglo-American relationship. It was not surprising, therefore, that Shelburne finally agreed in July 1782 to the necessity of accepting American independence.

Anglo-American negotiations were conducted in Paris. The fate of the lands between the Appalachians and the Mississippi proved to be more contentious than independence. Competing British, Spanish and American claims were decided in America's favour because neither of the other powers was as determined, Shelburne hoping for concessions in other spheres. On 30 November 1782 Anglo-American differences were settled. America received recognition of her independence, the boundaries she sought, and valuable Newfoundland fishing rights, while she only agreed to recommend to the individual states that the Loyalists be treated fairly, an undertaking that was scant compensation for Loyalist service, and promised to honour her debts. This promise caused many problems and the undertakings on behalf of the Loyalists were only fulfilled in part. Relations were to be complicated further by disputes

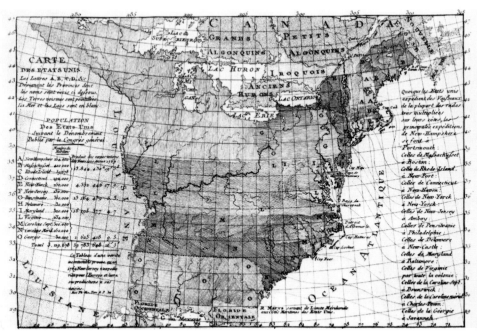

A French map of the Thirteen Colonies, engraved in 1783. It has a brief history of each state, providing such information as the landing of 120 Presbyterians at Plymouth, New England on 6 September 1621 having fled religious persecution in Europe; that New York was originally colonized mainly by the Dutch and that Quaker followers of William Penn had settled in Pennsylvania in 1681 to avoid persecution in England

over the drawing of the north-east frontier and over Newfoundland fishing rights. The activities of British officials, officers and traders on the frontier aroused American suspicion for many years.[15]

On the other hand America had cut free from the French alliance. The British had displayed considerable resilience in the last stages of the war: Rodney had defeated de Grasse at the Saintes, while a Spanish attack on Gibraltar had failed. Widespread opposition to peace in London was recorded in November 1782, 'for say they why should we make a peace at the period when our navy is on a respectable footing and able to cope with that of the House of Bourbon'.[16] However, by the armistice and preliminary peace agreement signed on 20 January 1783 the British yielded West and East Florida and Minorca to Spain, retaining Gibraltar and regaining the Bahamas. France retained Senegal and Tobago, and regained St Lucia, Goree and Pondicherry. Symbolic of the changed relationship was the abrogation of the article in the 1763 treaty which gave Britain the right to maintain a commissioner at the French port of Dunkirk to prevent the rebuilding of military installations there.

After the war the French found the Americans ungrateful, unwilling to accept a commercial relationship on French terms. French officials thought the Americans self-interested and unprepared to translate declarations of gratitude into action.[17] No lasting political or economic entente had been created between America and France and commercial links between Britain and America revived strongly after the conflict. New York was described in July 1790 as more like a suburb of London than an American town. The war had helped to cripple the finances of the French government and thus to set in train the political crisis of 1787–9 which resulted in the French Revolution. This launched Europe into near continuous conflict from 1792 until 1815. During this period the American state overcame its early internal divisions without the external intervention that had such a radicalizing impact on the revolutionary French state, as later on that of Russia. The French envoy Louis-Guillaume Otto reported in November 1790 that the Americans were unlikely to take a role in the Anglo-Spanish war that then seemed imminent over competing claims on the Pacific coast of Canada, as they needed ten years of peace in order to settle their government.[18] The last American warship had been sold in 1785 and, although the American navy was revived in the early nineteenth century in order to protect American trade during the Napoleonic Wars, America did not seek command of the sea or trans-oceanic commercial or political dominion.[19]

This, however, was also a period of marked American territorial expansion on the North American continent. A settlement in 1795 of the disputed frontier with Spanish West Florida brought America much of Mississippi and Alabama. In 1803, by the Louisiania Purchase, America gained all or much of the future states of Montana, North and South Dakota, Minnesota, Wyoming, Colorado, Nebraska, Iowa, Kansas, Missouri, Oklahoma, Arkansas and Louisiana. The Spanish stranglehold on the Gulf of Mexico was therefore broken, and the new state now reached from the Atlantic to the Rockies. Coastal Mississippi and Alabama were seized from Spain in 1810–13. From 1818 the Oregon Country, including the future states of Idaho, Oregon and Washington, was to be jointly occupied by America and Britain.

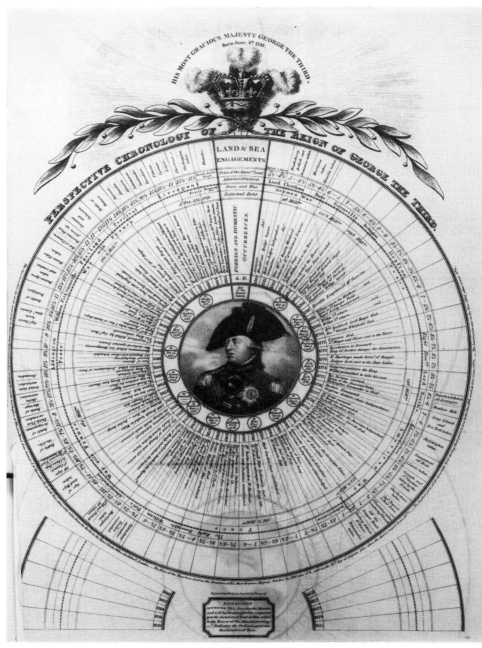

A perspective of the reign of George III

Protected by her navy from some of the consequences of the same period of European warfare, in which she of course also participated, Britain benefited by extending her territories worldwide, her gains by 1815 including Malta, St Lucia, Tobago, Trinidad, Ascension, Tristan da Cunha, Mauritius, the Seychelles, the Maldives, Ceylon, Singapore and Cape Colony, all bar the last islands. Her position in India and Australasia was also consolidated. Without the American War of Independence and the reforms this led to, the British, especially the Royal Navy, would not have been ready for the French Revolutionary and Napoleonic Wars. Britain's imperial triumph owed much to her earlier set-backs. The four decades from 1775 until the Congress of Vienna of 1815 therefore helped to give the British Empire and the English-speaking world very different shapes. The latter was no longer exclusively part of the empire, which now included a far greater number of non-English speakers, who were ruled, instead of being largely self-governing, as the American colonies had been. America, inhabited by an independent people of extraordinary vitality, was to be the most dynamic of the independent states in the western hemisphere, the first and foremost of the decolonized countries, the people that were best placed to take advantage of the potent combination of a European legacy, independence, and the opportunities for expansion and growth that were to play an increasingly important role in the new world created from 1776.

STRUGGLE REVIEWED

In December 1807 Archibald Robertson, a British army engineer who had served in the American war, wrote to Viscount Melville, who had sought his advice on strategy in the event of war breaking out with America:

> I deprecate the idea of making war again by land on that great continent, so distant from European support except in the defence of the British settlements should they be attacked. Our shipping alone can decidedly annoy them in every point, provided they had a safe anchorage to run to in case of a storm . . .

which he thought might be provided by the islands off the New England coast. The following month Robertson added:

> In the case of an American war taking place, I do not doubt but that a flying squadron with some troops in transports, threatening either the Chesapeake or Delaware Rivers might alarm and impede any intended movement of the enemy against Canada, without (on our part) any particular attempt to land in any place, but only threatening particular points thought of consequence by the enemy and after attracting their attention to one point shift the ground and threaten some other.[20]

Given British commitments in the war with Napoleonic France, a stress on naval action was reasonable, and indeed in the war of 1812 the British blockade nearly ruined American trade, but Robertson's suggestions also reflected the numerous failures of British armies operating abroad since 1775, first against the Americans and then against the French.[21] There had been exceptions: in

Egypt against the French and, more obviously, in India. There Cornwallis, Gerard Lake, who had served as a lieutenant-colonel in Cornwallis' North Carolina campaign in 1781 and at Yorktown, and Arthur Wellesley, who was to be created Duke of Wellington in 1814, won a number of victories over Tippoo Sahib of Mysore and the Mahrattas, including the storming of Bangalore in 1791, that of Seringapatam in 1799, which delivered hegemony in southern India to the British, and the battles of Assaye, Laswari and Argaum in 1803. In both Egypt and India the British were helped by the cooperation of important sections of the native population, many of whom fought directly under the British. Such cooperation was also to be instrumental in Wellesley's success in the Peninsular War with the French in Portugal and Spain (1808–13), as it had earlier been in the conquest of Canada, with American help, during the Seven Years War. Cooperation entailed not simply the assistance of soldiers but, more crucially, the presence of a generally friendly population from which supplies could be obtained and who could be relied upon not to obstruct military operations.

It was this that the British lacked in the American war. There were areas where Loyalism was strong and periods when obstructive local revolutionary activity was weak, as in New Jersey in December 1776 and South Carolina immediately after the fall of Charleston. These were, however, limited. Without reliable popular support, the British were obliged both to obtain the bulk of their supplies from Britain and to employ much of their army in garrison duty, an obligation made more necessary by the need to protect supply bases and the crucial trans-shipment points. Thus, only a part of the army was available for operations, while the seizure of new posts, whether ports, such as New York, Savannah and Charleston, or inland fortresses, such as Stony Point and Ticonderoga, forced them to deploy still more of the troops as garrison units. This had serious operational consequences in particular campaigns, and also helps to account for the stress on a decisive battle, because it was only by destroying the American field armies that troops could be freed from garrison duty in order to extend the range of British control. The pacification strategy was therefore not necessarily incompatible in conception with the idea of a decisive victory however much it might be difficult to reconcile the two in practice.[22] A successful resolution of the war would from the point of view of British taxpayers require pacification, but that appeared most likely to be a consequence of decisive victory. The alternative of attrition, military and economic, was difficult to implement after French entry into the war, although there are some signs that life was becoming pretty unendurable for Americans and difficult for the American war-effort by 1781. Nevertheless, the importance of decisive victory was certainly the lesson to be drawn from Ireland after the battles of the Boyne and of Aughrim (1690–1) and from Scotland after Culloden (1746).

Whether, in the context of the American war, a decisive battle was indeed an illusion is difficult to assess.[23] The feasibility of a strategy depended to a considerable extent on when it was considered or applied and with what strength. In 1776 a decisive victory, the destruction of Washington's army and possibly the death of the general, might well have been fatal to the cause of independence. In 1777 such a victory by Howe would have been significantly more important than Burgoyne's defeat, although it is by no means clear how this would have helped the British in New England. A substantial force landed subsequently near Boston might well have fared no better than Gage in 1775, though with bases in New York and Rhode Island the British would have been in a better position to blockade and raid the coast. Given the military difficulty of a conquest of New England and, at that stage, the apparent problems facing one of the south, especially after Clinton's failure at Charleston and the Loyalist defeat at Moore's Creek Bridge in 1776, it is not surprising that, irrespective of their clear political preference for conciliation, the Howes should have been so interested in negotiating an end to the conflict. Negotiations were not an illusion, as Prevost discovered at Charleston in 1779, but there were enough Americans who were not prepared to abandon their independence (whatever their disinclination to contribute to the military effort), to make such an option unlikely to succeed, short of a major British military success. Pacification of the south, where negotiations were most likely to succeed, could only be a means to an end, that of the defeat or demoralization of more militant regions. This was equally true of decisive victory in the south, apparently gained at Charleston and Camden in 1780. Such victory had been obtained earlier, in the clearing of Canada in 1776, but that was only a stage in the military struggle. The reconquest and pacification of Canada did not imply that the same was inevitable in the bordering regions of the Thirteen Colonies.

By stressing the British need for decisive victory, a greater emphasis can be placed on American skill and determination in avoiding such a defeat. Much can doubtless be ascribed to British indecision and to generals who were arguably insufficiently prepared to take risks, such as Howe, or who were too reckless, such as Burgoyne and Cornwallis, but there were major engagements and in these, after the campaign of 1776, whatever the fate of parts of the army, the main American force was not routed. The British were unable to exploit battlefield advantages, because of deficiencies on their part, principally caution, fatigue and the absence of cavalry, but also because of skilful American withdrawals and the toll inflicted in battle by the Americans, most obviously at Bunker Hill and Guilford. Although not a particularly good field general, Washington was an excellent leader and a good strategist. He was aggressive and always sought the offensive if it was at all feasible. Seeking unanimity outside Boston, he agreed to bind himself to the decisions of the Councils of War, which stopped his planned assaults across the ice on Boston, as later attacks on New York City and other operations. Following the disasters of 1776, Washington recognized that for many his army was the Revolution. Thereafter, he did not take risks unless success was all but guaranteed.

The Americans owed their independence to the willingness of some of the people to continue fighting when the struggle became more widespread, bitter and sustained than had at first seemed likely, before the British sent a major army to crush the revolution. The Americans subsequently had to face British determination to continue the struggle on land even after French intervention. Casualties were heavy. Although American deaths in battle amounted to about 6,000 men, the number of probable deaths in service was over 25,000, as a result of casualties in camp and among prisoners. This was 0.9 per cent of the population in 1780, compared to near 1.6 for the Civil War, 0.12 for World War One and 0.28 for World War Two.[24] These were heavy though far less than French losses of nearly 2 million compared to a population of about 28 million in 1789 in the, admittedly longer, Napoleonic and Revolutionary wars.

There were, of course, many parallels between the two revolutions. The Negroes, who rejected France and proclaimed the independent Republic of Haiti in 1804, had come to appreciate that the French had little to offer them, despite the abolition of slavery in 1794. In America freedom was also circumscribed, most obviously with the retention of slavery. The contrasts between the two revolutions are, however, striking. Although the Thirteen Colonies, like France, were both invaded and affected by civil war, the treatment of Loyalists was less savage than that of Royalists in France: in America the tumbrils never rolled. On the other hand, pre-war internal terrorism was quite commonplace and during the war American Revolutionary councils and militia could be quite harsh in their dealings with Loyalists, although their treatment of them varied considerably. American society was less mobilized for war than that of revolutionary France was to be, and more respect was paid to private property and pre-existing institutions. This was in part because there was less of a social contest in the American Revolution than in its French counterpart. French local government was reorganized institutionally and geographically, provincial assemblies being a major casualty. In America there was no equivalent centralization; in fact, avoidance of centralization was a principle of American revolutionary ideology. Nor was there any comparable attempt to export the Revolution, certainly not outside British America. The American Revolution was intensely conservative in its nature, and there was in a vague way a conscious desire to reaffirm the values of the British Glorious Revolution of 1688–9, which had been an essentially conservative episode in England, as these were then envisaged. This conservation should not, however, be exaggerated, and it was certainly not obvious to British observers, who tended to scorn what they saw as signs of democratic feelings. In January 1779 James Harris MP recorded:

> Saw Mr Ambrose Serle, Secretary to Lord Howe, and lately returned from North America. As a sample of the Bostonian spirit, he told me 'twas a common language in that country, when they were desirous to praise a man – 'that he was a good sort of man – that he had nothing of a *gentleman* in him'. He added this liberal, levelling spirit went so far that even their own (mock) Governor durst not keep a valet de chambre, but went regularly to the barber's shop to be shaved; and that, the rule there being that the *first* comer should be *first* served, the Governor, if he found a cobbler before him, was obliged to wait till that worthy cobler had been shaved first.[25]

Before their respective revolutions America lacked a strong identity comparable with that which France enjoyed, and in America, unlike France, there was to be no source of revolutionary activity able to terrorize those who supported the Revolution but had alternative, less centralist views of how the new state should be organized. Had the British been more successful, the Americans might well have resorted to more revolutionary military methods, such as guerrilla warfare and the strategy advocated by Charles Lee.[26] Greene succeeded in the south in combining partisan bands with the manoeuvres of a field army.[27] Alternatively, the Americans might have continued to rely on field armies, as the French Revolutionaries did, but those who took power could have taken a harsher attitude toward state rights and private property. The consequence might have been a very different American public culture, one that stressed the national state more than the individual, obligations more than rights. This might have engendered an ethos that was more genuinely egalitarian than that of freedom and property that was expressed in the constitution; although the ideological underpinnings of the Revolution were so strong, that it is possible that the Revolution would have been abandoned by many, if not most, Americans in the face of such a compromising of their principles. An alternative public culture would have arguably been one that is less attractive than that of America today, a country that does not know the tyranny of the state, a people who largely fulfil their collective myth of freedom.

SELECT BIBLIOGRAPHY

It is difficult to choose from among the wealth of fine studies on the conflict, the overwhelming majority by excellent American scholars. Restricting oneself to books and urging readers to find other references, both books and articles, in the bibliographies of the works cited, it is possibly best to note first Don Higginbotham, *The War of American Independence: Military Attitudes, Policies and Practice, 1763–1789* (New York , 1971) and by British scholars Eric Robson, *The American Revolution* (London, 1955) and Piers Mackesy, *The War for America 1775–1783* (London, 1964). R. Middlekauff, *The Glorious Cause. The American Revolution, 1763–1789* (Oxford, 1982) is somewhat unsympathetic towards the British. K. Perry, *British Politics and the American Revolution* (London, 1990) is a good recent survey. British policy in America can be followed in G.S. Brown, *The American Secretary. The Colonial Policy of Lord George Germain* (Ann Arbor, 1963), P.H. Smith, *Loyalists and Redcoats: A Study in British Revolutionary Policy* (Chapel Hill, 1964), G.A. Billias (ed.), *George Washington's Opponents* (New York, 1969), J.R. Alden, *General Gage in America* (Baton Rouge, 1948), I.D. Gruber, *The Howe Brothers and the American Revolution* (New York, 1972), R.J. Hargrove, *General John Burgoyne* (Newark, Delaware, 1983), W.B. Willcox, *Portrait of a General: Sir Henry Clinton in the War of Independence* (New York, 1964) and F. and M. Wickwire, *Cornwallis and the War of Independence* (London, 1971). For British supply problems, N. Baker, *Government and Contractors: The British Treasury and War Supplies 1775–1783* (London, 1971), R.A. Bowler, *Logistics and the Failure of the British Army in America 1775–1783* (Princeton, 1975) and D. Syrett, *Shipping and the American War, 1775–1783* (London, 1970). On the naval aspects, J.R. Dull, *The French Navy and American Independence: A Study of Arms and Diplomacy, 1774–1787* (Princeton, 1975), W.M. Fowler, *Rebels Under Sail* (New York, 1976), N. Tracy, *Navies, Deterrence and American Independence. Britain and Seapower in the 1760s and 1770s* (Vancouver, 1988), J. Black and P. Woodfine (eds.), *The British Navy and the Use of Naval Power in the Eighteenth Century* (Leicester, 1988), D. Syrett, *The Royal Navy in American Waters 1775–1783* (Aldershot, 1989). For the diplomatic dimension S.F. Bemis, *The Diplomacy of the American Revolution* (Washington, 1935), R.B. Morris, *The Peacemakers: The Great Powers and American Independence* (New York, 1965), R.W. Van Alstyne, *Empire and Independence. The International History of the American Revolution* (New York, 1965), J.H. Hutson, *John Adams and the Diplomacy of the American Revolution* (Lexington, 1980), R. Hoffman and P.J. Albert (eds.), *Diplomacy and Revolution: The Franco-American Alliance of 1778* (Charlottesville, 1981), J.R. Dull, *A Diplomatic History of the American Revolution*

(New Haven, 1985), P. Gifford (ed.), *The Treaty of Paris (1783) in a Changing States System* (Lanham, 1985), Hoffman and Albert (eds.), *Peace and the Peacemakers: The Treaty of 1783* (Charlottesville, 1986), H.M. Scott, *British Foreign Policy in the Age of the American Revolution* (Oxford, 1990).

J.M. Dederer, *War in America to 1775. Before Yankee Doodle* (New York, 1990) is crucial for the American background. General accounts of the war by American scholars include W.M. Wallace, *Appeal to Arms* (Chicago, 1951), C. Ward, *The War of the Revolution* (New York, 1952), J.R. Alden, *The American Revolution, 1775–1783* (New York, 1954) and H.H. Peckham, *The War of Independence* (Chicago, 1958). John Shy's *A People Numerous and Armed. Reflections on the Military Struggle for American Independence* (Oxford, 1976) is a crucial study. Other valuable wide ranging works include H.F. Rankin, *The North Carolina Continentals* (Chapel Hill, 1971), R.H. Calhoon, *The Loyalists in Revolutionary America, 1760–1781* (New York, 1973), J.G. Rossie, *The Politics of Command in the American Revolution* (Syracuse, 1975), D. Palmer, *The Way of the Fox: American Strategy in the War for America* (Westport, 1975), D. Higginbotham (ed.), *Reconsiderations on the Revolutionary War* (Westport, 1978), C. Royster, *A Revolutionary People at War: The Continental Army and American Character, 1775–1783* (Chapel Hill, 1979), W.M. Fowler and W. Coyle (eds.), *The American Revolution: Changing Perspectives* (Boston, 1979), Royster, *Light-Horse Harry Lee and the Legacy of the American Revolution* (New York, 1981), R.S. Allen, *The Loyal Americans: The Military Role of the Provincial Corps and their Settlement in British North America* (Ottawa, 1983), E.W. Carp, *To Starve the Army at Pleasure: Continental Army Administration and American Political Culture, 1775–1783* (Chapel Hill, 1984), R. Hoffman and P.J. Albert (eds.), *Arms and Independence. The Military Character of the American Revolution* (Charlottesville, 1984), D. Higginbotham, *George Washington and the American Military Tradition* (Athens, Georgia, 1985) and his *War and Society in Revolutionary America: The Wider Dimensions of Conflict* (Columbia, S.C., 1988), J. Ferling (ed.), *The World Turned Upside Down* (Westport, 1988), Calhoon, *The Loyalist Perception and Other Essays* (Columbia, S.C., 1989).

For many biographies are an attractive way to approach the subject. Among the numerous that can be mentioned are D.S. Freeman, *George Washington* (New York, 1948–57), W.M. Wallace, *Traitorous Hero: The Life and Fortunes of Benedict Arnold* (New York, 1954), N. Callahan, *Henry Knox: George Washington's General* (New York, 1958), T. Thayer, *Nathanael Greene: Strategist of the American Revolution* (New York, 1960), D. Higginbotham, *Daniel Morgan: Revolutionary Rifleman* (Chapel Hill, 1961), G.A. Billias (ed.), *George Washington's Generals* (New York, 1964), J.T. Flexner, *George Washington in the American Revolution* (Boston, 1967), R.J. Champagne, *Alexander McDougall and the American Revolution in New York* (Schenectady, 1975), P.D. Nelson, *General Horatio Gates* (Baton Rouge, 1976), J.R. Alden, *George Washington* (Baton Rouge, 1984), Nelson, *Anthony Wayne* (Bloomington, 1985), J.E. Ferling, *The First of Men: A Life of George Washington* (Berkeley, 1988).

Three areas of importance are covered in G. Lanctot, *Canada and the American Revolution 1774–1783* (London, 1967), R. Buel, *Dear Liberty: Connecticut's Mobilization for the Revolutionary War* (Middletown, 1980), and E.M. Eller (ed.), *Chesapeake Bay in the American Revolution* (Centreville, 1981). On Connecticut see also H.E. Selesky, *War and Society in Colonial Connecticut* (New Haven, 1990); on Virginia, J.E. Selby, *The Revolution in Virginia, 1775–1783* (Williamsburg, Va., 1988). On the war in West Florida, W.S. Coker and R. Rea (eds.), *Anglo-Spanish Confrontation on the Gulf Coast during the American Revolution* (Pensacola, 1982) and in the south J.R. Alden, *The South in the Revolution, 1763–1789* (Baton Rouge, 1957), J.J. Crow and L.E. Tise (eds.), *The Southern Experience in the American Revolution* (Chapel Hill, 1978), W. Roberts Higgins (ed.), *The Revolutionary War in the South: Power, Conflict and Leadership* (Durham, 1979), H. Lumpkin, *From Savannah to Yorktown: The American Revolution in the South* (Columbia S.C., 1981), J.J. Nadelhaft, *The Disorders of War. The Revolution in South Carolina* (Orono, 1981), J.M. Dederer, *Making Bricks Without Straw: Nathanael Greene's Southern Campaigns and Mao Tse-Tung's Mobile War* (Manhattan, Kansas, 1983), R. Hoffman, T.W. Tate and P.J. Albert (eds.), *An Uncivil War: The Southern Backcountry during the American Revolution* (Charlottesville, 1985), J.S. Pancake, *This Destructive War: The British Campaign in the Carolinas, 1780–1782* (Tuscaloosa, 1985), R. Berg, 'The Southern Campaigns: British Efforts to Retake the South', *Strategy and Tactics*, 104 (1985), L.E. Babits, 'Greene's Strategy in the Southern Campaign, 1780–1781', in M. Ultee (ed.), *Adapting to Conditions. War and Society in the Eighteenth Century* (Tuscaloosa, 1986). Indians are discussed in B. Graymont, *The Iroquois in the American Revolution* (Syracuse, 1972) and J.H. O'Donnell, *Southern Indians in the American Revolution* (Knoxville, 1973). On Negroes see, B. Quarles, *The Negro in the American Revolution* (Chapel Hill, 1961), and on the 'lower sort', S. Rosswurm, *Arms, Country and Class: The Philadelphia Militia and the 'Lower Sort' during the American Revolution 1775–1783* (New Brunswick, 1987). Recent work on an important dimension of the conflict can be approached through R. Kaplan, 'The Hidden War: British Intelligence Operations during the American Revolution', *WMQ* 47 (1990).

Recent work on the opposing armies includes J.B. Trussell, *The Pennsylvania Line* (Harrisburg, 1977), R. Atwood, *The Hessians. The Mercenaries from Hessen-Kassel in the American Revolution* (Cambridge, 1980), S.R. Frey, *The British Soldier in America: A Social History of Military Life in the Revolutionary Period* (Austin, 1981), R.K. Wright, *The Continental Army* (Washington, 1983). Work on eighteenth-century warfare includes R.F. Weigley, *The American Way of War* (New York, 1973) pp. 3–39; W.H. McNeill, *The Pursuit of Power* (Oxford, 1983) pp. 144–84, M.S. Anderson, *War and Society in Europe of the Old Regime, 1618–1789* (Leicester, 1988) pp. 157–204; J.M. Black, *Europe in the Eighteenth Century 1700–1789* (London, 1990) pp. 303–27; Black, *A Military Revolution? Military Change and European Society 1550–1800* (London, 1991) pp. 20–65.

It is always helpful and interesting to consult the accounts of participants. There are excellent editions of the papers of a number of American leaders, most recently *The Papers of George Washington. Revolutionary War Series*, vols. 1–3 (Charlottesville, 1985–8), as well as several of their British counterparts, most interestingly W.B. Willcox (ed.), *The American Rebellion: Sir Henry Clinton's Narrative of His Campaigns, 1775–1782*, (New Haven, 1954). Other useful sources include, E. Robson (ed.), *Letters from America* (Manchester, 1951),

M. Balderston and D. Syrett (eds.), *The Lost War. Letters from British Officers during the American Revolution* (New York, 1975), H.H. Peckham (ed.), *Sources of American Independence: Selected Manuscripts from the Collections of the William L. Clements Library* (Chicago, 1978), H.C. Rice and A.S.K. Brown (eds.), *The American Campaigns of Rochambeau's Army* (Princeton, 1972), J.C. Dohla, *A Hessian Diary of the American Revolution* edited by B.E. Burgoyne (Normal Ok., 1990). Peckham has also produced a more pointed record of suffering, *The Toll of Independence. Engagements and Battle Casualties of the American Revolution* (Chicago, 1974), while the war can be followed in D.W. Marshall and Peckham, *Campaigns of the American Revolution. An Atlas of Manuscript Maps* (Ann Arbor, 1976).

NOTES

1 Prologue

1. WW R1-522; BL. Egerton Mss. 982 f.12; WW R1-1321.
2. R.R. Palmer, *The Age of the Democratic Revolution* (Princeton, 1959); J. Godechot, *France and the Atlantic Revolution of the Eighteenth Century* (London, 1965). For a critical view, I.R. Christie, *Stress and Stability in Late Eighteenth-Century Britain* (Oxford, 1984) pp. 9–14.
3. C.R. Boxer, *The Portuguese Seaborne Empire 1415–1825* (1973) pp. 202–3; J. Lynch, *Bourbon Spain 1700–1808* (Oxford, 1990) pp. 329–74; J.H. Parry, *The Spanish Seaborne Empire* (Berkeley, 1990) pp. 327–45; A. Beer, *Joseph II, Leopold II und Kaunitz: Ihr Briefwechsel* (Vienna, 1873) pp. 107–8.
4. Huntington Library, Loudoun Papers 7087; P.D.G. Thomas, 'The Cost of the British Army in North America, 1763–1775', *WMQ* 45 (1988) p. 516; PRO. State Papers 78/294 f.166–7.
5. C.I. Archer, *The Army in Bourbon Mexico 1760–1810* (Albuquerque, 1977); J. Shy, *Towards Lexington: The Role of the British Army in the Coming of the American Revolution* (Princeton, 1965); N.R. Stout, *The Royal Navy in America, 1760–1775* (Annapolis, 1973).
6. B.C. Steiner, *Western Maryland in the Revolution* (Baltimore, 1902) p. 7; J. Shy, *A People Numerous and Armed. Reflections on The Military Struggle for American Independence* (Oxford, 1976) p. 178.
7. R.J. Dinkin, *Voting in Provincial America : A Study of Elections in the Thirteen Colonies, 1689–1776* (Westport, 1977).
8. R. Ryerson, *The Revolution is Now Begun* (Philadelphia, 1978); G.H. Nobles, *Divisions throughout the Whole: Politics and Society in Hampshire County, Massachusetts, 1740–1775* (Cambridge 1983); G.B. Nash, 'Artisans and Politics in Eighteenth-Century Philadelphia', and S. Rosswurm, ' "As a Lyen out of His Den": Philadelphia's Popular Movement, 1776–80', in M. and J. Jacob (eds.) *The Origins of Anglo-American Radicalism* (1984).
9. N.O. Hatch, *The Sacred Cause of Liberty: Republican Thought and the Millenium in Revolutionary New England* (New Haven, 1977); R.M. Bloch, *Visionary Republic : Millenial Themes in American Thought, 1756–1800* (Cambridge, 1985); J.C.D. Clark, 'The American Revolution: A War of Religion?', *History Today* 39 (December 1989); Clark, 'Revolution in the English Atlantic Empire', in E.E. Rice (ed.), *Revolution and Counter-Revolution* (Oxford, 1990) pp. 60–73.
10. B. Bailyn, *The Ideological Origins of the American Revolution* (Cambridge, Mass., 1967), and *The Origins of American Politics* (New York, 1968).
11. T.H. Breen, *Tobacco Culture: the Mentality of the Great Tidewater Planters on the Eve of the Revolution* (Princeton, 1985); J.W. Tyler, *Smugglers and Patriots: Boston Merchants and the Advent of the American Revolution* (Boston, 1986).
12. B. Donoughue, *British Politics and the American Revolution: The Path to War 1773–1775* (1964); P. Thomas, *British Politics and the Stamp Act Crisis: The First Phase of the American Revolution 1763–1767* (Oxford, 1975); I. Christie and B.W. Labaree, *Empire or Independence 1760–1776* (Oxford, 1976); J.L. Bullion, *A Great and Necessary Measure: George Grenville and the Genesis of the Stamp Act 1763–1765* (Columbia, Missouri, 1982); R.C. Simmons and Thomas (eds.), *Proceedings and Debates of the British Parliaments Respecting North America, 1754–1783* (New York, 1982–); Thomas, *The Townshend Duties Crisis: The Second Phase of the American Revolution 1767– 1773* (Oxford, 1987); K. Perry, *British Politics and the American Revolution* (1990); T.R. Clayton, 'Sophistry, Security and Socio-Political Structures in the American Revolution, or Why Jamaica did not rebel', *Historical Journal* 29 (1986).
13. F. Anderson, *A People's Army : Massachusetts Soldiers and Society in the Seven Years War* (Chapel Hill, 1984); D. Higginbotham, *War and Society in Revolutionary America: The Wider Dimensions of Conflict* (Columbia, South Carolina, 1988) pp. 35, 38; J.M. Dederer, *War in America to 1775* (New York, 1990).
14. A.H. Jones, *Wealth of a Nation to Be. The*

American Colonies on the Eve of the Revolution (New York, 1980) pp. 340–1.

15. G.B. Nash, *The Urban Crucible: Social Changes, Political Consciousness, and the Origins of the American Revolution* (Cambridge, Mass., 1979).

16. P.H. Smith (ed.), *Letters of Delegates to Congress, 1774–1789*, 1 (Washington, 1976).

2 The Problems of Suppressing Rebellion

1. M. Elliott, *Partners in Revolution. The United Irishmen and France* (New Haven, 1982); Black, *Culloden and the '45* (Stroud, 1990); WO.34/135 f.220; A.H. Tillson, 'The Localist Roots of Backcountry Loyalism', *Journal of Southern History* 54 (1988).

2. *Adams Family Correspondence* 2, 148; *Hamilton Papers* 1, 268; NeC 2, 330; BL.Add. 34416, f.60–1; R.O. DeMond, *The Loyalists in North Carolina During the Revolution* (Durham, North Carolina, 1940); P.H. Smith, 'The American Loyalists, Notes on Their Organization and Numerical Strength', *William and Mary Quarterly* 25 (1968); R.M. Calhoon, *The Loyalists in Revolutionary America, 1760–1781* (New York, 1973); R. Ranlet, *The New York Loyalists* (Knoxville, 1986); Smith, 'The New Jersey Loyalists and the British "Provincial" Corps in the War for Independence', in *The Loyalist Perception and Other Essays* (Columbia, South Carolina, 1989) pp. 147–75.

3. WO.34/122, f.31; Durham, Department of Palaeography, papers of 1st Earl Grey 25; Sheffield Archives, Spencer Stanhope Muniments 60542/10; WW R150-4; Me 172-111/29; S. Conway, 'To Subdue America: British Army Officers and the Conduct of the Revolutionary War', *WMQ* 43 (1986) pp. 381–407.

4. Edinburgh, National Library of Scotland MS. 16621 f.181; B.A. Uhlendorf (ed.), *Revolution in America: Confidential Letters and Journals 1776–1784 of Adjutant General Major Baurmeister of the Hessian Forces* (2nd edn., Westport, Conn., 1975) pp. 139, 185; J.S. Tiedemann, 'Patriots by Default: Queens County, New York, and the British Army, 1776–1783', *WMQ* 43 (1986) pp. 35–63; A. Starkey, 'War and Culture, a case study: The Enlightenment and the conduct of the British Army in America, 1775–1781', *War and Society* 8, (1990); Black, *A Military Revolution? Military Change and European Society 1550–1800* (1991).

5. WO.34/114 f.105–13; Cobbett, 20, 1151, 1246, 392; *Madison* 2, 181; Durham, Grey 23; Anon., *Some Reflections on the Trade Between Great Britain and Sweden* (1756) p. 18; WO.34/112 f.166.

6. Halifax SH 7/JL/38; WW R1-1668, 1686, 1693; *Franklin Papers* 22, 519.

7. PRO 30/11/85 f.33; NeC 2295.

8. HMC *Lothian* pp. 381–2; PRO 30/11/68 f.1–2; NeC 2291.

9. C. Duffy, *The Military Life of Frederick the Great* (1985) pp. 268–77.

10. NeC 2, 758; BL. Add.21687 f.322, 34416 f.118, 32413 f.47; PRO WO.34/112 f.41, 34/127 f.154, 34/111 f.37.

11. *Hamilton Papers* 1, 202, 219, 252, 276; WW R150-4, R1-1568, 1634; Durham, Grey, 23, 25; BL. Add. 34416 f.156, 271.

12. PRO 30/8/5; WO. 34/115 f.71.

13. *A State of the Expedition from Canada, as laid before the House of Commons, by Lieutenant General Burgoyne* (London, 1780) p. 114; R. Hoffman, *A Spirit of Dissension: Economics, Politics and the Revolution in Maryland* (Baltimore, 1973); *Madison Papers* 1, 129–30, 153; G.S. McCowen, *The British Occupation of Charleston, 1780–1782* (Columbia, SC, 1972) p. 99.

14. A.A. Lawrence, *Storm over Savannah* (Athens, 1951) p. 73.

15. B. Quarles, *The Negro in the American Revolution* (Chapel Hill, 1961); McCowen, *Charleston*, pp. 100–3; M. Duffy, *Soldiers, Sugar and Seapower, The British Expeditions to the West Indies and the War against Revolutionary France* (Oxford, 1987); M. Mullin, 'British Caribbean and North American slaves in an Era of War and Revolution, 1775–1807', in J.J. Crow and L.E. Tise (eds.) *The Southern Experience in the American Revolution* (Chapel Hill, 1978) pp. 235, 240–1.

16. Cobbett, 20, 1061–2.

17. J.R. Alden, *John Stuart and the Southern Colonial Frontier* (Ann Arbor, 1944); J.H. O'Donnell, *Southern Indians in the American Revolution* (Knoxville, 1973); M.D. Green, 'The Creek Confederacy in the American Revolution: Cautious Participants', in W.S. Coker and R.R. Rea (eds.) *Anglo-Spanish Confrontation on the Gulf Coast during the American Revolution* (Pensacola, 1982); Cobbett 20, 17; J.A. Houlding and G.K. Yates, 'Quebec, Saratoga and the Convention Army', *Journal of the Society for Army Historical Research* 48 (1990) p. 160.

18. Me 172-111/4, 11; B. Graymont, *The Iroquois and the American Revolution* (Syracuse, 1972).

19. Rutledge to Sumter, 16 December 1780, LC Sumter papers; PRO 30/11/72 f.71; *Madison Papers* 1, 249–50; R.A. Bowler *Logistics and the Failure of the British Army in America 1775–1783* (Princeton, 1975) pp. 231, 234.

20. Durham, Grey, 25; Sheffield, WW R150-8, Spencer Stanhope 60542/10, 12, 9; S. Conway, ' "The great mischief complain'd of " : Reflections on the Misconduct of British Soldiers in the Revolutionary War',

WMQ 47, (1990) pp. 384–5; *State of the Expedition* p. 112.

21. *Jefferson Papers* I, 28; Me 172-111/26; HMC. *Lothian* pp. 388–9.
22. NRO. 1314/6; BL. Add. 32413 f.14, 16–17; SRO.GD.26/9/513/7; Halifax SH 7/JL/14, 20.
23. Me 172-111/47.
24. HMC. *Lothian* p. 388; PRO 30/11/68 f.15.
25. NeC 2, 618.
26. Black, *Military Revolution* pp. 12, 64.

3   The Revolutionary War Effort

1. *Jefferson* 2, 3.
2. PCC. 172.
3. D. Higginbotham, 'The Early American Way of War: Reconnaissance and Appraisal', *WMQ* 44 (1987); J.M. Dederer, *War in America to 1775; Before Yankee Doodle* (New York, 1990).
4. J. Shy, *A People Numerous and Armed: Reflections on the Military Struggle for American Independence* (New York, 1976); D. Higginbotham, 'The American Militia: A Traditional Institution with Revolutionary Responsibilities', in Higginbotham (ed.), *Reconsiderations on the Revolutionary War* (Westport, 1978); C.R. Ferguson, 'Carolina and Georgia Patriot and Loyalist Militia in Action, 1778–1783', in J.J. Crow and L.E. Tise (eds.), *The Southern Experience in the American Revolution* (Chapel Hill, 1978); P.D. Nelson, 'Citizen Soldiers or Regulars', *Military Affairs* (1979).
5. *Madison* 1, 320–3.
6. NRO. 1314/6; *Jefferson* 2, 125–6.
7. *Jefferson* 2, 13; Nelson, *Anthony Wayne. Soldier of the Early Republic* (Bloomington, 1985) pp. 69–71; *Madison* 1, 266–7; Nelson, 'Major General Horatio Gates as a Military Leader: The Southern Experience', in W. Roberts Higgins (ed.), *The Revolutionary War in the South* (Durham, NC, 1979) pp. 150–1.
8. S.H.H. Carrington, *The British West Indies during the American Revolution* (Dordrecht, 1988).
9. Me 172-111/48.
10. *Hamilton* 2, 369; L.C. Sumter papers, 14 Ap. 1781; R.A. Bowler, 'Logistics and Operations in the American Revolution', in Higginbotham (ed.), *Revolutionary War*, p. 59.
11. *Reflections on the Present State of the American War* (London, 1776) p. 17.
12. W.W. Abbot (ed.), *The Papers of George Washington. Revolutionary War Series* 2 (Charlottesville, 1987) p. 28; D.R. Gerlach, *Proud Patriot. Philip Schuyler and the War of Independence* (Syracuse, 1987) p. 15.
13. NeC 4219; *Jefferson* 2, 195.
14. H.F. Rankin, *The North Carolina Continentals* (Chapel Hill, 1971) pp. 22, 38.

15. Rankin, pp. 28–9, 40.
16. *Franklin* 22, 181–2.
17. *Franklin* 22, 440.
18. E.S. Kite, 'The Continental Congress and France: Secret Aid and the Alliance 17 76–1777', *Records of the American Catholic Historical Society of Philadelphia* 39 (1928); *idem* 'French "Secret Aid". Precursor to the French Alliance, 1776–1777', *French American Review* 1 (1948); J.R. Dull, *A Diplomatic History of the American Revolution* (New Haven, 1985) pp. 61–3; *Adams Family Correspondence* 2, 25, 61; *Madison* 1, 160; *Diplomatic Corresp.* 2 (1889) p. 66; D. Higginbotham, *The War of American Independence* (New York, 1971) p. 308.
19. *Franklin* 22, 398.
20. *Hamilton* 1, 265–6; P. Mackesy, 'What the British Army Learned', in R. Hoffman and P.J. Albert (eds.), *Arms and Independence. The Military Character of the American Revolution* (Charlottesville, 1984) p. 199.
21. L.C. Greene Letterbook; E.W. Carp, *To Starve the Army at Pleasure: Continental Army Administration and American Political Culture, 1775–1783* (Chapel Hill, 1984).
22. *Hamilton* 2, 554.
23. C.H. Lesser (ed.), *The Sinews of Independence: Monthly Strength Reports of the Continental Army* (Chicago, 1976); Dederer, *War in America* pp. 210–11; PCC. 172.
24. J.C. Cavanagh, 'American Military Leadership in the Southern Campaign: Benjamin Lincoln', in Higgins (ed.), *Revolutionary War* pp. 106, 108, 114; Nelson, 'Gates' p. 140; G. Massey, 'The British Expedition to Wilmington, January–November, 1781', *North Carolina Historical Review*, 66 (1989) p. 392; L.C. Greene Letterbook.
25. L.C. Sumter papers, 30 Mar. 1781; PRO. 30/11/86 f.47.
26. *Hamilton*, 2, 632.
27. BL. Add. 36803 f.81.
28. LC. Peter Force 49.

4   Conflict

1. Hull, University Library, Department of Manuscripts DDHo 4/17.
2. *Franklin* 22, 359.
3. *Franklin* 24, 293; *Papers of George Washington, Revolutionary War Series* 2, 81; L. Diamant, *Chaining the Hudson. The Fight for the River in the American Revolution* (New York, 1989); *Hamilton*, 238–40; *Adams Family Corresp.* 2, 190–1; *Franklin* 22, 343.
4. *Franklin* 23, 118–19.
5. *Franklin* 22, 155–7, 185, 522–3; A. Roland, *Underwater Warfare in the Age of Sail* (Bloomington, 1978) pp. 67–79.
6. *Adams Family Corresp.* 1, 215; *Madison* 1, 153;

Hamilton 1, 316; WW R150–8; *A State of the Expedition from Canada, as laid before the House of Commons, By Lieutenant-General Burgoyne* (London, 1780) p. 120; BL.Add. 32627 f.15–16.

7. Cobbett 20, 984; BL.Ad. 21687 f.322; R. Atwood, *The Hessians* (Cambridge, 1980) p. 69; WO. 34/115 f.65–6.

8. *Lee* 2, 76; Nelson, *Wayne* p. 72.

9. *Franklin* 22, 275–6; Halifax SH 7 JL/1 p. 16; BL.Add. 32413 f.18; SRO.GD. 170/1063/25.

10. Rankin, *North Carolina* p. 65.

11. NRO. 1314/5; Cobbett, 20, 982, 791; G.A. Billias (ed.), *George Washington's Opponents* (New York, 1969) p. 163.

12. *Lee* 1, 417–18; L.C. Greene letterbook; HMC. *Stopford-Sackville* 1, 383–4; M.C. Searcy, *The Georgia–Florida Contest in the American Revolution, 1776–1778* (Tuscaloosa, 1985) p. 97.

13. P. Mackesy, 'Problems of an Amphibious Power: Britain against France, 1793–1815', *Naval War College Review* (1978) p. 20; BL.Add. 21687 f.322; NeC 2,600.

14. T. Keppel, *Life of Augustus, Viscount Keppel* (2 vols., 1842) I, 442–3; H.C.B. Rogers, *The British Army of the Eighteenth Century* (1977) pp. 70–4.

15. Higginbotham, *War and Society in Revolutionary America* (Columbia, South Carolina, 1988) p. 133; Cavanagh, 'Lincoln', p. 114.

16. PRO.30/11/76 f.12; Durham, Grey, 25, pp. 2–3, 9.

17. Washington to Hancock, 23 Sept. 1777, PCC 169.

18. PRO. 30/11/76 f.12; Washington to Hancock, 5 October 1777, PCC 169; Gist to —, 10 October 1777, LC Peter Force.

19. Washington to Hancock, 5 Oct. 1777, PCC 169; *Adams Family Corresp.* 2, 336.

5   1775: The First Year of the War

1. Bedford CRO, Lucas papers, L 30/14/314/4.

2. J. Fortescue (ed.), *The Correspondence of King George the Third from 1760 to December 1783* (1928) 3, 153.

3. NRO. 1314/7; Halifax SH 7/JL/1 p. 15.

4. WW R150–4.

5. Halifax SH 7/JL/41; Exeter CRO, 64/12/29/1/107.

6. NeC 4234; M. Balderston and D. Syrett (eds.), *The Lost War. Letters from British Officers during the American Revolution* (New York, 1975) p. 33; Sheffield City Library, Spencer Stanhope papers 60542/9, 13.

7. Spencer Stanhope 60542/8.

8. NeC 2,649, 2,317, 2,348; Halifax SH 7/JL/43, 46; NRO. 1314/3a, 4; Spencer

Stanhope 60542/10, 12; *Leeds Mercury* 19 September, 10, 24 October 1775; Balderston and Syrett, *Letters* pp. 35, 39, 49–53, 57.

9. *Washington* 2, 3, 112; *Franklin*, 22, 295; *Adams Family Corresp.* 1, 261.

10. J.K. Martins and M.E. Lender, *A Respectable Army. The Military Origins of the Republic, 1763–1789* (Arlington, Illinois, 1982) xi–xii; *Washington*, 2, 55.

11. *Franklin* 22, 292–3.

12. WW R1–1590, 1575.

13. A.C. Land (ed.), *Letters from America by William Eddis* (Cambridge, Mass., 1969) p. 113; BL.Add. 32627 f.6.

14. *Adams Family Corresp.* 1, 195, 212; *Maddison* 1, 149.

15. WW R 150–2; *Leeds Mercury* 18 July 1775; NRO. Berwick office 1955 A No. 98.

16. *Eddis* pp. 110, 113.

17. W.H. Moomaw, 'The British leave colonial Virginia', *Virginia Magazine of History and Biography* 66 (1958); A.J. Mapp, 'The "Pirate" Peer: Lord Dunmore's Operations in the Chesapeake Bay' in E.M. Eller (ed.), *Chesapeake Bay in the American Revolution* (Centreville, 1981).

18. *Franklin* 22, 247; D. Syrett, *The Royal Navy in American Waters 1775–1783* (1989) pp. 14, 20.

19. *Reflections on the Present State of the American War* (London, 1776) p. 5; *Franklin* 22, 293–5.

20. Fortescue, 3, 265–72; P. Smith, *Loyalists and Redcoats. A Study in British Revolutionary Policy* (Chapel Hill, 1964) p. 22; NeC 2, 381; I.D. Gruber, 'Britain's Southern Strategy', in Higgins (ed.), *Revolutionary War* p. 210.

21. Exeter CRO. Q/51/20 p.589; *Present State* p. 151. Sympathy for the Revolutionary cause and support for conciliation is stressed in J.E. Bradley, *Popular Politics and the American Revolution in England. Petitions, the Crown, and Public Opinion* (Macon, Georgia, 1986).

22. *Franklin* 22, 180; D.R. Gerlach, *Proud Patriot: Philip Schuyler and the War of Independence, 1775–1783* (Syracuse, 1987) p. 31.

23. Spencer Stanhope 60542/11.

6   1776: The British Attack

1. BL. Add. 24162 f. 144.

2. PCC. 58.

3. B.W. Fowle, *The Maryland Militia during the Revolutionary War: A Revolutionary Organization* (University of Maryland PhD, 1982) p. 30; Shy *People Numerous and Armed* p. 142.

4. H.M. Lydenberg (ed.), *Archibald Robertson, His Diaries and Sketches in America 1762–1780* (New York, 1930) p. 79; Bowler, *Logistics* pp. 107–8.

5. NeC 2,300; Harris Memoranda, 1 May 1776, London, History of Parliament transcripts;

C. Rose (ed.), *Correspondence of Charles, 1st Marquess Cornwallis* (1859) p. 21.

6. E. Robson, 'The Expedition to the Southern Colonies, 1775–1776', *English Historical Review* (1951); NeC 2342, 2321.
7. BL.Add. 21687 f.245.
8. BL.Add. 21687 f.258, 261–2.
9. BL.Add. 32413 f.12.
10. BL.Add. 32413 f.14–15.
11. Me 172-111/1.
12. A.S. Everest, *Moses Hazen and the Canadian refugees in the American Revolution* (Syracuse, 1976).
13. BL.Add. 34416 f.273.
14. Franklin 22, 438; Exeter CRO 997Z/Z 12.
15. A.T. Mahan, *The Influence of Sea Power upon History 1660–1783* p. 342; NeC 2,323, 2,326, 2,322; BL.Add. 32413 f. 19–21, 25; NeC 2,326; Me 172-111/3, 6; Fortescue 3, 406.
16. Cobbett 20,678; HMC. *Lothian* p. 296; NeC 2,325.
17. SRO.GD.26/9/513/16; I. Gruber, 'America's First Battle: Long Island, August 27, 1776' in C. Heller (ed.), *America's First Battles, 1776–1965* (Lawrence, 1986) pp. 1–32.
18. *Franklin* 22, 584.
19. Cobbett 20, 679.
20. SRO.GD.26/9/513/15; NeC 2,323; Cobbett 20, 680.
21. SRO.GD.26/9/513/12,11; R.K. Showman (ed.), *The Papers of Nathanael Greene* I (Chapel Hill, 1976) pp. 352–9; NeC 2,370, 2,342; W.B. Willcox (ed.), *The American Rebellion. Sir Henry Clinton's Narrative of his Campaigns* (New Haven, 1954) p. 55; NeC 2,372; *Cornwallis Corresp.* 11, 25; Cobbett 20, 681, 742.
22. WW R1-1706; Cobbett 20, 749; V.L. Collins (ed.) *A Brief Narrative of the Ravages of the British and Hessians at Princeton in 1776–1777* (Princeton, 1906).
23. Bedford CRO. L30/14/410/11; Munich, Bayerisches Hauptstaatsarchiv, Bayr. Ges. Wien 705, 20 November, 18 December.
24. *Bristol Journal*, 1 February, 1 March 1777.
25. W.S. Stryker, *The Battles of Trenton and Princeton* (Boston, 1898); S.S. Smith, *The Battle of Trenton* (Monmouth Beach, 1965).
26. SRO.GD.26/9/513/8.
27. Germain to Howe, 19 Ap. 1777, PRO. 30/8/5.

7 1777: Phliadelphia and Saratoga

1. Georginia Lady Chatterton, *Memorials . . . of Admiral Lord Gambier* (2 vols., London, 1861) 1, 106.
2. PRO. 30/8/7.
3. NeC 2,371; General Gist to Samuel Chase, 8 March 1777, LC series 7E transcripts, Peter Force, entry 50; B.W. Fowle, *The*

Maryland Militia (University of Maryland PhD, 1982) pp. 31–2, 173–7.

4. Germain to John Stuart, 2 Ap. 1777, PRO. 30/8/5.
5. G.A. Billias, 'John Burgoyne: ambitious general', in Billias (ed.), *George Washington's Opponents* (New York, 1969) pp. 142–92; R.J. Hargrove, *General John Burgoyne* (Newark, Delaware, 1983).
6. Huntington Library, Lo. 7086; PRO. 30/8/5.
7. W.B. Willcox, 'Too many cooks: British planning before Saratoga', *Journal of British Studies* (1962) pp. 56–90.
8. HMC. *Stopford-Sackville* 2, 49–50.
9. HMC. *Stopford-Sackville* 2, 52–3.
10. HMC. *Stopford-Sackville* 2, 60–3; NeC 2,810.
11. Quoted in G.S. Brown, *The American Secretary. The Colonial Policy of Lord George Germain, 1775–1778* (Ann Arbor, 1963) p. 109.
12. NeC 2369, 2346; *Hamilton* 1, 220.
13. Gruber, 'British Strategy: The Theory and Practice of Eighteenth-Century Warfare', in Higginbotham (ed.), *Reconsiderations on the Revolutionary War* (Westport, 1978) p. 26.
14. Cobbett 20, 689.
15. *Hamilton* 1, 274–5; Balderston and Syrett (eds.), *Lost War* p. 130.
16. Cobbett 20, 690.
17. Durham, Grey 2239a; 3rd Earl of Malmesbury (ed.), *Letters of the First Earl of Malmesbury* (2 vols., 1870) I, 363; W.H. Moomaw, 'The denouement of General Howe's campaign of 1777', *English Historical Review* (1964) p. 504; Gruber, *Howe Brothers* pp. 235–6.
18. NeC 2,810; BL.Add. 32413 f.48–9; Houlding and Yates, 'Quebec . . .' p. 157. Although it has been suggested that Carleton was unhelpful, both A.G. Bradley, *Sir Guy Carleton* (Toronto, 1926) ch. 9 and P. Smith, 'Sir Guy Carleton', in G.A. Billias (ed.), *George Washington's Opponents* (New York, 1969) pp. 127–8, say that he did all he could to help Burgoyne prepare for the campaign of 1777.
19. Me 172-111/5.
20. NeC 4226.
21. Cobbett 20, 794.
22. Me 172/111/4.
23. *State of the Expedition* pp. 107–8.
24. *State of the Expedition* p. 114.
25. Me 171-110/5; NeC 2356, 2353.
26. *A Brief Examination of the Plan and Conduct of the Northern Expedition in America, in 1777. And of the Surrender of the Army under the Command of Lieutenant-General Burgoyne* (London, 1779) pp. 8–9.
27. *Remarks on General Burgoyne's State of the Expedition from Canada* (London, 1780) p. 56.
28. *State of the Expedition* p. 121; M.M. Mintz, *The Generals of Saratoga* (New Haven, 1990) pp. 191–7; Houlding and Yates, 'Quebec . . .' p. 159.

29. *State of the Expedition* p. 124; Houlding and Yates, 'Quebec . . .' p. 160.
30. Willcox (ed.), *American Rebellion* p. 70; NeC 2,721, 2,357, 2,344, 2,340, 2,351, 2,357.
31. NeC 2,344.
32. Howe to Germain, 30 Nov. 1777, PRO. 30/8/7.
33. *Hamilton* 1, 347, 353.
34. *Hamilton* 1, 311.
35. NeC 2337; Willcox (ed.), *American Rebellion* pp. 81–2.
36. *Hamilton* 1, 338–9.
37. BL.Add. 24177 f.92.
38. HMC. *Lothian* p. 300.
39. PCC. 169.
40. *Adams Family Corresp.* 2, 329.
41. Washington to Hancock, 3 September 1777, PCC 169. There is a good reproduction of a contemporary map of the countryside between Head of Elk and Philadelphia in D.W. Marshall and H.H. Peckham, *Campaigns of the American Revolution. An Atlas of Manuscript Maps* (Ann Arbor, 1976) p. 58.
42. PCC. 169.
43. SRO.GD.21/492/4 f.14–15; Cobbett 20, 698–9.
44. Washington to Hancock, 23 September 1777, PCC; Cobbett 20, 699; Gist to John Smith, 23 Sept. 1777, LC Peter Force 50; *Hamilton* 1, 330.
45. PCC. 169; SRO.GD.21/492/4 f.21–2.
46. Cobbett 20, 702; Atwood, *Hessians* pp. 118–30.
47. 7 October 1777, PCC. 169; SRO.GD.21/492/4 f.22,26; S.S. Smith, *Fight for the Delaware* (Monmouth Beach, 1970) pp. 41–2.
48. Refers to meeting on 29 October.
49. PCC. 169.
50. Navy Records Society, *Private Papers of John Earl of Sandwich* 1, 327–35.
51. Huntington Library, Loudoun papers 8903; *Malmesbury* I, 368.

8   1778: France Enters the War

1. NeC 2,648; BL.Add. 34416 f.33.
2. J. Dull, *The French Navy and American Independence: A Study of Arms and Diplomacy, 1774–1787* (Princeton, 1975) p. 120; O.T. Murphy, *Charles Gravier, Comte de Vergennes. French Diplomacy in the Age of Revolution: 1719– 1787* (Albany, 1982) pp. 252–60. See more generally H. Doniol (ed.), *Histoire de la participation de la France à l'établissement des Etats-Unis d'Amérique: Correspondance diplomatique et documents* (Paris, 1886–99); R. Hoffmann and P.J. Albert (eds.), *Diplomacy and Revolution: The Franco-American Alliance of 1778* (Charlottesville, 1981).
3. Balderston and Syrett (eds.), *Lost War* p. 148.
4. PCC. 169; NeC 2,374; PRO. 30/55/8.
5. PRO. 30/55/10 f.66.
6. Cobbett 20, 359; PRO. 30/55/8.
7. PRO. 30/55/10.
8. BL.Add. 34426 f.154–5; W. Hackman, 'English Military Expeditions to the Coast of France, 1757–1761' Michigan, (PhD , 1968).
9. HMC. *Carlisle* pp. 322–33.
10. Paris, Archives du Ministère des Affaires Etrangères, Correspondance Politique Angleterre 528 f.384.
11. NeC 4,219; WO 34/110 f.144–6.
12. NeC 4,219.
13. HMC. *Stopford-Sackville* 2, 94–9.
14. Fortescue 4, 30–1.
15. NeC 2,355; PRO. 30/55/10.
16. PRO. 30/55/10.
17. J.M. Palmer, *General von Steuben* (New Haven, 1937); *Madison* 1, 220; *Hamilton* 1, 426.
18. Washington to Hancock, 20 March, 10 April 1778, PCC. 169.
19. *Diplomatic Correspondence* 2, 554.
20. NRO. 2DE 12/5/24; Nelson, *Anthony Wayne* pp. 75–6.
21. Germain to Clinton, 1 July 1778, PRO. 30/55/11.
22. Clinton to Germain, 5 July 1778, PRO. 30/55/11; BL.Add. 34416 f.153.
23. *Hamilton* 1, 504–6.
24. BL.Add. 34416 f. 153; Clinton to Germain, 5 July 1778, PRO. 30/55/11; NeC 2,645; HMC. *Carlisle* p. 383.
25. *Jefferson* 2, 201; W.S. Stryker, *The Battle of Monmouth* (Princeton, 1927).
26. BL.Add. 34416 f.154.
27. G.S. Brown, 'The Anglo-French Crisis, 1778: A Study of Conflict in the North Cabinet' *William and Mary Quarterly* (1956); Gruber, *Howe Brothers* pp. 281–5.
28. Cobbett 20, 332.
29. WW R140–6.
30. Cobbett 20, 340–1.
31. NeC 2,611; Grey memorandum on Rhode Island, Durham, Grey 23; BL.Add. 34416 f.154.
32. NeC 2,614; HMC *Carlisle* pp. 387–8.
33. HMC *Carlisle* p. 387; BL.Add. 34416 f.155; NeC 2,644; *Cornwallis* 1, 36.
34. NeC 2,648, 2,635, 2,614, 2,637.
35. *Journals of the Continental Congress* 12, 1091; BL.Add. 34416 f.241; PRO.WO. 34/112 f.3–4.
36. BL.Add. 34416 f.67–9.
37. Willcox (ed.), *American Rebellion* pp. 112, 119; BL.Add. 34416 f.156.
38. BL.Add. 34416 f.123–4.
39. Bowler, 'Logistics and Operations in the American Revolution', in Higginbotham (ed.), *Reconsiderations on the Revolutionary War* p. 59; R.K. Showman (ed.), *The Papers of Nathanael Greene* 3 (Chapel Hill, 1983).
40. Cavanagh 'Lincoln' in Higgins (ed.), *Revolu-*

tionary War in the South p. 106; Calhoon, *Loyalist Perception* p. 157.

41. P.H. Smith (ed.), *Letters of Delegates to Congress, 1774–1789* vols. 10, 11 (Washington, 1983–4); *Diplomatic Correspondence* 2, 675.
42. *Gloucester Journal* 21 December 1778.
43. Me 172-111/7, 11; *Malmesbury* I, 397–8.
44. NeC 2,646; Willcox (ed.), *American Rebellion* p. 120. WO 34/111 f.184–5.
45. Cobbett 20, 22, 87.
46. Me 172-111/7, 11.
47. Cobbett 20, 7–8, 17–18, 34, 42–4.
48. BL.Add. 34416 f.155.

9 1779: Georgia and the Highlands

1. BL.Add. 34416 f. 425.
2. BL.Add. 34416 f. 479.
3. J. Shy, 'British Strategy for Pacifying the Southern Colonies, 1778–1781', in J.J. Crow and L.E. Tise (eds.), *The Southern Experience in the American Revolution*, (Chapel Hill, 1978) p. 157.
4. BL.Add. 34416 f. 241.
5. Fortescue, *George*, 4, 250–3.
6. NUL Me 172-111/7.
7. PRO.WO. 34/112 f/164-6; NeC 2,604, 2,633; BL.Add. f.241.
8. C.R. Ferguson, 'Functions of the Partisan-Militia in the South During the American Revolution: An Interpretation', in W.R. Higgins (ed.), *The Revolutionary War in the South* (Durham, North Carolina, 1979) p. 253.
9. E.J. Cashin, ' "But Brothers, It is Our Land We are Talking About" Winners and Losers in the Georgia Backcountry', in R. Hoffmann, T.W. Tate and P.J. Albert (eds.), *An Uncivil War. The Southern Backcountry during the American Revolution*, (Charlottesville, 1985) p. 258.
10. BL.Add. 34416 f. 241.
11. BL.Add. 34416 f. 271; PRO.WO. 34/112 f.5.
12. *Hamilton* 12, 34, 120.
13. Cobbett 20, 460.
14. Willcox (ed.), *American Rebellion*, pp. 126–7; PRO.WO. 34/112 f.38; *Hamilton*, 12, 55; NeC 2,603, 2,618, 2,605–6.
15. R. Fallaw and M.W. Stoer, 'The Old Dominion under fire: The Chesapeake Invasions, 1779–1781', in E.M. Eller (ed.), *Chesapeake Bay in the American Revolution* (Centerville, 1981) pp. 443–51; NeC 2,605.
16. *Hamilton*, 12, 57.
17. HMC. *Stopford-Sackville*, 2, 128–9.
18. D. Syrett, *The Royal Navy in American Waters 1775–1783* (Aldershot, 1989) p. 124.
19. WO. 34/115 f.63–7; NeC 2, 606; H.P. Johnston, *The Storming of Stony Point* (New York, 1900); WO. 34/118 f.171–2.
20. J. Calef (ed.), *The Siege of Penobscot* (New York, 1971).

21. *Hamilton*, 12, 171, 176–7, 207.
22. J. Dull, *The French Navy and American Independence*, (Princeton, 1975) pp. 161–2 fn. 15.
23. Lincoln Journal, 5, 9, 12 Sept. 1779, LC.
24. Lincoln Journal, LC.
25. F.B. Hough, *The Siege of Savannah* (Albany, 1866); C.C. Jooe (ed.), *The Siege of Savannah* (Albany, 1874); WO. 34/119 f.248–9.
26. WO. 34/117, f.109, 34/118, f.169–70; BL. Add. 34416, f.425; NeC 2, 634.
27. WO. 34/119, f.66; BL. Add. 34416, f.417, 419, 437, 452, 455; NeC 2, 634.
28. BL.Add. 34416, f.426–7, 430, 462, 478.
29. WO. 34/119, f.228; BL. Add. 34416, f.449, 454, 478.

10 1780: The Siege of Charleston; Impasse in the North

1. Me 172-111/23, 25.
2. NeC 2,623; BL.Add. 34416 f.425.
3. *Hamilton* 2, 158–9.
4. NeC 2,631; Me 172-111/21.
5. G.F. Jones, 'The 1780 Siege of Charleston as Experienced by a Hessian Officer', *South Carolina Historical Magazine* 88 (1987) pp. 27, 30.
6. *Ibid.*, p. 32.
7. *Ibid.*, p. 64.
8. NeC 2,598; [F.B. Hough], *The Siege of Charleston* (Albany, 1867); *Original Papers Relating to the Siege of Charleston* (Charleston, 1898); B.A. Uhlendorf (ed.), *The Siege of Charleston* (Ann Arbor, 1938); W.T. Bulgar, 'Sir Henry Clinton's "Journal of the Siege of Charleston, 1780"', *South Carolina Historical Magazine* 66 (1965); Eller, 'Washington's Maritime Strategy and the Campaign that Assured Independence', in Eller (ed.), *Chesapeake Bay* p. 482.
9. Me 172-111/21.
10. NeC 2,598; *Cornwallis* 1, 45.
11. J.J. Nadelhaft, *The Disorders of War. The Revolution in South Carolina* (Orono, Maine, 1981) pp. 53–4.
12. NeC 2620; *Cornwallis* 1, 48. The British commander at Wilmington followed the same policy in 1781, Massey 'British Expedition to Wilmington', pp. 400–1.
13. HMC. *Polwarth* 5, 371; PRO. 30/11/72 f.16; G. Cornwallis-West, *The Life and Letters of Admiral Cornwallis* (London, 1927) p. 102; Me 172-111/22.
14. PRO. 30/11/72 f.40.
15. *Hamilton* 2, 385–6; WO. 34/126 f.71.
16. PRO. 30/11/72 f.16; *Cornwallis* 1, 47.
17. PRO. 30/11/72 f. 27, 40, 30/11/76 f.2, WO. 34/127 f.82.
18. BL.Add. 32627 f.13–14.
19. *Cornwallis* 1, 47.

20. PRO. 30/11/72 f.40, 42, 44; *Cornwallis* 1, 58–9.
21. L.C. Draper, *King's Mountain* (Cincinnati, 1881); NeC 2,609–10.
22. LC Greene letter book.
23. Greene to Sumter, 12 December 1780, LC Sumter papers.
24. PCC. 172, 7 December, Greene to Morgan, 16 December 1778; T.B. Myers (ed.), *Cowpens Papers* (Charleston, 1881) pp. 9–10.
25. Greene to Gist, 20 November 1780, LC Greene letter book.
26. LC Sumter papers.
27. PCC. 172.
28. *Cornwallis* 1, 67–9.
29. NeC 2,625.
30. NeC 2,610.
31. *Cornwallis* 1,74.
32. *Hamilton* 2, 259, 265; S.S. Bradford, 'Hunger Menaces the Revolution, December 1779– January 1780', *Maryland Historical Magazine* 61 (1966).
33. *Hamilton* 2, 303.
34. Me 172–111/24–5.
35. NeC 2,625, 2,624; PRO. WO. 34/127 f.8, 81.
36. Mundy, *Life and Correspondence of Admiral Lord Rodney* (London, 1830) 1, 400.
37. *Cornwallis* 1, 66; NeC 2,610.
38. *Rodney* 1, 432.

11   1781: Yorktown

1. PRO. 30/11/74 f.16–17; LC Sumter.
2. A.T. Patterson, *The Other Armada. The Franco-Spanish Attempt to Invade Britain in 1779* (Manchester, 1960); D. Baugh, 'Why did Britain lose command of the sea during the war for America?', in Black and P. Woodfine (eds.), *The British Navy and the Use of Naval Power in the Eighteenth Century* (Leicester, 1988) p. 152.
3. John Rutledge to Greene, 16 December 1780, LC Sumter.
4. PRO. WO 34/136 f.74; N.O. Rush, *The Battle of Pensacola* (Tallahassee, 1966); Coker and Rea (eds.), *Anglo-Spanish Confrontation*; C. Fernandez-Shaw, 'Participation de la Armada Espanola en la Guerre de la Independencia de Los Estados Unidos', *Revista de Historia Naval* 3 (1985).
5. Massey, 'British Expedition to Wilmington' p. 391; H. Smith (ed.), *Letters of Delegates to Congress, 1774–1789* 15, 16 (Washington, 1988–9); *An Answer to that part of the narrative of Lieutenant General Sir Henry Clinton which relates to the conduct of Lieutenant General Earl Cornwallis* (London, 1783) iii–v.
6. PRO. 30/11/74 f.24.
7. PRO. 30/11/74 f.26.
8. PRO. 30/11/68 f.53–5.
9. NeC 2,335.
10. *Jefferson* 4, 312.
11. S.J. Idzerda, *Lafayette in the Age of the American Revolution* 3 (Ithaca, 1980) pp. 333–4, 417.
12. PRO. 30/11/68 f.1.
13. BL.Add. 32627 f.21; PRO. WO 34/132 f.128; Rankin, 'Cowpens: Prelude to Yorktown', *North Carolina Historical Review* 31 (1954); T. Fleming, *Cowpens National Battlefield* (National Park Service Handbook 135, Washington DC, 1988).
14. Rankin, *North Carolina* pp. 275–6; F. and M. Wickwire, *Cornwallis and the War of Independence* (London, 1971) pp. 278–81.
15. LC Sumter; PCC. 172, 31 January, 15 February.
16. LC Sumter.
17. PRO. 30/11/85 f.33; Cornwallis 1, 87–91.
18. PRO. 30/11/74 f.2–3, 49.
19. PRO. 30/11/86 f.1.
20. LC Sumter; BL.Add. 32627 f.24; Massey, 'British Expedition to Wilmington' pp. 410–11.
21. PRO. 30/11/86 f.41.
22. NeC 2,295.
23. PRO. 30/11/74 f.17.
24. *Narrative of. . . Clinton* p. 50.
25. PRO. 30/11/74 f.15.
26. PRO. 30/11/68 f.8–10.
27. PRO. 30/11/68 f.11–12, 15–18; *Jefferson* 4, 14–15.
28. PRO. 30/11/68 f.24–6.
29. Willcox (ed.), *Rebellion* pp. 532–3.
30. PRO. 30/11/68 f.28, 40, 44.
31. PRO. 30/11/74 f.26–7, Cornwallis 1, 103–4. The strategic controversy can be pursued in B.J. Stevens (ed), *The Campaign in Virginia 1781. . . the Clinton–Cornwallis Controversy* (London, 1888); Willcox, 'The British Road to Yorktown: A Study in Divided Command', *American Historical Review* 52 (1946).
32. PRO. 30/11/74 f.34.
33. PRO. 30/11/68 f.43.
34. PRO. 30/11/74 f.33.
35. PRO. 30/11/68 f.53–5.
36. *Narrative of. . . Clinton* p. 110.
37. NeC 2,289.
38. PRO. 30/11/74 f.76–7.
39. PRO. 30/11/74 f.82.
40. Dull, *French Navy* pp. 242–5.
41. J.T. Flexner, *George Washington in the American Revolution* (Boston, 1967) p. 440.
42. *Hamilton* 2, 667.
43. PRO. 30/11/68 f.72–3.
44. Dull, *French Navy* p. 245.
45. F.J.P. Grasse-Tilly (ed.), *Correspondence of General Washington and Comte de Grasse* (Washington, 1931) pp. 33–4.
46. PRO. 30/11/68 f.75, 77.
47. Undated memorandum, 'Admiral Graves's Justification', Durham, Grey, 56; Syrett,

Royal Navy pp. 192–200; K. Breen, 'Graves and Hood at the Chesapeake', *Mariner's Mirror* 66 (1980); J. A. Sullivan, 'Graves and Hood', *Mariner's Mirror* 69 (1983).

48. PRO. 30/11/74 f.91.
49. PRO. 30/11/74 f.88.
50. PRO. 30/11/68 f.83, 87.
51. PRO. 30/11/68 f.91.
52. PRO. 30/11/74 f.101.
53. PRO. 30/11/74 f.103.
54. NeC 2,303, 2,287.
55. NeC 2,307.
56. PRO. 30/11/74 f.108. *Caldwell Papers* II ii, 344–5.
57. NeC 2,290, 2,288, 2,297, 2,599; Willcox, 'Rhode Island in British Strategy, 1780–1781', *Journal of Modern History* 17 (1945) p. 318; *Sandwich Papers* 3,251; Willcox, *American Rebellion* pp. 479–81.
58. Syrett, *Royal Navy* p. 218.
59. *Narrative of . . . Clinton*; p. 66.

12 Epilogue

1. Gateshead, Public Library, Ellison mss A.24 no. 17.
2. Dull, *American Independence* p. 299.
3. R.G. Mitchell, 'After Yorktown: The Wayne–Greene Correspondence, 1782', in H.H. Peckham (ed.), *Sources of American Independence* (2 vols., Chicago, 1978) 2, 385.
4. WO. 34/142 f.48; Gateshead A.63 no. 41.
5. Quoted in I.R. Christie, *The End of North's Ministry 1780–1782* (London, 1958) pp. 319–20.
6. Me 172-111/33; *Morning Chronicle* 15, 18 July, *St James's Chronicle* 23 July, *Gazetteer* 24 July 1782.
7. Dull, *American Independence* p. 308.
8. G. Lanctot, *Canada and the American Revolution 1774–1783* (London, 1967) p. 208.
9. Mitchell 2,367; E. Jones, 'The British Withdrawal from the South, 1781–1785', in W.R. Higgins (ed.), *Revolutionary War* p. 267.
10. E.W. Carp, 'The Origins of the Nationalist Movement of 1780–1783: Congressional Administration and the Continental Army', *Pennsylvania Magazine of History and Biography* 107 (1983) p. 390.
11. D. Syrett, *Shipping and the American War, 1775–83* (London, 1970) pp. 231–41.
12. BL.Add. 32627 f.27.
13. LC Sumter.
14. C.R. Ritcheson, 'The Earl of Shelburne and Peace with America, 1782–1783: Vision and Reality', *International History Review* 5 (1983); L.S. Kaplan, 'The American Revolution in an International Perspective: Views from Bicentennial Symposia', *Ibid.*, 1 (1979).
15. J.L. Cross, *London Mission: The First Critical Years* (East Lansing, 1968); R.C. Stuart, *United States Expansionism and British North America, 1775–1871* (Chapel Hill, 1988) p. 35; Ritcheson, *Aftermath of Revolution: British Policy toward the United States, 1783–1795* (Dallas, 1969); J.L. Wright, *Britain and the American Frontier, 1783–1815* (Georgia, 1975); Ritcheson, 'Thomas Pinckney's London Mission, 1792–1794. A Reappraisal', in P.J. Korshin and R.R. Allen (eds.), *Greene Centennial Studies* (Charlottesville, 1984).
16. BL.Add. 35527 f.81.
17. P.P. Hill, *French Perceptions of the Early American Republic 1783–1793* (Philadelphia, 1988).
18. Paris, Ministère des Affaires Etrangères, Correspondance Politique Etats Unis 35 f.136, 188.
19. J.B. Hattendorf, 'The American Navy in the World of Franklin and Jefferson, 1775–1826', *War and Society* 2 (1990) pp. 10, 17.
20. H. Lydenberg (ed.), *Archibald Robertson. His Diaries and Sketches in America* (New York, 1930) pp. 36, 38.
21. Mackesy, *The Strategy of Overthrow 1798–1799* (London, 1974).
22. Ira Gruber has written a number of studies of British strategy, including 'The Origins of British Strategy in the War for American Independence', in S.J. Underdal (ed.), *Military History of the American Revolution* (Washington, 1976); 'Classical Influences on British Strategy in the War for American Independence', in J.W. Eadie (ed.), *Classical Traditions in Early America* (Ann Arbor, 1976); 'British Strategy: The Theory and Practice of Eighteenth-Century Warfare' in D. Higginbotham (ed.), *Reconsiderations on the Revolutionary War* (Westport, 1978); 'Britain's Southern Strategy', in W.R. Higgins (ed.), *Revolutionary War in the South*; 'The Anglo-American Military Tradition and the War for American Independence' in K.J. Hagan and W.R. Roberts (eds.), *Against All Enemies* (Westport, 1986).
23. Gruber, 'Military Tradition', pp. 43–4.
24. H.H. Peckham (ed.), *The Toll of Independence. Engagements and Battle Casualties of the American Revolution* (Chicago, 1974) pp. 130–3.
25. L.G. Schwoerer, 'The Bill of Rights: epitome of the Revolution of 1688–89', in J.G.A. Pocock (ed.), *Three British Revolutions: 1641, 1688, 1776* (Princeton, 1980) p. 225; Harris memoranda, January 1779, London, History of Parliament transcripts; T. Aruga, 'The Diplomatic Thought of the American Revolution', *Hitotsubashi Journal of Law and Politics* 9 (1981) pp. 40–1; P. Higonnet, *Sister Republics. The Origins of French and American Republicanism* (Princeton, 1988) is somewhat limited.
26. J. Shy, *A People Numerous and Armed. Reflections on the Military Struggle for American Independence* (Oxford, 1976).
27. R.F. Weigley, *The American Way of War* (New York, 1973) p. 36.

INDEX

Adams, Abigail, 81
Adams, John, 15, 60, 70, 142, 144
Adams, Samuel, 9
Alabama, 243
Alaska, 2
Albany, NY, 27, 32, 117–18, 120, 127, 129, 131–5
Allen, Ethan, 88, 90
Amboy, NJ, 112, 122
Amherst, Jeffrey, Lord, 32, 134, 151, 154, 181
amphibious operations, 49, 86, 105, 149–50, 172, 205
André, John, 200–1
Annapolis, MD, 85–6
Arbuthnot, Admiral Marriot, 180–2, 189, 199, 201, 208, 221–2, 224
Argentina, 2
Armed Neutrality, 204
arms, 48–50, 136
army, American, beginnings of, 81–3; see also Continental army
Arnold, General Benedict, 38, 53, 88–9, 92, 100, 128–9, 131, 134, 183, 198–201, 208, 220
artillery, 53, 58–9, 65, 77–8, 96–7, 101, 108, 111, 140, 178, 226, 228
Ashe, John, 175
Ashley River, 187
Assaye, 246
Assunpink Creek, NJ, 111
Aughrim, 246
Augusta, GA, 172, 174, 195, 209–10, 217

Bahamas, 240, 243
Balfour, Lt.-Col. Nesbitt, 216
Ballinamuck, 13
Baltimore, MD, 25, 83
Bangalore, 246
Barras, Comte de, 225–6, 228, 233
Baton Rouge, 204
Battle of the Clouds, 137–8
Baum, Lt.-Col. Frederick, 127
Baurmeister, Major Carl Leopold, 18
Bavarian Succession, War of, 27, 47
bayonets, 62–4, 78, 218
Beaufort, SC, 56, 175
Beaumarchais, Pierre-Augustin Caron de, 49
Bedford, NY, 105

Bedford Pass, NY, 103
Belton, Joseph, 59
Bemis Heights, NY, 64, 129, 132, 134, 144
Bennington, VT, 31, 35, 127–8, 195
blockade, 71, 150, 245
Bolivar, Simon, 2
Boone, Governor Thomas, 1
Bordentown, NJ, 111
Boston, MA, 5, 9, 17, 20, 22, 24, 27, 29, 31, 38–9, 44, 49, 54–5, 59–60, 63, 68, 71–2, 74–5, 79–83, 86–8, 93–4, 96, 115, 118–19, 163–4, 176, 207, 235, 247
Boston Massacre, 9
Boston Port Act, 11
Boston Tea Party, 2, 11
Bouquet, Henry, 67, 81
Bourne, William, 59
Boyd, Col. James, 174
Boyne, 246
Braddock, Gen. Edward, 67
Brandywine, PA, 62, 114, 120, 134, 136–8, 140, 155
Brant, Joseph, 36
Brazil, 2–3
Breed's Hill, MA, 29, 38, 75–7
Brest, Brest fleet, 161, 207
Breymann, Lt.-Col. Heinrich von, 128
Briar Creek, 175
British Legion, 187, 210
Bronx, 102, 105
Brooklyn, NY, 29, 69, 103–4
Brown, Lt.-Col. Thomas, 66, 174
Bunbury, Sir Charles, 20
Bunker Hill, MA, 25, 27, 29, 38, 64–5, 68, 71, 75–9, 247
Burford, Col. Abraham, 189
Burgoyne, Gen. John, 19, 25, 29, 31–2, 35, 38, 65–6, 75, 77–9, 101, 112, 115, 117–21, 123–9, 131–5, 247
Burlington, NJ, 110
Bushnell, David, 59–60
Butler, John, 36

Caledonian Volunteers, 17
Camden, SC, 56, 69, 191, 195, 198, 216–17

Camden, battle of, 29, 56, 68, 191–4, 196, 204, 210, 247
Campbell, Alexander, 64
Campbell, Lt.-Col. Archibald, 16, 28, 166, 171–2, 174–6
Campbell, Lord William, 84, 96, 148
Canada, 7, 13, 19–20, 23–5, 27–9, 31, 37–8, 41–4, 65–6, 71, 78, 83, 88–93, 95, 97–101, 115, 119, 122, 125, 128–9, 131, 154, 165, 170, 172, 179, 201, 203, 235, 240, 243, 245–7
Cape Fear, NC, 87, 95–6, 198
Cape Fear River, 215
Cape Hatteras, 167, 185
Caribbean see West Indies
Carleton, Gen. Sir Guy, 64, 66, 90, 92, 98–101, 117, 119, 125–6, 128, 147–8, 238–40
Carlisle, Frederick Howard, 5th Earl of, 46, 151–2, 166, 172, 238
Carolinas, 15, 26, 35, 49, 180, 188–9, 224
Castine, ME, 177, 189
Casualties, American, 247–8
Catawba River, 34, 212
Cathcart, Charles, 9th Lord, 3, 117
Catherine the Great, 87, 204
cavalry, 39, 64–7, 69, 187–8, 210, 217, 247
Chambly, 90, 98, 100
Champlain, Lake, 25, 39, 88–9, 93, 98–101, 126
Charleston, SC, 17, 20, 22, 25, 33–4, 39, 45, 53, 56, 62, 66, 68–9, 86–7, 93, 96–7, 108–9, 115, 148–9, 166, 170, 173, 175, 181, 183–9, 191, 195, 196, 204–5, 216–17, 223, 233–6, 238–40, 246–7
Charlestown, MA, 74–5, 77
Charlotte, NC, 41, 191, 195, 204, 209
Chatham, 1st Earl of see Pitt, William,
Chatterton's Hill, NY, 107
Cheraw, NC, 209
Cherokee Indians, 35–6
Cherry Valley, NY, 37
Chesapeake, 34, 47, 96–7, 115, 120, 123–4, 160, 164, 173, 176–7, 180–4, 186, 195, 197–8, 201–2, 206–9, 215, 219–33, 235, 245

Chesney, Alexander, 84, 210, 217, 240
Chester, Peter, 204
chevaux de frise, 60, 140
Clark, Elijah, 190
Clark, George Rogers, 36
Clarke, Lt. John, 76
Clinton, Gen. Sir Henry, 16, 20, 22, 24, 26–9, 31, 37, 39–40, 56, 65–6, 69–70, 75–6, 78–9, 87, 94, 96–7, 101, 105–6, 108–10, 115, 127–9, 131–5, 146–50, 153–4, 157–60, 165–70, 176–7, 179–85, 187–90, 195, 198–9, 201, 203, 205–9, 220–8, 238
Clive, Robert, 34
coastal raids, 149–50, 176–7, 199
Cockburn, Admiral Sir George, 144
Coercive Acts, 11, 88
Collier, Commodore Sir George, 176–8
Concord, MA, 1, 24, 49, 63, 71–3, 83, 85, 146
Congress, Continental, 6, 10–12, 25, 42, 44–5, 48, 53, 55, 60, 64, 80–1, 95, 155–6, 167–8, 172, 196, 205
Connecticut, 53, 64, 82, 106, 118, 135, 150, 172, 199
Connecticut River, 119
Continental army, 42–6, 55, 57, 63, 81, 83, 128, 136, 167, 179, 184, 188, 191, 199, 210, 214
Continental currency, 47, 50
Cooper River, SC, 187–8
Cork, 95
Cornell, Ezekiel, 189
Cornwallis, Gen., 2nd Earl, 13–14, 17, 26–7, 29, 31–2, 36, 38–9, 53, 55–7, 62, 68, 70, 95, 108, 110–12, 129, 134, 136–7, 160, 174, 183, 189–91, 194, 198, 201–7, 209–10, 212–17, 219–34, 246–7
Cowan's Ford, NC, 211–12
Cowpens, SC, 66, 210–12, 214
Coxe's Mill, NC, 191
Craig, Maj. James, 219
Creek Indians, 34, 174
Cresap, Michael, 60
Crow Creek, NC, 48–9, 215
Crown Point, NY, 89, 98, 100–1, 112, 115, 126
Cruden, John, 33
Cuba, 19
Culloden, 17, 246

Dalrymple, William, 201
Dan River, 212–13
Danbury, CT, 150, 172

Dartmouth, William Legge, 2nd Earl of, 87
Davidson, Gen. William, 212
Deane, Silas, 110
Declaration of Independence, 42–3, 102
Declaratory Act, 9
Deep River, NC, 191
Delaware, 44, 192
Delaware River, 22, 58, 69, 108–11, 120, 123–4, 134–5, 138, 140–3, 156–7, 173, 222, 236, 245
Denbigh, Basil Feilding, Earl of, 145
Denmark, 204
Detroit, 36–7
deserters, 39, 44, 47, 53, 62, 150
Dickinson, Gen. Philemon, 142
Digby, Admiral Robert, 227–8, 240
Digby, Lt. William, 39, 63, 98, 100
disease, 97–8, 179
Dominica, 166
Donkin, Maj. Robert, 17
Donop, Col. Karl von, 140
Dorchester Heights, MA, 75, 80–1
Drayton's Landing, SC, 187
Duane, James, 20
Dunkirk, 243
Dunmore, John Murray, 4th Earl of, 33, 37, 83–4, 86, 94

East Bridgewater, MA, 49
East Florida Rangers, 66, 174
East India Company, 69
East River, NY, 102
Easton, 49
Ebenezer, GA, 236
Eddis, William, 83, 85
Eden, Robert, 86
Eden, William, 152, 166, 171–2
Egypt, 246
Elizabeth River, 198
Ellison, Gen. Cuthbert, 234
Estaing, Charles-Hector, Comte d', 22–3, 160, 162–4, 166–7, 170, 178–82, 207, 233–4
Eutaw Springs, SC, 218

Fairfield, CT, 177
Fairhaven, MA, 150
Falkland Islands, 9
Falmouth, ME, 86
Ferguson, Maj. Patrick, 33, 61, 195
Finance
  American, 50–1
  British, 204
Fishing Creek, SC, 194
Flatbush Pass, NY, 103
Florida, East, 13, 25–6, 28, 41, 78, 86, 115, 149, 154, 157, 165–6, 168, 175, 241, 243

Florida, West, 13, 25, 28, 41, 78, 154, 157, 165–6, 204, 243
Forbes, Gen. John, 67, 81
Fort Ann, NY, 125–6
Fort Clinton, NY, 117, 130, 132, 135
Fort Constitution, NY, 50, 117, 130, 132
Fort Duquesne, 67
Fort Edward, NY, 125, 132
Fort Granby, SC, 195
Fort Johnson, SC, 187
Fort Johnston, NC, 84
Fort Lee, NJ, 60, 108, 110
Fort Mercer, 140–2
Fort Mifflin, 140–2
Fort Montgomery, NY, 117, 130–2
Fort Motte, SC, 195, 217
Fort Moultrie, SC, 188
Fort Nelson, 176
Fort Stanwix, NY, 35, 128
Fort Washington, NY, 60, 63–4, 69, 106–8, 117
Fort Watson, SC, 195
fortifications, 51, 64–5, 68, 74, 125
'Forty-five rebellion, 13, 15, 17–18, 61, 93, 246
Forty Fort, PA, 37
Fox, Charles James, 24, 162
France, 6, 15, 29, 49, 70, 93, 99, 135–6, 140, 145–8, 152, 154, 165, 168, 198, 202, 204, 243, 248
Franklin, Benjamin, 24, 49, 58–9, 80, 85–6, 104
Franklin, William, 85
Fraser, Gen. Simon, 98, 134
Frederick the Great, 27, 64, 144, 155, 159
Fredericksburg, VA, 49
Freeman's Farm, NY, 129, 131, 144
French army, 178–9, 190, 199, 201
French Revolution, 243, 245, 248–9
Fulton, Robert, 60

Gage, Gen. Thomas, 11, 17, 26–7, 31, 60, 65, 67, 69, 71–6, 79, 85, 93–4, 247
Gale, Benjamin, 59
Galloway, Joseph, 172
Gálvez, Governor Bernardo de, 204
Gansevoort, Col. Peter, 128
Gardiner's Island, Long Island, 224
Gardinerstown, ME, 92
Gates, Gen. Horatio, 44, 46–7, 64, 117, 120, 128–9, 131–4, 143, 190, 196, 204, 216
George III, 1, 5, 7, 32, 71, 84, 87–8, 101, 147, 151–2, 232, 238–9
George, Lake, 125–6
Georgetown, SC, 189
Georgia, 15–16, 25, 28, 31, 34, 66,

86, 115, 153, 166, 171, 173–7, 181–2, 194, 204, 215, 238, 240
Germain, Lord George, 18, 27, 32, 53, 66, 87, 95, 112–15, 117–21, 134, 148, 153–4, 156, 161, 165–7, 169, 189, 221, 232, 236, 239
German Flats, NY, 37
Germantown, PA, 69–70, 120, 134, 138, 140, 142, 144, 155
Gibraltar, 28, 204, 243
Gibraltar, Straits of, 161–2
Gist, Gen. Mordecai, 69
Glorious Revolution, 248
Gloucester, VA, 231
Glover, Col. John, 107
Gordon Riots, 204
Goree, 19–20, 243
Gosforth, William, 58
Gosport, 86, 176
Gowanus Bay, 103
Grant, Gen. James, 28, 173, 179
Grasse, Admiral, Comte de, 207–8, 222, 225, 228, 230, 233–5, 243
Graves, Admiral Samuel, 86
Graves, Admiral Thomas, 224–8, 233
Gravesend Bay, 102
Great Bridge, 86
Green Spring, 223
Greene, Gen. Nathanael, 41, 47, 49, 51–3, 55, 66–7, 107–8, 137, 158, 167, 190, 196–7, 203, 205–6, 209–10, 212–20, 234, 240–1
Grenada, 23, 178
Grey, Gen. Charles, 19, 22, 31, 164
Guadeloupe, 19, 235
Guan, Heights of, 103
Guilford Court House, NC, 39, 70, 198, 206, 213–15, 218, 247

Hadden, Lt. James, 40, 47
Haiti, 2, 207, 248
Haldimand, Gen. Frederick, 28, 148, 240
Halifax, NC, 216
Halifax, Nova Scotia, 23, 28, 95, 97, 154, 172, 177–80, 224
Hamilton, Alexander, 29, 53, 57, 120, 155, 158, 199
Hamond, Capt. Andrew Snape, 124
Hampton Roads, VA, 86, 208, 224
Hancock, John, 94
Hanging Rock, SC, 194
Harlem Heights, NY, 106–7
Harris, James, 95, 248
Hartford, CT, 172
Hartley, David, 88
Harvey, Gen. Edward, 27
Harvie, John, 44
Havana, 19, 94

Hayes, John, 17, 98, 168, 172, 183, 195, 238
Hazen, Moses, 99
Head of Elk, MD, 124, 135
Henry, Patrick, 36, 45, 83–4, 155
Herkimer, Gen. Nicholas, 35, 128
Hessians, 28–9, 47, 62, 68, 107–11, 140
Highlands, 29, 31, 50, 108, 117, 119–20, 123, 130–2, 135, 144, 147, 157, 172, 174, 176–7, 181–2, 199, 201, 221
Hillsborough, NC, 193, 213, 216
Hobkirk's Hill, SC, 216–7
Hood, Admiral Samuel, 226, 232
Howe, Gen. George, 3rd Viscount, 150
Howe, Admiral Richard, 4th Viscount, 14, 22, 24, 102–3, 129, 150, 152, 162–5
Howe, Gen. Robert, 149, 166, 188
Howe, Gen. Sir William, 14, 17, 24–5, 27–9, 31–2, 38, 40, 55, 64–6, 69–70, 75, 77–81, 87, 93–5, 99–110, 114–15, 117–25, 134–8, 140, 142, 144, 148–52, 155–6, 162, 246–7
Hubbardtown, NY, 125
Hudson River, 16, 25, 58, 93, 99, 107–8, 117, 119, 121, 125–6, 128–35, 144, 147, 154, 164, 172, 201, 226
Huger, Gen. Isaac, 187
Hungary, 5, 25

Illinois, 36
India, 19, 37, 146, 154, 219, 245–6
Indians, 33–7, 61, 78, 83, 100, 125–8, 134, 172, 174–5, 235
Innes, Alexander, 17
Intolerable Acts, 11–12
Ireland, 13, 18, 24, 27–8, 219, 246
Iroquois, 36
Isle aux Noix, 98, 100

Jacobites, 13, 15, 18, 61, 93
Jägers, 61–2
Jamaica, 34, 179, 204, 234–5
Jamaica Pass, 103
James Island, 185
James River, VA, 208, 220, 223, 227
Jefferson, Thomas, 39, 44, 208, 222
John's Island, 175
Johnson, Guy, 34
Johnstone, George, 152
Joseph II, Emperor, 5

Kalb, Baron Johann de, 191–2
Kennebec River, ME, 92
Kentucky, 36
Keppel, Admiral Augustus, 162
Kettle Creek, SC, 174

King's Ferry, NY, 177
King's Mountain, SC, 33, 61, 195–6, 210
Kingsbridge, NY, 165, 201
Kingston, NY, 133
Kip's Bay, NY, 105
Knox, Gen. Henry, 53, 80
Knyphausen, Gen. Wilhelm von, 137

Lafayette, Marie Joseph, Marquis de, 40, 53, 158, 208, 220–1, 223, 228
Lake, Lt.-Col. Gerard, 246
Lancaster, PA, 49, 137
Laurens, Henry, 45, 166
Lee, Charles, 37, 42, 62, 64–5, 67, 80, 82, 94, 96–7, 108, 157–60
Lee, Henry 'Light-Horse Harry', 67, 179, 209–10, 212–14, 217
Lee, Richard Henry, 45, 47
Leeds Mercury, 61, 76
Lenud's Ferry, SC, 188
Leslie, Gen. Alexander, 33, 40, 198, 220, 233, 238
Leslie, Capt. William, 103–5
Lexington, MA, 1, 71–3, 83, 85, 146
Lincoln, Gen. Benjamin, 56, 67, 166–7, 175, 178–9, 184–90, 235
Lister, Ensign Jeremy, 24, 63, 74, 79
Livingston, Robert, 15
logistics
  American, 19, 36–8, 41, 44, 48, 50–7, 74, 82, 97, 122, 138, 142–3, 150, 155, 166, 172, 191, 199, 205, 235
  British, 17, 19, 38–9, 79, 100, 127
Long Island, NY, 69, 102–4, 172, 177, 222
Long Island, battle of, 62, 68, 103–4, 155, 188
Louisbourg, 19–20, 41, 94
Louisiana Purchase, 243
Lovell, James, 156
Lovell, Gen. Solomon, 177
Loyalists, 7, 15–18, 22–5, 28, 32–3, 36–7, 48–9, 61, 70, 85–8, 94–5, 110, 113, 115, 117, 123, 127, 147, 151–2, 156, 167–9, 171–2, 174–5, 190, 195–7, 206, 212–13, 215, 219, 221–2, 224, 231, 235, 240, 242, 247
Luzerne, Anne-César, Chevalier de la, 226

Maclean, Col. Allen, 92
McCrea, Jane, 35
McDougall, Gen. Alexander, 29
Madison, James, 33, 49
Mahan, Alfred, 99
Maine, 38, 92, 177

Manchac, 204
Manchester, VA, 220
Manhattan, NY, 103–6, 164, 201
Manila, 19, 154
Maria Theresa, 144
Marion, Gen. Francis, 196–7, 209–10, 217
Martha's Vineyard, 163
Martin, Governor Josiah, 48, 84, 86
Martinique, 19, 207
Maryland, 4, 32, 60, 86, 94, 115, 136, 143, 156, 173, 199, 222
Massachusetts, 11–12, 71, 82, 178
Mathew, Gen. Edward, 176–7
Mellish, Charles, 17, 48, 151–3
Menotomy, MA, 73
Middlebrook, NJ, 122
militia
  Colonial, 42, 67
  Revolutionary, 16, 29, 35, 42–6, 50, 53, 55–6, 62, 82, 94, 105–6, 110, 115, 117, 122, 127–8, 134, 136, 142–3, 156, 174–5, 192, 194, 210, 212, 217, 220, 228
Minorca, 28, 161, 204, 243
Mississippi, 243
Mobile, 204
Mohawk Indians, 35
Mohawk River, 119, 126, 128, 135
Monck's Corner, SC, 188
Moncrief, James, 33
Monmouth, NJ, 63, 110, 157–60
Montgomery, Gen. Richard, 64, 89–90, 92, 101
Montreal, 20, 58, 90, 92, 94, 98
Moore, John, (later) Sir John, 178
Moore, John, 194
Moore's Creek Bridge, NC, 16, 94, 96, 247
Morgan, Gen. Daniel, 51, 65, 67, 91, 128–9, 131, 134, 196, 209–10, 212, 214
Morning Chronicle, 238–9
Morning Herald, 234
Morristown, NJ, 112, 122, 199
Moultrie, Col. William, 56, 96
Mount Pleasant, SC, 188
Murray, Sir Alexander, 104
Murray, James, 38, 60
mutinies, 53, 234

Nantucket Shoals, 167, 222
Natchez, 204
Navies
  American, 100, 140, 142, 150, 177–8, 188, 243
  British, 5, 13, 23, 40, 76, 96, 100–2, 104, 108, 121, 123, 140, 153–4, 160–6, 175, 178, 180, 197, 199, 202, 224–8, 245

French, 13–14, 22, 40, 56, 70, 160–6, 178–9, 199, 201, 207–8, 217, 221, 225–8
Negroes, 33–4, 37, 83, 86, 166, 175, 216, 227, 248
Nelson, Thomas, 41
Newark, NJ, 108
New Bedford, MA, 150, 163
New Brunswick, NJ, 108, 112, 122
Newburgh, NY, 172
Newburyport, MA, 92
Newcastle, DE, 124
New England, 17, 49, 53–4, 60, 63, 119, 121, 123, 129, 134–5, 147–50, 153, 165, 168, 173, 238
Newfoundland, 25, 41, 153, 178, 226, 242–3
New Hampshire, 1, 31, 82, 127, 173
New Hampton,
New Haven, CT, 177
New Jersey, 15, 25, 27, 40, 46–7, 53, 69, 85, 93, 110, 112, 115, 118, 120, 122–3, 140, 142, 147, 155–7, 160, 165, 172, 174, 176, 199, 207, 210, 246
New Orleans, 181
Newport, RI, 20, 22, 29, 59, 86, 108, 150, 162–3, 165, 167–8, 178, 180, 183–4, 199, 201, 208, 221–2, 224–6
New York, 15, 17, 25–6, 36, 48, 54, 62, 66, 93, 117, 174
New York City, 14, 18, 20, 22, 24, 28, 31, 53, 55, 59, 64, 68, 78–9, 82, 85, 87–8, 93–7, 105–7, 112, 114–15, 118–19, 123, 127, 129, 134–5, 146–7, 154, 156, 158, 162, 165, 168–72, 176, 178–80, 185, 198–9, 201, 203, 205, 207, 221–2, 224–8, 235, 238–40, 243, 247
New York Volunteers, 17
Newtown, NY, 36
Ninety-Six, SC, 84, 195, 217–19
Norfolk, VA, 96, 176, 202
North Carolina, 16, 32, 39, 41, 46–9, 51, 56, 64, 66, 86–8, 94–7, 183–4, 191, 193–6, 203, 206, 210, 212–13, 215, 219, 226, 246
North Edisto Inlet, 185
North, Frederick, Lord, 11–12, 17, 57, 71, 87, 204, 239, 241
Norwalk, CT, 177
Nova Scotia, 18, 25, 28, 41, 153, 177, 240

Ogeechee River, 174
Old Point Comfort, VA, 224–5
Orangeburg, SC, 195, 217
Oregon, 243
Oriskany, NY, 128

Oswego, NY, 119, 128
Otto, Louis-Guillaume, 243

Paine, Thomas, 58
Paoli massacre, 138
Paris, Peace of, 13
Parker, Capt. Hyde, 172
Parker, Sir Peter, 95–6
Parliament, 1, 6–7, 12, 17, 20, 24, 35, 87–8, 109, 151, 175
Pattison, Gen. James, 62, 177, 179
Paulus Hook, 63, 179
Pee Dee River, SC, 209
Peekskill, NY, 57, 108
Pelham Bay, NY, 107
Pells Point, NY, 107
Penobscot Bay, ME, 177
Penobscot River, 178
Pennsylvania, 32, 36, 45, 47, 53, 55, 59–60, 62, 94, 110, 117, 122, 135–8, 140, 142, 147, 156, 207, 221–2
Pennsylvania Associators, 49, 110
Pensacola, 28, 166, 181, 204–5
Percy, Gen. Hugh, Earl, 39, 44, 64, 72–4, 79
Petersburg, VA, 198, 216, 219–20
Philadelphia, 6, 11, 20, 22, 24–5, 27, 29, 31, 40, 66, 68–9, 108–9, 113–15, 118–20, 122–4, 134–8, 140, 142, 144, 147, 149, 153–7, 165, 168, 176, 185, 203, 207, 221–4
Philippines, 19
Phillips, Gen. William, 100, 119, 125, 208–9, 215, 219–20
Phillipsburg, NY, 222
Pickens, Gen. Andrew, 197, 217
Pigot, Sir Robert, 163
pikes, 49
Pitt, the Elder, William, 18, 48, 154
Plassey, 34
Pondicherry, 20, 243
Port Royal Island, 175, 178
Porter, Sir James, 71
Portland, ME, 86
Portsmouth, VA, 39, 176, 202, 208, 225
Portugal, 2–3, 19
Potomac River, 179
Preston, Maj. Charles, 90
Prevost, Gen. Augustine, 33, 166, 174–5, 178, 184, 186, 195, 247
Princeton, NJ, 111–13, 119
Pringle, John, 199
privateering, 46, 150
Providence, RI, 49, 118
Public Advertiser, 88, 241
Pulaski, Count Casimir, 66
Pyle, Col. John, 213

Quakers, 94

Quebec, 19, 58, 88, 91–2, 94, 97–9, 125, 134, 162, 166
Quebec Act, 7, 88
Queen's County, NY, 18
Queen's Rangers, 17

Rall, Col. Johann Gottlieb, 111
Ramsour's Mill, NC, 194, 212
Raritan River, NJ, 110, 112
Rawdon, Francis, Lord, 65, 206, 215–19
Red Bank *see* Fort Mercer
Rhode Island, 22–3, 28, 66, 86, 97, 108, 110, 114–15, 118–19, 122, 134, 144, 163–4, 166, 172, 174, 178–81, 199, 201, 222, 226, 236, 247
Richelieu River, 89–90
Richmond, Charles, 3rd Duke of, 24, 61–2, 64
Richmond, VA, 198, 208, 221
Riedesel, Gen. Frederick, 131, 134
riflemen/rifles, 49, 60–5, 128–9, 134, 195
Rittenhouse, David, 60
Rivington, James, 85–6
Rivington's New York Gazeteer, 85–6
Roanoke River, 212, 216
Robertson, Archibald, 95, 245
Robertson, Gen. James, 172, 236
Rochambeau, Jean Comte de, 163, 199, 221–2, 226–8, 235, 240
Rockingham, Charles, Marquis of, 24, 31, 239, 242
Rocky Mount, 194
Roderique Hortalez and Co., 49
Rodney, Admiral George, 162, 201, 222, 230, 235–6, 243
Rogers, Maj. Robert, 32
Russia, 2, 18, 29, 87, 204, 243
Rutledge, Edward, 105
Rutledge, John, 36, 175

St Augustine, 86, 166, 184, 239, 241
St Clair, Gen. Arthur, 125, 235
St Johns, 89–90, 98, 101, 125
St Lawrence River, 39, 92, 98
St Leger, Lt.-Col. Barry, 32, 35, 128
St Lucia, 154, 157, 166, 168, 173, 179, 243
St Vincent, 178
Saints, Battle of the, 162, 164, 235–6, 243
Salisbury, NC, 49, 52, 191
Saltonstall, Commodore Dudley, 177–8
Sandwich, John, 4th Earl of, 27, 153–4, 161
Sandy Hook, NY, 160, 162, 166, 176, 180, 182, 185, 198, 208, 226–7, 230
Santee River, SC, 188

Sarah Farley's Bristol Journal, 169
Saratoga, NY, 25, 69–70, 114, 117, 132–5, 140, 144–5, 147, 151, 168
Savannah, GA, 16, 20, 22–3, 25, 33–4, 66, 68, 86, 149, 166–7, 169–70, 172, 174, 178–9, 184–6, 188, 219, 233–6, 238–40, 246
Savannah River, 34, 175
Saxe, Marshal, 27, 165
scalping, 35–6, 74
Scammell, Alexander, 57
Schuylkill River, PA, 138, 156
Schuyler, Gen. Philip, 44, 48, 89, 96–7, 128, 134
Scots/Scotland, 13, 15, 17–18, 48, 78, 87, 215, 246
Seneca Indians, 35
Senegal, 243
sepoys, 34, 37
Seringapatam, 246
Serle, Ambrose, 248
Seven Years War, 2–3, 8, 13, 19, 32, 38, 62, 64, 82, 126, 134, 148, 150, 238
Shallow Ford, NC, 212
Shelburne, William, 2nd Earl of, 34, 240, 242
ships
  Cruiser, 84
  Eagle, 59
  Fowey, 84
  Phoenix, 60
  Scarborough, 84
  Tamar, 84
  Turtle, 59–60
shoes, 138, 142–3, 212
Shuttleworth, Lt. Ashton, 38
Sill, Maj. Francis, 17, 38, 78
Simmon's Island, SC, 185
Smallwood, Gen. William, 70
Sorel, 98
South Carolina, 15–16, 31, 33–4, 39, 51, 55–6, 61, 64, 83–4, 87, 101, 115, 153, 170, 173, 175, 177–9, 181–2, 193–4, 196–7, 199, 203–4, 206, 215–18, 238, 246
Spain, 2–3, 5, 9, 147, 167–8, 198, 204, 239, 241, 243
Springfield, 49
Stamp Act, 4, 7–9
Stanley, Hans, 135
Stark, Brig. -Gen. John, 127
Staten Island, 40, 95, 101, 142, 199, 226
Steuben, Fredrich Wilhelm von, 63, 155, 158, 208
Stevens, John, 58
Stewart, Lt.-Col. Alexander, 218
Stillwater, NY, 129

Stirling, William Alexander 'Lord', 199
Stono Ferry, SC, 56, 67, 175
Stony Point, 62–3, 177, 179, 181, 246
Stormont, David Murray, 6th Viscount, 4, 93
Stuart, John, 34–5
submarines, 58–60
Suffolk, 176
Sullivan, Gen. John, 36–7, 98, 136, 163–4
Sullivan's Island, SC, 96, 170, 188
Sumter, Gen. Thomas, 194, 196–7, 212, 215, 217
Sussex County, NJ, 15
Sweden, 204

Tait, David, 174
Tarleton, Lt.-Col. Banastre, 33, 66, 187–9, 192, 195, 210, 212
tea, 6, 9
temperature, 38–40, 101, 160, 195
Thomas, Jeremiah, 33
Throg's Neck, NY, 106
Ticonderoga, NY, 25, 29, 35, 80, 88–9, 100–1, 112, 117, 119–20, 125, 127–9, 144, 147, 246
Tippoo Sahib, 246
Tobago, 226, 243
Tonyn, Governor Patrick, 168, 241
Toulon, 161–2
Townshend, Charles, 8–9
Trading Ford, NC, 212
Trenton, NJ, 49, 108, 110–11, 113, 117, 119, 140, 195
Trois Rivières (Three Rivers), 58, 98
Tryon, Governor William, 84, 177
Tybee Island, 185, 240

United Provinces, Dutch, 204
Ushant, 162

Valley Forge, PA, 50, 63, 144, 147, 150, 155–6
Valcour Island, 25, 100
Vaudreuil, Admiral, 235, 240
Vaughan, Gen. Sir John, 132–3
Venezuela, 2
Vergennes, Charles Gravier, Comte de, 146
Vermont, 180
Verplanck's Point, NY, 130–1, 177, 181
Vienna, 144
Vincennes, 36
Virginia, 4, 17, 26–7, 33, 35, 40, 44, 49, 53, 56, 60, 66, 83, 86, 94, 115, 118, 134, 142–3, 156, 166–7, 173, 180, 183, 201, 203, 206, 208, 212, 220–2, 224–6, 234–5

Virginia Capes, 39, 164–5, 208, 227, 232

Wadsworth, Jeremiah, 167
Wallace, Sir James, 132
Warner, Col. Seth, 125
Warren Tavern, PA, 137
Washington, DC, 144
Washington, Gen. George, 2, 19, 25, 27, 29, 31, 37, 40, 42, 44–51, 53, 56–7, 69–70, 80–2, 86, 92–5, 99, 102, 111–13, 117, 122, 132, 134–8, 140, 142–4, 146–7, 155–60, 163, 165, 167–8, 172–3, 176–7, 179–85, 196, 199, 201, 205, 208, 210, 221–35, 240, 246–7
Washington, Col. William, 111, 209, 214

Watchung Mountains, 122, 165, 181
Waxhaws, 66, 189, 195
Wayne, Gen. Anthony, 45, 62, 67, 138, 156–8, 160, 177, 179, 223, 235
Wethersfield, CT, 221
Wellington, Arthur Wellesley, Duke of, 93, 246
Wentworth, Sir John, 1, 31, 84
West Indies, 7, 15, 20, 23, 28, 34, 41, 43, 56, 70, 146–7, 152–4, 162, 165–6, 170, 178–9, 185, 198, 201, 204–5, 233–5, 238, 240
West Point, NY, 58, 177, 183, 198–201
Westchester County, NY, 38
Westover, VA, 208
Whitemarsh, PA, 144
White Plains, NY, 107–8, 165

Williams, Otho, 67, 192
Williamsburg, VA, 39, 83–4, 220–1, 223–5, 227, 230
Williamson's Plantation, SC, 194
Wilmington, DE, 124, 150
Wilmington, NC, 205, 215–16, 219, 234, 240
Winnsborough, SC, 196
Wolfe, Gen. James, 93, 166
Wright, Sir James, 84, 148, 240
Wrottesley, Sir John, 149, 169
Wyoming Massacre, 36

Yadkin River, NC, 212
Yonge, Sir George, 20
York River, 231
Yorktown, VA, 13–14, 29, 31, 53, 63, 84, 165, 198, 203, 207–9, 219, 223, 225–34, 236, 238, 246

ILLUSTRATED
HISTORY PAPERBACKS
FROM ALAN SUTTON PUBLISHING LIMITED

THE PICTS AND THE SCOTS
LLOYD AND JENNY LAING

ISBN 0 7509 0677 4
'excellent'
The Guardian

**THE MAN BEHIND THE IRON
MASK**
JOHN NOONE

ISBN 0 7509 0679 0
'a lively and minutely argued
historical whodunnit'
The Daily Telegraph

**INVISIBLE POWER: THE
ELIZABETHAN SECRET
SERVICES 1570–1603**
ALAN HAYNES

ISBN 0 7509 0676 6
'a superb analysis'
The Mail on Sunday

WOMEN IN ANCIENT EGYPT
BARBARA WATTERSON

ISBN 0 7509 0680 4
'the domestic sphere is scrutinized
as well as life outside the home'
History Today

**KING ARTHUR'S PLACE IN
PREHISTORY**
W A. CUMMINS

ISBN 0 7509 0664 2
'a strongly argued and attractive
book'
The Times Literary Supplement

WAR FOR AMERICA
JEREMY BLACK

ISBN 0 7509 0675 8
'candid and detailed . . . a
disturbingly convincing study'
The Times

**THE CROMWELLIAN
GAZETTEER**
PETER GAUNT

ISBN 0 7509 0063 6
'details county by county all the
sites and buildings associated with
the Parliamentary cause'
This England

**HENRY VIII AND THE
INVASION OF FRANCE**
CHARLES CRUICKSHANK

ISBN 0 7509 0678 2
'recommended for its depth of
scholarship and facility of style'
The Economist

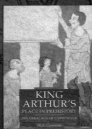

ILLUSTRATED
HISTORY PAPERBACKS
FROM ALAN SUTTON PUBLISHING LIMITED

THE MAKING OF THE TUDOR DYNASTY
RALPH A. GRIFFITHS AND ROGER S. THOMAS
ISBN 0 86299 427 6
'informative and beautifully illustrated'
The Ricardian

THE WARS OF THE ROSES
J.R. LANDER
ISBN 0 7509 0018 0
'Using extracts from contemporary sources . . . Lander provides a new approach to the hostilities'
British Book News

THE BATTLES OF BARNET AND TEWKESBURY
P.W. HAMMOND
ISBN 0 7509 0374 0
'A portrayal of an England torn by political strife'
British Book News

THE BATTLE OF BOSWORTH
MICHAEL BENNETT
ISBN 0 86299 426 8
'the best account we are going to have for a long time'
G.R. Elton

MARGARET OF YORK, DUCHESS OF BURGUNDY
CHRISTINE WEIGHTMAN
ISBN 0 7509 0378 3
'the author's researches are thorough, her illustrations copious and apt'
Encounter

LAMBERT SIMNEL AND THE BATTLE OF STOKE
MICHAEL BENNETT
ISBN 0 7509 0377 5
'will deservedly become the standard account of the rebellion'
The Ricardian

THE ENGLISH CIVIL WAR
MAURICE ASHLEY
ISBN 0 7509 0019 9
'For a sound general account of the period . . . look no further'
British Army Review

THE BATTLE OF NASEBY AND THE FALL OF KING CHARLES I
MAURICE ASHLEY
ISBN 0 7509 0376 7
'a vivid and detailed account'
The Times

CULLODEN AND THE '45
JEREMY BLACK
ISBN 0 7509 0375 9
'thoroughly researched'
History

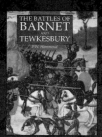

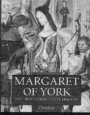

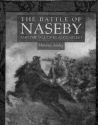